In this book, Jeffrey Knopf investigates domestic sources of state preferences about whether to seek cooperation with other countries on security issues. He does so by examining whether public protest against nuclear weapons influenced US decisions to enter strategic arms talks. The analysis builds on the domestic structure approach to explaining foreign policy, using it as the starting point to develop a new framework that can be employed to trace the influence of societal actors. The book's finding that protest had a major impact suggests that prevailing conceptions of the relationship between domestic politics and international cooperation need to be broadened. Existing approaches typically assume that state preferences are set by political leaders or powerful interests, thereby treating the rest of society only as a constraint on state action. In contrast, this book demonstrates that ordinary citizens can also serve as a direct stimulus to the development of a state interest in cooperation.

CAMBRIDGE STUDIES IN INTERNATIONAL RELATIONS: 60

Domestic society and international cooperation

Cambridge Studies in International Relations is a joint initiative of Cambridge University Press and the British International Studies Association (BISA). The series will include a wide range of material, from undergraduate textbooks and surveys to research-based monographs and collaborative volumes. The aim of the series is to publish the best new scholarship in International Studies from Europe, North America, and the rest of the world.

CAMBRIDGE STUDIES IN INTERNATIONAL RELATIONS

60 *Jeffrey W. Knopf*
Domestic society and international cooperation
The impact of protest on US arms control policy

59 *Nicholas Greenwood Onuf*
The republican legacy in international thought

58 *Daniel S. Geller and J. David Singer*
Nations at war
A scientific study of international conflict

57 *Randall D. Germain*
The international organization of credit
States and global finance in the world economy

56 *N. Piers Ludlow*
Dealing with Britain
The Six and the first UK application to the EEC

55 *Andreas Hasenclever, Peter Mayer, and Volker Rittberger*
Theories of international regimes

54 *Miranda A. Schreurs and Elizabeth C. Economy (eds.)*
The internationalization of environmental protection

53 *James N. Rosenau*
Along the domestic–foreign frontier
Exploring governance in a turbulent world

52 *John M. Hobson*
The wealth of states
A comparative sociology of international economic and political change

51 *Kalevi J. Holsti*
The state, war, and the state of war

50 *Christopher Clapham*
Africa and the international system
The politics of state survival

49 *Susan Strange*
The retreat of the state
The diffusion of power in the world economy

Series list continues after index

Domestic society and international cooperation

The impact of protest on US arms control policy

Jeffrey W. Knopf

PUBLISHED BY THE PRESS SYNDICATE OF THE UNIVERSITY OF CAMBRIDGE
The Pitt Building, Trumpington Street, Cambridge CB2 1RP, United Kingdom

CAMBRIDGE UNIVERSITY PRESS
The Edinburgh Building, Cambridge CB2 2RU, United Kingdom
40 West 20th Street, New York, NY 10011–4211, USA
10 Stamford Road, Oakleigh, Melbourne 3166, Australia

First published 1998

Printed in the United Kingdom at the University Press, Cambridge

Typeset in Palatino 10/12½ pt [CE]

A catalog record for this book is available from the British Library

Library of Congress Cataloging in Publication data

Knopf, Jeffrey W.
Domestic society and international cooperation : the impact of protest on US arms control policy / Jeffrey W. Knopf.
p. cm. – (Cambridge studies in international relations; 60)
Includes bibliographical references and index.
ISBN 0 521 62240 9 (hb.) – ISBN 0 521 62691 9 (pbk.)
1. Nuclear arms control – Government policy – United States.
2. Antinuclear movement – United States.
3. Security, International.
I. Title. II. Series.
JZ5665.K59 1998
327.1′747′0973 – dc21 97–27919 CIP

To my parents, Carol and Paul Knopf

Contents

Illustrations

Figures

Tables

Preface

The research that led to this book arose out of a personal curiosity about the impact of protest against nuclear weapons. In looking for guidance on this question, I found that most international relations experts view peace and other protest movements as quite marginal actors in world politics. The research results presented here will demonstrate that this is not so. Citizen activism can make a difference.

The choice to focus on a type of actor that is usually neglected turned out to have other benefits as well, as it drew my attention to patterns that many studies of international politics overlook. This book thus contends that many major theories of international relations entail an unduly narrow and misleading view of domestic politics. Domestic society is generally treated as a source of constraints on foreign policymakers, or else as a source of incentives that lead policy to diverge from the national interest. This study will show that the opposite is also possible. Societal activism can be the trigger to foreign policy initiatives that most analysts would regard as consistent with state interests. Studies of international cooperation in particular have tended to view the domestic arena as a source of obstacles to cooperation. This book will show that social protest can also be the reason some states develop a preference for cooperation in the first place.

Because assessing the impact of protest movements is quite difficult, this book builds on the domestic structure approach to explaining foreign policy to develop an original framework for tracing activism's influence in individual cases. By using this framework, this book is able to identify causal links between domestic activism and US decisions to enter into three major sets of strategic arms control talks during the Cold War. In all, this book makes three important contributions. Empirically, it demonstrates that popular campaigns against the nuclear arms race had a significant impact on US arms control policy. Theoretically, it shows that the common treatment of domestic politics as a constraint is too one-sided, because societal activism can also serve as a direct stimulus to the development of new state preferences. Finally, this study extends the range of applications of the domestic structure framework, by developing a new technique by which it can be used to examine individual cases.

This book has been substantially revised and broadened from a Ph.D. dissertation completed in 1991. An earlier version of some of the material in chapters 3 and 7 appeared as "The Nuclear Freeze Movement's Effect on Policy," in Thomas R. Rochon and David S. Meyer's edited work, *Coalitions and Political Movements: The Lessons of the Nuclear Freeze* (© 1997 by Lynne Rienner Publishers, Inc.). My research was made possible by financial support from the Political Science Department and Center for International Security and Arms Control at Stanford University, the School of International Relations and Center for International Studies at the University of Southern California, John D. and Catherine T. MacArthur Foundation fellowships administered by the Stanford Arms Control Center, a US Arms Control and Disarmament Agency Hubert H. Humphrey fellowship, and grants from the Institute for the Study of World Politics and the Stanford Center on Conflict and Negotiation.

A great many individuals also provided invaluable assistance. Alexander George served as the supervisor of the dissertation and continued to provide helpful comments and encouragement as I completed the transformation of that product into a book manuscript. Eileen Crumm, through her comments on a number of draft chapters and countless conversations, gave me tremendous help in figuring out how to re-focus the original research to make it more relevant to a post-Cold War world. Sue Peterson, Matt Evangelista, Thomas Risse, John Odell, and an anonymous reviewer for Cambridge University Press read the penultimate draft in its entirety, and this final product has benefited a great deal from their thoughtful suggestions. I also wish to thank the following for their helpful comments: Hayward Alker, Cheryl Boyer, Richard Brody, Alison Brysk, Peter Cowhey, Miriam Fendius Elman, John Ferejohn, Kurt Taylor Gaubatz, Judy Goldstein, Scott Johnson, Steve Krasner, Ed Mansfield, Lee Metcalf, David Meyer, Paul Papayanou, Mark Peceny, Tom Rochon, Scott Sagan, Etel Solingen, Michael Ward, and participants in a UCSD

Program in International and Security Affairs seminar. I also thank Andrew Bertolino, Darold Higa, Evan Schulz, and Guy Ziv for research assistance, and Geert Poppe for doing the index. In addition, I thank John Haslam and Karen Anderson Howes at Cambridge University Press for their guidance and assistance on the final revisions and manuscript preparation. Finally, I wish to express my deepest possible gratitude to Christina Milburn, just for being there.

Abbreviations

ABM	anti-ballistic missile
ACDA	Arms Control and Disarmament Agency
AEC	Atomic Energy Commission
AFSC	American Friends Service Committee
BAS	*Bulletin of the Atomic Scientists*
CIA	Central Intelligence Agency
CLW	Council for a Livable World
CNVA	Committee on Non-Violent Action
COPDAB	Conflict and Peace Data Bank
CTB	comprehensive test ban
DDRS	*Declassified Documents Reference System*
DOD	US Department of Defense
FAS	Federation of American Scientists
FBI	Federal Bureau of Investigation
FRUS	*Foreign Relations of the United States*
GATT	General Agreement on Tariffs and Trade
IAEA	International Atomic Energy Agency
ICBM	intercontinental ballistic missile
INF	intermediate-range nuclear forces
IPE	international political economy
IR	international relations
JCAE	Joint Committee on Atomic Energy (US Congress)
JCS	Joint Chiefs of Staff
kt	kiloton
LR	likelihood ratio
LTBT	Limited Test Ban Treaty
MAD	mutual assured destruction
MIRV	multiple independently targetable reentry vehicle

MIT	Massachusetts Institute of Technology
mt	megaton
NATO	North Atlantic Treaty Organization
NIMBY	"not in my backyard"
NPT	Non-Proliferation Treaty
NSC	National Security Council
NSSM	National Security Study Memorandum
NYT	*New York Times*
PD	prisoner's dilemma
PRE	proportionate reduction in error
PSAC	President's Scientific Advisory Committee
PSR	Physicians for Social Responsibility
SALT	Strategic Arms Limitation Talks
SANE	Committee for a Sane Nuclear Policy
SDI	Strategic Defense Initiative
START	Strategic Arms Reductions Talks
UNDC	United Nations Disarmament Commission
WEIS	World Events Interaction Survey

Introduction

Protest and other public advocacy efforts designed to influence international politics have become commonplace. In recent decades, there have been campaigns to promote environmental protection, human rights, and disarmament, and to restrict immigration and economic integration. This activity has been widely noted, but its impact remains poorly understood. This book asks whether such citizen activism can be an important source of state preferences in foreign policy. In particular, can social protest be a reason why states develop a preference for seeking international cooperation?

This study explores this question empirically by examining what impact, if any, peace movements had on US decisions to seek nuclear arms control with the Soviet Union. During the Cold War, the United States and the Soviet Union entered three distinct sets of direct, bilateral negotiations on control of their strategic weapons programs. The United States and USSR began talks on a nuclear test ban in 1958, began a decade of Strategic Arms Limitation Talks (SALT) in 1969, and resumed discussion of such weapons in 1982 under the umbrella of the Strategic Arms Reduction Talks (START).

These diplomatic efforts sometimes arose against a background of protest. In the late 1950s, there was extensive protest against nuclear testing and the radioactive fallout it was producing, and, in the early 1980s, a massive movement arose around the demand for a nuclear weapons freeze. To what extent are these talks and protest activities related? This study finds that, in all three cases where the United States entered new arms talks, the actual or potential mobilization of domestic opposition strongly affected the US decision. In contrast, absence of organized public support for nuclear cooperation made the pursuit of arms control less likely.

This finding is highly suggestive. Examining nuclear weapons policy poses a hard test for the impact of social protest, because a key national security issue is involved. Cooperation is more difficult to establish on security than on non-security issues,[1] and central decisionmakers are normally expected to retain control over policy without much hindrance from societal opposition.[2] These considerations suggest that superpower arms control is one of the least likely[3] areas for finding that citizen activism can foster cooperation. Of course, there was much more scope for public protest to affect arms policy in the United States than in the Soviet Union. Still, it is important to recognize that mainstream international relations (IR) theory leads one to doubt whether popular movements can affect core security policies even in democracies like the United States. Showing that they did so will therefore suggest that grassroots actors can serve as a direct stimulus to new foreign policy preferences in many other, though not all, situations.

Theoretical approach

To make it possible to evaluate protest's impact on policy, this book builds on the domestic structure approach to explaining foreign policy. This approach initially treated state institutions as an intervening variable between systemic conditions and foreign economic policies,[4] but several recent studies have also used it to investigate the impact of public opinion or transnational actors on security issues.[5]

1 Robert Jervis, "Security Regimes," in Stephen D. Krasner, ed., *International Regimes* (Ithaca: Cornell University Press, 1983); Charles Lipson, "International Cooperation in Economic and Security Affairs," *World Politics* 37 (October 1984), pp. 1–23.

2 Kenneth N. Waltz, *Foreign Policy and Democratic Politics: The American and British Experience* (Boston: Little, Brown, 1967), chap. 10; William Zimmerman, "Issue Area and Foreign-Policy Process: A Research Note in Search of a General Theory," *American Political Science Review* 67 (December 1973), pp. 1204–12; Stephen D. Krasner, *Defending the National Interest: Raw Materials Investments and US Foreign Policy* (Princeton: Princeton University Press, 1978), p. 70.

3 On the concept of "least likely" cases, see Harry Eckstein, "Case Studies in Political Science," in Nelson Polsby and Fred I. Greenstein, eds., *Handbook of Political Science*, vol. VII (Reading, MA: Addison-Wesley, 1975), pp. 113–20.

4 Peter J. Katzenstein, ed., *Between Power and Plenty: Foreign Economic Policies of Advanced Industrial States* (Madison: University of Wisconsin Press, 1978).

5 Matthew Evangelista, "Issue-Area and Foreign Policy Revisited," *International Organization* 43 (Winter 1989), pp. 147–71; Thomas Risse-Kappen, "Public Opinion, Domestic Structure, and Foreign Policy in Liberal Democracies," *World Politics* 43 (July 1991),

Most of these applications of the domestic structure framework have focused on explaining differences between countries or issue-areas in the impact of societal actors. In this study, I develop a new technique for using this approach to evaluate the role of non-state actors in individual cases. This technique involves adapting well-established models of domestic policymaking to the foreign policy issue in question.

Specifically, by examining the processes that afford organized publics in the US influence on domestic policy issues, this study identifies three sources of policy influence (or causal mechanisms) that could be used by citizens' campaigns on arms issues. It will show that one or more of these influence pathways came into play in each of the three cases of arms talks initiation. At times, there was a mobilization of public opinion that created electoral incentives for action. At other times, activist groups contributed resources that changed the balance among competing coalitions in Congress. And, at other times, activism raised ideas that altered the course of bureaucratic debates. Influence is not automatic. But, this book will show that, with the framework developed here, it is possible to identify specific circumstances under which public advocacy campaigns can be a direct stimulus to the pursuit of cooperation.

Implications

The impact of societal activism and democratic foreign policy

This study has two important larger implications. First, it reveals that people who are not seated at the pinnacle of political or economic power can make a difference in world politics. Indeed, by examining a

pp. 479–512; Peter J. Katzenstein and Nobuo Okawara, *Japan's National Security: Structures, Norms, and Policy Responses in a Changing World* (Ithaca: Cornell University East Asia Program, 1993); Matthew Evangelista, "The Paradox of State Strength: Transnational Relations, Domestic Structures, and Security Policy in Russia and the Soviet Union," *International Organization* 49 (Winter 1995), pp. 1–38; Thomas Risse-Kappen, ed., *Bringing Transnational Relations Back In: Non-State Actors, Domestic Structures, and International Institutions* (Cambridge: Cambridge University Press, 1995); Eric Mlyn, *The State, Society, and Limited Nuclear War* (Albany: State University of New York Press, 1995); Susan Peterson, *Crisis Bargaining and the State: The Domestic Politics of International Conflict* (Ann Arbor: University of Michigan Press, 1996); Jeffrey T. Checkel, *Ideas and International Politics: Soviet/Russian Behavior and the End of the Cold War* (New Haven: Yale University Press, 1997).

hard case, this study suggests that citizen activism may be influential in a number of other settings. This is important because there have been many such efforts besides the anti-nuclear protests examined here. In the United States, the movement against the Vietnam War remains the most dramatic example. Since then, there have also been major protests against support for apartheid in South Africa and against Reagan administration policies in Central America.

Outside the United States, many countries in Western Europe have also experienced large-scale protest against nuclear weapons. In the Middle East, Israel has had an active peace movement and the Palestinian *intifada* appears to have played a major role in stimulating peace talks. Transnational networks of groups are also active on other global issues such as human rights, the environment, hunger, and refugees. Activism does not always seek to advance liberal causes or international cooperation, however. In many countries, popular campaigns have arisen to limit immigration or regional economic integration. During the Cold War, there was also sometimes opposition to arms control in the United States that included a grassroots element, most notably the effort to block SALT II.

A major lesson of this book is that these protest campaigns need to be taken seriously as players in international politics. Beyond this general implication, this study also develops an effective way to assess their impact. The theoretical framework I develop here is potentially generalizable. With suitable changes to take account of the move to different issues or different countries, the basic technique utilized by this book could be used to evaluate the foreign policy impact of citizen activism in a variety of other cases.

By examining societal inputs into foreign policy, this book both reinforces and goes beyond current research on the international behavior of democracies. The finding that democracies may never fight wars against each other has stimulated a major research program. Most hypothesized explanations for the democratic peace involve the constraints and transparency created by democratic institutions and/or the norms into which democratic leaders are socialized.[6] These variables, however, do not necessarily require analysts to examine the preferences being expressed by ordinary citizens.

[6] Bruce M. Russett, *Grasping the Democratic Peace: Principles for a Post-Cold War World* (Princeton: Princeton University Press, 1993); John M. Owen, "How Liberalism Produces Democratic Peace," *International Security* 19 (Fall 1994), pp. 87–125.

Therefore, while this book strengthens the argument that democracies may be likely partners in security cooperation, it also points to a need to broaden the research focus. This study suggests that there might be benefits from going deeper into society to examine the impact of active public participation in foreign policy debates. There is no reason to believe that public opinion is always a force for peace, but this does not mean that it is never part of the reason for cooperation. It is ironic that the IR research most concerned with democracy has devoted little attention to identifying the conditions under which societal inputs might favor cooperative outcomes. The current study begins that task.

Expanding the role of domestic politics

The second major implication of this study is that there is an important omission in much IR theory. Current theory views the role of domestic politics in a partial and distorted way. As a result, the most common perspectives are all likely to underestimate the role of societal actors, especially non-elites. Specifically, most theories adopt one of three views of domestic politics. Domestic factors are most often treated as constraints that explain failures by states to act on behalf of apparent national interests. On occasion, theorists also discuss domestic incentives for state leaders to use foreign policy strategically to enhance their domestic standing. In this approach, domestic conditions can be a stimulus to international initiatives, but the stimulus is indirect, not a direct answer to the demands of societal actors. Finally, a third perspective does assume that domestic actors directly shape state preferences. But advocates of this approach, which is most common in political economy, typically focus on leading socioeconomic interest groups. They therefore draw attention only to the role of elites.[7]

I do not argue that these other approaches are wrong. Each clearly captures the role of domestic factors part of the time. But even this set of alternatives is unduly restrictive. In addition to these commonly discussed impacts of domestic politics, societal actors who are not part of the foreign policy elite can also be a direct stimulus to changing state preferences, even on the "high politics" of national security. By virtue of their efforts, citizens' campaigns can trigger new

[7] I describe all this literature more fully, and provide citations, in the next chapter.

foreign policy departures and put new issues on the agenda for international negotiations. This "direct stimulus" scenario needs to be added to the set of ways in which we conceptualize the impact of domestic politics.

This study thus goes beyond a simple claim that "domestic politics matters." Because of the influence of neo-realism, with its purely system-level focus, much recent research has been concerned merely with establishing that internal factors are important. This common goal has obscured the fact that theories which incorporate internal factors can still differ in how they describe the role of domestic inputs. So far, the possibility that a state's interest in cooperation could arise in a bottom-up manner, from public pressure, has not been given much consideration by IR theory. If this omission is unwarranted, it could have unfortunate consequences. It could lead state leaders to think that they can or should ignore the hopes and fears of ordinary citizens. And it could lead such individuals to conclude that there is no point in participating in campaigns to promote their concerns. Hence, if protest sometimes makes a difference, it will be important for our theories of foreign policy to allow for that possibility.

Although the IR literature has not given much consideration to whether non-elite societal actors can alter state preferences, recent research on public opinion and US foreign policy lends credence to this possibility. Correlational analyses have suggested that public opinion sometimes leads directly to changes in policy.[8] This foreign policy research has not yet been integrated, however, into international relations theories dealing with state preferences or with cooperation. Moreover, this research has not specified the mechanisms by which public opinion exerts this apparent influence. The theoretical framework developed in chapter 3 will suggest one way of accomplishing these tasks.

Caveats

In discussing public inputs, I do not mean to imply an interest only in mass public opinion. In the terminology of the public opinion literature, most of the participants in the movements I study were instead

[8] For good summaries of the key research in this area, see Robert Y. Shapiro and Benjamin I. Page, "Foreign Policy and Public Opinion," and Thomas W. Graham, "Public Opinion and US Foreign Policy Decision Making," both in David A. Deese, ed., *The New Politics of American Foreign Policy* (New York: St. Martin's Press, 1994).

part of the attentive public.[9] They generally were well educated and enjoyed relatively high social status. Thus, when I talk about preferences arising from the bottom up or from the efforts of ordinary citizens, this does not mean that the working masses or the poor were responsible for policy. These claims must be understood in the context of prevailing explanations of foreign policy, especially on security issues, which focus on government officials or major economic interests. Because the actors I examine were mostly not part of any such "power elite," focusing on them provides a more bottom-up explanation than is typical. For this same reason, I do not focus only on protests or only on organizations with grassroots memberships. Individuals with some social prestige can also be part of a bottom-up explanation if they do not have regular access to security policymakers, so that they instead engage in public advocacy designed to rally other segments of society. Famous individuals who contribute in this way to societal pressures will be treated as another element of citizen activism.

Finally, I want to be explicit about what this book does not argue. First, in contrast to some versions of liberal idealism, I am not arguing that citizen influence is always a good force in world politics. I am sympathetic to the peace movements studied in this book. However, the continuing prevalence of ethnic conflict makes it clear that mobilized publics can also have quite negative consequences, and some would say the same of peace movements. Still, if protest campaigns sometimes have an impact even on security cooperation, this would be an important finding. It would mean existing theories err when they assume away this possibility. The key point, therefore, is simply that, whether it is a positive or negative force, the potential influence of social protest needs to be better incorporated into theories of state preference formation.

Second, I am not seeking to replace system-level theories with a purely domestic-level approach. I assume that variables at both levels

[9] Gabriel A. Almond, *The American People and Foreign Policy* (New York: Frederick A. Praeger, 1960), pp. 139, 233; James N. Rosenau, *Public Opinion and Foreign Policy* (New York: Random House, 1961), p. 41.

I have not framed this research as a study of the attentive public, however, because the earlier literature envisioned a largely passive role for it. The attentive public was seen as an audience before which elites debated competing visions for foreign policy. The members of society I study are more active. They organize and campaign for their own preferred foreign policy agenda, rather than limiting their role to choosing between alternatives offered by elites.

matter and am attempting to build on some recent ideas about how to combine them. Realists have generally justified a focus on states and statesmen by arguing that they are more powerful than any other actors.[10] But one need not claim that the state is becoming unimportant to argue that non-state actors have an impact. The "interactive"[11] perspective of several newer approaches thus rejects the debate on international *versus* domestic determinants of state choice, by assuming that the two levels often interact in ways that shape policy choices and bargaining outcomes.

The present study adopts this interactive perspective. Thus, it does not argue that external factors are irrelevant, nor does it claim that society is dominant and that state officials lack any autonomy. Instead, I assume that some domestic or transnational actors may hold a different view from state leaders about what policy is best in current international circumstances. The question is influence, whether societal actors can get central decisionmakers to change state policy. I do not assume that they always succeed; state officials may maintain independence from social pressure instead. However, there is no reason to assume that the state is always insulated from grassroots concerns. Therefore, this study treats the importance of social protest as variable, and it seeks to identify the circumstances under which impact is most likely. By showing that societal activism does sometimes change policy, this study makes a case that inputs from below can be an important source of state preferences.

Research design

This study uses a combination of statistical and case study methods. The first cut in assessing activism's impact is a quantitative analysis of

[10] Robert Gilpin, "The Politics of Transnational Economic Relations," in Robert O. Keohane and Joseph S. Nye, Jr., eds., *Transnational Relations and World Politics* (Cambridge, MA: Harvard University Press, 1972), pp. 53–55, 67–69; Kenneth N. Waltz, *Theory of International Politics* (Reading, MA: Addison-Wesley, 1979), esp. chap. 4; Waltz, "Reflections on *Theory of International Politics*: A Response to My Critics," in Robert O. Keohane, ed., *Neorealism and Its Critics* (New York: Columbia University Press, 1986), p. 329.

[11] Christer Jönsson, *Superpower: Comparing American and Soviet Foreign Policy* (London: Frances Pinter, 1984), p. 30; Andrew Moravcsik, "Introduction: Integrating International and Domestic Theories of International Bargaining," in Peter B. Evans, Harold K. Jacobson, and Robert D. Putnam, eds., *Double-Edged Diplomacy: International Bargaining and Domestic Politics* (Berkeley: University of California Press, 1993), pp. 15–17.

US decisions to enter arms talks. This analysis tests whether protest activity proves to be significant when the most relevant system-level variables are controlled for. Statistical correlations by themselves, though, often do not make clear the causal connections involved. Therefore, in order to corroborate the statistical results and explore the causal mechanisms by which citizen activism could have brought them about, I employ case studies as a second mode of analysis, following the method of structured, focused comparison.[12]

In selecting cases, I limited the universe of possible cases to those where US–Soviet arms talks were not already taking place, so that I could focus on the initial development of a preference for cooperation. I also excluded negotiations in the early years of the Cold War on the Baruch Plan, because these do not appear to have involved a genuine interest in or realistic opportunity to achieve cooperation.[13] From the remaining candidate cases, in order to avoid biasing the results, I selected cases that vary in the independent variable of interest (activism), while being sure variation in the dependent variable (cooperation) was not artificially correlated with values of the explanatory variable.[14] This book thus examines four cases: Eisenhower's first presidential term; Eisenhower's second term; a period covering the tail end of the Johnson administration and start of Nixon's first term; and Reagan's first term.

[12] Alexander L. George, "Case Studies and Theory Development," in Paul Gordon Lauren, ed., *Diplomacy: New Approaches* (New York: Free Press, 1979); Alexander L. George and Timothy J. McKeown, "Case Studies and Theories of Organizational Decision Making," in *Advances in Information Processing in Organizations*, vol. II (Greenwich, CT: JAI Press, 1985).

[13] Michael Mandelbaum, *The Nuclear Question: The United States and Nuclear Weapons, 1946–1976* (New York: Cambridge University Press, 1979), pp. 23–27; Gregg Herken, *The Winning Weapon: The Atomic Bomb in the Cold War, 1945–1950* (New York: Alfred A. Knopf, 1981), chaps. 8–9.

Nevertheless, it appears that an important part of the impetus for seeking these negotiations came from an organized campaign by atomic scientists, and was further bolstered by public opinion polls (Alice Kimball Smith, *A Peril and a Hope: The Scientists' Movement in America, 1945–1947* [Cambridge: MIT Press, 1970; Chicago: University of Chicago Press, 1965], esp. chap. 11; Thomas W. Graham, "The Politics of Failure: Strategic Nuclear Arms Control, Public Opinion, and Domestic Politics in the United States, 1945–1980," Ph.D. dissertation, MIT [1989], chap. 4). Hence, excluding this case does not bias the study against international factors or in favor of domestic factors; adding it would likely only reinforce the conclusions I reach anyway.

[14] This reflects guidelines recommended in Gary King, Robert O. Keohane, and Sidney Verba, *Designing Social Inquiry: Scientific Inference in Qualitative Research* (Princeton: Princeton University Press, 1994), pp. 142–46.

Two of these cases – Eisenhower's second term and Reagan's first – witnessed the major growth phases of the test ban and freeze movements, respectively. They hence involve a high level of activism. The other two cases involve a much lower level of protest. For reasons I will explain further in chapter 2, I initially coded preferences about cooperation in terms of whether or not the cases resulted in formal, bilateral negotiations. From this perspective, three cases involved development of an interest in cooperation and one did not. Eisenhower's second term and the inaugural Nixon and Reagan terms all saw major US–Soviet arms talks initiated. But no superpower negotiations dedicated to control of their nuclear arsenals ever got underway in the first case.[15]

Despite an effort to include also one case where protest was present but arms talks did not occur, the pattern among actual cases empirically turned out to be quite suggestive. There are no cases combining a high level of domestic activism with an outcome of no talks; the cases with the largest citizens' movements all result in a decision to seek cooperation. However, there is one (and only one) case where domestic pressures appear limited but strategic arms talks were initiated nonetheless. I thus made sure to include this case, Nixon's first term, which completed efforts by the Johnson administration to launch SALT. In fact, closer examination of the Nixon case in chapter 6 will reinforce the suggestion that domestic pressures play an important role. While no major anti-nuclear weapons movement existed, some protest did arise against proposed deployment of an anti-ballistic missile (ABM) system. Worries about potential growth of this opposition, I will show, helped persuade President Nixon to begin SALT talks.

Outline of the study

Chapter 1 reviews cooperation theory and other relevant research on state preference formation. It shows that studies do frequently adopt one of the three perspectives introduced above – domestic politics as a

[15] In the case studies themselves, I investigate more directly whether the available evidence supports my preliminary codings that the first three cases represent cooperative preferences and the other one does not. For purposes of having some variation in outcomes, however, selecting some cases where talks resulted and some where no talks resulted seemed the most likely way to ensure variation in the dependent variable.

constraint, as an indirect stimulus to strategic initiatives by statesmen, or as a source of preferences that reflect the interests of elites. It then shows how some applications of a domestic structure approach and some recent work from a "social constructivist" perspective are more open to a bottom-up account of state action. It explains how the rest of this study builds on and extends these recent research developments.

Chapter 2 begins the empirical part of the study. It summarizes existing arms control theory in order to identify the variables that will serve as the main controls when assessing the impact of peace movements. It then presents a preliminary statistical test of whether societal pressures affect US decisions to seek arms talks. The book then turns to case studies. Chapter 3 outlines the theoretical framework that will be used to assess whether there are causal connections between protest and policy. This framework draws on existing research to identify three specific processes by which domestic groups might exert influence on arms control policy: electoral pressure, shifting congressional coalitions, and raising ideas that are utilized by bureaucratic actors. The four case studies then appear, in chronological order, in chapters 4 through 7.

The final chapter summarizes the findings and their implications. Overall, this study demonstrates that ordinary citizens, when they participate in larger campaigns on behalf of arms restraint, have been able to alter US preferences. Domestic society is not just a source of impediments to sound statecraft; it can also be the spur to efforts to achieve what many analysts identify as mutual interests in security cooperation. To show that this finding is in many respects novel or unexpected, it is necessary to discuss existing conceptions of the role of domestic politics in relevant bodies of international relations theory. The next chapter takes up this task.

1 The domestic politics of cooperation: three views

This chapter describes the roles most commonly envisioned for domestic factors in current research on interstate cooperation. Its purpose is to show how the empirical findings in the rest of this study will add a new possibility to existing ideas about how states develop a preference for cooperation. Current research programs tend to conceptualize the impact of domestic politics in one of three ways. They treat the domestic arena either as a source of constraints, as an indirect stimulus to strategic action by state leaders, or as a source of preferences derived from the interests or ideas of societal elites. For all their differences, each of these perspectives assumes preferences are set at or near the peak of state power.

This common top-down orientation makes it worthwhile to investigate whether state preferences can also reflect the impact of societal activism that involves a grassroots component. I will refer to this alternative as a bottom-up approach. By this, I mean that participation by some members of the public is a critical input in the process. Prestigious individuals who might not be considered part of the general public may also be involved, provided they do not hold government office and are seeking to generate broader societal interest in cooperation. As long as the concerns of some part of society at large are being channeled into public advocacy efforts, and this activity has a major effect on the formation of state preferences, I will argue that a bottom-up process has shaped the state's definition of its interests.

This alternative is meant to supplement, not to replace, the other perspectives. The goal of this chapter is to show that existing approaches are incomplete in ways that lead to biased inferences about the role of domestic factors. Because the main theories do not direct attention to the possibility that ordinary citizens can shape state preferences, they tend to conceive of the impact of societal pressures only as something deleterious to the national interest. I argue, in contrast, that sometimes the role of societal actors is to help states define their interests in new and potentially productive ways.[1]

I begin with a discussion of cooperation theory, as that is the most directly relevant body of literature.[2] This overview will show that the starting assumptions of cooperation theory lead it to treat domestic politics only as a possible source of constraints, rather than as something that could also provide a direct stimulus to seeking cooperation. Although I focus on cooperation theory, the treatment of domestic factors as a constraint reflects a traditional mode of analyzing foreign policy.[3] Thus, while there are important exceptions, this discussion will apply to much of the IR literature.

[1] I recognize that not everyone thinks nuclear arms control with the Soviet Union was in US interests. In this study, I work under the assumption that it was. To make this case fully would be a lengthy digression, which is not necessary for the point I seek to establish here. The key point is that most mainstream analysts themselves believe that the superpowers had a mutual interest in cooperation to reduce the chance of nuclear war. To the extent that protest stimulated efforts to achieve such cooperation, therefore, it would be a mistake for these same analysts to work with assumptions that make it difficult for them to imagine ordinary citizens playing this role.

[2] Cooperation is defined in this literature as a mutual adjustment of behavior by states in order to coordinate their policies in an area where, because of the potential costs or risks of such action, policy coordination would not automatically occur (Robert O. Keohane, *After Hegemony: Cooperation and Discord in the World Political Economy* [Princeton: Princeton University Press, 1984], pp. 51–52; Helen Milner, "International Theories of Cooperation Among Nations: Strengths and Weaknesses," *World Politics* 44 [April 1992], p. 467).

[3] Ole R. Holsti, "Public Opinion and Containment," in Terry L. Deibel and John Lewis Gaddis, eds., *Containing the Soviet Union: A Critique of US Policy* (Washington, DC: Pergamon-Brassey's, 1987), p. 23; Alexander L. George, "Domestic Constraints on Regime Change in US Foreign Policy: The Need for Policy Legitimacy," in Ole R. Holsti, Randolph M. Siverson, and Alexander L. George, eds., *Change in the International System* (Boulder: Westview Press, 1980).

This view has been strongly challenged by recent public opinion research; for good summaries, see Robert Y. Shapiro and Benjamin I. Page, "Foreign Policy and Public Opinion," and Thomas W. Graham, "Public Opinion and US Foreign Policy Decision Making," both in David A. Deese, ed., *The New Politics of American Foreign Policy* (New York: St. Martin's Press, 1994). While it implies that public opinion can be more than a constraint, this recent foreign policy research has not been integrated into international relations theory on preferences for cooperation.

Cooperation theory: domestic politics as constraint

What is now known as neo-liberal cooperation theory arose from an attempt to refute neo-realist pessimism about the prospects for cooperation in an anarchic international system.[4] To answer this skepticism, cooperation theorists attempted to show that cooperation could emerge even if one grants neo-realist assumptions.[5] Cooperation theorists thus assumed that states behave as if they are unitary, rational actors responding to conditions in their external environment. These assumptions led to the utilization of game theory, with an initial emphasis on modeling international relations as a game of prisoner's dilemma (PD).[6]

However, from the outset of the research program, there has also been interest in applying cooperation theory to empirical cases. The two key works in this research program, Robert Axelrod's *Evolution of Cooperation* and Robert Keohane's *After Hegemony*, both contain empirical case studies. The first major follow-up to these works, Kenneth Oye's edited volume on *Cooperation Under Anarchy*, was specifically devoted to applying their ideas to empirical cases. Several subsequent books also assess elements of cooperation theory against empirical data.[7]

[4] Kenneth N. Waltz, *Theory of International Politics* (Reading, MA: Addison-Wesley, 1979), pp. 105–07; Joseph Grieco, *Cooperation Among Nations: Europe, America, and Non-Tariff Barriers to Trade* (Ithaca: Cornell University Press, 1990). For a counterargument that structural realism is actually consistent with cooperation, see Charles L. Glaser, "Realists as Optimists: Cooperation as Self-Help," *International Security* 19 (Winter 1994/95), pp. 50–90.

[5] Thus, in *After Hegemony*, Robert Keohane claims, "My argument anticipates [Realist] objection[s] by adopting the Realist model . . . I propose to show, on the basis of their own assumptions, that the characteristic pessimism of Realism does not follow" (p. 67).

[6] In PD, two players must decide whether to cooperate (C) or defect (D). Although each player would receive a higher payoff from mutual cooperation than mutual defection, the rational choice for each player, deciding in isolation in a single game, is to defect. Mutual defection results because the payoffs are such that, whatever the other player's move, one gains more by defecting than cooperating (DC > CC and DD > CD, but CC > DD). The key breakthrough of cooperation theory was to show ways in which cooperation could emerge once the game is iterated.

[7] Robert Axelrod, *The Evolution of Cooperation* (New York: Basic Books, 1984); Keohane, *After Hegemony*; Kenneth A. Oye, ed., *Cooperation Under Anarchy* (Princeton: Princeton University Press, 1986); Oran Young, *International Cooperation: Building Regimes for Natural Resources and the Environment* (Ithaca: Cornell University Press, 1989); Grieco,

Although it was not cooperation theorists' intent to imply that internal politics and actors can be ignored, the research program retained an emphasis on the system level when it moved into these empirical applications.[8] This has made its treatment of domestic factors one-sided, leading the studies to overlook certain ways in which the societal level may be important. Specifically, basing analysis at the system level creates a tendency to think of domestic factors only as constraints. Because the premise of cooperation theory is that the international situation creates an interest in cooperation, the only role it can envision for domestic factors is as something that intervenes to prevent states from acting on their interests. Hence, most empirical applications of cooperation theory only ever introduce domestic politics to explain failures to cooperate.[9]

Of course, systemic approaches have been criticized many times. Hence, several commentaries have taken cooperation theory to task for neglecting domestic-level factors,[10] especially as these relate to

Cooperation Among Nations; Steve Weber, *Cooperation and Discord in US–Soviet Arms Control* (Princeton: Princeton University Press, 1991); Lisa L. Martin, *Coercive Cooperation: Explaining Multilateral Economic Sanctions* (Princeton: Princeton University Press, 1992); Michael Mastanduno, *Economic Containment: CoCom and the Politics of East–West Trade* (Ithaca: Cornell University Press, 1992).

[8] I am aware of only one serious attempt to incorporate domestic factors into a formal model of the origins of preferences regarding cooperation (Vinod K. Aggarwal and Pierre Allan, "The Origin of Games: A Theory of the Formation of Ordinal Preferences and Games," in Michael D. Intriligator and Urs Luterbacher, eds., *Cooperative Models in International Relations Research* [Boston: Kluwer Academic Publishers, 1994]). However, their deductions are of only limited assistance empirically. When Aggarwal and Allan apply their model to the US–Soviet relationship, they conclude that the two states were in a prisoner's dilemma throughout the entire Cold War (pp. 314–16). But a model that posits constant preferences is insufficient to account for superpower behavior, since the two states seemed to vary quite a bit over time in their actual level of willingness to work toward cooperation.

[9] Keohane, *After Hegemony*, pp. 140–41, 178–79; Robert Jervis, "From Balance to Concert," p. 68, Stephen Van Evera, "Why Cooperation Failed in 1914," esp. p. 95, and John Conybeare, "Trade Wars," pp. 150, 171, all in Oye, *Cooperation Under Anarchy*; Young, *International Cooperation*, chap. 7; Grieco, *Cooperation Among Nations*, pp. 188–89; Weber, *Cooperation and Discord*; Mastanduno, *Economic Containment*; Martin, *Coercive Cooperation*, chaps. 5, 8.

[10] Even Axelrod and Keohane have recognized this as a problem and called for incorporating domestic factors into cooperation theory (Robert Axelrod and Robert O. Keohane, "Achieving Cooperation Under Anarchy: Strategies and Institutions," in Oye, *Cooperation under Anarchy*, pp. 241–42; Keohane, "Institutional Theory and the Realist Challenge After the Cold War," in David A. Baldwin, ed., *Neorealism and Neoliberalism: The Contemporary Debate* [New York: Columbia University Press, 1993], pp. 294–95).

the question of state preferences.[11] The problem these critiques most commonly point to is that states may not necessarily recognize or be able to implement the interest-maximizing behavior identified by game theoretic analysis. Ironically, though, emphasizing the fact that states may fail to follow the predictions of game theory often leads the critics to discuss domestic politics in exactly the same way system-level theorists do, as constraints. For example, Joanne Gowa and Matthew Evangelista both bring up empirical cases where cooperation failed to emerge due to internal barriers to the development of cooperative preferences.[12] The idea that societal concerns could sometimes be a stimulus to pursuing cooperation, meaning that domestic politics could be part of the explanation *for* cooperation

[11] Duncan Snidal, "The Game *Theory* of International Politics," in Oye, *Cooperation under Anarchy*, pp. 40–44; Robert Jervis, "Realism, Game Theory, and Cooperation," *World Politics* 40 (April 1988), pp. 324–29; Milner, "International Theories of Cooperation," p. 493; Stephan Haggard and Beth A. Simmons, "Theories of International Regimes," *International Organization* 41 (Summer 1987), p. 513.

A committed neo-realist might argue that this criticism is misguided. Kenneth Waltz draws a sharp distinction between a theory of international politics and a theory of foreign policy (*Theory of International Politics*, pp. 71–72, 121–23). A theory of international relations takes state objectives as given and seeks to predict the outcome of interaction between states with these given preferences. Explaining where preferences actually come from, in contrast, would be the task of a theory of foreign policy.

Cooperation theory is clearly in the former vein. To criticize the theory for not exploring where payoff estimates come from, therefore, could be construed as unfair, as this was never intended to be part of the theory. This point can be granted, however, without in any way diminishing the importance of the task set for this study. Knowing why and when a state will choose to pursue cooperation is surely as interesting and relevant a question as knowing what will be the outcome of interaction between two or more such states.

Moreover, not considering the internal process of preference formation biases possible conclusions about the role of domestic factors. Even Waltz acknowledges that it is sometimes necessary to consider the impact of internal conditions on a state's foreign policy. However, he describes these factors as important only in relation to failures by states to act on their interests (*Theory of International Politics*, pp. 124–25). This means that domestic politics is only ever introduced as a source of harmful constraints, not as the potential origin of policies consistent with state interests.

[12] Joanne Gowa, "Anarchy, Egoism, and Third Images: *The Evolution of Cooperation* and International Relations," *International Organization* 40 (Winter 1986), p. 181; Matthew Evangelista, "Cooperation Theory and Disarmament Negotiations in the 1950s," *World Politics* 42 (July 1990), pp. 502–28.

when it does occur, simply does not arise in most studies of cooperation.[13]

This reveals a problem with the common argument, accepted even by many neo-liberals, that the international structure should serve as the "first cut" in any analysis.[14] Starting at the system level implicitly relegates societal pressures, such as peace movements, to a *ceteris paribus* clause. This is appropriate as long as one is simply trying to determine what predictions follow from a particular set of assumptions about the system. The danger is that the analyst will only look to see if *ceteris paribus* was violated when the initial predictions do not come true. But the assumption that initial behavior (the attempt to cooperate) follows directly from systemic conditions means that theorists will not feel a need to turn to domestic factors to explain success. If we really only ever wanted to make predictions about international outcomes, this neglect might be acceptable, for reasons of parsimony. However, there are times when the impact of societal pressures is itself an object of concern, and even when systemic theory is the goal it is hard to imagine that our images of domestic actors will not be affected if every reference to them in the literature concerns a case where their influence was counterproductive. By treating domestic politics only as a constraint, therefore, cooperation theory may bias our inferences about the role played by societal actors. When domestic factors are used only to explain residual variance, we will tend to overlook those times when they are the initial stimulus to a state's pursuit of its interests.[15]

[13] Even a generally impressive recent book by Beth A. Simmons largely fits this pattern (*Who Adjusts? Domestic Sources of Foreign Economic Policy During the Interwar Years* [Princeton: Princeton University Press, 1994]). Simmons' study emphasizes the domestic level, in an effort to explain why states defected from the international economic regime of the 1920s. Although it is quite nuanced, her account still treats domestic politics exclusively as something that interferes with interstate cooperation, either through constraints or by encouraging non-cooperative policies.

[14] Robert O. Keohane, "The World Political Economy and the Crisis of Embedded Liberalism," in John H. Goldthorpe, ed., *Order and Conflict in Contemporary Capitalism* (Oxford: Clarendon Press, 1984), p. 16; Joseph S. Nye, Jr., "Nuclear Learning and US–Soviet Security Regimes," *International Organization* 41 (Summer 1987), pp. 372–73.

[15] For a broader critique of treating domestic factors as a residual category, see Andrew Moravcsik, "Introduction: Integrating International and Domestic Explanations of International Bargaining," in Peter B. Evans, Harold K. Jacobson, and Robert D. Putnam, eds., *Double-Edged Diplomacy: International Bargaining and Domestic Politics* (Berkeley: University of California Press, 1993), pp. 9–15.

Research on preferences: elite interests and social norms

Although cooperation theory remains incomplete on the question of how states initially determine that they want to seek cooperation, other theories have addressed issues of state preference formation. Two broad research programs are especially relevant. One emphasizes the material interests of powerful societal groups, the other the role of ideas or norms. However, much of this research remains close to a top-down approach. It traces state preferences to certain key elites and does not investigate whether broader citizens' movements can also be a significant source of cooperative preferences. Some exceptions have begun to emerge among work with a "social constructivist" perspective. This work has yet to develop a clear account of how non-state actors actually achieve influence, though. Since this book seeks to advance some of the same arguments constructivists are making, I begin by describing the elitist approaches, then discuss how this book relates to recent constructivist studies.

Political economy approaches

The idea that state policies might reflect organized societal interests has a long pedigree in political economy. Much of the recent work in this vein has built on Peter Gourevitch's notion of the "second image reversed." These studies have traced preferences for protectionism or free trade to the interests of coalitions of business firms or economic sectors, and the changing balance of power among them.[16] There have also been some attempts to go beyond economic policy and relate states' security strategies to coalitions of important economic interests.[17]

[16] Peter Gourevitch, "The Second Image Reversed: The International Sources of Domestic Politics," *International Organization* 32 (Autumn 1978), pp. 881–912; Gourevitch, *Politics in Hard Times: Comparative Responses to International Economic Crisis* (Ithaca: Cornell University Press, 1986); Jeff Frieden, "Sectoral Conflict and US Foreign Economic Policy, 1914–1940," in G. John Ikenberry, David A. Lake, and Michael Mastanduno, eds., *The State and American Foreign Economic Policy* (Ithaca: Cornell University Press, 1988); Helen Milner, *Resisting Protectionism* (Princeton: Princeton University Press, 1988); Ronald Rogowski, *Commerce and Coalitions* (Princeton: Princeton University Press, 1989).

[17] Jack Snyder, *Myths of Empire: Domestic Politics and International Ambition* (Ithaca: Cornell University Press, 1991); Etel Solingen, "The Political Economy of Nuclear Restraint," *International Security* 19 (Fall 1994), pp. 126–69.

This literature offers an often persuasive account of state preferences broadly construed. Because the focus is on ruling coalitions, however, there is not much consideration of whether domestic oppositions can also have an impact. The emphasis is on societal elites, rather than average citizens. Thus, although the political economy approach lends credence to the idea that domestic factors are important, it is not especially helpful on the question of how far down the social ladder there are actors who can influence state preferences on cooperation, which is the question being investigated in this study.

Epistemic communities

There have also been some attempts to address specifically the question of where preferences for cooperation come from. The best-known approach, associated with Peter Haas, emphasizes the role of epistemic communities – groups of technical specialists who share common causal understandings and policy prescriptions.[18] In response to the question of why states decide to pursue cooperation, this approach answers that epistemic communities create a new interpretation of state interests that convinces state leaders that cooperation is desirable. Although it moves a step below national leaders, this approach still leans toward a top-down analysis. Haas and his colleagues generally suggest that the reason epistemic communities succeed is because some of their members gain positions in relevant bureaucratic agencies.[19] Preferences are thus ultimately traced to the deference given to technical elites once they hold government office, rather than to the efforts of non-elite actors outside the state.

Several studies have found, though, that the power of epistemic communities depends heavily on favorable domestic political conditions, such as sponsorship from above or support from below.[20]

[18] Peter M. Haas, ed., *Knowledge, Power, and International Policy Coordination*, a special issue of *International Organization* 46 (Winter 1992). For the definition, see Peter Haas, "Introduction: Epistemic Communities and International Policy Coordination," p. 3.

[19] Peter Haas, "Introduction," pp. 27, 30; Emanuel Adler and Peter M. Haas, "Conclusion: Epistemic Communities, World Order, and the Creation of a Reflective Research Program," *International Organization* 46 (Winter 1992), p. 374.

[20] Jeff Checkel, "Ideas, Institutions, and the Gorbachev Foreign Policy Revolution," *World Politics* 45 (January 1993), pp. 271–300; Sarah E. Mendelson, "Internal Battles and External Wars: Politics, Learning, and the Soviet Withdrawal from Afghanistan," *World Politics* 45 (April 1993), pp. 327–60; John Kurt Jacobsen, "Much Ado About

Because epistemic communities probably cannot succeed on their own, there is no way to tell whether they will be able to influence state preferences without a more fully elaborated model of the policy-making process. This problem is nicely illustrated by the one attempt that has been made to apply this approach to the case of nuclear arms control. Emanuel Adler argues that a US-based epistemic community formulated the ideas that came to govern US–Soviet arms control.[21] The 1980s pose a problem for Adler's argument, though, because President Reagan removed the members of the traditional arms control community from the bureaucracy.

Adler suggests that the community's ideas survived and were revived through the help of Congress.[22] But this undermines the initial premise that capturing part of the bureaucracy constitutes the route to influence. The argument also runs the danger of being non-falsifiable. Whenever we see arms control, it must be due to the success of the epistemic community. It would be better to specify in advance the routes by which such a group might gain influence and conditions under which these routes can be effective, rather than seek a new *ad hoc* explanation every time we see a practice consistent with the ideas of some epistemic community. In chapter 3, I undertake this step. The theoretical framework I develop there will thus provide one possible way to study the impact of epistemic communities.

Constructivist approaches

Other work that stresses how state interests emerge from a process of interpretation shares this ambiguity about the sources of influence. Several recent works argue that neo-realism, neo-liberalism, and domestic political economy approaches all share a "rationalist" orientation that takes interests as unproblematic. They put forward a constructivist alternative that sees state interests and even identities as being molded, at least in part, by norms and culture rather than material conditions. Some of this work still traces preferences to actors

Ideas: The Cognitive Factor in Economic Policy," *World Politics* 47 (January 1995), pp. 297–99, 304, 309–10.

21 Emanuel Adler, "The Emergence of Cooperation: National Epistemic Communities and the International Evolution of the Idea of Nuclear Arms Control," *International Organization* 46 (Winter 1992), pp. 101–45.

22 Ibid., pp. 140–42.

who are part of the state, such as military organizations.[23] Other works in this vein focus on non-state actors, however. Audie Klotz has even studied a case of social protest, the transnational movement against apartheid.[24]

The relationship between these works and the approach I develop here is complementary. The constructivist studies have focused on demonstrating non-spurious correlations between norms and state behavior. Most note that norms are often contested, but, so far, they have not clearly identified the political processes within states that enable non-state actors to bring about compliance with the norms they favor. Recognizing this as a problem, constructivists have acknowledged the need for more work on identifying the mechanisms by which norms gain influence and the conditions under which these processes are effective.[25] The general approach and specific framework I develop in chapter 3 could help constructivists fill in this gap.

At the same time, social constructivism could deepen the analysis in this study by helping explain the content of protest movements' ideas and why some draw wider public support than others. I take these factors as given and seek to explain why and how the resulting campaigns succeed or fail in influencing state policy, which is something constructivist accounts do not do well. While some of the new constructivist work is a welcome exception, overall, most attempts to explain how states develop a preference for cooperation have not seen a need to incorporate the hopes and fears of ordinary people. The question of how far below the elite level one can go and still find societal actors capable of contributing to state preference formation thus remains open.

[23] Jeffrey W. Legro, "Culture and Preferences in the International Cooperation Two-Step," *American Political Science Review* 90 (March 1996), pp. 118–37.

[24] Audie Klotz, *Norms in International Relations: The Struggle Against Apartheid* (Ithaca: Cornell University Press, 1995).

[25] Martha Finnemore, *National Interests in International Society* (Ithaca: Cornell University Press, 1996), pp. 130, 135–37; Ronald L. Jepperson, Alexander Wendt, and Peter J. Katzenstein, "Norms, Identity, and Culture in National Security," pp. 53–57, 64, and Paul Kowert and Jeffrey Legro, "Norms, Identity, and Their Limits: A Theoretical Reprise," both in Katzenstein, ed., *The Culture of National Security: Norms and Identity in World Politics* (New York: Columbia University Press, 1996).

Domestic structure: statesman-centered and pluralist versions

One other research program in IR has an interactive perspective that could be useful in understanding domestic processes relevant to state preference formation. The domestic structure or institutionalist approach arose out of work in political economy, especially that of Peter Katzenstein.[26] While the initial emphasis was on the impact of domestic institutions, this approach has since also incorporated attention to coalitions, as stressed in the second image reversed.[27] In addition, the two-level game approach, developed by Robert Putnam to model the relation of international and domestic bargaining processes, largely emphasizes the same factors.[28] I will therefore discuss two-level games under the general rubric of the domestic structure approach.

Within this body of research, one can identify a range of perspectives on the role of domestic factors. One of these introduces a third alternative to the two discussed so far, which emphasized domestic constraints and the influence of societal or technical elites, respectively. In this third view, domestic politics can be an indirect stimulus to state action, but actual foreign policy goals are still set at the top. After describing this statesman-centered[29] perspective, I will introduce a more pluralist version of domestic structure analysis that has recently begun to emerge.

Statesman-centered analysis

The intuition behind the domestic structure approach is that states facing similar international conditions may nonetheless respond differently because of differences in their domestic political institutions. As a result, this approach has been used primarily to explain

[26] Peter J. Katzenstein, ed., *Between Power and Plenty: Foreign Economic Policies of Advanced Industrial States* (Madison: University of Wisconsin Press, 1978).

[27] Thomas Risse-Kappen, "Public Opinion, Domestic Structure, and Foreign Policy in Liberal Democracies," *World Politics* 43 (July 1991), pp. 479–512.

[28] Robert D. Putnam, "Diplomacy and Domestic Politics: The Logic of Two-Level Games," *International Organization* 42 (Summer 1988), pp. 427–60.

[29] Although I prefer to use gender-neutral language, the body of literature being discussed here has itself adopted the label "statesman-centered." For the sake of clarity, I follow this existing usage whenever I am discussing this approach.

policy variation across countries, or across issues handled by different governing regimes or institutional settings within a country.[30] The initial focus in this literature was on state strength, or how much capacity central decisionmakers have to resist pressure from societal groups. In asking this question, this "statist" perspective reflected the traditional view of the domestic arena as a source of constraints on the ability of state leaders to pursue the national interest.[31]

However, some elaborations of this approach (though not those of Katzenstein himself) have adopted a statesman-centered framework in which societal factors might also serve as a stimulus to state action.[32] But the stimulus is indirect. In this framework, foreign policy initiatives are described not as a result of societal demands, but are instead seen as reflecting efforts by national leaders to achieve domestic goals of their own. In other words, an interest in cooperation may emerge because national leaders who are seeking to retain political power or win a domestic policy debate find international cooperation a useful strategy to those ends.[33] The link between domestic conditions and international action is thus indirect, a function of the state leader's goals rather than a direct reflection of societal concerns.

[30] Katzenstein, *Between Power and Plenty*; G. John Ikenberry, "The Irony of State Strength: Comparative Responses to the Oil Shocks in the 1970s," *International Organization* 40 (Winter 1986), pp. 105–37; Ikenberry et al., *The State and American Foreign Economic Policy*; Thomas Risse-Kappen, ed., *Bringing Transnational Relations Back In: Non-State Actors, Domestic Structures, and International Institutions* (Cambridge: Cambridge University Press, 1995); Susan Peterson, *Crisis Bargaining and the State: The Domestic Politics of International Conflict* (Ann Arbor: University of Michigan Press, 1996).

[31] Stephen D. Krasner, *Defending the National Interest: Raw Materials Investments and US Foreign Policy* (Princeton: Princeton University Press, 1978); G. John Ikenberry, *Reasons of State: Oil, Politics, and the Capacities of American Government* (Ithaca: Cornell University Press, 1988); Mastanduno, *Economic Containment*. In an interesting twist, however, Ikenberry (*Reasons of State*, p. 81) points out that there are times when domestic constraints could motivate a search for international cooperation.

[32] Putnam, "Diplomacy and Domestic Politics"; Evans et al., *Double-Edged Diplomacy*, esp. Moravcsik, "Introduction"; Michael Mastanduno, David A. Lake, and G. John Ikenberry, "Toward a Realist Theory of State Action," *International Studies Quarterly* 33 (December 1989), pp. 457–74.

[33] The diversionary theory of war fits this same logic, only for non-cooperative action. It suggests that economic or political hard times might cause leaders to initiate a foreign conflict in order to divert attention from domestic problems (Jack S. Levy, "The Diversionary Theory of War: A Critique," in Manus I. Midlarsky, ed., *Handbook of War Studies* [Boston: Unwin Hyman, 1989]; Patrick James and John R. Oneal, "The Influence of Domestic and International Politics on the President's Use of Force," *Journal of Conflict Resolution* 35 [June 1991], pp. 307–32).

The emphasis in this approach is on the strategies that are available to state leaders because of their position at the intersection of domestic and international politics. Given this emphasis, it becomes natural to assume that it is leaders who place new items on the international agenda,[34] because of the utility of negotiations on those items for advancing leaders' strategic goals. The assumption that state leaders have control over agenda-setting once again makes preference formation a top-down process, because it implies that the decision to seek cooperation always comes from the top.[35] It would thus be useful to step outside the statesman-centered perspective, to see if state preferences sometimes also arise directly from the expression of societal concerns.[36]

Toward a bottom-up alternative

Not all applications of the domestic structure approach adopt a top-down perspective, however. Some have been attentive to the possibility that a bottom-up process could alter state interests. Several recent studies have even examined the impact of public opinion or other non-state actors specifically on security policies. These studies all suggest that differences in influence reflect differences in domestic

[34] Thus, Peter B. Evans concludes, "State leaders are in the driver's seat as international agendas are being formulated" ("Building an Integrative Approach to International and Domestic Politics," in Evans et al., *Double-Edged Diplomacy,* p. 399; see also pp. 403–05). Elsewhere, I have shown that this conclusion is actually incorrect for the empirical case Evans cites in support of this assertion (Jeffrey W. Knopf, "Beyond Two-Level Games: Domestic–International Interaction in the Intermediate-Range Nuclear Forces Negotiations," *International Organization* 47 [Autumn 1993], pp. 620–21).

[35] Some attempts to formalize two-level games do not assume statesmen have agenda control and allow for domestic groups to make international proposals (for example, Jongryn Mo, "Two-Level Games with Endogenous Domestic Coalitions," *Journal of Conflict Resolution* 38 [September 1994], pp. 402–22). But such formal models simply assume this is true. They do not explore the conditions under which this would actually be the case empirically, nor do they indicate which groups would be likely to have this agenda-setting power. These are of course central questions in this study.

[36] A statesman-centered approach does not logically require that cooperative initiatives reflect efforts to manipulate domestic audiences. Leaders interested in retaining power would also be motivated to respond to direct societal demands for action. However, statesman-centered accounts rarely seem to consider such a possibility. To do so would be to yield the main initiative to actors who are not at the "center" of the analysis, and probably also does not seem as interesting as the clever use of two-level strategies by state leaders.

structures or arise from domestic institutional change.[37] By showing that the domestic structure approach can accommodate a more pluralistic set of actors, this research suggests that this approach would make a useful starting point for the present study. But what these studies have done is still incomplete as a framework for investigating the influence of domestic actors in individual cases. Most of these studies use state structure as an explanation for why the impact of societal or transnational actors differs across countries or governing regimes. But none of these studies specify the precise causal processes that permit societal or transnational actors to gain influence when domestic structure is favorable.[38]

Without an ability to follow the causal process, though, there is no way to know in any particular case whether a domestic or transnational actor will achieve the usual or maximum potential level of influence. To explain the importance of societal inputs in individual cases, rather than the variation in typical influence levels across domestic structures, the causal connections need to be specified more fully. Otherwise, one cannot tell whether non-state actors will actually be able to take advantage of the influence opportunities provided by a particular domestic structure. Knowledge of the "policy networks" that link state and society within a given system is still important, because this determines what institutional avenues are available (and not available) for influencing policy. But once one has identified those pathways and how they work, domestic structure recedes into the

[37] Risse-Kappen, "Public Opinion, Domestic Structure"; Thomas Risse-Kappen, "Ideas Do Not Float Freely: Transnational Coalitions, Domestic Structures, and the End of the Cold War," *International Organization* 48 (Spring 1994), pp. 185–214; Susan Peterson, "How Democracies Differ: Public Opinion, State Structure, and the Lessons of the Fashoda Crisis," *Security Studies* 5 (Autumn 1995), pp. 3–37; Matthew Evangelista, "The Paradox of State Strength: Transnational Relations, Domestic Structures, and Security Policy in Russia and the Soviet Union," *International Organization* 49 (Winter 1995), pp. 1–38; Eric Mlyn, *The State, Society, and Limited Nuclear War* (Albany: State University of New York Press, 1995); Jeffrey T. Checkel, *Ideas and International Politics: Soviet/Russian Behavior and the End of the Cold War* (New Haven: Yale University Press, 1997).

[38] Risse-Kappen rightly stresses the importance of entering into larger coalitions. But this still begs the questions of who the right coalition partners are, how much leverage they can provide, and under what conditions. Peterson and Mlyn both make an assumption that the legislature is the representative of societal interests. But they do not address the issues of when the legislature is responsive, and to whom. Moreover, as I will show in chapter 3, there can be more than one pathway to influence within a domestic structure, so it would be a mistake to focus only on legislatures.

background. For a given country deciding whether to pursue cooperation on a given issue, state structure, as a fixed entity, cannot explain variations in outcome. In contrast, the processes permitted by that structure, because they might be manipulated differently by different groups, can help explain varying state interest in international cooperation.[39]

These recent applications of a domestic structure approach have provided a useful start toward understanding the impact of domestic actors on state preferences. I thus seek to build on this approach, by specifying more fully how one could evaluate the impact of societal pressures in specific cases. In particular, I seek to add a fuller depiction of the causal processes that could be at work within the policy networks contained in a given domestic structure. I therefore supplement this approach with explanatory models drawn from the study of domestic politics, in order to create a theoretical framework that can be applied to individual case studies. Hence, the theoretical framework for this study, which I describe in chapter 3, relies on political processes that have been shown to be effective in shaping US domestic policy, and identifies conditions under which they might give societal groups influence on arms control policy. This framework is intended to improve the ability of domestic structure models to trace the causal processes that would have to come into play to give societal actors influence.

Overall, both cooperation theory and recent attempts to integrate domestic factors into theories of foreign policy and interstate bargaining have made tremendous contributions to our understanding of international politics. Yet important gaps remain in our knowledge of how states develop a preference for seeking cooperation, and of the domestic processes involved. The main rationalist approaches tend to assume some variant of a top-down process and hence have not examined whether non-elite societal actors can also play a major role. Some constructivist and domestic structure research is more open to

[39] This would still not be a complete explanation of state preferences, because it would not account for the content of groups' goals. As noted above, recent constructivist research suggests one possible way to account for why movements arise around certain goals. The social movement literature also has much to say about why protest emerges and makes the demands that it does. I take protest campaigns and their goals as given, and seek to explain how such non-state actors get their preferred version of state interests adopted. This is a question on which constructivism and social movement theory are fairly weak.

this possibility, but remains vague about the political mechanisms by which influence is achieved. The approach I develop in this study is intended to build on and extend some of this recent work. Its goal is to develop a framework that makes it possible to determine when citizen activism has an impact on state preference formation. I defer development of this framework until chapter 3. In the next chapter, I provide an initial statistical assessment of activism's impact. The results of this analysis will give added reason to move into case studies, using the modified version of the domestic structure framework introduced in chapter 3.

2 Protest and arms control: a first look

The previous chapter showed that research on international cooperation and state preference formation generally overlooks one of the roles that grassroots societal actors might play. Even when they take internal factors into account, existing studies rarely consider whether the direct stimulus to seeking cooperation can come from below. The rest of this book presents the results of empirical research designed to test this possibility. The analysis focuses on US decisions to enter nuclear arms talks during the Cold War. It will show that protest against nuclear weapons was a significant source of state preferences for cooperation to control strategic arms. As a first step in making this case, this chapter presents a quantitative test of the hypothesis that domestic protest can affect states' willingness to pursue cooperation. Subsequent chapters then use case studies to corroborate the statistical results and identify the causal processes involved. In order to clarify the variables that must be controlled for, I begin by summarizing the main explanations for arms control in the existing literature.

As noted in the introduction, one reason to examine strategic arms control is because the issue poses a relatively hard test for the impact of societal activism. Another benefit of examining arms control is a useful parallelism between arms control theory and the larger literature on cooperation. Existing explanations for arms control mirror the explanations most prevalent in cooperation theory, as well as some of the other statesman-centered approaches described in the previous chapter. This makes it possible to identify specific factors that must be controlled for if one is to assess whether system-level or statist approaches can explain interest in cooperation, independent of domestic actors' concerns in this area.

Arms control: existing explanations

A number of studies have sought to draw lessons inductively from the history of arms control. These studies tend to explain success in reaching agreement somewhat differently from failures to cooperate. Arms control theory often introduces domestic politics to explain breakdowns in the attempt to cooperate, thus corresponding to much of cooperation theory in conceptualizing domestic factors as a constraint. But, again consistent with top-down approaches, this literature generally explains successful accords by system-level factors or statesmen's own initiatives.[1]

In fact, there is remarkable agreement in the literature about the chief factors that account for arms control. The three variables most widely stressed are the military balance, the state of political relations between the adversaries, and the leadership exercised by their heads of state. These variables are usually described as necessary conditions for the successful conclusion of treaties, so they might not be as decisive in the initiation of talks, which is the focus here. However, there is no literature that focuses on arms control initiation *per se*, and these variables largely capture the factors emphasized in the various system-level and statesman-centered theories described in the last chapter. Therefore, these variables are not only the best available, there is good reason to believe they should control effectively for how the major theories of cooperation would explain the outcomes being studied here.

The most commonly reiterated conclusion in studies of arms control is that accord is possible only when the military forces of the two sides are in rough parity and/or the agreement affects both sides equally.[2]

1 There is one significant exception to the portrait of domestic factors as only a constraint or an indirect stimulus in US arms control policy. Fen Osler Hampson has argued that domestic political factors have often been important in bringing the United States to the bargaining table initially ("Headed for the Table: United States Approaches to Arms Control Prenegotiation," in Janice Gross Stein, ed. *Getting to the Table: The Processes of International Prenegotiation* [Baltimore: Johns Hopkins University Press, 1989]). The analysis in this book, by using multiple methods and a structured framework for assessing case study evidence, will confirm and deepen Hampson's preliminary observations in this area.

2 Michael Mandelbaum, *The Nuclear Question: The United States and Nuclear Weapons, 1946–1976* (New York: Cambridge University Press, 1979), pp. 12, 39, 197; Joseph Kruzel, "From Rush–Bagot to START: The Lessons of Arms Control," *Orbis* 30 (Spring 1986), pp. 203, 210; Albert Carnesale and Richard N. Haass, "Conclusions: Weighing the Evidence," in Carnesale and Haass, eds., *Superpower Arms Control: Setting the*

This is clearly consistent with the neo-realist emphasis on relative gains. It suggests that cooperation on arms occurs only when it would give neither side a relative advantage. The military balance will thus serve as a control for neo-realist explanations of cooperation.

Most arms control studies also argue that agreement is likely only after there has been some improvement in political relations between the adversaries, and that objectionable behavior in other areas often derails arms talks.[3] This point reflects a traditional realist objection to liberal hopes that arms control will help reduce tensions. Yet the notion that a prior warming of relations is necessary can also be seen as congruent with neo-liberal cooperation theory. Neo-liberal depictions of how cooperation emerges often emphasize the importance of playing strategies that both begin with and reciprocate cooperative moves.[4] Indeed, bargaining strategy has been explicitly introduced as a key variable in several studies of attempted US–Soviet cooperation. Different studies find different variants of an initially concessionary strategy to be the most effective, but they agree that such strategies play an important role by improving the political atmosphere so as to facilitate action on mutual interests.[5] Arms

Record Straight (Cambridge, MA: Ballinger, 1987), p. 330; Philip J. Farley, "Strategic Arms Control, 1967–1987," in Alexander L. George, Farley, and Alexander Dallin, eds., *US–Soviet Security Cooperation: Achievements, Failures, Lessons* (New York: Oxford University Press, 1988), pp. 232–33; Lloyd Jensen, *Bargaining for National Security: The Postwar Disarmament Negotiations* (Columbia, SC: University of South Carolina Press, 1988), p. 247.

3 Mandelbaum, *The Nuclear Question*, pp. 39–40; Kruzel, "From Rush–Bagot to START," p. 200; Carnesale and Haass, *Superpower Arms Control*, pp. 339–41; Alexander L. George, "Factors Influencing Security Cooperation," in George et al., *US–Soviet Security Cooperation*, pp. 655, 667; April Carter, *Success and Failure in Arms Control Negotiations* (Oxford: Oxford University Press, 1989), pp. 1, 16–17, 279–81 – but, for a contrary view, see Jensen, *Bargaining for National Security*, pp. 79–80.

4 The classic statement is Robert Axelrod, *The Evolution of Cooperation* (New York: Basic Books, 1984).

5 Deborah Welch Larson, "Crisis Prevention and the Austrian State Treaty," *International Organization* 41 (Winter 1987), pp. 27–60; Joshua S. Goldstein and John R. Freeman, *Three-Way Street: Strategic Reciprocity in World Politics* (Chicago: University of Chicago Press, 1990); Steve Weber, *Cooperation and Discord in US–Soviet Arms Control* (Princeton: Princeton University Press, 1991); Alexander L. George, "Strategies for Facilitating Cooperation," in George et al., *US–Soviet Security Cooperation*, pp. 705–09.

Larson suggests that publicly announced unilateral concessions might sometimes work by fostering "domestic political pressures" to abide by "social norms to reciprocate" ("Crisis Prevention," p. 33). But she does not indicate when or how such pressures would actually be effective in influencing security policy. The theoretical framework I develop in chapter 3 will attempt to do this, by identifying specific

control theory's stress on the need for a prior improvement of relations can thus control for the role assigned in neo-liberal cooperation theory to strategies that begin with an initial cooperative move.

Finally, most accounts of arms control also see a need for the "political will" to agree.[6] This variable introduces a role for domestic factors, but is usually conceptualized in a manner consistent with one of the realist perspectives introduced in chapter 1. In particular, most accounts translate this into a need for leadership at the top to overcome domestic obstacles to security cooperation, thus again treating the domestic arena only as a source of constraints.[7] Some studies, though, have also noted the possibility of an indirect stimulus, in which societal conditions could trigger a new international initiative. These studies suggest that worsening political or economic situations sometimes created incentives for US leaders to seek cooperation with the Soviet Union as a way to counteract declines in public support produced by these domestic problems.[8] Thus, even when it introduces domestic factors, the arms control literature still resembles both cooperation theory and statesman-centered approaches in viewing preference formation as a top-down process. Willingness to cooperate is taken to be a function of central decisionmakers' independent calculations or initiatives, not something that might result from the concerns expressed by a citizens' campaign.

In sum, based on existing arms control theory, this study will use the military balance, the state of political relations, and domestic economic conditions as control variables in the statistical analysis. I describe how I operationalize and measure these variables below, in connection with my discussion of the results of that analysis. I will

conditions when another state's strategy might be able to change US policy by appealing to a domestic audience.

6 Mandelbaum, *The Nuclear Question*, p. 12; Jensen, *Bargaining for National Security*, p. 254.

7 Thus, the most comprehensive exploration of the domestic politics of arms control in the United States that I have come across treats domestic factors solely as "impediments" to arms control (Steven E. Miller, "Politics over Promise: Domestic Impediments to Arms Control," *International Security* 8 [Spring 1984], pp. 67–90).

8 Robin F. Marra, Charles W. Ostrom, Jr., and Dennis M. Simon, "Foreign Policy and Presidential Popularity," *Journal of Conflict Resolution* 34 (December 1990), pp. 588–623; James D. Morrow, "Electoral and Congressional Incentives and Arms Control," *Journal of Conflict Resolution* 35 (June 1991), pp. 245–65.

also consider these variables as possible alternative explanations in the case studies. However, the variables stressed in existing arms control theory do not capture the third top-down perspective introduced in the previous chapter, in which a direct stimulus to action can arise from domestic elites other than central decisionmakers. I therefore control for this view as well in the case studies. I do so by considering whether decisions to seek arms cooperation can be fully explained by efforts within Congress or relevant bureaucratic agencies without taking into account societal activism. In the statistical test presented below, the main goal is simply to assess whether it is possible to explain efforts to pursue arms limitation solely on the basis of systemic and statesman-centered variables, with no need to take account of any domestic actors besides state leaders. Before presenting the statistical results, though, it is also necessary to discuss the dependent variable. How can the abstract concept of state preferences be given clear meaning in the arms control area?

Operationalization of the dependent variable

The focus of this study is the development of a preference for cooperation. In game theoretic research, preference is a relative term. The concern is simply whether cooperation is seen as a better move or outcome than defection, not what the absolute payoffs are. In this study, the key question is whether attempting to achieve mutual cooperation becomes preferred to continuing a competition in arms buildups. Unfortunately, this is not an easy thing to determine empirically, because a lack of cooperative behavior does not necessarily indicate a lack of interest in cooperation. Non-cooperative actions may arise because a state actively prefers unilateral or even mutual defection to making a cooperative move. But even when a state holds a preference ordering like that of the prisoner's dilemma (PD) game which is the focus of much cooperation research, and wants to achieve a mutual cooperation outcome, defection could still result if the state is playing a strategy like tit-for-tat, which calls for punishing a previous defection by the other side. Thus, a conflictual move need not imply that a state actually attaches a higher payoff to continued competition than it would to mutual cooperation.

To avoid the problem that a preference for cooperation may not be manifested in cooperative behavior, I draw on the distinction between opportunity and willingness enunciated by Most and

Starr.[9] From this perspective, the charge that cooperation theory ignores domestic sources of preferences is equivalent to saying that a system-level opportunity to cooperate may not be matched by actor willingness to do so. But states that would prefer cooperation, even if they are engaged in a pattern of conflictual moves at the moment, must at some point demonstrate willingness to adopt a cooperative policy if they want to realize their preference for cooperation. Thus, a question that can be addressed empirically is what leads states to take action that shows an interest in cooperation. Therefore, following the Most and Starr terminology, the dependent variable I examine in this study is willingness to cooperate.[10] I operationalize willingness as a decision to pursue formal negotiations in a format that is also acceptable to the other side. This coding requires simply that the United States either makes a proposal for arms talks that elicits a positive Soviet response or agrees to a Soviet proposal for talks.[11]

This coding is intended to deal with two possible sources of uncertainty about a state's willingness to pursue cooperation. First, a public offer of arms talks might not reflect an actual preference for cooperation. The offering party may be making a proposal that it expects will not be accepted, simply to win propaganda points. I seek to get around this problem by adopting a "proof is in the pudding" principle. That is, I look for those cases where arms talks actually result and either lead to an agreement or significant progress toward a possible deal. If a country makes a concerted effort to reach a deal, it is

[9] Benjamin A. Most and Harvey Starr, *Inquiry, Logic, and International Politics* (Columbia, SC: University of South Carolina Press, 1989).

[10] Obviously, the phrase "willingness to cooperate" has positive connotations that may not always have been warranted. In any given situation, the opponents of an arms control proposal may have had the better assessment of US interests. To avoid unintended connotations would require adopting new jargon, however, and I felt it better to work with existing terminology. Readers should therefore keep in mind that "unwillingness to cooperate" should not automatically be seen as a bad thing; it will depend on one's own assessment of the merits of proposed arms talks.

[11] This coding omits tacit forms of cooperation that some other studies have addressed (for example, George W. Downs and David M. Rocke, *Tacit Bargaining, Arms Races, and Arms Control* [Ann Arbor: University of Michigan Press, 1990]). However, tacit cooperation has usually concerned only a single weapons program, while attempts to deal more comprehensively with security problems arising from an arms race have generally required formal negotiations. Hence, a preference for cooperation on more than a single limited aspect of the competition will be reflected in a formal offer to go to the table.

likely that its initial offer (or acceptance of the other side's invitation) indicated a real interest in cooperation.

But a country may make a sincere offer that does not lead to talks because the other side lacks interest in cooperation. This second problem is more difficult to resolve, but I believe the coding adopted here is the best option for the case of US–Soviet arms talks. This is because the Soviet Union generally maintained a high level of readiness to engage in arms talks. The USSR was thus unlikely to decline negotiations except when a US offer seemed designed solely to secure an American advantage, meaning it did not reflect a preference for mutual cooperation.

Soviet eagerness for talks reflected a political view of the purposes of arms control. In the Soviet view, independent of their effect on the military balance, arms control negotiations and agreements could be useful as an avenue to other goals, such as gaining equal status or creating disunity in the Western alliance.[12] But even where Soviet willingness did not reflect purely cooperative aims, the USSR nearly always maintained a high level of readiness to engage in talks. This means the Soviets were likely to turn down US offers only when they felt the American proposal was purely self-serving and not meant to make possible a mutually beneficial outcome.[13] Thus, for purposes of coding in this study, it is plausible to treat the absence of negotiations as indicating a lack of serious US interest in cooperation, since the United States could normally find negotiating terms acceptable to the Soviets when it wanted to do so.

Thus, operationally, the dependent variable for this study is a decision to seek or agree to arms talks on a basis that is also acceptable to the other side. I focus specifically on negotiations that targeted the strategic nuclear programs of the superpowers. These are the negotiations that, according to mainstream arms control theory, objectively should have matched the mixed-motive situation represented by

12 Franklyn Griffiths, "The Soviet Experience of Arms Control," in Stein, *Getting to the Table*.

13 An example is the Open Skies proposal of 1955. As I will document in chapter 4, its advocates in the Eisenhower administration were largely motivated by relative gains seeking. They thought that the proposal would either give the United States an intelligence advantage or a propaganda advantage, and fully expected that the Soviet Union would find the plan unacceptable. The fact the USSR rejected the idea of even starting talks on the plan thus really is a fair reflection of an absence of US willingness at that time to make concessions that could bring about a more balanced "CC" outcome.

prisoner's dilemma. Other negotiations, such as those that produced the Non-Proliferation Treaty (NPT), were closer to games of co-ordination or even harmony, in that neither side had much to gain from avoiding or defecting from an agreement. Talks that would limit development or deployment of strategic nuclear weapons, on the other hand, did arouse ongoing doubts about the desirability and feasibility of cooperation. Willingness to cooperate in this area was always problematic, which makes explaining it an interesting puzzle.

I turn now to a statistical analysis designed to test the hypothesis that domestic protest campaigns affected the willingness of the United States to seek control of strategic weapons. This analysis uses logistic regression on a pooled time-series data set. I introduce the analysis by describing the data set for the dependent variable.

The data

Data on the dependent variable

Given the focus on strategic arms control, I analyze a data set that includes the origins of three series of negotiations, each of which produced formal agreements with strategic implications: the test ban, SALT, and START talks. There are a few other negotiations that could have been added, but a mix of technical and substantive concerns suggests that they are best left out. For example, I exclude negotiations on the Baruch Plan, offered by the United States in 1946, for two reasons. First, it is not clear that this offer counts as indicating a preference for cooperation by the criteria developed above. The USA proposed the plan in the United Nations, which left the Soviet Union with no choice about whether it wanted to discuss such a plan. All indications are that the USSR saw little promise in the proposal, so it is not clear that there would have been any negotiations had the United States first sought direct bilateral talks instead.[14] Second, some of the data sets I use to measure the control variables do not extend back as far as 1946. This means it would be quite difficult to include the Baruch Plan in the statistical analysis even if it seemed appropriate to do so.

[14] Mandelbaum, *The Nuclear Question*, pp. 23–27. As explained in the introduction, n. 13, excluding this case does not bias the results in favor of the importance of societal actors.

In addition, I do not include talks that followed directly from and were seen as a continuation of an earlier set, such as SALT II or START II. Since these talks were planned in the course of the preceding negotiations, there is no period before they began in which the USA lacked willingness to cooperate and therefore no new decision to seek cooperation to explain. Instead, the decision to pursue cooperation in these cases came earlier, when the first SALT and START talks began. It is that decision that is the focus here.

The data set therefore contains three instances of development of a preference for seeking cooperation on controlling strategic arms. The decision whether or not to seek talks is a dichotomous variable. For the statistical analysis, I measure all the variables on a quarterly basis. I chose this time period because anything shorter might have been too brief to capture trends in protest or the other independent variables, while a longer time period would reduce the number of observations so much as to make statistical inference quite difficult. Thus, the dependent variable is coded 1 in any quarter where the United States makes an offer of talks that is accepted, or agrees to a Soviet offer, and acceptance of this invitation directly leads to a new set of talks. It is coded 0 otherwise.

Once an invitation that produces talks is issued or accepted by the United States, I exclude all subsequent quarters for the duration of that set of talks and the period during which any resulting treaty is being considered for ratification. For these observations, the question becomes what maintains a preference for cooperation, and this may have a somewhat different answer than the question of what leads to that preference in the first place. The latter question is the focus here. Hence, all quarters in which a possible arms agreement was formally under consideration are excluded. This means that each series of observations begins with the conclusion of deliberations on the previous possible agreement (either treaty ratification, treaty withdrawal, or the last formal negotiating session of failed talks) and continues until the next successful talks invitation. The periods covered by the three time series are indicated in figure 2.1. In all, they comprise sixty-seven quarterly observations.

Usefulness of this data for drawing inferences

This data set may seem limited to just three cases, which contain no variation on the dependent variable. That is not the case. Because each time series concludes with negotiations getting underway, this creates an impression that there are only three observations, with no cases of failure to cooperate. However, this impression is simply an artifact of the fact each series runs until there is a 1 observation.

In fact, the data set contains several cases where arms talks were considered but willingness to cooperate did not result. For example, the time series include periods in which certain other actors promoted arms control yet failed to persuade the US government to enter talks. In one such case, some protest arose against President Truman's decision in 1950 to launch a crash program to develop the H-bomb. However, no talks on a possible ban on the hydrogen bomb ever resulted. In another case, in their first two meetings in early 1981 with Reagan's first secretary of state, Al Haig, Soviet diplomats asked the United States to resume arms talks. Their request was rebuffed.[15] Thus, there are cases in the data when certain actors tried to stimulate a US interest in cooperation but failed.

There are also cases in the time series when the US government deliberated arms control and chose to make proposals that were driven almost entirely by the desire for propaganda or other relative gains. Because officials knew the USSR would reject these proposals and indeed designed them in ways that virtually precluded the possibility of agreement, they should be viewed as separate cases where the outcome is an absence of willingness to cooperate. One example is the Open Skies proposal of 1955, for reasons I discuss in note 13 in this chapter. Another is Lyndon Johnson's 1964 proposal for a freeze on production of strategic nuclear delivery vehicles, to be verified by on-site inspection. Officials later admitted they made the proposal precisely because they knew it would lead nowhere.[16]

All of these examples account for some of the zeros within each time series prior to the 1 observation. They mean that the data set contains more than just three cases. These zero observations also mean that there is variation on the dependent variable. Because it includes cases when cooperation was decidedly not already on the table, this analysis can evaluate whether the system-level factors taken to explain cooperation when it occurs can also account for what leads to an interest in cooperation in the first place.

15 Alexander M. Haig, Jr., *Caveat: Realism, Reagan, and Foreign Policy* (New York: Macmillan, 1984), pp. 104–08.

16 John Newhouse, *Cold Dawn: The Story of SALT* (New York: Holt, Rinehart, and Winston, 1973), pp. 69–70.

Is arms control cooperation?

Before describing the data on the independent variables, it is worth considering whether even the positive observations in this data set really represent willingness to cooperate. Critics on both the left and the right have suggested that superpower arms control was nothing but a sham.[17] They suggest that superpower arms talks never significantly restrained the arms competition, and perhaps were never meant to. From this perspective, even the treaties that were signed do not reflect any serious cooperation to limit arms.

There is an important element of truth in this argument. The arms talks were in part symbolic exercises, designed to provide assurance to the rest of the world that the superpowers were concerned about the arms race. But Robert Jervis has argued that this symbolism extended to the rival governments as well; the United States and USSR used arms talks to reassure each other that neither wanted a nuclear war.[18] Thus, even on the symbolic level, there was an element of real cooperation involved.

Moreover, each set of talks did produce some meaningful restrictions. Every treaty was opposed by some weapons scientists and conservative pro-defense groups, which would have been unlikely had each contained nothing of substance. Edward Teller testified against the Limited Test Ban Treaty (LTBT) of 1963 because he believed it would leave the United States behind in certain areas, especially development of an ABM.[19] The ABM treaty, signed as part of SALT I in 1972, also became a major target of conservatives in the 1980s precisely because it would hamstring President Reagan's Strategic Defense Initiative (SDI). Finally, the START I treaty actually required both sides to cut their existing arsenals significantly.

To be sure, arms control never achieved the fondest hopes of its adherents. But the fact that cooperation is less than perfect does not mean no cooperation was involved. By that logic, the General Agreement on Tariffs and Trade (GATT) regime would also not be a case of

[17] Alva Myrdal, *The Game of Disarmament*, rev. and updated edn. (New York: Pantheon Books, 1982); Colin S. Gray, *House of Cards: Why Arms Control Must Fail* (Ithaca: Cornell University Press, 1992).

[18] Robert Jervis, *The Meaning of the Nuclear Revolution* (Ithaca: Cornell University Press, 1989), pp. 221–25.

[19] Ivo H. Daalder, "The Limited Test Ban Treaty," in Carnesale and Haass, *Superpower Arms Control*, pp. 22–25.

cooperation, because first the Americans and then the Europeans managed to exclude agriculture from the trade regime. Students of international political economy (IPE) have no problem treating trade as an area of cooperation despite the less than perfect reach of free trade. Even if it is often limited in extent, security cooperation should not be coded any differently.

Operationalization of the independent variables

Anti-nuclear weapons protest serves as the main independent variable in the following analysis, with other variables serving as controls. I developed a measure of protest activity from stories listed in annual editions of the *New York Times Index*. I operationalize the amount of protest as the total number of stories found under relevant headings in the index, where the stories concern demonstrations or public calls for government action by non-governmental groups, and these events occur in the United States. In line with the measurement of the other variables, I initially counted the relevant stories on a quarterly basis.

Graphs of quarterly protest for each of the three time periods in the data set are contained in figure 2.1. The observation points are identified on the x-axis by the last two digits of the calendar year and the number of the quarter in question (so 503 means the third quarter of 1950). The quarters in which the USA issued the invitations that led to arms talks are indicated by arrows in each diagram. All three graphs give a strong visual impression that the decision to seek cooperation occurred at or near the peak level of protest activity in each period. The statistical analysis presented below is designed to see whether this observation holds up when other factors are controlled for.

There still remains the question of the proper specification of the protest variable. Theory does not suggest any precise answer, but common sense suggests some parameters. I believe it unlikely that policy would respond to the amount of protest in just a single quarter. Policymakers would probably want to see whether a new protest campaign had more staying power than that, meaning that the protest measure should cover at least two quarters. At the other end of the spectrum, I find it hard to imagine policymakers responding to events that happened much more than six months before. If protest peaked more than half a year earlier and was not maintained, policymakers would probably no longer be worried about it. The upper and lower

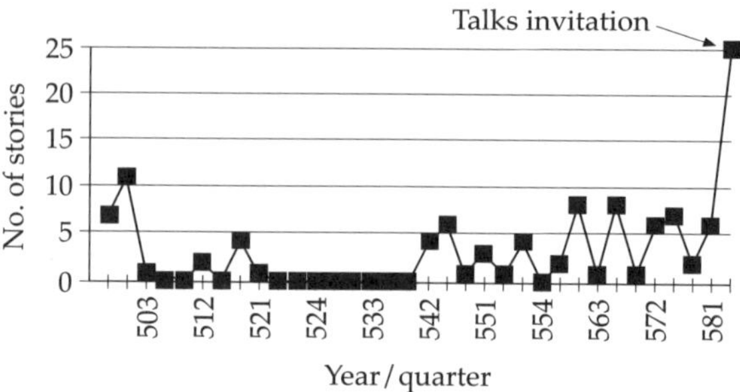

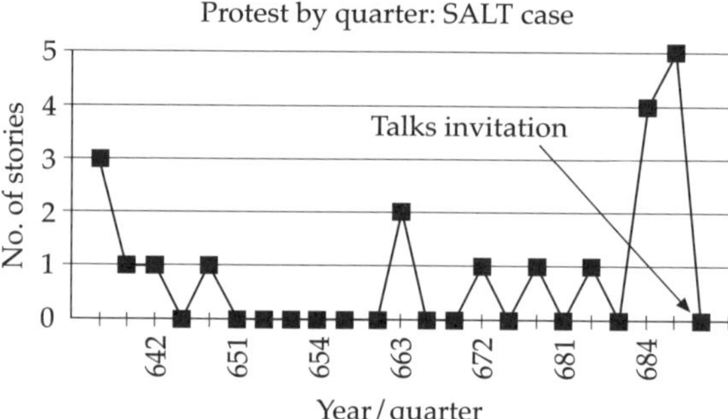

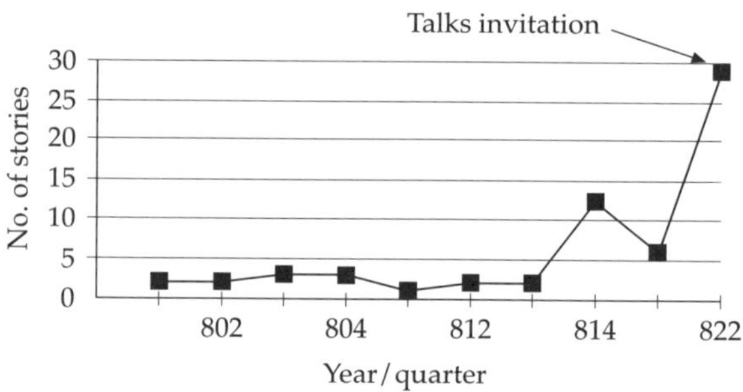

Figure 2.1 Protest levels in three time periods

bounds on the measure of protest suggested by common sense hence converge on a period of six months. I therefore operationalize societal activism with a count of all the stories on anti-nuclear weapons protest in the current and previous quarter.[20]

For reasons described above, I use three other variables as controls: the military balance, the political atmosphere, and domestic economic conditions. There are several reasonable ways to measure each. I begin with the specifications of those that previous statistical analyses found to perform best. I then discuss more briefly the results of trying plausible alternative measurements. I describe the different ways of measuring the control variables that I use in conjunction with my discussion of the results they produce.

Results

Because the dependent variable in this study is dichotomous, standard OLS regression is inappropriate.[21] I therefore employ multivariate logistic regression to test whether protest against nuclear weapons contributes to US willingness to pursue cooperation. I begin by using current knowledge to specify what should theoretically be the best form of the equation to be estimated. Because the theoretical grounds for preferring this particular specification are not especially strong, however, I test the robustness of these preliminary results by trying other ways of measuring the control variables that appear reasonable given prior findings in the relevant literature.

Theoretically best specification

In all tests, I measure willingness to cooperate (the dependent variable) and societal protest (the main independent variable) in the manner outlined above. Previous quantitative studies of arms races and arms control suggest that the following would be the strongest way to measure the control variables. First, for the military balance, I use a measure based on warhead levels. Comparative analysis has

20 I also tested variants of the protest measure covering one and three quarters, and involving a lag of one quarter. They generally did not change the results, suggesting the findings below are robust across different specifications of the main independent variable.

21 John H. Aldrich and Forrest D. Nelson, *Linear Probability, Logit, and Probit Models* (Beverly Hills: Sage Publications, 1984).

found stronger arms race reactivity in weapons stockpiles than in overall defense spending.[22] And stockpile levels, not military spending, were also the focus of arms control talks. I use data on total deliverable nuclear warheads collected by Ward and Davis as the basis for constructing this stockpile measure.[23]

The time lag for this measure reflects research by McGinnis and Williams. They have found that reaction to changes in the other side's capabilities is virtually instantaneous, suggesting that decisionmakers constantly update their information.[24] On this basis, I use a military balance measure that is contemporaneous, not lagged. Finally, there is the problem of what to do with a variable measured in annual installments when the other observations are quarterly. Based on McGinnis and Williams' notion of constant updating and adjusting, I prorate each year's increase or decrease equally across the four quarters, reaching the reported total for the year in the fourth quarter. Since the arms control literature suggests that cooperation should occur under conditions of parity, I transform this stockpile data into a measure of how close the two sides' warhead levels are to being equal. This measure of warhead parity varies between 0 and 1, with 1 indicating parity and 0 indicating that all warheads are possessed by only one side.[25]

To measure the state of political relations, I rely on events data. I use a data set on US–Soviet relations created by Sheen Rajmaira by merging two sources of events data. Rajmaira recoded events in the WEIS (World Events Interaction Survey) data set for 1979–88, applying COPDAB (Conflict and Peace Data Bank) coding rules, and joined these with the COPDAB data, which run through 1978.[26] The co-

[22] Michael D. Ward, "The Political Economy of Arms Races and International Tensions," *Conflict Management and Peace Science* 7 (Spring 1984), pp. 1–23. (An analysis that agrees that arms races take place in terms of stockpiles, but finds no US–Soviet race in nuclear arsenals, is Robert Ayanian, "Nuclear Consequences of the Welfare State," *Public Choice* 49 [1986], pp. 201–22).

[23] Michael D. Ward and David R. Davis, "Risky Business: US–Soviet Competition and Corporate Profits," in Alex Mintz, ed., *The Political Economy of Military Spending in the United States* (London: Routledge, 1992), tabs. 5.3 and 5.6.

[24] Michael D. McGinnis and John T. Williams, "Change and Stability in Superpower Rivalry," *American Political Science Review* 83 (December 1989), pp. 1101–23.

[25] The calculation is: warhead parity = 1 – ABS(US warheads – Soviet warheads)/(US warheads + Soviet warheads).

[26] I obtained this data on-line from osiris.colorado.edu/pub/statlib/datasets/copdab48-88/us-soviet.data, where Michael Ward helpfully informed me he had posted it.

operative and conflictual diplomatic actions in this data set have been weighted and aggregated quarterly. Based on Goldstein and Freeman's study of superpower reciprocity, a measure of net cooperation by the other side, lagged one quarter, seems likely to be the strongest specification.[27] I thus operationalize the political atmosphere as the total weighted cooperation minus total weighted conflict directed at the United States by the Soviet Union in the previous quarter.

Finally, to control for the domestic political motivations US leaders might have to seek arms talks, independent of any organized societal demands for cooperation, I draw on research by James Morrow on US concessions in the SALT talks. His analysis of the impact of economic conditions suggests that inflation, lagged one quarter, is the best measure to control for the president's incentives to seek cooperation arising from economic conditions.[28] The equation I estimate, as theoretically most likely to be the best specified, is thus:

> decision to seek talks = a + b_1 (six-month protest count) + b_2 (warhead parity) + b_3 (net Soviet cooperation, lagged one quarter) + b_4 (inflation, lagged one quarter) + e

The results are reported in table 2.1. Three features of the results are noteworthy. First, the protest variable is statistically significant, at better than the .01 level using a one-tailed test. Quite surprisingly, though, none of the control variables is even close to being significant (they do, however, have the expected signs). Second, the goodness-of-

27 Joshua Goldstein and Freeman, *Three-Way Street*.

28 Morrow, "Electoral and Congressional Incentives," p. 260. Inflation data are taken from US Department of Commerce, Bureau of Economic Analysis, *Handbook of Cyclical Indicators* (Washington, DC: Government Printing Office, 1984), p. 103, tab. 320C.

It might seem to make more sense to control for the president's approval ratings directly. However, this would run a serious danger of multicollinearity. It has been shown that respondents' views on foreign policy issues are part of what shape overall approval ratings (Miroslav Nincic and Barbara Hinckley, "Foreign Policy and the Evaluation of Presidential Candidates," *Journal of Conflict Resolution* 35 [June 1991], pp. 333–55). Thus, declining polls might be due partly to public displeasure with the president's arms control policy. If so, approval rating would be correlated with protest levels, and including both variables in the analysis would lead to underestimating the true impact of societal concerns. A significant body of evidence suggests that the state of the economy, because of its separate impact on approval, does affect US foreign policy, so this seems an appropriate proxy (see, for example, Patrick James and John R. Oneal, "The Influence of Domestic and International Politics on the President's Use of Force," *Journal of Conflict Resolution* 35 [June 1991], pp. 307–32).

Table 2.1. *Logistic regression analysis of decisions to seek arms talks: theoretically best specification*

Variable	Coefficient	S.E. of coefficient	Significance[a]
Protest	0.226	0.093	0.008
Warhead parity	0.154	2.446	0.475
Net Soviet cooperation$_{t-1}$	0.000	0.011	0.494
Inflation$_{t-1}$	0.108	0.266	0.342
Constant	– 5.987	2.084	0.004

N = 64

Model chi-square	df	Significance
12.665	4	0.013

d (calculated from OLS regression) = 2.02

Cross-classification table: predicted vs. observed results

Observed	Predicted 0	Predicted 1	Percent correct
0	61	0	100.0%
1	1	2	66.7%
		Overall	98.4%

Proportionate reduction in error = .667

[a]One-tailed p-values, except for constant.

fit of the equation, which is measured in logistic regression by a model chi-square, is also significant, indicating that the model as a whole does fit the observed data. Since autocorrelation is always a potential problem in time-series data, I also obtained the Durbin–Watson statistic by running the model using OLS regression. The value of d is quite close to 2, indicating that there is no problem from autocorrelation.

Finally, table 2.1 includes a cross-classification table in which the predicted and observed values of the dependent variable are compared. The high percentage of correct predictions overall is not very meaningful because the data is so skewed. Much more telling is the proportionate reduction in error (PRE) produced by the model. If one used a naive model in which one simply predicted the modal outcome, there would be only three errors in sixty-four cases – the modal prediction, which is no successful talks invitation, is correct for sixty-one of the sixty-four quarters in the analysis. But when one uses the independent variables in the equation to predict outcomes, two of the three positive cases are also correctly predicted, while there are no false positives.[29] This produces a PRE of 0.667, which is extremely good for a dependent variable with so few positive observations.

These results are very surprising. If correct, they suggest that decisions about whether it is a propitious moment to seek arms control are strongly related to the pressure or encouragement arising from below, in the form of societal protest. The first question to ask before reading too much into these results is whether they are robust, or are instead an artifact of the particular specifications of the independent variables.

Further tests of robustness

In this section, to save space, I will simply summarize the results of the robustness testing, without presenting the actual regression data.[30] Because the theoretical reasons for using the above specifications of the control variables were not decisive, it was important to check the sensitivity of the results to the model specification used. To do this, I ran a logistic regression on every combination of ways of measuring the control variables that earlier relevant quantitative studies had found to be important. While simply looking for what "fits best" is an inappropriate way to construct theory, running through these alternative specifications was a useful way to assess the robustness of the results reported above. Thus, for each control variable, I tried several alternatives. These involved measuring the variable from a different data source and/or using alternative specifications of the variable. For example, for the military balance, in place of warheads I also tried military spending data, measured several different ways.

Results produced by the various combinations of alternative oper-

[29] The test ban and START talks are the correct predictions, while the equation misses the invitation to begin SALT.

[30] For a thorough discussion of the alternative measurements tried and why, plus details and further analysis of the regression results that seemed least consistent with the above results, see Jeffrey W. Knopf, "Domestic Sources of Preferences for Cooperation in Arms Control: The Impact of Protest on US Decisions to Enter Arms Talks," paper presented at the annual meeting of the American Political Science Association, Chicago, August 31–September 3, 1995.

ationalizations fell into two categories. By far the majority of combinations produced results similar to those reported in table 2.1. In these logistic regressions, the protest variable proved statistically significant but all or most of the control variables did not. Several combinations, however, produced results that raised doubts about the conclusion that protest is significant. In these cases, while the measures of the control variables used still did not prove significant, incorporating them had the effect of pushing protest above the usual cutoffs for accepting a variable's importance.

I subjected these cases to further analysis, following a procedure recommended by Hosmer and Lemeshow in the standard textbook on logistic regression. When existing theory is not strong enough to dictate the appropriate model, and one is interested in exploring how well different equations fit the data, Hosmer and Lemeshow recommend using a forward stepwise regression as a check on which variables should actually be excluded on grounds of statistical insignificance.[31] One then includes in the final equation only those variables for which a likelihood ratio (LR) chi-square test on the overall model, when that variable is added, performs better than a prespecified cutoff. Hosmer and Lemeshow suggest not making the selection criterion too stringent, so I followed their recommendation and used a significance level of .20 as the cutoff value.

When I applied this forward stepwise procedure to the cases where none of the variables, including protest, appeared significant at first, the results changed. This procedure always led the protest variable to be selected into the final equation, while excluding all three control variables. In the univariate model this produced, protest was again significant at better than a .01 level. More importantly, this analysis revealed that the protest measure is by itself capable of generating the two correct positive predictions of the original multivariate model. The entire reduction in error the first equation produced is apparently due to the societal protest variable.

In these tests, the failure of the military balance to have a significant impact was the most puzzling. From a systemic perspective, this should theoretically have been the strongest variable. For this reason, I took special efforts to improve the impact of the military balance as a control. I concluded the most likely source of the problem was the

[31] David W. Hosmer and Stanley Lemeshow, *Applied Logistic Regression* (New York: John Wiley & Sons, 1989), pp. 106–18.

nature of parity. Especially once the two sides had second-strike nuclear arsenals, parity could be said to exist at a range of different stockpile levels, so that it was not really affected by slight changes in the military balance. If so, looking at the impact of quarterly variance was inappropriate. I therefore constructed two different indices of the military balance, designed to damp out short-term fluctuations and capture a cruder, more long-term notion of whether the two sides were in or approaching parity.[32] Entered into a logistic regression with protest and net Soviet cooperation, neither of these broader parity measures proved significant, while protest still achieved a p-value below .01. I could discover no way of measuring the military balance that was significantly correlated with decisions to start arms control that also caused the impact of protest to disappear.

Discussion

The statistical results are very suggestive, if not completely consistent. The amount of anti-nuclear weapons protest generally turns out to be strongly related to US decisions to enter arms talks. It appears to account for two of the three cases where the USA entered new sets of strategic arms control negotiations. In contrast, the analysis reveals no significant relation between interest in cooperation and the military balance, the state of superpower political relations, or domestic economic conditions. This result is not as robust as would be ideal, with the significance of protest displaying some sensitivity to how the control variables are operationalized. On balance, though, the analysis favors the conclusion that protest matters. When prior research is used to specify the theoretically best model, the results clearly support this conclusion. Likewise, while some alternative measurements of the controls raise doubts, the additional screening made possible through forward stepwise selection techniques consistently supports the finding that protest is significant.

[32] Both indices involved a three-point scale. The first assigned one point if the smaller side's warheads were at least 75 percent of the larger side's in the current year, one point if they met this threshold in the previous year, and one point if the smaller side had closed the gap more quickly in the current year than the year before. The second scale assigned one point each for warhead and military spending levels on the smaller side that were at least 75 percent the size of the larger side's, plus one point if the average gap on these two measures was less in the current year than the year before. Both indices were designed to capture a rough static measure of parity plus a dynamic evaluation of whether the trend was moving toward greater parity.

Although the other variables do not come out as statistically significant, one should not read too much into this result. Given the strong support they have received in previous analyses, it would be a mistake to conclude that the control variables, especially the military balance, have no relationship to the prospects for arms control. The problem may simply be that different variables operate on different time frames. As suggested above, the judgment as to whether or not parity exists probably does not vary much from quarter to quarter. It is more likely that parity, or its absence, characterizes the nuclear balance over multi-year periods, so parity might still have been necessary for arms control to succeed.

These same considerations also suggest that parity is a weak predictor, however. If the nuclear balance can be in an appropriate condition for arms control for years at a time, what accounts for actual decisions to seek an agreement? It might be possible to have favorable international circumstances for some time before developing the willingness to cooperate. The results of the analysis here suggest that a push from below, in the form of grassroots activism, may in some cases be necessary to get states to seek cooperation. If so, systemic factors like parity are at most necessary conditions for security cooperation, not sufficient ones, and domestic factors must also be included.

While the statistical results provide some evidence for the impact of protest, they are not decisive. The number of observations and amount of variance on the dependent variable are both less than ideal, and the correlation between protest and decisions to seek arms control is also less than perfect. Moreover, as any introductory statistics textbook will point out, correlation does not prove causality. To provide a further check on these findings and identify what causal mechanisms may be at work, the rest of this study employs comparative case analysis. In the case studies, I consider whether interpretations of parity or the political atmosphere that are less tied to particular numerical measurements can account for decisions to seek cooperation. I also consider other control variables that are not part of mainstream arms control theory, but have been emphasized in historical interpretations of the individual cases. The next chapter describes the theoretical framework that structures the case studies.

3 A framework for assessing activism's influence

In this chapter, I develop a general framework that will be applied to the case studies in subsequent chapters. The case studies are intended to build on the quantitative analysis of the previous chapter. That analysis found that protest is correlated with the development of a preference for cooperation. The case studies examine whether there is a causal relation behind this apparent association of protest activity and decisions to seek arms control. The goal of the theoretical framework developed in this chapter is to make it possible to identify reliable evidence on that question.

The literature review in chapter 1 suggested that the domestic structure approach is the most promising starting point for thinking about how and when a citizens' campaign might gain influence. That approach identifies those aspects of a country's political institutions and culture that could provide access for societal actors, and indicates which kinds of coalition partners would prove most useful. A wide range of work on domestic sources of US foreign policy highlights three key institutions: regular, national elections; an independent legislature; and a large, decentralized bureaucracy. However, existing work on domestic structure has not specified in much detail the circumstances under which opportunities for citizens' groups to gain access through these institutions are most favorable, nor what is required to take advantage of such opportunities.

To do this, I draw on existing research on American domestic politics to identify three causal mechanisms or pathways through which a citizens' campaign could gain leverage on arms policy. These potential influence mechanisms, each of which corresponds to one of the institutions mentioned above, involve generating electoral pressure, changing coalitions in Congress, and feeding ideas into the bureaucracy, respectively. By indicating the conditions under which activism could use these causal mechanisms to influence security policy, this framework enhances our ability to employ the domestic structure approach to explain the impact of grassroots inputs in individual cases.

This framework enables me to look for two kinds of evidence in the case studies. First, I examine whether popular movements were able to utilize one or more of these influence mechanisms. Once I establish that one of these pathways may have operated, I then look for confirmation of this conclusion in a variety of historical source materials. Requiring correspondence between these two forms of evidence makes it possible to have greater confidence in the results of the case studies. In each case, I also consider whether other factors can better explain decisions that appear due to activism.

Theoretical framework

As a type of actor, citizens' campaigns on arms control are best viewed as social movements.[1] However, social movement research has not focused on how such movements gain influence. Instead, social movement theory seeks mostly to explain the rise and nature of movements, rather than their impact on policy.[2] The few studies that do focus on political impact, moreover, generally define the question as the determinants of movement success or failure.[3] That is inappropriate in this case. Failure to obtain its own stated objectives need not mean that a movement has failed to exert any influence on

[1] US anti-nuclear weapons movements have been explicitly examined as social movements, and used to test competing theories about social movements, in Frances B. McCrea and Gerald E. Markle, *Minutes to Midnight: Nuclear Weapons Protest in America* (Newbury Park, CA: Sage Publications, 1989); David S. Meyer, *A Winter of Discontent: The Nuclear Freeze and American Politics* (New York: Praeger, 1990); Robert Kleidman, *Organizing for Peace: Neutrality, the Test Ban, and the Freeze* (Syracuse: Syracuse University Press, 1993).

[2] Thomas R. Rochon, "Political Movements and State Authority in Liberal Democracies," *World Politics* 42 (January 1990), p. 300.

[3] The key work is William A. Gamson, *The Strategy of Social Protest*, rev. edn. (Belmont, CA: Wadsworth Press, 1990).

state preferences. In the case studies, the important question is whether there is change from an existing policy baseline (in particular, one that initially does not favor arms talks). If so, the question then becomes whether societal activism is a significant cause of that change, which it might be even if the movement in question did not succeed in getting all its policy demands adopted.

Because the social movement literature does not provide enough guidance on the particular questions asked in this study, I turn instead to more general theories of American politics that deal with the actors that are the most similar to social movements. I thus adapt some models for assessing the influence of arms control activism from studies of how public opinion and interest groups can affect domestic policy. I have identified three processes that are well established in the study of American politics that could lead to a movement impact on arms policy: (1) mobilizing public opinion to exert electoral pressure, (2) working with sympathetic political elites to alter the amount of support for the president's policy in Congress, and (3) generating ideas that have utility for agencies in the executive.

Attributes of the influence pathways

I distinguish these influence mechanisms in terms of three attributes. First, I identify for each a necessary "pre-condition" or set of circumstances that must exist before that mechanism could be activated and provide access.[4] Second, each causal pathway involves an interaction between a citizens' campaign and some other actor, and can therefore be distinguished by the other actor involved. Finally, for each pathway I specify a particular kind of policy effect that will be produced. These potential effects of activism will be measured by whether there is change in a policy baseline established by an incumbent presidential administration before any protest campaign took off.

These three attributes serve to establish independent indicators for

[4] This can be viewed as a way of giving a concrete definition in this issue-area to the concept of "political opportunity structure," which has lately become prevalent in the social movement literature. See Herbert Kitschelt, "Political Opportunity Structures and Political Protest: Anti-Nuclear Movements in Four Democracies," *British Journal of Political Science* 16 (January 1986), pp. 57–85; Sidney Tarrow, *Power in Movement: Social Movements, Collective Action, and Politics* (Cambridge: Cambridge University Press, 1994).

identifying when citizen activism could have produced a change in US arms control preferences. In other words, rather than rely solely on anecdotal evidence or on a simple correlation between policy and activist demands, I use the theoretical framework to identify in advance the times at which activist influence is most likely and the type of impact the citizens' movement should have. Thus, in using this framework, I first examine whether a situation existed that would make it possible for one of the three potential influence mechanisms to operate, i.e., whether the necessary pre-condition was in place. I then examine whether there was interaction between activist groups and the other actor entailed by that mechanism, and finally assess whether arms control policy was adjusted in the manner associated with the mechanism in question. If all three conditions are not met, I conclude that no influence was exerted through that pathway. In contrast, if conditions match those the model suggests will make influence possible, and if policy takes the shape predicted under those conditions, this correspondence constitutes one form of evidence for a conclusion that activism influenced that policy decision.

Before accepting this conclusion, I look for corroboration in other sources. These include government documents, decisionmakers' memoirs and statements to the media, interviews I have conducted with policymakers involved in the more recent cases, and a wide range of secondary sources. In the case studies, this means that I take the conservative approach of requiring two distinct kinds of evidence before concluding that a citizens' movement had an impact. As a final check on such a conclusion, I also examine potential alternative explanations that are suggested by existing studies on the case in question. Before describing the potential influence mechanisms I have identified, I first describe the types of policy changes they might produce. The type of policy effect expected becomes one of the three attributes used to tell whether a causal mechanism might have influenced arms control preferences.

Two types of policy effect

Arms control involves several different kinds of choices. The most obvious are questions such as whether to accept another side's offer or modify an offer of one's own. However, before these sorts of matters even come up for decision, a host of prior choices have to be made. Most basically, there must first be decisions about whether to enter negotiations at all and, if so, what topics these talks should cover.

These decisions will normally be the ones most closely associated with the development of a willingness to cooperate.

It proves most useful to divide these aspects of arms control policy into two different levels, which I label the general and the specific. The general level concerns national priorities. In particular, it involves the question of whether the United States should attach greater importance to arms control, or should instead de-emphasize it while pursuing a buildup of nuclear arms or focusing on other policy areas altogether. As a related concern, the general level also includes the scope of US objectives, such as whether to seek far-reaching reductions or only modest limitations on nuclear arms. In short, the general level consists of the priority arms restraint enjoys as a policy objective.

Once arms control is accepted as a goal or inevitability, more specific questions arise. What types of weapons or activities is it most important to regulate or eliminate first? What should be the content of US proposals that address these goals? These questions make up the specific level of policy. Thus, one level of policy involves the place of arms control on the national agenda and the scope of the goals that are set for it. A second level is the arms control agenda itself, in the form of the particular negotiating objectives that receive top priority and the details of the proposals for reaching those objectives.

These two levels are closely related to the dependent variable of this study. For reasons explained in the previous chapter, preferences are operationalized in terms of the willingness to cooperate, which is taken to mean decisions to enter formal negotiations in a format acceptable to the other side. Where no such talks are underway, development of a preference for cooperation would require change in one or both of the two levels of arms policy. The United States would have to give arms restraint greater priority than arms buildup and/or endorse a specific negotiating agenda that holds out sufficient promise of mutual benefits to interest the other side. Thus, shifts at one or both of the two levels of policy will determine whether serious negotiations become possible, so that these policy effects correspond closely to how the dependent variable has been operationalized.

Three influence mechanisms

Having distinguished two possible areas of policy that could be influenced by activism, I now describe three possible mechanisms for exerting influence and specify which level of arms control policy each would affect. The first mechanism is based on the idea that influence is gained by exerting pressure, and focuses on the electoral arena. The other two mechanisms come from alternatives to the pressure model that emphasize information and ideas as useful resources, focusing on the legislative and bureaucratic arenas, respectively. I will describe these mechanisms primarily from the perspective of campaigns seeking to promote arms restraint, but these same processes would also be vital to campaigns against arms control. It would hence be possible to apply this theoretical framework to the study of pro-defense groups, such as those involved in the late 1970s in the effort to defeat SALT II.

Mechanism 1: mass electoral pressure

One obvious potential route to influence is electoral pressure. However, elections are not normally referenda on international co-operation. Thus, it is necessary to specify conditions under which electoral incentives could affect arms control policy. To do this, I draw on findings derived through spatial modeling of elections. This approach represents candidates' positions and voters' preferences as points on a graph, to investigate how much voter concerns will constrain party platforms. The results of spatial modeling suggest that a citizens' campaign could meet the criteria to apply electoral pressure, but only at the general level of arms control policy, not at the specific level.

The key finding is the "median voter theorem," associated primarily with the work of Anthony Downs. This theorem predicts that, when majority rule determines the outcome, two parties in electoral competition will converge on the position of the median voter, provided that policy preferences are distributed along a single dimension (like left versus right). However, once voters' choices reflect multiple dimensions (for example, economics and civil rights), the center can be defeated by other positions. Early models even suggested that it would be possible for outcomes to cycle over the entire policy space, making prediction nearly impossible.[5]

The median voter and cycling results have been softened somewhat by recent research based on more realistic initial assumptions.

[5] Anthony Downs, *An Economic Theory of Democracy* (New York: Harper & Row, 1957), pp. 115–18; Peter C. Ordeshook, *Game Theory and Political Theory: An Introduction* (Cambridge: Cambridge University Press, 1986), pp. 160–75; Dennis C. Mueller, *Public Choice II* (Cambridge: Cambridge University Press, 1989), chaps. 5, 10.

However, it is still possible to anticipate pressure to move toward the center in unidimensional situations, but harder to predict a particular outcome in situations involving multiple dimensions. For example, current findings suggest that, although complete convergence on the median may not occur, there will still be movement toward the center in unidimensional situations, provided certain circumstances are met. Greater convergence occurs when an issue becomes more salient to voters, as voters' sensitivity to party differences increases, or when parties have more information about voters.[6] Rather than making prediction impossible, therefore, this work is more useful for indicating the circumstances under which electoral pressures will produce movement in the direction of voter concerns. In line with what common sense would suggest, this work implies that an issue must become important to voters and that this fact must become clear to the parties. Whether or not two parties converge onto the exact same position is not as important as the ability to predict a direction of movement, and for the one-dimensional case this ability is not undermined by relaxing the initial assumptions.[7]

A number of other studies have tackled the multidimensional case. They have produced the conclusion that cycling will be limited to a

[6] Henry W. Chappell, Jr., and William R. Keech, "Policy Motivation and Party Differences in a Dynamic Spatial Model of Party Competition," *American Political Science Review* 80 (September 1986), pp. 881–99; Donald Wittman, "Spatial Strategies When Candidates Have Policy Preferences," in James M. Enelow and Melvin J. Hinich, eds., *Advances in the Spatial Theory of Voting* (Cambridge: Cambridge University Press, 1990), pp. 67–70 and 77–78; Ken Kollman, John H. Miller, and Scott E. Page, "Adaptive Parties in Spatial Elections," *American Political Science Review* 86 (December 1992), pp. 929–37.

[7] This prediction of the median voter theorem has been challenged more explicitly by directional voting theory, which predicts that voters will prefer more extreme rather than more centrist candidates (George Rabinowitz and Stuart Elaine Macdonald, "A Directional Theory of Issue Voting," *American Political Science Review* 83 [March 1989], pp. 93–121). However, other studies that have tested the two approaches generally support the original Downsian model (Glenn Plott, Keith T. Poole, and Howard Rosenthal, "Directional and Euclidean Theories of Voting Behavior: A Legislative Comparison," *Legislative Studies Quarterly* 17 [1992], pp. 561–72; Roy Pierce, "Directional Versus Proximity Models: A Second Opinion," and Irwin L. Morris, "Issue Voting and the Coexistence of Directional and Proximity Voters," papers presented at the annual meeting of the American Political Science Association, Washington, DC, September 2–5, 1993). While research is ongoing in this area, the evidence so far still supports the median voter result, suggesting that it is a plausible basis for an electoral pressure mechanism.

subset of the pareto-optimal outcomes.[8] This basically means that the president could not gain electorally by moving to a more extreme position than any major grouping in the public favors. But as long as his proposals stay within the parameters of existing debate, there is no reason to expect that public pressure on one dimension would necessarily bring about movement on that dimension.

This can be illustrated through a concrete example. To begin with, even a cursory review of arms control policy debates in the United States reveals that the specific level did involve multiple dimensions. There were debates about the level of verifiability to require, about whether or not numerical limits had to be strictly equal, and about whether arms control should give more emphasis to quantitative or qualitative restrictions, to name just a few. Now, suppose one finds a case where there was popular concern that the president was not doing enough to slow modernization. The president could respond on that dimension, deciding to seek stricter limits on the qualitative arms race. But the president could also respond by raising verification concerns, using fear of Soviet cheating to restrict the US proposal to more easily monitored quantitative ceilings. Or the president could make the issue one of equality, arguing that preventing modernization would lock in a Soviet advantage. By invoking either of these other two dimensions, the president could avoid having to alter policy on qualitative restrictions. This example, suggested by the Reagan years, shows that there were many different packages of trade-offs at the specific level that could achieve majority support, rather than just a single median point. Even accepting the limits on cycling in multiple dimensions, there are good reasons to believe that presidents would still have been able to avoid being forced to move toward the specific-level proposals of their opponents.[9]

[8] Ordeshook, *Game Theory and Political Theory*, pp. 183–87; Dennis C. Mueller, *Public Choice II*, pp. 185–89; John Ferejohn, "The Spatial Model and Elections," in Bernard Grofman, ed., *Information, Participation, and Choice: "An Economic Theory of Democracy" in Perspective* (Ann Arbor: University of Michigan Press, 1993), p. 110.

[9] This idea of freedom to maneuver in multiple dimensions has been challenged by one other new direction in spatial voting research, the development of probabilistic election models. In these models, there are conditions that can lead to an equilibrium in either uni- or multidimensional situations (James M. Enelow, James W. Endersby, and Michael C. Munger, "A Revised Probabilistic Spatial Model of Elections: Theory and Evidence," in Grofman, *Information, Participation and Choice*, pp. 127–28; Dennis C. Mueller, *Public Choice II*, chap. 11; Peter J. Coughlin, "Candidate Uncertainty and Electoral Equilibria," in Enelow and Hinich, *Advances in the Spatial Theory*). However,

Based on the spatial modeling literature, therefore, it appears that the electorate could exert pressure on arms control policy, but only when the issue can be reduced to one dimension. In the time period covered by this study, the general level of policy, which concerns the priority given to arms control overall, was indeed characterized by a single dimension. During the Cold War, opinion research repeatedly found that public preferences on nuclear arms reflected a mix of two opposing core values, which analysts labeled somewhat imprecisely as peace and strength.[10] The two opposed poles arose because arms control policy was buffeted by two different fears, fear of the Soviet Union and fear of nuclear war. As Michael Nacht once put it, "Some see nuclear weapons as protecting the United States from the Soviet threat, while others see their possession as the principal threat."[11] And these two concerns pulled in opposite directions, since one could not simultaneously build up to meet the Soviet threat and disarm to address the nuclear threat. Since one could map preferences at the general level onto a line between the two extremes of pure buildup and pure restraint, opinion at this level did fall along a single dimension.

In addition, there is evidence that opinion at this level could meet the other conditions necessary to trigger the median voter theorem. Most importantly, candidates would have to believe that their positions on this issue might determine the vote of a reasonable portion of the public.[12] Recent studies find the public can meet these criteria. They have shown that sizable numbers of voters do sometimes perceive defense or foreign policy as the country's most important issue and that this significantly affects their evaluations of the presi-

the equilibria in these models have been defined in terms of complicated mathematical formulae, and I see no obvious way to apply them to the empirical situations I examine in the case studies. I therefore prefer to stick to the original estimate that electoral pressure will be effective only at the general level.

10 William Schneider, "Public Opinion," in Joseph S. Nye, Jr., ed., *The Making of America's Soviet Policy* (New Haven: Yale University Press, 1984).

Labeling the dovish preference "peace" neglects the hawkish perspective that peace comes through strength. A more accurate label for this preference is "restraint." This is hence the term I employ.

11 Michael Nacht, *The Age of Vulnerability: Threats to the Nuclear Stalemate* (Washington, DC: The Brookings Institution, 1985), p. 53.

12 Unless a particular issue is uniquely important, it will simply become part of a multidimensional space with other issues, allowing the pull of the median to be offset.

dent and other candidates.[13] There is even evidence that the public reacted specifically to presidential positions on the spectrum between buildup and restraint in ways that favored movement toward the center. Examining opinion on US–Soviet relations during the Carter and Reagan years, Miroslav Nincic found that, "desiring both, the public ... tend[ed] to reward behavior enhancing that value (either peace or strength) which appear[ed] currently most slighted in US foreign policy."[14] Taken as a whole, this evidence demonstrates that public opinion on arms control could meet all the conditions necessary to invoke median voter dynamics.

This creates a possibility that a citizens' movement could take advantage of the median voter theorem, at least during the Cold War period. Within a case that takes place in this context, a president might not set the balance between the goals of strength and restraint where most of the public would prefer. I will call this situation, when presidential policy diverges from the median public position, an "opinion disjunction." Under these circumstances, there are likely to be advocacy groups arguing that the United States should adopt a "tougher" or a "softer" stance (depending on which way the president is out of line). Other citizens may then decide that a way to voice their own concerns is to give support to organizations that advocate this change of course.[15] If the resulting growth of activism suggests that arms control might be an important enough issue to some segments of the public to make a difference in electoral outcomes, this would likely force an incumbent administration to shift its policies toward the center. The White House might be driven by concerns that the opposition party will pick up the votes of those dissatisfied with existing arms policy in either the next congressional or presidential election, or that the president's approval rating will go down,

[13] John H. Aldrich, John L. Sullivan, and Eugene Borgida, "Foreign Affairs and Issue Voting: Do Presidential Candidates 'Waltz Before a Blind Audience'?," *American Political Science Review* 83 (March 1989), pp. 123–41; Miroslav Nincic and Barbara Hinckley, "Foreign Policy and the Evaluation of Presidential Candidates," *Journal of Conflict Resolution* 35 (June 1991), pp. 333–55.

[14] Miroslav Nincic, "The United States, the Soviet Union, and the Politics of Opposites," *World Politics* 40 (July 1988), p. 458.

[15] It does not matter how this opinion disjunction arises. It might be produced by activist groups' public education efforts. But movement success in changing public preferences is not necessary, only that an opinion disjunction emerges for whatever reason.

lessening his legislative influence.[16] Hence, electoral pressure could operate at most points in an administration's term.

I call this situation "mechanism 1" or the "electoral pathway." The pre-condition for this mechanism is a disjunction between the priority the administration gives to arms control and the median position among an electorally relevant body of public opinion. The subsequent interaction that must occur is for citizen activism to mobilize a portion of the dissatisfied public. If the intensity of resulting activism signals to administration officials that they are out of line with mainstream Americans about how hard-line to be toward the USSR and that this could matter electorally, they will have an incentive to change policy. Specifically, when a citizens' campaign activates mechanism 1, administration policy at the general level will move toward the position supported by the citizens' movement, thereby increasing or decreasing the priority given to making progress in arms control. But, for the reasons described earlier, mechanism 1 will not necessarily enable one to predict some particular change at the specific level of policy.

Of course, electoral pressure does not operate only on the president. Because members of Congress have to run for office in geographic districts, even when a movement lacks the national strength to threaten a president's electoral chances, it may be enough of a force in many localities to make the legislature sit up and take notice. Mechanism 1 could thereby influence an administration's approach to arms control by affecting the assertiveness and policy preferences of Congress on nuclear arms issues. If, in response to public pressure, Congress threatens to or does vote against administration defense or arms control programs, the president would likely take steps to meet public concerns and take the pressure off Congress. Where Congress is responding solely to public concerns and not disputes of its own with the president, the general-level shifts in administration policy entailed by mechanism 1 should be adequate to bring Congress back into the fold. The essence of the electoral pathway, in short, is that the

16 Douglas Rivers and Nancy L. Rose, "Passing the President's Program: Public Opinion and Presidential Influence in Congress," *American Journal of Political Science* 29 (May 1985), pp. 183–96; Charles W. Ostrom, Jr., and Dennis M. Simon, "The President and the Politics of Military Force," in Joseph R. Goldman, ed., *American Security in a Changing World* (Lanham, MD: University Press of America, 1987), pp. 100–01.

president sees broad public concerns as the source of his problems and can, by addressing them, remove the opposition to his policies.

Finally, it should be noted that it is not logically necessary for there to be activism in order for electoral pressure to arise. Public opinion could theoretically meet all the conditions necessary to engage mechanism 1 without a citizens' movement being involved. In cases where electoral pressure appears important, therefore, I evaluate whether or not interaction between mass opinion and activism was an integral factor in creating signals of the public's dissatisfaction. Even if public opinion is important independently of protest, this would still clearly be a case of bottom-up preference formation, and hence be supportive of the more general argument of this study.[17]

Mechanism 2: shifting elite coalitions

Of course, members of Congress and other political elites do not necessarily have to perceive electoral incentives before they would challenge a president's arms control policies. They might also be motivated by genuine policy concerns or certain personal ambitions, such as gaining greater influence in Washington.[18] Under these circumstances, organizations seeking a change in US arms policy can play a different role than in the electoral pathway. By pooling their resources and coordinating their activities with elites who share some of their policy goals, citizens' groups can stimulate action by and enhance the capabilities of like-minded political elites.[19] Rather than

[17] There is evidence that public opinion may sometimes have this kind of effect. Page and Shapiro have shown that large changes of opinion about foreign policy issues are often followed by a shift in policy in the same direction (Benjamin I. Page and Robert Y. Shapiro, "Effects of Public Opinion on Policy," *American Political Science Review* 77 [March 1983], pp. 175–90). And in the area of arms control specifically, Thomas W. Graham has found that policies tended to align with public opinion when there was a majority of at least 60 percent and especially 70 percent or more favoring a particular arms control goal ("The Politics of Failure: Strategic Nuclear Arms Control, Public Opinion, and Domestic Politics in the United States, 1945–1980," Ph.D. dissertation, MIT [1989]). These studies do not specify the causal mechanism involved, so the electoral pathway described here provides one possible way of tracing when public opinion is likely to be effective.

[18] Richard F. Fenno, *Congressmen in Committees* (Boston: Little, Brown, 1973).

[19] To my knowledge, the interest group literature has never put the point quite this way, but a number of strands in the literature that I discuss below can be synthesized because they all relate to capability-enhancement. I owe the idea that this is an important influence technique to Eileen Crumm ("The Value of Economic Incentives in International Politics," *Journal of Peace Research* 32 [August 1995], pp. 313–30).

exerting pressure through the manipulation of electoral incentives, advocacy groups in this second pathway become part of the dynamics of elite coalition formation.

Leverage is possible through this process because the president needs the support of a majority of Congress for certain elements of his program that are related to arms control policy, such as weapons' appropriations and appointments of negotiators, and of course two-thirds of the Senate if he wants a treaty ratified. For this reason, the president will normally also be concerned about the stance of other elites who might affect congressional opinion, such as nuclear scientists. Because presidents need a winning coalition in Congress and value an elite consensus behind their policies, there is a route for activist influence even if arms control is not a major concern with most voters. Here, citizens' groups must work with political elites whose positions they prefer to the likely alternative. This process gains effectiveness if it alters the degree of support for the administration's policies in Congress or among others, such as recognized national security experts, whose support an administration regards as vital. I call this process "mechanism 2" or the "elite coalition-shift pathway." While I will discuss the mechanism 2 process as working against the president, in principle coalition-building by activists could also be with an administration facing Senate opposition to a treaty both activists and the president support (it could also involve groups and legislators that both oppose arms control).

While mechanism 1 is based mostly on a single finding, the median voter theorem, mechanism 2 draws on several recent developments in studies of interest groups and agenda setting. In recent decades, the apparent effectiveness of public interest groups has prompted a search for alternative bases of influence to the money or privileged access of special interests. A number of studies have now coalesced around explanations that involve information and ideas.[20] Rather than pressuring elected officials who are averse or neutral toward a group's policy goals, these studies imply, a key function of citizens'

[20] Thus, John T. Tierney concludes that there has been "a gradual supplementing, if not a complete supplanting, of the 'politics of interests' with a 'politics of ideas,' in which the power of a good idea or a symbolically appealing cause can be just as persuasive or forceful in the policymaking process as a vested interest" ("Organized Interests and the Nation's Capitol," in Mark P. Petracca, ed., *The Politics of Interests: Interest Groups Transformed* [Boulder: Westview Press, 1992], p. 216).

groups may instead be to provide assistance to elites who are favorably disposed to their objectives.

The body of research from which I draw the elite coalition-shift pathway has been built on a path-breaking analysis by E. E. Schattschneider.[21] Schattschneider argued that a losing coalition can sometimes reverse a decision against them by broadening the scope of conflict. In a larger arena, the previous losers may now have majority support. This suggests a movement's activities might be able to alter the degree of support behind the president's policies by, for example, getting an issue moved from a committee that is unsympathetic to their concerns to the floor of Congress, or by involving new actors who do not normally comment on arms policy but carry a certain moral authority, like churches. By contributing to a broadening of the debate, advocacy groups may shift the balance between competing coalitions on arms control policy.

Research on agenda setting and interest groups emphasizes two stages of congressional action where this can occur. First, ideas and information provided by advocacy groups can be an important cueing mechanism. In other words, activist organizations may actually be responsible for getting sympathetic elites to act in the first place.[22] No member of Congress can possibly be fully informed about all of the issues and policy options that the legislature might consider. Advocacy groups can at times, therefore, point out alternative interpretations of a given situation or policy that persuade members, especially those of an entrepreneurial bent, that it would be desirable to take action.[23] In a recent study of agenda setting, Baumgartner and Jones even argue that redefining an issue is the main way in which

[21] E. E. Schattschneider, *The Semisovereign People: A Realist's View of Democracy in America* (New York: Holt, Rinehart, and Winston, 1960).

[22] Mechanisms 1 and 2 can be complementary here, as electoral concerns can reinforce this process. Eileen Burgin found that one of the strongest causes of decisions by Congress members to get involved in foreign policy issues is learning that supporters in their district re-election constituency are interested in the issue ("The Influence of Constituents," in Randall B. Ripley and James M. Lindsay, eds., *Congress Resurgent: Foreign and Defense Policy on Capitol Hill* [Ann Arbor: University of Michigan Press, 1993]).

[23] Richard A. Smith, "Advocacy, Interpretation, and Influence in the US Congress," *American Political Science Review* 78 (March 1984), pp. 44–63; Jane J. Mansbridge, "A Deliberative Theory of Interest Representation," in Petracca, *Politics of Interests*, p. 32; Thomas L. Gais, Mark A. Peterson, and Jack L. Walker, "Interest Groups, Iron Triangles, and Representative Institutions in American National Government," *British Journal of Political Science* 14 (April 1984), p. 178.

Schattschneider's notion of the expansion of conflict is brought about.[24] Both their study and others have found that interest groups can be important facilitators of this process.[25]

In the second stage, after congressional action has been triggered (regardless of whether activism is responsible), citizens' groups can contribute to the shifting of elite coalitions in other ways. Many of these involve supplementing officeholders' own staff resources. This function has long been recognized, but its importance only recently appreciated.[26] Indeed, recent studies of relations between interest groups and Congress have found legislators thirsting for the information and assistance that interest groups can supply.[27] For example, activist groups can provide their legislative allies with intelligence about other members of Congress and arguments they can use in congressional debate. They can serve as go-betweens to forge an alliance among elite actors who would not otherwise have worked together. By testifying at hearings, or even more by organizing public demonstrations, these groups can also show that there is outside support for the positions their allies favor. By strengthening their congressional allies' ability to argue and strategize on behalf of an arms control initiative, advocacy groups also increase their chances of doing so successfully.[28]

24 Frank R. Baumgartner and Bryan D. Jones, *Agendas and Instability in American Politics* (Chicago: University of Chicago Press, 1993).

25 Jack L. Walker, Jr., *Mobilizing Interest Groups in America: Patrons, Professions, and Social Movements* (Ann Arbor: University of Michigan Press, 1991), pp. 14, 128–35; Robert H. Salisbury, "The Paradox of Interest Groups in Washington – More Groups, Less Clout," in Anthony King, ed., *The New American Political System*, 2nd ver. (Washington, DC: AEI Press, 1990), p. 211.

26 A classic study of interest group efforts in the late 1950s concluded that lobbies function largely as "service bureaus" for sympathetic politicians rather than as sources of pressure on opponents (Raymond A. Bauer, Ithiel de Sola Pool, and Lewis Anthony Dexter, *American Business and Public Policy: The Politics of Foreign Trade*, 2nd edn. [Chicago: Aldine-Atherton, 1972], p. 353). Mary Milling Lepper labeled this the support function of advocacy groups (*Foreign Policy Formulation: A Case Study of the Nuclear Test Ban Treaty of 1963* [Columbus, OH: Charles E. Merrill, 1971]).

27 Norman J. Ornstein and Shirley Elder, *Interest Groups, Lobbying and Policymaking* (Washington, DC: Congressional Quarterly Press, 1978), pp. 84–85; Kay Lehman Schlozman and John T. Tierney, *Organized Interests and American Democracy* (New York: Harper and Row, 1986), pp. 263, 274–75, 290–304, 331; Mark P. Petracca, "The Rediscovery of Interest Group Politics," in his *Politics of Interests*, p. 25; Baumgartner and Jones, *Agendas and Instability*, p. 195.

28 Schlozman and Tierney, *Organized Interests*, pp. 263, 290, 295–301; Ornstein and Elder, *Interest Groups*, pp. 59–60; Petracca, "Rediscovery of Interest Groups," p. 25; Roger W.

Of course, all the techniques available to a campaign that favors arms restraint are also available to groups that oppose that goal. Thus, examining mechanism 2 in any specific situation will require paying attention to whether there is countermobilization on the other side. If there is, it will be necessary to assess the relative resources brought to bear by each side and the relative attractiveness to elites of their ideas. Since the coalition-shift pathway depends on the expansion of conflict, however, the fact that other arms control opponents join the fray, thereby widening the conflict even further, will not necessarily undercut this mechanism. For the president, any expansion of the debate to include Congress creates some pressures to modify policy to give it wider appeal.

This section has discussed a number of specific steps by which grassroots activism can affect congressional action on arms control. All of them share a common theme, though. Each involves increasing the capabilities of legislators to pursue goals that activists support, thereby creating a possibility of altering the winning coalition on arms policy. The necessary pre-condition for this pathway is a division among the elite. For activism to change policy, such divisions must be followed by some interaction between the movement and like-minded elites. The actual elite-level debate could concern either the balance between the competing goals of strength and restraint or the specific details of how to proceed in arms talks. Thus, in contrast to mechanism 1, which operates only at the general level of policy, mechanism 2 can affect either the general or the specific level. In specific cases, however, which level of policy is affected by mechanism 2 will follow directly from which level forms the focus of debate among elites. Thus, it will still be possible in any given instance to anticipate where policy adjustment should occur. Finally, protest does not have to be present for Congress to promote change in US arms policy. In cases where Congress is important, therefore, I will also evaluate whether it would have exerted the same leverage in the absence of societal activism.

Mechanism 3: bureaucratic use of movement ideas

The third process by which movements might gain influence is drawn from literature on policy communities and the impact of ideas. In

Cobb and Charles D. Elder, *Participation in American Politics: The Dynamics of Agenda-Building*, 2nd edn. (Baltimore: Johns Hopkins University Press, 1983), pp. 141–43; Baumgartner and Jones, *Agendas and Instability*, pp. 104–09.

order to generate clear predictions about arms policy from this approach, I combine insights from this literature with aspects of the bureaucratic politics approach to explaining foreign policy. The intersection of these two approaches yields a third influence mechanism, based on bureaucratic utilization of outside ideas. The key literature here began with the observation that, in certain issue-areas, experts who do not necessarily represent any particular interest are becoming more prominent than traditional special interest lobbyists. Scholars have labeled these groups of experts, who are driven by ideas about good policy, "issue networks" or "policy communities."[29]

Within these communities, one can identify various policy "entrepreneurs" who seek to promote particular ideas. A process of selection within the larger political system then determines which ideas actually rise on the agenda. Mechanism 3 is based on a selection process identified by Jack Walker and John Kingdon.[30] Walker and Kingdon took their inspiration from the "garbage can model" of administrative behavior developed by Cohen, March, and Olsen. In the garbage can approach, organizations are seen as "collections of choices looking for problems,"[31] so that problems and solutions constitute separate sets of ideas that can get joined together in many different ways. In agenda setting in US politics, this joining occurs when the development of a new problem or a significant political change creates a "window" that entrepreneurs can use to sell their pet proposals as a possible solution under the new conditions.[32]

29 Hugh Heclo, "Issue Networks and the Executive Establishment," in Anthony King, ed., *The New American Political System* (Washington, DC: American Enterprise Institute, 1978); Jack L. Walker, "The Diffusion of Knowledge, Policy Communities, and Agenda Setting," in John E. Tropman, Milan J. Dluhy, and Roger M. Lind, eds., *New Strategic Perspectives on Social Policy* (New York: Pergamon Press, 1981).

30 John W. Kingdon, *Agendas, Alternatives, and Public Policies* (Boston: Little, Brown, 1984); Jack L. Walker, "Setting the Agenda in the US Senate: A Theory of Problem Selection," *British Journal of Political Science* 7 (October 1977), pp. 423–45. Two studies have sought to apply their ideas to Soviet foreign policymaking. See Matthew Evangelista, "Sources of Moderation in Soviet Security Policy," in Philip E. Tetlock, Jo L. Husbands, Robert Jervis, Paul C. Stern, and Charles Tilly, eds., *Behavior, Society, and Nuclear War*, vol. II (New York: Oxford University Press, 1991); Kimberly Marten Zisk, *Engaging the Enemy: Organization Theory and Soviet Military Innovation* (Princeton: Princeton University Press, 1993).

31 Michael D. Cohen, James G. March, and Johan P. Olsen, "A Garbage Can Model of Organizational Choice," *Administrative Science Quarterly* 17 (March 1972), pp. 1–25, quote from p. 1.

32 Kingdon, *Agendas, Alternatives*, esp. chap. 8; Paul C. Light, *The President's Agenda: Domestic Policy Choice from Kennedy to Reagan*, rev. edn. (Baltimore: Johns Hopkins

In arms control, the US negotiating position is developed by the executive, not by Congress. This means that the critical response for entrepreneurs seeking to take advantage of policy windows will come from the foreign policy bureaucracy. A degree of bureaucratic politics can be anticipated in arms control, moreover, because a number of different agencies are routinely involved in policy formulation in this area. These include the State Department, the Arms Control and Disarmament Agency (ACDA, established in 1962), the Defense Department's civilian wing and the Joint Chiefs of Staff (JCS), the National Security Council (NSC), and often the CIA. Studies of bureaucratic politics have revealed that agencies like these tend to assess policy options in terms of how they might affect the agency's ability to carry out those missions most vital to the agency's identity and future well-being.[33] This virtually guarantees that there will sometimes be differences in how the agencies involved view possible arms control proposals. For example, diplomatic agencies will usually be more favorable to arms negotiations than their military counterparts. Given the frequency of divisions within the executive, Steven Miller observes, "arms control proposals are usually the result of internal bargaining."[34]

University Press, 1991), chaps. 4 and 8, esp. pp. 192–95; Walker, "Diffusion of Knowledge," pp. 89–91; Martha Derthick and Paul J. Quirk, *The Politics of Deregulation* (Washington, DC: The Brookings Institution, 1985), pp. 38–39, 245; Deborah A. Stone, "Causal Stories and the Formation of Policy Agendas," *Political Science Quarterly* 104 (Summer 1989), p. 298; Baumgartner and Jones, *Agendas and Instability*, pp. 160, 241–42.

33 Graham T. Allison, *Essence of Decision: Explaining the Cuban Missile Crisis* (Boston: Little, Brown, 1971); Morton H. Halperin, with the assistance of Priscilla Clapp and Arnold Kanter, *Bureaucratic Politics and Foreign Policy* (Washington, DC: The Brookings Institution, 1974), esp. chap. 3.

34 Steven E. Miller, "Politics over Promise: Domestic Impediments to Arms Control," *International Security* 8 (Spring 1984), p. 82.

There have been several rather strong critiques of the bureaucratic politics approach. But the main criticisms do not invalidate the point I am making here – that disputes between the agencies formally charged with arms control policymaking are likely. For example, Steve Krasner and Ed Rhodes have argued that the policies bureaucrats advocate often do not match the parochial interests of their agencies (Stephen D. Krasner, "Are Bureaucracies Important? [Or Allison Wonderland]," *Foreign Policy* 7 [Summer 1972], pp. 159–79; Edward Rhodes, "Do Bureaucratic Politics Matter? Some Disconfirming Findings from the Case of the US Navy," *World Politics* 47 [October 1994], pp. 1–41). Instead, personal values or ideas about good policy seem to determine the positions advocated. But even if policy preferences reflect officials' personal beliefs, this can still lead to differences of opinion among top government officials. As I will discuss shortly, for mechanism 3 to operate all that

There are conditions under which domestic advocacy efforts could impinge on this internal bargaining. For example, agency officials are recruited from outside and, once in government, they may retain ties to a policy community or issue network to which they previously belonged. Thus, they may come into office already supporting certain favored proposals of the policy community. Or there may be outsiders in the issue network whose views and recommendations they value and would listen to even after they are inside the government. In essence, this is the influence scenario envisioned in the epistemic communities approach.[35] But this is not the only route to influence. Actual appointment of community members to bureaucratic positions is not necessary for outside ideas to affect internal government deliberations. I would argue, therefore, that the epistemic communities approach is best treated as a special case of the more general pathway for ideas to affect bureaucratic debates that I develop here.

There are a couple of reasons why appointment from an issue network to the bureaucracy need not be the critical step. First, citizens' groups may themselves employ some of the experts who act as entrepreneurs within the community.[36] This is especially likely with organizations that claim to represent groups with recognized technical expertise, such as the Federation of American Scientists (FAS) or Union of Concerned Scientists. At times, the specialists who work in

matters is that bureaucratic actors disagree. The source of such differences – be it organizations' interests or individuals' ideas – does not matter.

Robert J. Art has criticized bureaucratic politics for implying that such disputes are resolved on the basis of internal power or resources ("Bureaucratic Politics and American Foreign Policy: A Critique," *Policy Sciences* 4 [December 1973], pp. 467–90). He argues that bureaucratic outcomes often depend on outside political forces, such as allies in Congress or support in public opinion. However, mechanism 3 is entirely consistent with this argument. Its premise is that bureaucratic actors can gain an advantage by using ideas developed outside the executive machinery. Hence, existing critiques of bureaucratic politics as a theory of foreign policy do not challenge the validity of an influence mechanism whose premise is the existence of intra-bureaucratic debate.

35 Peter M. Haas, "Introduction: Epistemic Communities and International Policy Coordination," pp. 27, 30, and Emanuel Adler and Peter M. Haas, "Conclusion: Epistemic Communities, World Order, and the Creation of a Reflective Research Program," p. 374, both in Haas, ed., *Knowledge, Power, and International Policy Coordination*, a special issue of *International Organization* 46 (Winter 1992).

Though the term used is slightly different, the concept of epistemic communities appears to be an application of the policy community idea to international actors and issues.

36 Walker, *Mobilizing Interest Groups*, p. 70; Mansbridge, "A Deliberative Theory," p. 40.

these advocacy groups may develop a proposal that catches on in the policy community. This proposal, even though it arises outside a bureaucratic agency, might nevertheless turn out to be an ideal vehicle to advance that agency's own mission or interests. In such a case, an agency might respond positively to an outside proposal even if it has not hired any members of the policy community.

There is also a second way to attract the interest of an executive branch actor, a process that is especially likely for mass-based groups. A major part of what activist campaigns actually seek to do is make others perceive some condition as a major problem requiring government action. Movement success in this endeavor can open a window of opportunity for a particular agency or individual to promote a proposal they have already been working on as a solution to the newly identified problem.[37] By defining the nuclear arms race or certain nuclear policies as important problems, therefore, protest movements could be a source of windows for government officials to advance their own arms proposals.[38] Alternatively, the proposals that movements or specialist groups advocate might serve to meet problems that already occupy policymakers. Or the two processes might happen in conjunction, with mass-based and expert groups reinforcing one another's efforts. While epistemic communities need not be involved, if they are, this process provides one mechanism by which the community's ideas could prevail with respect to US arms control preferences.

Whatever sequence is involved in this process, the key element is that arguments arising from or made salient by outside activism are used by officials inside the policymaking system to gain an advantage in debates with other executive actors. I call this situation "mechanism 3" or the "bureaucratic utilization pathway." The pre-condition neces-

[37] Kingdon, *Agendas, Alternatives*, p. 155; Patrick O'Heffernan, *Mass Media and American Foreign Policy* (Norwood, NJ: Ablex Publishing, 1991), pp. 45, 48, 92–94.

[38] This does not necessarily mean that activists will oppose "being used" in this way. They may still regard the officials who utilize their arguments as allies whom they are only too glad to help. But mechanism 3 can also result in unintended consequences. Officials who are not terribly sympathetic to the proposals of an activist campaign might still use the problem that campaign has identified as a way to advance quite different pet proposals of their own. The "Star Wars" proposal of President Reagan appears to be such a case, as certain officials used public criticisms of nuclear deterrence to argue for a new emphasis on strategic defense (Jeffrey W. Knopf, "Domestic Politics, Citizen Activism, and US Nuclear Arms Control Policy," Ph.D. dissertation, Stanford University [1991], pp. 459–66).

sary for mechanism 3 to operate is divisions on arms control within the administration. A movement gains influence here only when the possible arguments it raises then interact with the course of the bureaucratic debate. Because the solutions or problems arising from activism will be tied to agency efforts to promote particular proposals, the bureaucratic utilization pathway will affect the specific level of policy. It will cause certain objectives to move up on the administration's arms control agenda or boost one idea for how to achieve an existing goal over the alternatives. Finally, as with the first two pathways, the actor that activism must interact with, in this case bureaucratic agencies, can also matter on its own. Thus, to evaluate the bureaucratic pathway, it will be especially important to investigate whether executive branch officials actually mention a citizens' campaign or its ideas in their internal discussions.

Impact of transboundary interactions

The three influence pathways I have identified draw on models developed in the study of American domestic politics. But arms control is not a domestic issue; it is a subject of international negotiations. As a result, the processes set in motion by the influence mechanisms will not usually play out in isolation from external developments. As suggested in the previous chapter, the military balance and other international-level factors might affect the same policy choices targeted by activists. But such external factors are not just variables to control for; they can also become "entangled"[39] in the very domestic processes that activism seeks to affect. In other words, a popular campaign's ability use the influence mechanisms to alter policy may itself be affected by developments outside US borders.

For example, the Soviet Union at times sought to bolster US (and European) protest movements, in the hope this would enable the USSR to make progress toward various policy objectives of its own. In addition, allied governments or other world leaders concerned about US–Soviet relations and the arms race (or, alternatively, a lack of US resolve) might also have sometimes tried to shift US government policy by giving encouragement to a US citizens' movement. Nor is it just foreign governments that might have been interested in forging

[39] Robert D. Putnam, "Diplomacy and Domestic Politics: The Logic of Two-Level Games," *International Organization* 42 (Summer 1988), p. 427.

some connection with US advocacy efforts. Like-minded groups and movements in other countries might also have seen benefits in collaborating with their American counterparts. Thus, it is important to consider the possible impact of interactions between domestic US activism and advocacy efforts by governmental and societal actors abroad.

There are several forms such interaction could take. One possibility emerges from work on two-level games. The two-level game approach draws attention to strategies by which leaders in one state could affect their opposite number's domestic constraints. One such strategy, "reverberation," seems especially likely to be relevant in arms control. Reverberation occurs when persuasive appeals to domestic groups on the other side help gain their support for the deal one is proposing.[40] Robert Putnam notes, however, that "reverberation can also be negative, in the sense that foreign pressure may create a domestic backlash." This is especially likely when appeals to domestic opinion come from an adversary.[41] This means Soviet attempts to increase support for protest movements' demands will not necessarily have been helpful to those campaigns and may even have ended up undercutting them. But there is no need to assume that this was automatically the case, and in the case studies I look for evidence of both positive and negative reverberation.

Reverberation represents only one possible form of interaction across national borders. It is a "cross-level" relation, in that it connects agents at the state level on one side with agents at the societal level on the other.[42] It is also possible to have transnational or transgovernmental relations, which each link a different set of actors. Transgovernmental processes come into play when officials on one or both sides are internally divided and one or both seek to bolster the influence of the like-minded faction in the other government. Transnational connections involve links between domestic actors on both sides, by which I mean actors outside the executive branch or its

[40] Ibid., p. 454; Andrew Moravcsik, "Introduction: Integrating International and Domestic Theories of International Bargaining," in Peter B. Evans, Harold K. Jacobson, and Robert D. Putnam, eds., *Double-Edged Diplomacy: International Bargaining and Domestic Politics* (Berkeley: University of California Press, 1993), pp. 16, 29.

[41] Putnam, "Diplomacy and Domestic Politics," pp. 455–56.

[42] Jeffrey W. Knopf, "Beyond Two-Level Games: Domestic–International Interaction in the Intermediate-Range Nuclear Forces Negotiations," *International Organization* 47 (Autumn 1993), pp. 599–628.

equivalent.[43] While they differ in the exact actors involved, transgovernmental, transnational, and cross-level connections all involve some form of coalition across state borders. It is useful to be able to refer to this kind of situation generically, so I will use the term "transboundary connections" to connote interactions involving subnational actors on at least one side.

For such a connection to have an impact, though, Thomas Risse-Kappen observes, two conditions must be met. "To influence policies, transnational actors need, first, channels into the political system of the target state and, second, domestic partners with the ability to form winning coalitions."[44] Domestic citizens' groups provide one possible such partner, though not the only one. Whether they can form a winning coalition will depend on the channels into the system the activist campaign is itself using. For this reason, I assume that linkages between activism and external actors matter only if they operate in conjunction with one of the three influence mechanisms outlined above. For example, if elite opinion about arms control is divided, a foreign initiative might serve as a vehicle advocacy groups can use to rally like-minded members of Congress. In other words, transboundary connections would trigger mechanism 2, with activist groups taking advantage of the opportunity created by the actions of external actors as a way to shift the elite coalition pattern at home. Since they must cause a response in some aspect of the domestic policymaking process to have an effect, I will always examine the impact of transboundary connections in terms of how they affect activism's ability to exert leverage through the three basic influence mechanisms.

Does this process entail Soviet manipulation?

When this process involves interaction between Soviet public diplomacy and an American activist campaign, it raises an obvious

43 Robert O. Keohane and Joseph S. Nye, Jr., eds., *Transnational Relations and World Politics* (Cambridge, MA: Harvard University Press, 1972); Keohane and Nye, "Transgovernmental Relations and International Organizations," *World Politics* 27 (October 1974), pp. 39–62; Knopf, "Beyond Two-Level Games"; Thomas Risse-Kappen, ed., *Bringing Transnational Relations Back In: Non-State Actors, Domestic Structures, and International Institutions* (Cambridge: Cambridge University Press, 1995).

44 Thomas Risse-Kappen, "Ideas Do Not Float Freely: Transnational Coalitions, Domestic Structures, and the End of the Cold War," *International Organization* 48 (Spring 1994), p. 208.

concern. If Soviet leaders could gain leverage on US policy by playing to a domestic American audience, was this because they were fooling citizens' groups into supporting measures deleterious to American security? This was certainly the fear of many right-wing observers, who often claimed that Western peace movements were the witting or unwitting victims of Soviet "active measures" and "disinformation."[45]

While this charge may at times have had some validity, there is no reason to presume it was always true. First, regardless of whether the Soviet intent was to exploit peace movements to Western disadvantage, critics supplied little evidence that the USSR actually had any control over or gained any benefits from US (or West European) protest campaigns.[46] In fact, when the FBI investigated charges of Soviet influence in the US freeze movement in the 1980s, it concluded that the USSR did not "have . . . a dominant role in the US peace and nuclear freeze movements, or . . . control or manipulate the movement."[47]

It is certainly true that some instances of Soviet public diplomacy were designed to hurt Western interests, but even here there is no need to assume Soviet intent was always wholly negative. This view would make sense only if US–Soviet relations had been zero-sum. Applied to arms control, this would imply that any agreement acceptable to the USSR must automatically have been harmful to US security. But most observers believe that the superpowers had a mutual interest in avoiding nuclear war. Therefore, the mere fact that the Soviets expressed interest in a proposal does not necessarily mean that the Soviets believed that proposal would give them an advantage over the United States. Soviet public diplomacy may sometimes have been motivated, at least partially, by the belief that an advocacy campaign's proposals could form a basis for mutually advantageous cooperation.[48]

[45] Richard H. Shultz and Roy Godson, *Dezinformatsia: Active Measures in Soviet Strategy* (Washington, DC: Pergammon-Brassey's, 1984); Raymond S. Sleeper, ed., *Mesmerized by the Bear: The Soviet Strategy of Deception* (New York: Dodd, Mead, 1987).

[46] As Leon V. Sigal pointed out with reference to Soviet propaganda efforts in the early 1980s against Euromissile deployment, "while evidence of such a campaign is incontrovertible, evidence of its success is not" (*Nuclear Forces in Europe: Enduring Dilemmas, Present Prospects* [Washington, DC: The Brookings Institute, 1984], p. 64).

[47] Report quoted in the *New York Times* (*NYT*), March 26, 1983, pp. 1, 7.

[48] In fact, both motivations could have been present simultaneously. Soviet (or US) public diplomacy could reflect both a genuine interest in cooperation and the desire

Because both possibilities exist, assessment must be made on a case-by-case basis, and I leave it to the reader reach his or her own judgment. The important point is that one cannot assume in advance that an interaction between Soviet diplomacy and US activism would be deleterious to American security (one also cannot assume *a priori* that it would not be harmful). In the case studies themselves, I simply look for evidence of efforts, arising from either side, to establish links between Soviet arms diplomacy and an American advocacy campaign. I assess the effect on US policy of this transboundary connection without trying to evaluate whether this effect was or was not in the United States' interest.

Summary of the theoretical framework

I have outlined three possible pathways through which activism might influence American arms control policy. Together, they permit assessment of whether citizen activism influences the willingness of the administration in power to pursue cooperation on arms control. In none of the three mechanisms does activism directly change a president's perceptions of the desirability of arms control. Rather, each mechanism involves an interaction between a citizens' campaign and some other actor involved in the shaping of arms control decisions.

By emphasizing the importance of interaction, the framework for this study is consistent with other works utilizing the domestic structure approach. That approach assumes that, in order to affect policy choices, societal actors must first gain access to some aspect of the political process that normally guides policymaking. It therefore draws attention to the existing institutions in a system that could provide societal actors with such access. In the United States, the institutions that might be relevant to arms policy are democratic elections, an independent legislature, and a large federal bureaucracy. For purposes of evaluating activism's impact, therefore, it is necessary to see whether a citizens' movement interacted with the key actors in these institutions (for purposes of controlling for alternative explana-

to achieve it on relatively favorable terms. This would especially be likely if public diplomacy was produced by logrolling the preferences of factions with different images of the adversary. Jack Snyder has argued that Soviet foreign policy often resulted from such a logroll (*Myths of Empire: Domestic Politics and International Ambition* [Ithaca: Cornell University Press, 1991], chap. 6).

tions, though, it is also important to consider whether these other actors mattered independently).

Studies of domestic structure have long been especially interested in the policy networks within different institutions that actually link state and society.[49] The three influence mechanisms identified here fill in the details of how these policy networks operate in the case of US arms control policy. Mechanism 1, the electoral pathway, involves the entwining of advocacy group efforts with trends in public opinion. Although the interaction is with public opinion, the link created in the policy network associated with this mechanism is between societal actors and the president and his political aides. Activist success in connecting with wider public concerns leads White House officials who are attentive to their party's electoral interests to find some way to respond to those demands of the citizens' movement that are resonating with voters.

The other two pathways are more straightforward, in that the policy network linking society to the state itself contains the other actor with which activism must interact. Mechanism 2, the elite coalition-shift pathway, involves interaction between advocacy groups and members of Congress or other political elites. The combination of their efforts creates, or threatens to create, a new winning coalition on arms control policy. Mechanism 3, the bureaucratic utilization pathway, involves an interaction between citizen activism and debates within the executive branch. In this pathway, activism influences an administration's arms control agenda because an idea raised by a movement, be it a specific proposal or assertion of a new problem, is seen by a bureaucratic agency to serve its own policy goals or organizational interests. Finally, each of these pathways can be affected by transboundary connections between international actors and domestic activism.

The theoretical framework can be represented visually. Figure 3.1 contains a diagram of the arms control policymaking process that indicates where each of the three mechanisms I have discussed would provide access to the process for citizens' groups. The arms control policy outputs of a particular administration at any given time will

[49] Peter J. Katzenstein, "Introduction: Domestic and International Forces and Strategies of Foreign Economic Policy," in his *Between Power and Plenty: Foreign Economic Policies of Advanced Industrial States* (Madison: University of Wisconsin Press, 1978), p. 19; Thomas Risse-Kappen, "Introduction," in his *Bringing Transnational Relations Back In*, p. 22.

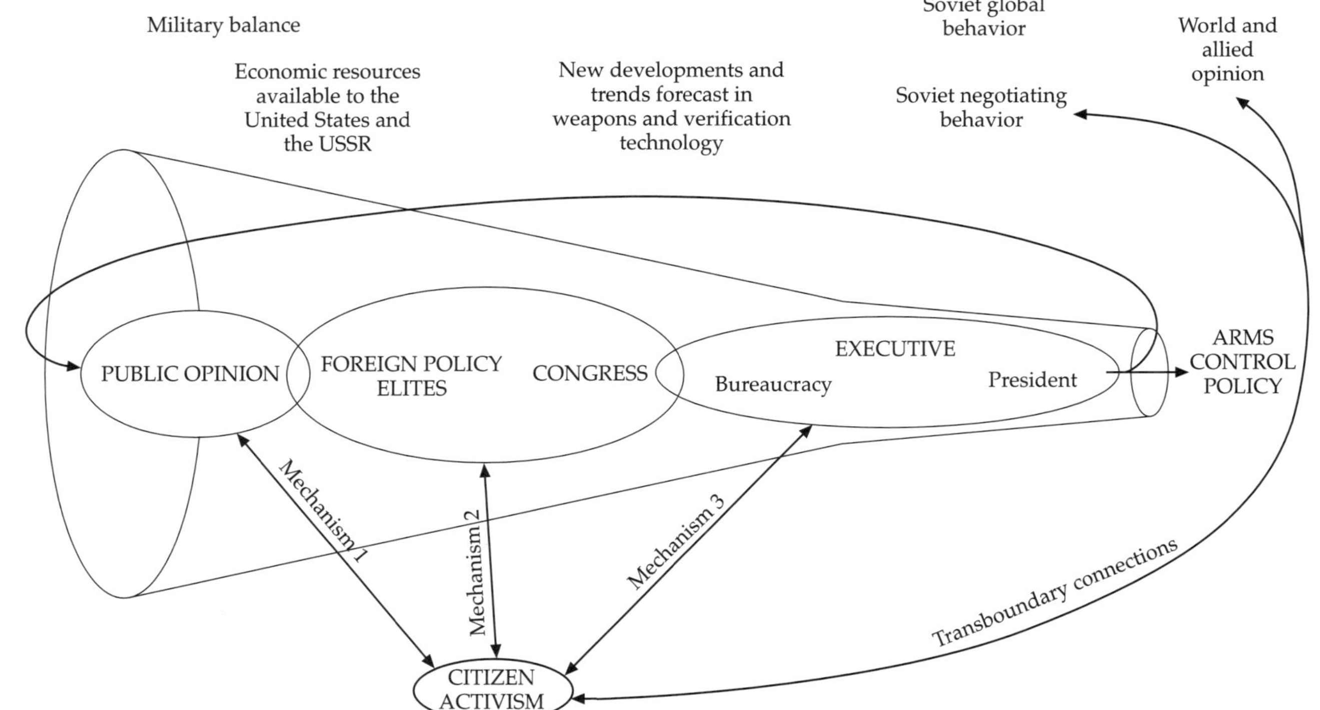

Figure 3.1 Potential influence pathways for arms control activism

reflect the effects of a number of inputs, a situation I depict as a chain of inputs existing inside a funnel. The relevant actors are arranged, moving from left to right, from those whose impact is typically most diffuse and indirect to those who have the greatest direct influence, so that the narrowing of the funnel represents the concentration of decisionmaking authority. In line with the notion of opinion leadership, moreover, each actor in this diagram is able to influence the opinions of all the actors to its left; e.g., the president can shape and mold congressional or public opinion as well as be influenced by them. To simplify matters, I represent this fact by a single feedback arrow from the end of the chain to its beginning. In addition, the entire funnel exists within, and is influenced by, a larger strategic environment. The military balance, Soviet global behavior, US economic resources, and anticipated developments in technology are all part of this environment.

I isolate the role of citizens' movements in this model by pulling advocacy groups out of the chain and putting them off to one side. There is no arrow going straight from the societal activism to policy outputs, because such efforts do not directly alter policy in the framework I have developed. Rather, citizens' movements derive influence through their interaction with other actors in the diagram. I circle the three groupings of actors in the funnel that are involved in mechanisms 1 through 3 and draw an arrow between activism and each one. Finally, I represent the possible effect of transboundary connections with an arrow to relevant actors in the strategic environment.

The theoretical framework presented in this chapter structures the empirical research in the following chapters. Table 3.1 contains a summary of the three influence mechanisms that make up the framework. Evaluation of activism's impact in each case begins with examination of whether a situation existed that would make it possible for one of the mechanisms to operate, i.e., whether the necessary pre-condition was in place. If so, I then examine whether the interaction between citizens' groups and the other actor entailed in that mechanism occurred. Then, if I find there was such interaction, I see whether the expected kind of policy effect followed. Where I do not find evidence for all three components of at least one of the influence mechanisms, I conclude that activism had no impact at that point in time.

Where the appropriate prior condition for a mechanism exists, the interaction specified in that influence mechanism occurs, and policy

Table 3.1. *Attributes of the three potential influence mechanisms*

Mechanism number and name	Necessary pre-condition	What activism must interact with	Source of leverage	Level of policy affected
1: Electoral pathway	Disjunction between administration approach to USSR and median public opinion	Expressions of mass or attentive public opinion	Electoral pressure	General
2: Elite coalition-shift pathway	Policy debate at elite level or absence of elite consensus	Actions of Congress or foreign policy elites	Changing the relative strengths of elite coalitions	General or specific (whichever is focus of elite debate)
3: Bureaucratic utilization pathway	Divisions within the executive branch	Goals or interests of an agency or advisor	Utilization of movement ideas by executive branch officials	Specific

changes in the expected direction, I take this as one piece of evidence for a conclusion that popular protest made a difference. Before drawing any final conclusions, I also consider the extent of corroborating evidence in a range of primary and secondary sources. Finally, I screen the historical record of that time period for other variables that might have caused the policy change in question and evaluate whether these alternative explanations can fully account for the decision.

In cases where there is no basis for concluding that activism affected policy, two further tasks become necessary. First, I ascertain whether the United States developed a willingness to seek arms control nonetheless. In any cases that fit this outcome, the second task will be to determine whether this decision can be explained by the control variables highlighted in the traditional explanation for arms control. In cases where there is no leverage exerted by activism and interest in arms talks also does not result, the second task becomes more counterfactual. I seek to determine whether greater societal support for arms control might have changed the outcome. In these cases, careful examination of the president's own preferences becomes important. If the president seemed to have some interest in arms control but could not manage to arrange arms talks, this will provide a basis for speculating on whether activism could have made a difference. Where the president was dead set against arms control, or the Soviets were clearly hostile to arms talks, the more likely conclusion will be that protest could not have changed the outcome.

In each case study, I assess each of the three pathways in the manner I have described. The cases are not intended to test one pathway at a time, but rather to ascertain whether any of the mechanisms provided a citizens' movement with influence. Neither do the three mechanisms represent alternative explanations of policy, meant to be tested against each another. The three pathways are not mutually exclusive, meaning more than one can be involved at any given point in time. In these cases, therefore, the chief question is whether the required evidence exists to indicate that a citizens' campaign effectively utilized either any single mechanism or some combination of mechanisms. If so, this particular set will constitute one possible explanation of policy, to be weighed against other plausible explanations for policy change in the same time period. In all, I will examine four cases, which vary in both outcome and in the level of protest activity. Empirical assessment begins with Eisenhower's first term.

4 Eisenhower's first initiatives: a matter of priorities

This chapter examines a period in which there was very little citizen activism and no productive arms talks got underway. The analysis is therefore shorter than in the other case studies, but examination of Dwight D. Eisenhower's first presidential term is still useful. In particular, this case will illustrate some limitations of conventional analyses of arms control and cooperation that add to the case for looking also at the degree of societal interest. This case will also establish a policy baseline for the next chapter's assessment of the impact of protest against nuclear testing in Eisenhower's second term.

Looking at the factors stressed in traditional arms control theory, conditions in Eisenhower's first term were favorable to cooperation, but not decisively so. By 1955, both superpowers had hydrogen bombs and long-range delivery capabilities. If not complete parity, this at least created the mutual vulnerability that arms control theorists see as the most essential motivation for arms control. In addition, political relations also changed in a direction more favorable to arms control. The death of Josef Stalin and end of the Korean War led to a thaw in US–Soviet relations, which created conditions more conducive to cooperation.

While these developments made arms control conceivable, they did not make it inevitable. Continuing US doubts about Soviet intentions and trustworthiness meant that the balance of system-level incentives remained indeterminate. This case thus reflects the common observation that systemic factors alone may not explain policy, because they do not obviously push state interests in a particular direction. In conditions where it is not clear whether cooperation is in the national interest, many of the theories discussed in earlier chapters propose an emphasis on the ideas or interests of national leaders. The main lesson of this chapter will be the potential liabilities of associating state preferences with the personal beliefs or public pronouncements of the head of government.

In this period of Cold War consensus and congressional deference, President Eisenhower enjoyed considerable autonomy from domestic constraints in foreign policy.[1] This case should therefore be favorable for statesman-centered analysis. Yet such an approach still proves incomplete and potentially misleading. To begin with, the domestic political interests often stressed in institutionalist approaches were simply not relevant here. Eisenhower had no need to take international action to deflect public attention from domestic problems or widen the "win set" for a preferred policy.

Given the absence of strong international or domestic constraints as well, Eisenhower's decisions would thus seem to be primarily a function of his own ideas or cognitive understandings.[2] Yet, identifying US preferences with the president's own views on arms control would lead to an exaggerated estimate of US willingness to cooperate. President Eisenhower held ideas about nuclear weapons that clearly favored arms control, and he expressed these ideas publicly on several occasions. However, Eisenhower also had other beliefs that worked against cooperative goals, including both suspiciousness of the Soviets and desire for foreign policy consensus. Because he faced bureaucratic opposition to arms control, especially from the military and atomic energy establishment, and no strong clamor for arms control elsewhere in the domestic arena, the president allowed his arms control policy to be limited by bureaucratic constraints. As a result, Eisenhower's personal interest in reducing the nuclear danger was at best only incompletely translated into actual American willingness to pursue cooperation.

Therefore, although Eisenhower's first term saw several dramatic expressions of interest in cooperation, closer examination will reveal that they do not indicate much willingness to pursue it seriously. This chapter will focus on the two major proposals for which the Eisenhower administration is best known in the arms control field: the

[1] I thank Sue Peterson for clarifying this point for me.

[2] For a summary of the ways in which ideas can be related to state preferences and international cooperation, see Judith Goldstein and Robert O. Keohane, eds., *Ideas and Foreign Policy: Beliefs, Institutions, and Political Change* (Ithaca: Cornell University Press, 1993).

"Atoms for Peace" proposal of December 1953 and the "Open Skies" idea unveiled in July 1955. The chapter will show that these initiatives were largely rhetorical and involved a strong dose of striving for relative advantage, which minimized the chances that they could lead to an agenda that would interest Soviet leaders.

While it is not fair to say that US policy in this period involved no willingness to cooperate, this chapter will show that efforts to limit the nuclear competition took a back seat to the desire to maintain an American position of strength in that competition. This preference was not surprising nor even necessarily wrong. But it does suggest that willingness to cooperate must be assessed in terms of its overall place in defense and foreign policy priorities. Showing how Eisenhower allowed other priorities, some with no direct bearing on arms control, to override his desire for cooperation will make apparent why it is not always accurate to equate state preferences with the goals or ideas of state leaders with regard to the issue in question. It will also raise the question of whether stronger signals of societal interest might have convinced Eisenhower to take more concrete steps on behalf of arms restraint. To make it possible to speculate intelligently on this question, this chapter begins by describing the conflicting impulses guiding Eisenhower's arms policies when he took office, in order to establish a policy baseline for this period.

Policy baseline: Eisenhower and nuclear weapons

The presidency of Dwight Eisenhower is full of paradoxes when it comes to nuclear weapons. Eisenhower's eight years in office saw the main expansion of the American nuclear arsenal, including the introduction of the hydrogen bomb and the intercontinental ballistic missile (ICBM). Indeed, when it comes to nuclear weapons, his administration may be best known for its strategy of massive retaliation and use of atomic threats in efforts to end the Korean War and the Chinese shelling of Quemoy and Matsu. Yet, President Eisenhower also felt grave concern about nuclear weapons and strongly doubted that a nuclear war could have a winner. In his inaugural address in January 1953, which came shortly after he had been briefed on the USA's first test of a thermonuclear device, Eisenhower's only reference to science was the observation that it "seems ready to confer upon us . . . the power to erase human life from this planet." When an aide complained that this passage was too negative, Eisenhower replied, "Just listen to the stories of the hydrogen bomb."[3]

His horror at the power of thermonuclear weapons led to great skepticism about the feasibility of fighting a nuclear war. At a Cabinet meeting less than two months after his inauguration, Eisenhower exclaimed "Any notion that 'the bomb' is a cheap way to solve things is awfully wrong . . . It is cold comfort for any citizen of Western Europe to be assured that – after his country is overrun and he is pushing up daisies – someone still alive will drop a bomb on the Kremlin." Similarly, in a press conference in March 1955, Eisenhower proclaimed, "The concept of atomic war is too horrible for man to endure and to practice, and he must find some way out of it."[4]

Eisenhower's heartfelt comment on this occasion could easily be taken to refer to his personal situation. For contradictory impulses in this area entangled the president in some serious dilemmas. Although Eisenhower hoped to avoid a dangerous nuclear arms race, he also placed the burden of the country's security firmly on the shoulders of its nuclear arsenal. The only true fiscal conservative among US Cold War presidents, Eisenhower zealously sought to reduce federal spending, including the defense budget. Because nuclear weapons offered "more bang for the buck," the administration cut back spending on more expensive conventional forces and gave primary emphasis to nuclear deterrence.[5]

To make the threat of nuclear retaliation remotely credible as a dissuasion to communist mischief seemed to require maintaining American superiority (the concept of stability through MAD – mutual assured destruction – had not yet taken hold). Needless to say, desire to keep the lead is not easily reconciled with the usual observation that arms control or cooperation require parity or equality of results.

[3] Gregg Herken, *Cardinal Choices: Presidential Science Advising from the Atomic Bomb to SDI* (New York: Oxford University Press, 1992), pp. 69–70.

[4] Emmet John Hughes, *The Ordeal of Power: A Political Memoir of the Eisenhower Years* (New York: Atheneum, 1963), p. 101; McGeorge Bundy, *Danger and Survival: Choices About the Bomb in the First Fifty Years* (New York: Vintage Books, 1988), p. 254.

[5] The emphasis on nuclear weapons also reflected a feeling that any major war would inevitably go nuclear, making conventional superiority less meaningful, and desire to use the nuclear threat to avoid getting bogged down in more Koreas. So strong was Eisenhower's commitment to rely on the nuclear threat that he intervened during the drafting of the NSC document that formalized his "New Look" strategy to change the document's description of the strategic bomber force from "a major deterrent" to "the major deterrent" (Bundy, *Danger and Survival*, p. 247).

Yet, when it came to possible trade-offs between the goals of strength and mutual restraint, Eisenhower consistently put an unassailable military position first. The president's instructions to Lewis Strauss when the latter was appointed chairman of the Atomic Energy Commission (AEC) in 1953 nicely capture Eisenhower's dual concerns: "[M]y chief concern and your first assignment is to find some new approach to the *dis*arming of atomic energy . . . that will be safe for the free world and attractive to the Russians . . . Meanwhile, we have to continue to keep our lead in weapons development. I am counting on you for that, too." Disarmament was seen as desirable. But until a surefire way to achieve it safely was found, top priority would go to staying ahead in the arms race. As Eisenhower put it in the speech in which he proposed Open Skies, "[I]n pursuit of his hope [for peace, the statesman] must not betray the trust placed in him as guardian of the people's security."[6]

Reliance on nuclear weapons to provide that security created a tendency to evaluate proposals in terms of who would be left with an advantage. The administration's view of the nature of the struggle with the Soviet Union added to that tendency. For, beyond the military realm, Eisenhower and his aides believed that the United States was locked in a psychological battle with the USSR for world opinion. Thus, after taking office, Eisenhower appointed a special advisor on psychological warfare. This advisor, C. D. Jackson, was assisted by an Operations Coordinating Board whose mission was to see that foreign policy actions "were conducted with a view to [ensuring] the impact on world opinion . . . most favorable to the United States."[7] In this context, no arms proposal was ever just a proposal. Instead, both US and Soviet offers were evaluated in terms of which scored the most propaganda points. This inclination introduced an additional relative gains concern that further complicated the search for cooperation.

Finally, Eisenhower, along with the rest of his administration and the majority of ordinary Americans, was highly skeptical of Soviet

[6] Lewis L. Strauss, *Men and Decisions* (Garden City, NY: Doubleday & Co., 1962), pp. 336–37; Statement by President Eisenhower on Disarmament, Geneva, July 21, 1955, in Robert L. Branyan and Lawrence H. Larsen, *The Eisenhower Administration, 1953–1961: A Documentary History* (New York: Random House, 1971), 2 vols., vol. I, p. 646.

[7] Former Eisenhower official, quoted in Richard A. Melanson, "The Foundations of Eisenhower's Foreign Policy: Continuity, Community, and Consensus," in Melanson and David Mayers, eds., *Reevaluating Eisenhower: American Foreign Policy in the 1950s* (Urbana: University of Illinois Press, 1987), p. 56.

intentions, including Soviet willingness to cooperate in good faith. For this reason, the president and his aides believed that the United States should not agree to any arms control measure for which there was not an iron-clad guarantee of enforcement (verification, in later parlance). They also tended to make any US offer of cooperation contingent on a prior demonstration of Soviet good faith. Though perfectly understandable, these caveats contributed even more to making US offers highly one-sided. In sum, the administration tended to package cooperative gestures in such a way that they were overwhelmed by concerns reflecting the competitive side of the relationship.

This dynamic can be seen in Eisenhower's famous "Chance for Peace" speech. This speech, on April 16, 1953, was intended to take advantage of any opening for change following the death of Josef Stalin a month before. Eisenhower's personal desire for peace clearly showed through in the address, which included a remarkably moving warning about the costs of the arms race: "Every gun that is made, every warship launched, every rocket fired signifies, in the final sense, a theft from those who hunger and are not fed, those who are cold and are not clothed." Without making any specific new offers, Eisenhower pledged American readiness to enter into a disarmament agreement, after which the United States would devote much of the savings to world aid and reconstruction.[8]

All of this was made contingent, however, on Soviet behavior. "We care nothing for mere rhetoric. We are only for sincerity of peaceful purpose attested by deeds." Eisenhower went on to list a number of deeds the USSR would have to carry out to prove its sincerity. These ranged from an Austrian peace treaty and a Korean armistice to stopping guerrilla movements in Southeast Asia and granting independence to the countries of Eastern Europe. Eisenhower said that progress depended on only one question: "What is the Soviet Union ready to do?" Since the administration knew many of these demands were unacceptable to the USSR, making an arms agreement contingent on prior Soviet actions of this kind made the speech's expression of readiness to talk disarmament moot.[9]

[8] The best accounts of Eisenhower's own goals, combined with extensive quotes from the speech, are Hughes, *Ordeal of Power*, pp. 102–13; and Harold Stassen and Marshall Houts, *Eisenhower: Turning the World Toward Peace* (St. Paul, MN: Merrill/Magnus Publishing Corp., 1990), pp. 168–71.

[9] Stassen and Houts, *Eisenhower*, pp. 171–73; Stephen E. Ambrose, *Eisenhower: The President* (New York: Simon and Schuster, 1984), p. 94.

The administration's baseline policy can thus be summarized as follows. At the general level, the president attached fairly high priority to finding some kind of agreement that could reduce the chance of nuclear war. However, the administration gave even greater priority to maintaining a position of nuclear strength, unless the USSR first changed its behavior in ways that would prove it no longer intended to threaten Western security. At the specific level, the administration was not committed to anything more than the search for new ideas. However, in evaluating prospective proposals, the administration would look primarily at whether they could be fully verified, would still leave the United States in a secure position militarily, and would be received favorably by world opinion. Their potential attractiveness to Soviet leaders did not rate as highly on this list. This set of priorities did not rule out arms control completely, but it did give opponents of arms control a number of levers they could use to block progress.

Domestic context

This policy baseline was more unfavorable than favorable to the pursuit of cooperation, but not so much so as to make cooperation inconceivable. A strong societal impulse might therefore have been able to change the balance in US preferences. One possible source of such an impulse would have been a citizens' campaign, but no such campaign emerged. In fact, earlier stirrings of activism for nuclear disarmament in the years after World War II all but disappeared in the early to mid-1950s, making this the case with the lowest level of activism among the four in this book.

Several factors account for the decline of protest. The deepening of the Cold War, culminating in the North Korean invasion of the South, convinced many Americans who had earlier supported arms limitation that such a goal no longer made sense. Communist-sponsored peace offensives that were obviously self-serving then split what remained of the peace movement in the late 1940s and early 1950s, further weakening it. Finally, the conditions created by McCarthyism largely repressed whatever activist impulse remained.[10] In Eisenhower's initial years in office, therefore, the absence of any popular

[10] Lawrence S. Wittner, *Rebels Against War: The American Peace Movement, 1941–1960* (New York: Columbia University Press, 1969), chaps. 7–8.

movement makes it moot even to consider whether activism could have engaged any of the influence mechanisms outlined in chapter 3.

Even if there was no societal activism on behalf of arms restraint, neither does this period fit the common view of public opinion as a constraint. Rather, the public was willing to support arms limitation, provided it was done carefully. In two polls in 1953, a roughly two-to-one margin favored seeking international control of atomic weapons through the UN. Enthusiasm about arms control was limited, however, by growing skepticism about whether the Soviets could be trusted to keep agreements. Thus, an April 1954 survey found that a substantial majority – 69 percent – wanted to continue efforts to reach an agreement, but without any weakening of US demands for inspection. If public opinion affected policy, this would limit the kinds of concessions the administration could make, but it in no way constrained the president from seriously pursuing an arms deal.[11]

Organized advocacy groups and diffuse public opinion were thus neither a strong stimulus nor a strong constraint in this period. In this domestic context, any US willingness to cooperate would have to come from the top, as traditional perspectives expect. Despite some favorable developments, ultimately Eisenhower's own hesitations combined with bureaucratic politics to prevent any major shift in US preferences. Because President Eisenhower had sufficient autonomy to set an agenda that would make serious arms talks possible, and chose not to do so, one cannot argue that social protest would have been necessary for arms control to occur. But Eisenhower's unwillingness to make arms control a priority leaves open the possibility that popular activism would have made the pursuit of arms cooperation more likely. In the absence of societal pressure, this case will show, the factors emphasized by other approaches were not sufficient to bring about US willingness to cooperate on restraining nuclear arsenals. Even when leaders have considerable autonomy and cognitions which suggest that state interests require cooperation, a preference for putting cooperation ahead of continued competition may not result. Showing how this can occur will strengthen the case for attaching greater import to whether there are clear expressions of societal support for cooperative policies.

[11] Survey data from Thomas W. Graham, "The Politics of Failure: Strategic Nuclear Arms Control, Public Opinion, and Domestic Politics in the United States, 1945–1980," Ph.D. dissertation, MIT (1989), app. 3, p. 346, and app. 7, pp. 397, 404.

Atoms for Peace

During Eisenhower's first term, the United States took several initiatives to express interest in finding a way out of the nuclear danger. However, the United States did little to find areas of common ground with the Soviet Union that could make actual progress possible. In this situation, what was theoretically a preference for cooperation was rarely manifested in practice. This dynamic did much to limit the chances of Eisenhower's first major proposal, which became known as Atoms for Peace.

When Eisenhower took office, he inherited an existing, thoroughly unproductive set of talks from his predecessor. After the collapse of initial negotiations on US and Soviet proposals for eliminating nuclear weapons, the Truman administration had proposed establishing a UN Disarmament Commission (UNDC), which began operations in early 1952. A subcommittee of this group comprising the United States, Britain, France, Canada, and the Soviet Union was also created. In a step that complicated already dim prospects for agreement, the UNDC talks merged the nuclear issue with discussions of conventional force reductions. Under a policy adopted by the NSC in 1951, though, the USA approached these talks primarily as an exercise in public relations anyway.[12]

Over the course of 1953, the feeling grew in the new administration that the United States had to make some new proposal. The initial impetus came from a review of American disarmament policy submitted in January by a panel of State Department consultants, chaired by the atomic scientist Robert Oppenheimer. The panel's report argued that, because of secrecy, the American people did not understand that both the United States and the Soviet Union would soon effectively be able to destroy one another with nuclear weapons. Because the panel saw no chance of progress in existing United Nations disarmament talks – an assessment the Eisenhower team accepted – its primary recommendation was simply greater "candor" with the American people, in order to stimulate a better-informed debate that could produce a more realistic policy.[13]

[12] Matthew Evangelista, "Cooperation Theory and Disarmament Negotiations in the 1950s," *World Politics* 42 (July 1990), pp. 515, 517.

[13] Richard G. Hewlett and Jack M. Holl, *Atoms for Peace and War, 1953–1961: Eisenhower and the Atomic Energy Commission* (Berkeley: University of California Press, 1989), pp. 41–43; Bundy, *Danger and Survival*, pp. 288–89.

In response, Eisenhower ultimately decided to give a speech that would describe the nuclear danger in general terms, coupled with some more positive proposal. Eisenhower later wrote in his diary that he hoped

> to make a clear effort to get the Soviet Union working with us in some phase of this whole atomic field that would have only peace and the good of mankind as a goal. If we were successful in getting even the tiniest of starts, it was believed that gradually this kind of talk and negotiation might expand into something broader . . . Underlying all of this, of course, is the clear conviction that as of now the world is racing toward catastrophe.[14]

The president's personal interest in finding a basis for cooperation was clear, but ultimately the level of willingness to cooperate reflected in American policy was diluted by the administration's other objectives in this area. Primary among these was the ongoing search for both propaganda and military advantage. The interest in propaganda was present from the start. At the first NSC meeting called to discuss the Oppenheimer Panel report, Vice President Richard Nixon responded that the United States should "make some kind of sensational offer on the disarmament side, which the Soviets would of course not accept, and which would therefore put them on the spot." Secretary of State John Foster Dulles concurred, reasoning that "we had squeezed all the juice out of our last proposal."[15]

Eisenhower also wanted to reassure the people of the USA and the world, though, that some good would come of atomic technology. He therefore suggested to aides that maybe the United States and USSR could both donate a certain amount of fissionable material to an international agency, which would use it to help other countries develop atomic power plants and other peaceful applications of atomic energy. Yet, at the same time, Eisenhower also saw the plan as a way to advance certain Cold War objectives. Thus, in the memo that first outlined the idea, National Security Advisor Robert Cutler indicated that Eisenhower had in mind a plan where "the amount X [of materials contributed] could be fixed at a figure which we could handle from our stockpile, but which would be difficult for the

[14] Robert H. Ferrell, ed., *The Eisenhower Diaries* (New York: W. W. Norton & Co., 1981), pp. 261–62.

[15] Herken, *Cardinal Choices*, p. 70.

Soviets to match."[16] Eisenhower also sought to use the proposal as a new test of Soviet intentions. The president told Dulles he wanted to make a "fair offer" to the USSR which, if rejected, would prove "we had no alternative but to look upon the Soviet Union as a potential aggressor." He reasoned that such a step would be necessary to convince the American people to support the buildup of nuclear weapons over the long term.[17]

Eisenhower presented the proposal in a speech to the United Nations on December 8, 1953. Though the plan was not directly related to disarmament, the president and some of his aides hoped that, if Atoms for Peace got established, it might eventually serve arms control purposes by forcing the superpowers to dismantle some of their nuclear weapons in order to make their required contributions of fissionable materials. Eisenhower also really believed that Atoms for Peace had some chance of being accepted. For one thing, as he pointed out in his speech, it bypassed the problem of inspection,

[16] Memorandum by Robert Cutler, September 10, 1953, in *Foreign Relations of the United States* (*FRUS*), 1952–54, vol. II, p. 1213.

Some historians have claimed that Eisenhower was actually willing to make contributions at a ratio of at least five by the United States to one by the USSR in order to keep the plan from working to Soviet disadvantage (Ambrose, *Eisenhower*, p. 149; John Newhouse, *War and Peace in the Nuclear Age* [New York: Vintage Books, 1990; Alfred A. Knopf, 1988], p. 108). This appears to be based on the way Eisenhower described the plan to the British and French prime ministers in a meeting in which he asked their support for making the proposal (Ambrose, *Eisenhower*, p. 147). But I can find no evidence anywhere in the publicly available records that Eisenhower sought to make this ratio the official policy of his own administration or ever offered it to the Soviets. US willingness to contribute more was not highlighted in the original speech that proposed the plan (Speech by President Eisenhower on Peaceful Uses of Atomic Energy, General Assembly of the United Nations, December 8, 1953, in Branyan and Larsen, *The Eisenhower Administration*, vol. I, pp. 194–200), which merely notes that the ratios would be subject to negotiation. Moreover, the first draft proposal that the United States conveyed to the Soviets specified that "[t]he USSR would make an equivalent donation" of fissionable materials to that of the United States (*Department of State Bulletin*, vol. 31, October 4, 1954, p. 481). Finally, both Eisenhower's private diary and his memoirs emphasize that the United States could have donated two or three times as much material as the Soviet Union and "still [have] improve[d] our relative position" (Ferrell, *The Eisenhower Diaries*, p. 262; Dwight D. Eisenhower, *The White House Years: Mandate for Change, 1953–1956* [Garden City, NY: Doubleday & Co., 1963], p. 254). Neither source says anything about being willing to adjust the ratio so that it would not hurt the USSR.

[17] Ambrose, *Eisenhower*, pp. 133–34; Henry Sokolski, "The Arms Control Connection," in Joseph F. Pilat, Robert E. Pendley, and Charles K. Ebinger, eds., *Atoms for Peace: An Analysis After Thirty Years* (Boulder: Westview Press, 1985), pp. 40–41.

which had prevented agreement on all previous proposals. To maximize the chances that the Soviets would take it seriously, Dulles instructed the US ambassador in Moscow to inform Foreign Minister Molotov that the speech was a serious statement of "US willingness to talk privately on [the] whole atomic armament problem."[18]

How much willingness to cooperate was actually involved here? Soviet rejection cannot be taken as a measure of US willingness in this case because the USSR probably lacked much willingness to cooperate itself at this time. But neither can US willingness be judged equal to Eisenhower's own evident sincerity in hoping to move stalled arms talks off "dead center."[19] For one thing, the president had been informed that the proposal might have only a limited effect on the nuclear arms race even under the best circumstances. Strauss had suggested in his initial response to Eisenhower's idea that, with the introduction of the H-bomb, "the relative importance of a stockpile of *fissionable* material is reduced since it is only required as a primer while quite different substances, *not fissionable*, support the thermonuclear explosion."[20]

The outer bounds of US willingness are also suggested by other alternatives the administration considered and rejected. Before settling on Atoms for Peace, the administration deliberated a more far-reaching proposal favored by Secretary Dulles. The State Department draft plan proposed setting limitations on both nuclear and conventional arms, along with making some new suggestions for resolving outstanding political disputes. However, the plan came under fire from several quarters in the administration. This included not only the usual opponents of negotiating with the Soviet Union, but some supporters of a new initiative who felt that the State Department plan was too complicated to serve the administration's other goals for a presidential speech. For example, National Security Advisor Cutler argued that the speech's audience "would be unable to grasp" what the president was talking about, adding "If this great proposal is to be

[18] Strauss, *Men and Decisions*, p. 358; Newhouse, *War and Peace*, p. 107; Thomas F. Soapes, "A Cold Warrior Seeks Peace: Eisenhower's Strategy for Nuclear Disarmament," *Diplomatic History* 4 (Winter 1980), p. 63.

[19] Letter from Eisenhower to his brother Milton concerning Atoms for Peace, quoted in Soapes, "A Cold Warrior Seeks Peace," p. 62.

[20] Memorandum for the President by the Chairman of the United States Atomic Energy Commission, September 17, 1953, *FRUS*, 1952–54, vol. II, p. 1219 (emphasis in original).

made as a last best hope of the world, its message must be clear beyond a doubt to John Q. Citizen." In short, the plan's simplicity was more important than its attractiveness to the Soviet Union. The State Department alternative finally died in late October, when Dulles himself recommended against announcing any new disarmament proposal for fear that it would undermine efforts to increase European defense cooperation.[21]

Once the administration had decided to go with Eisenhower's own suggestion, responsibility for fleshing it out into an actual proposal fell to AEC chair Strauss. He suggested stopping all uranium mining and production of plutonium for ten years while requiring fixed monthly donations of fissionable materials to a new international atom bank. But the Defense Department objected vehemently to halting production of materials needed to expand the US nuclear arsenal. Hence, even the idea of a moratorium on fissile materials production did not survive to be included in the president's speech.[22] The actual Atoms for Peace proposal, while clearly sincere, was thus also quite modest compared to the other options the administration considered and rejected. In particular, it was several steps further removed from imposing any restrictions on the arms race.

The plan's tenuous link to actual arms limitation strongly limited the proposal's appeal to the Soviet Union. The Soviet reply thus complained – accurately – that Atoms for Peace would "neither check the growing production of atomic weapons nor limit the possibilities of their use." However, finding an agenda the United States could live with that might also be acceptable to the USSR did not rate highly among the administration's criteria for its arms proposals. Commenting on how the administration developed the Atoms for Peace idea, McGeorge Bundy observes that "No one seems to have addressed the question of the likelihood of Soviet enthusiasm for such a bargain." In sum, while the administration made a big show of professing its willingness to cooperate, it did little to find out what type of cooperation might be feasible.[23]

21 Memorandum by the Special Assistant to the President, October 19, 1953, *FRUS*, 1952–54, vol. II, p. 1233; Robert R. Bowie, "Eisenhower, Atomic Weapons, and Atoms for Peace," in Pilat et al., *Atoms for Peace*, pp. 20–22; Bundy, *Danger and Survival*, pp. 290–92.

22 Hewlett and Holl, *Atoms for Peace and War*, pp. 65–67; Bowie, "Eisenhower, Atomic Weapons," p. 22.

23 Statement by the Soviet Government on President Eisenhower's "Atoms for Peace"

The administration's follow-up after the speech likewise focused on the proposal's other objectives, rather than the effort to get talks going. For one thing, Eisenhower's speech was received with tremendous enthusiasm by the non-communist world, leading to a flurry of activity to push this propaganda victory as far as possible. In February 1954, C. D. Jackson declared the effort a success, noting "The President's speech . . . [had] placed the USSR in a defensive position." In a profound piece of irony, given that the policy process had begun with the Oppenheimer Panel's recommendation for greater candor about the nuclear threat, Lewis Strauss also used Atoms for Peace to try to reduce popular fear of nuclear weapons. As part of the follow-up to the proposal, Strauss suggested an international scientific meeting on peaceful uses of the atom, which took place in 1955. After the conference, Strauss declared it had successfully countered "the mesmerism of the bomb." "No other event . . . has done so much toward taking the horror – the terror – out of the atom."[24]

Still, by the criteria developed in chapter 2, this episode cannot be judged as showing no US preference for cooperation. For one thing, intermittent negotiations with the Soviet Union on Eisenhower's proposal did get going, after the Soviets agreed to discuss the American idea so long as talks alternated with sessions on the preferred Soviet proposal for a ban on nuclear weapons. Moreover, both superpowers eventually concurred in a multilateral agreement to create an International Atomic Energy Agency (IAEA). However, as Robert Strong notes, "By the time the IAEA was finally in operation [in October 1957,] nearly four years after the speech was given, the stockpiles of weapons and fissionable materials on both sides were so large that no commitment to the international development of atomic energy could be regarded as an arms control measure." The delay in reaching agreement was partly due to Soviet foot-dragging, but American slowness in developing a workable proposal also contributed, so it is unlikely that the IAEA could have had any bearing on the arms race even had the Soviets been more cooperative.[25]

Address, December 21, 1953, in US Department of State, Bureau of Public Affairs, Historical Office, *Documents on Disarmament* (Washington, DC: Government Printing Office, 1960), vol. I, 1945–56, p. 405; Bundy, *Danger and Survival*, p. 290.

24 Peter Pringle and James Spigelman, *The Nuclear Barons* (New York: Holt, Rinehart, and Winston, 1981), pp. 122–24; Bundy, *Danger and Survival*, pp. 293–95, 303; Hewlett and Holl, *Atoms for Peace and War*, p. 232.

25 Robert A. Strong, "Eisenhower and Arms Control," in Melanson and Mayers,

While Soviet unwillingness to engage on the American agenda was a major obstacle in this period, neither can it be said that the United States showed much sympathy for the proposed Soviet agenda. When it became clear that the Soviet Union would continue to push for nuclear disarmament as its alternative to Atoms for Peace, the president and his top advisors met to determine their policy on such negotiations. The minutes from the January 1954 meeting indicate that "everyone present was of the opinion that no effective agreement could be reached with the Soviets on the control of nuclear weapons at this time." The group therefore decided that all the United States would do was "listen to any proposals which the USSR cared to submit on the control or abolition of nuclear weapons, [but] we would not be drawn into any negotiation on this subject."[26]

There were good reasons to fear that complete nuclear disarmament might leave a conventional imbalance that would increase the danger to Western Europe. But the repeated use of the word "control" in this document, in addition to "abolition," suggests that the Eisenhower administration was unwilling even to explore whether the Soviets might accept some deal that stopped short of eliminating nuclear arms. Instead, Dulles was authorized to seek talks on peaceful uses of the atom provided they would "take place entirely separately" from any negotiations on weapons.[27] Thus, when the Soviets agreed to alternating discussions on Atoms for Peace and atomic disarmament, the United States had already made a policy decision not to take the second set of talks seriously.

Administrative and policy changes in 1955

The American reticence about disarmament talks in 1954 was part of an evolution in US policy that finally led the United States the next year to give up altogether on finding a comprehensive approach to the arms problem. In spring 1955, the United States officially dropped disarmament as its policy goal, in favor of more modest arms control

Reevaluating Eisenhower, pp. 247–48; Richard G. Hewlett, "From Proposal to Program," in Pilat et al., *Atoms for Peace*, p. 28; Hewlett and Holl, *Atoms for Peace and War*, pp. 219–21, 309–15.

26 Summary of Meeting in the White House, January 16, 1954, in *Declassified Documents Reference System* (Woodbridge, CT: Research Publications; *DDRS*), 1979-331B (the first number is the series year, the second the item number).

27 Ibid.

measures. Ironically, this policy shift came about in part because of Soviet expressions of interest in recent Western disarmament proposals. In autumn 1954, the Soviet government indicated it would be willing to make a British–French proposal of that summer the basis for discussions of a draft treaty. Since the United States had not taken UNDC talks at all seriously, the administration was suddenly forced to review its own policy.

A major internal split quickly developed. Neither side in the debate believed cooperation was possible, but they disagreed sharply about what policy would best protect US interests.[28] Frustration at this infighting among his advisors prompted Eisenhower to make an organizational change. In March 1955, Eisenhower appointed Harold Stassen to be his special assistant on disarmament, with Cabinet rank. The president gave Stassen the task of integrating the different ideas of the various agencies involved into a single administration disarmament program.[29] Creating a Cabinet-level position in charge of arms talks represented an attempt to raise the priority attached to arms restraint at the general level. There would now be an official advocate of progress in this area with formally equal rank to the opponents of seeking disarmament. However, the impact on US willingness to seek cooperation ultimately proved slight, as Eisenhower rarely supported Stassen against administration opponents of arms cooperation.

While Stassen was conducting a comprehensive review of US disarmament policy, the USSR unveiled a new disarmament plan on May 10. The Soviet proposal incorporated many aspects of the British–French plan and made some moves to address traditional Western concerns about compliance, though it still fell short of what the United States deemed necessary in the area of monitoring.[30] Besides being caught by surprise by the Soviet offer, the administra-

[28] See Evangelista, "Cooperation Theory and Disarmament," p. 517; Memorandum from the Joint Chiefs of Staff to the Secretary of Defense, June 23, 1954, *FRUS*, 1952–54, vol. II, pp. 680–81; Paper Prepared in the Department of State, November 15, 1954, *FRUS*, 1952–54, vol. II, pp. 775–76.

[29] Sherman Adams, *Firsthand Report: The Story of the Eisenhower Administration* (New York: Harper and Bros., 1961), p. 177; Stassen and Houts, *Eisenhower*, pp. 275–83.

[30] Overall, though, the deputy US representative to the talks was sufficiently encouraged to declare that "to a measurable degree, the gaps between us seem to have been lessened" (Evangelista, "Cooperation Theory and Disarmament," pp. 502–03, 514). For the Stassen Panel's analysis of the Soviet offer, see Progress Report Prepared by the President's Special Assistant, May 26, 1955, *FRUS*, 1955–57, vol. XX, pp. 96–97.

tion felt additional urgency about formulating a new policy because the president was scheduled to go to his first summit meeting with Soviet leaders in Geneva in July, and the administration did not have any worked-out proposal that it could make at the summit. Hence, a quick decision on disarmament was necessary.[31]

Stassen and his advisors submitted their initial report on May 26, 1955. The most important part of the report recommended a new direction for US disarmament policy. The Stassen report argued that the United States should abandon nuclear disarmament as its official goal in favor of more limited forms of arms control, a recommendation the administration accepted.[32] In the long run, this represented a move toward greater willingness to cooperate, as it gave up a stance geared more to propaganda concerns and replaced it with one that increased the chances of finding an agenda acceptable to both sides. In the short run, however, the main result of the administration's discussion of the Stassen report was just the opposite.

Though for different reasons, both the military and the State Department argued against any direct counteroffers or other efforts to make progress on the existing UNDC proposals, leading the administration to reject pursuing the possible agenda created by the USSR's May 10 proposal. Hence, when talks in the UN Disarmament Subcommittee resumed after the Geneva summit, Harold Stassen, recently appointed chief US delegate, announced that his government was placing a reservation on all its pre-summit positions. This in effect repudiated not only the Soviet May 10 offer but the earlier British–French proposal as well. Indeed, during the Geneva summit, Dulles allegedly told his staff that he wanted the disarmament negotiations "closed out quietly." Forced to consider whether it was willing to pursue an agenda for arms limitations in which the Soviets actually expressed an interest, the administration decided that the answer was no. In place of its previous positions, the administration now tried to substitute a narrower agenda centered on a plan for aerial inspection, which came to be known as Open Skies.[33]

31 Bundy, *Danger and Survival*, p. 296.

32 Progress Report Prepared by the President's Special Assistant, May 26, 1955.

33 Matthew Evangelista has found evidence that the USSR's May 10 proposal may have reflected a genuine change in Soviet policy and may actually have been negotiable, so the US decision not to pursue it further may have been a missed opportunity for cooperation: Evangelista, "Cooperation Theory and Disarmament," pp. 503, 506–14,

Open Skies

Despite (and because of) its decision to avoid further engagement on existing disarmament proposals, the administration sought a new proposal the president could bring with him to the Geneva summit. This produced the second new offer of Eisenhower's term, the Open Skies proposal. Under this plan, both sides would exchange information about their military facilities and permit aerial overflights of their territory so that the other could confirm this information. The president believed that this would reduce the danger of surprise attack by making it harder to keep military preparations secret.

While Stassen's advisory group had suggested something along the same lines, the specific proposal that gained Eisenhower's formal approval came out of a conference organized by Nelson Rockefeller, who had replaced Jackson as the special assistant for psychological warfare. Once it became clear that the summit would happen, Rockefeller brought a group of administration officials and outside specialists to Quantico, Virginia, in early June to discuss what Eisenhower should propose in Geneva. The idea of mutual aerial inspection became one of the Quantico Panel's recommendations. When Rockefeller met with the president on July 6 to promote the idea, Eisenhower responded enthusiastically and ordered Dulles to begin work on refining the proposal.[34]

Open Skies is paradigmatic of the way arms control policy worked in Eisenhower's first term. It is a proposal that emerged only because – indeed precisely because – it met the concerns of nearly every administration official involved in arms policy. It was as if everyone's objectives were logrolled together, and only those ideas that fit in the intersection of their conflicting goals survived. Although for the president these goals included a sincere desire to find a basis for cooperation, most other administration officials gave priority to achieving the strongest possible position in the ongoing superpower competition, a goal that suggested underlying "deadlock" preferences. The peculiar quality of Open Skies is that it actually managed to square this circle.

For example, the Quantico Panel believed that trends in the military

519–21; Hewlett and Holl, *Atoms for Peace and War*, p. 300; Adams, *Firsthand Report*, p. 88.

34 W. W. Rostow, *Open Skies: Eisenhower's Proposal of July 21, 1955* (Austin: University of Texas Press, 1982), pp. 26–35; Ambrose, *Eisenhower*, pp. 258–59.

balance had turned unfavorable and was thus most concerned about finding a way to rally the country behind a greater military effort. They reasoned that, if the United States put forward hard proposals on German reunification and disarmament and the Soviets rejected them, this could be used to convince the American public to support higher defense spending. In some ways, an even more extreme position was taken by Secretary of State Dulles, who opposed making any effort to reach an agreement at Geneva. Dulles worried especially that the president's generous personality would lead him to accept some Soviet proposal at the summit disadvantageous to Western security.[35]

But the secretary also felt that some proposal had to be made, and in these circumstances Open Skies was about the best he could hope for. In a memo written for an NSC meeting on June 30 to discuss Stassen's report, Dulles laid out his thinking. He argued that American advantages in military capability and economic productivity meant continuation of the status quo was more desirable "than any plan that rested upon agreement and supervision." But – even in the absence of any organized domestic campaign – the secretary felt that there were counterpressures. "[I]nstinctive abhorrence" at the destructiveness of nuclear weapons had combined with Soviet propaganda to "create a popular and diplomatic pressure for limitation of armament that cannot be resisted by the United States without our forfeiting the good will of our allies and the support of a large part of our own people . . . We must, therefore, propose or support some plan for the limitation of armaments." But, in order not to lose the advantages of the current situation, Dulles recommended that "there should not be any effort to agree upon any over-all plan until first a measure of inspection has been tried out and found to be workable."[36]

Because even officials more favorable to cooperation recognized the possibility of Soviet cheating, the argument that inspection should be tried and proven first became an effective way to come out against any proposal that involved actual arms limitation. In memos written prior to the June 30 NSC meeting, Defense Secretary Wilson and the JCS both expressed the opinion that attempting to preserve a position of military strength would be better for US security than any possible

[35] Rostow, *Open Skies*, pp. 26–33, 160.
[36] Draft Memorandum by the Secretary of State, June 29, 1955, *FRUS*, 1955–57, vol. XX, pp. 140–42.

arms limitation plan. At the meeting itself, though, Wilson and Admiral Radford, chairman of the Joint Chiefs, stressed verification concerns, arguing that it would be necessary to change Soviet attitudes about inspection before any arms deal would be possible. At that point, Dulles suggested that "heavy initial emphasis from now on be placed on the problem of inspection and policing," and Eisenhower agreed that the main focus after the meeting should be on studying possible inspection schemes. Dulles made his recommendation directly after expressing concern that British and French pressures to make concessions would turn any other proposal to US disadvantage. Both this statement and his memo make it clear that the secretary saw inspection largely as a way to avoid pressure actually to agree to some disarmament. His eventual concurrence in making the Open Skies proposal thus did not imply any interest in seeing cooperation develop.[37]

The competitive aspects of Open Skies also won over Admiral Radford, the JCS chair. When Rockefeller briefed him on Open Skies, Radford replied, "I see what you guys are doing – you are trying to open up the Soviet Union." Radford then dictated a memo indicating his support for the proposal. He argued that the United States would gain "a decided intelligence advantage" if the Soviet leaders accepted it and "a decided public opinion advantage" if they did not.[38] In reality, virtually no administration official thought the Soviet Union would accept the plan. The Radford memo predicted that "the USSR would probably turn down a US [aerial inspection] proposal." Another member of the US delegation to the Geneva summit, Vernon Walters, later noted that "no one had any illusions that the Russians with their passion for secrecy would ever accept it." The head of the State Department Policy Planning Staff also remembers thinking that Open Skies "was . . . never in the least negotiable."[39]

One important exception to this line of thought was the president himself who, in instructing Dulles to develop the proposal on July 6,

[37] Evangelista, "Cooperation Theory and Disarmament," pp. 519–20; Hewlett and Holl, *Atoms for Peace and War*, pp. 297–99.

[38] Rostow, *Open Skies*, pp. 52–53, and fn. 28, p. 197. Some other officials also anticipated that making a public proposal for both sides to open up their air space might forestall criticism when the United States later began flights of the nearly operational U-2 reconnaissance plane: Strong, "Eisenhower and Arms Control," p. 249.

[39] Rostow, *Open Skies*, p. 53; Evangelista, "Cooperation Theory and Disarmament," p. 522; Newhouse, *War and Peace*, p. 115.

expressed hope that it "might open a tiny gate in the disarmament fence." The president explained in a letter he wrote shortly after the summit to General Alfred Gruenther: "[I]f we assume that the kind of inspection to which I referred would eliminate the danger of devastating *surprise* attack, the agreement for such inspection and this result would yield an immense gain in mutual confidence and trust. This means that we would thus have established a truly realistic basis for studying disarmament." These hopes account for probably the most useful thing Open Skies did, which was to give Eisenhower a chance to tell the Soviet leaders of his personal desire for peace. When he made the proposal, Eisenhower took off his glasses and turned to look directly at the Soviet table. He said he had been "searching" for a way to "convince everyone of the great sincerity of the United States in approaching this problem of disarmament." Then, after outlining his aerial inspection scheme, the president promised this "would be but a beginning."[40]

While more hopeful than his aides, however, even Eisenhower suspected that nothing immediate would come of his proposal. According to Stassen, in the days after the summit, Eisenhower told him that "he knew that full implementation of the 'Open Skies' proposal would be years, perhaps decades away. Because of their backgrounds in a closed society, the Soviet leaders could not view it on its face as a genuine peace offer."[41] For the president, the emphasis was really on improving the climate, in the hope that the Soviet leaders would eventually change their attitudes.

Eisenhower and his aides were certainly right about the short term, as the Soviet Union quickly rejected Open Skies. As the session in which Eisenhower made his proposal broke up, Nikita Khrushchev, who emerged at the summit as the main Soviet leader, told Eisenhower that he regarded Open Skies as "nothing more than a bald espionage plot against the USSR." The Soviets made their rejection official in the coming months. On September 19, Premier Bulganin wrote Eisenhower that the Soviets would not agree to aerial inspection unless it accompanied an agreement on arms reductions and also involved each side's allies, on the grounds that they would have

[40] Rostow, *Open Skies*, p. 62; Soapes, "A Cold Warrior Seeks Peace," pp. 65–66 (emphasis in original); Ambrose, *Eisenhower*, pp. 264–65; Stassen and Houts, *Eisenhower*, pp. 338–39.

[41] Stassen and Houts, *Eisenhower*, p. 352.

to be included to make it effective as a safeguard against surprise attack.[42]

All administration officials recognized that Open Skies was unbalanced in the USA's favor. Because the United States was already an open society, the United States would learn much more about the USSR under the plan than the other way around. Given Eisenhower's evident interest in cooperation, this raises the question of why the United States didn't package Open Skies with some concessions more favorable to the Soviet Union. As Bundy observes, "There is no evidence that anyone concerned with the Open Skies proposal ever addressed the question of finding a way to offer a balancing incentive in return for Soviet agreement to aerial inspection."[43]

US actions in the aftermath of the summit make the answer clear. For many US officials, Soviet rejection of the plan was actually seen as preferable to the effort to find a compromise agreement. At an NSC meeting after Bulganin's reply seemed not to shut the door entirely, Stassen wanted to probe Soviet willingness to accept a trial inspection system over limited bands of territory. But Dulles, with Eisenhower absent due to his first heart attack, overruled him. Eisenhower's proposal had "put the Russians on the hook," the secretary said, and he wanted to keep them there.[44]

The administration therefore pushed an effort to get the UN General Assembly to endorse Eisenhower's original proposal. The president's UN representative, Henry Cabot Lodge, wrote that UN endorsement "would give us a spectacular gain in the cold war, get for us the initiative as the great leaders for peace in the world, and would also win resounding and widespread support from US public opinion."[45] Of course, it is not clear that Soviet agreement could have been obtained even if the United States had offered balancing concessions. John Newhouse suggests that the Soviet leaders turned down Open Skies because they feared it would reveal just how far behind in the arms race they really were, a fact they had gone to some

[42] Eisenhower, *Mandate for Change*, p. 521; Letter from the Soviet Premier to President Eisenhower, September 19, 1955, US Department of State, *Documents on Disarmament*, vol. I, pp. 516–21.

[43] Bundy, *Danger and Survival*, p. 302.

[44] Hewlett and Holl, *Atoms for Peace and War*, p. 301.

[45] Letter from the Representative at the United Nations to the Secretary of State, October 26, 1955, *FRUS*, 1955–57, vol. XX, p. 223.

lengths to conceal.[46] But the point here is that US willingness to try was also not very high.

Final efforts

Eisenhower was not willing to give up, however. Hence, over the next two years, the administration continued making new proposals, basically by cobbling together watered-down versions of its previous offers. But a closer look at the effort suggests US willingness to cooperate must still be judged as fairly low. In particular, the administration remained too suspicious to respond favorably to any Soviet movement in the American direction. Instead, when the USSR did make concessions, the administration seemed unable to take yes for an answer. In November 1956, for example, the Soviets informed the United States that they would now be willing to discuss a trial of Open Skies over test strips of NATO and Warsaw Pact territory. Then, in April 1957, at talks of the UN Disarmament Subcommittee in London, the Soviet negotiator unveiled a specific offer. It would have opened up more US than Soviet territory to overflights, but was still regarded as an important concession.[47]

This potential opening fell victim, however, to in-fighting within the administration. After the administration worked out a possible compromise response, Stassen ignored instructions to consult with allied governments first and gave his Soviet counterpart a memo outlining the new US proposal before it had gotten final approval. Secretary of State Dulles, who had always wanted to retain control over US foreign policy and had long regarded Stassen's independence as a threat, used Stassen's mistake as an opportunity to re-assert his authority. Stassen was called back to Washington for a reprimand, and Dulles eventually went to London to take charge of the negotiations himself. When the United States finally presented the official proposal it had worked out with its allies, it was not as forthcoming as what Stassen had earlier seemed to offer. Both sides now hardened their positions, and the talks collapsed in mutual recriminations.[48] Open Skies was never seriously entertained again until the Cold War was largely over.

Soviet offers in this period remained tilted to their own advantage,

[46] Newhouse, *War and Peace*, pp. 109–10, 115.

[47] Adams, *Firsthand Report*, pp. 325–27.

[48] Ibid., pp. 327–29; Ambrose, *Eisenhower*, pp. 401–04; Hewlett and Holl, *Atoms for Peace and War*, pp. 394–97, 458–61.

and the concessions the USSR was willing to make to get cooperation were also limited. Nonetheless, it is striking how difficult the US administration found it to respond positively to Soviet concessions. Their wariness about Soviet intentions, though based on a reasonable foundation, created a sort of catch-22. On the one hand, the administration was unwilling to take Soviet concerns into account in its own proposals, fearing that this might lead to an agreement that lessened US deterrent ability. On the other hand, suspiciousness also created skepticism when the Soviets did anything that recognized US concerns.

For example, the USA had long opposed nuclear disarmament proposals because they would leave a conventional imbalance in Europe. In March 1956, the USSR announced that it was dropping its insistence on banning the bomb and instead proposed troop reductions to equal levels. The proposal was partly aimed at removing US military bases from Europe and limiting West German rearmament, but it was nonetheless a move toward the US position. But the administration saw it as just another hostile move in the Cold War. As one State Department analyst put it:

> USSR has excellent propaganda position by this move. It can point to the fact it is willing to reduce to an equal level in conventional forces but leave nuclear restrictions for later negotiations. It can imply it has sufficient nuclear strength now to take this step, which is bound to impact upon European and other public opinion which has regarded US nuclear superiority as a shield.[49]

When the Soviets wanted to ban the bomb it was propaganda, and when they dropped that position it was also propaganda. Such a viewpoint made it almost impossible for the administration to regard any Soviet proposal as serious, short of their simply acceding unconditionally to one-sided US demands.[50] In essence, the United States was not prepared to enter into serious negotiations on any agenda except one devoted to implementing Eisenhower's own favored proposals. Since US officials knew these proposals by themselves

[49] Adams, *Firsthand Report*, pp. 318, 324; Hewlett and Holl, *Atoms for Peace and War*, p. 336; Office Memorandum to Harold Stassen from Howard Meyers, March 27, 1956, *DDRS*, 1993-707.

[50] Khrushchev in fact complained several times that, whenever the Soviet leaders made concessions they thought would improve the chances for an agreement, the West kept moving away (Hewlett and Holl, *Atoms for Peace and War*, p. 336; Evangelista, "Cooperation Theory and Disarmament," p. 522).

were unacceptable to the USSR, this meant that the administration was ultimately not willing to cooperate. Even Stephen Ambrose, in a largely favorable biography of the president, concludes:

> The truth was that the United States was no more ready to enter into genuine disarmament than were the Russians. Despite all Eisenhower's eloquence on the subject, despite his firm conviction that an arms race could only lead to disaster, he could not bring himself, or his nation, to trust the Russians. On disarmament, he did exactly the opposite of what he had promised to do – he was picayunish and recalcitrant.[51]

Conclusions

Eisenhower's first term contains a lot of activity that seems to indicate an interest in cooperation. The administration continued talks in the UNDC begun under Truman, while the president gave several major speeches and made two new proposals, Atoms for Peace and Open Skies, with the avowed purpose of breaking the deadlock on disarmament. Yet no cooperation to limit nuclear weapons took place, nor did any new negotiations get underway that later led to such an outcome. Part of the explanation lies with Soviet behavior, which often emphasized propaganda over substance and usually reflected the most suspicious possible interpretation of US offers. Yet US behavior was often not very different. Despite many expressions of interest in cooperation, actual willingness to cooperate was more apparent than real. The administration placed so many caveats on its willingness to cooperate that no cooperation was possible.

This outcome suggests several limitations on some common ways of analyzing cooperation. In the first place, it suggests that ideas or a cognitive understanding of an issue-area that favor cooperation are not sufficient.[52] Eisenhower in fact saw the arms race in terms that largely anticipated the arms control theorists of the next decade. In a letter in 1956, he wrote, "when we get to the point, as we one day will, that both sides know that in any outbreak of general hostilities . . . destruction will be reciprocal and complete, possibly we will have sense enough to meet at the conference table with the understanding

51 Ambrose, *Eisenhower*, p. 404.

52 Cognitive evolution has been stressed by Ernst B. Haas ("Why Collaborate? Issue-Linkage and International Regimes," *World Politics* 32 [April 1980], pp. 357–405) and is a key element of the epistemic communities approach discussed in chapter 1.

that the era of armaments has ended."[53] Yet, despite an analysis that could have come straight from Schelling or McNamara, Eisenhower's views on the arms race did not fully translate into a willingness to cooperate.

Part of the explanation lies with the president's other beliefs and values, including some not directly relevant to nuclear arms policy. Cognitive evolution that creates a perception that cooperation on a certain issue would be in a state's interest is not enough to create a preference for cooperation, even at the individual level. One could of course respond that an explanation in terms of ideas would still be possible if one took the president's other beliefs into account. However, most attempts to explain cooperation in terms of ideas or learning look only at perceptions of the issue in question, not broader belief systems. Moreover, in this case, the relevant other ideas included beliefs about the domestic arena. This therefore opens up the possibility that organized societal support for arms restraint might have made a difference.

Specifically, an understanding of the arms race favorable to cooperation was checked in part by the value Eisenhower attached to foreign policy consensus. Eisenhower repeatedly proved reluctant to move without a broader base of support, especially from his own foreign policy advisors. Though the president would at times overrule his advisors, he much preferred consensus, even for the smallest moves. For instance, at a 1956 NSC meeting that gave Stassen approval to suggest trying aerial inspection on test strips (an idea that died with the collapse of UNDC talks the following year), Eisenhower "said this idea was very appealing to him but only if all would agree we must move . . . in this matter." John Newhouse in fact blames the lack of progress in arms control on Eisenhower's disinclination to challenge prevailing sentiment. He argues that the president's failure to achieve anything in this area was due "mainly [to] his own reluctance to push against the current. Eisenhower rarely met opposition head-on or stretched the political tolerances of his policies."[54]

Thus, though analysts frequently associate state preferences with those of the leader, in this case the leader let his own preferences be

[53] Strong, "Eisenhower and Arms Control," p. 258.

[54] Memorandum of Discussion at the 275th Meeting of the National Security Council, February 7, 1956, *FRUS*, 1955–57, vol. XX, p. 324; Newhouse, *War and Peace*, p. 92.

limited by what the rest of the political system would support. This suggests a possible limitation of the statesman-centered approaches discussed in chapter 1. Their tendency to equate state preferences with the goals of the national leader can be misleading. Focusing only on the president's desires in this case would lead to an erroneous estimate of US willingness to cooperate. The many eloquent words Eisenhower spoke on this subject were not matched by US deeds during his first term.

Moreover, this was true despite a situation of considerable leader autonomy. Congress rarely challenged the president on foreign policy in this pre-Vietnam era, while, as the beginning of this chapter showed, societal attitudes on arms policy were fairly permissive. In these circumstances, acceptance of bureaucratic constraints was more a matter of choice than necessity for Eisenhower. Thus, even when leaders have the power to set the agenda, making the assumption that they control the agenda can lead to an inaccurate assessment of state preferences, because a leader may choose not to act on his personal preferences in the absence of broader domestic support. Eisenhower's desire to remain within the parameters of existing opinion raises the possibility that greater public activism might have changed things. Even mild activism might have convinced the president that his cooperative impulses enjoyed greater domestic support than he realized, making him more willing to go ahead, while a sizable campaign might have forced bureaucratic opponents of arms control to yield to political pressures.

Probably the greatest inhibiting factor to cooperation, therefore, was the nationwide suspicion of Soviet intentions. It was not hard to argue that cooperation would be desirable. But willingness to pursue it also required that some reasonable proportion of the country thought it was feasible. Yet, Soviet behavior and the secretive nature of the Soviet system provided strong grounds for skepticism on this score. However, in a kind of vicious circle, these doubts about co-operation's feasibility also contributed to American behavior that further reduced whatever prospects existed for cooperation. On the one hand, it made the administration inclined to see every Soviet proposal as some kind of trick designed to weaken the West. No doubt some were, but the Soviet offer of May 1955 and later offer to try aerial inspection on test strips represented movement toward US positions. However, because most administration officials were so suspicious of all Soviet offers, the United States almost never reciprocated such concessions. Without reciprocity of cooperative bids by the other side, cooperation is unlikely to get established.

US suspiciousness of the Soviets also limited the USA's own initiatives, because all US offers to cooperate required that the USSR first prove itself a trustworthy negotiating partner by making significant changes in its behavior. Thus, the Chance for Peace speech promised efforts to negotiate disarmament, but only if the Soviets proved their good faith by making concessions on several Cold War political disputes. Similarly, although neither proposal directly addressed arms levels, both Atoms for Peace and Open Skies required the Soviet government to accept the American proposals first, before the United States would respond to the Soviet demand for talks on arms limitations *per se*. In short, each US offer asked the USSR to address a major US security concern, without indicating any US willingness to address Soviet concerns in the same stage of the process. Short of a prior Soviet effort to redress the main sources of Cold War tension, US expressions of a preference for cooperation in theory would not be translated into a willingness to pursue cooperation in practice.

This points to a final limitation of conventional analysis suggested by this case study. Simply comparing the relative preference for mutual cooperation and mutual defection as outcomes in an issue-area can be inadequate. Action in foreign policy does not always follow from a state's preference ordering within an issue. There are always other issues that require attention and competing objectives that must be balanced within any single issue. Thus, the operative question is always the question of priorities. One may have a preference for cooperation in a certain issue-area, but that will mean little unless achieving such cooperation rates highly relative to other policy goals one holds. In Eisenhower's first term, the biggest problem is not that the administration did not see cooperation on arms as desirable, but that it did not rank such cooperation as highly as several competing objectives. As John Lewis Gaddis observes, "the Eisenhower administration accorded negotiations on arms control a priority lower than such other components of its strategy as maintenance of a credible nuclear deterrent, the preservation of harmony among allies, and the determination to score 'points' at the expense of the Russians in the arena of psychological warfare."[55]

[55] John Lewis Gaddis, *Strategies of Containment* (New York: Oxford University Press, 1982), p. 193.

The last goal proved especially costly, because it affected the way in which the administration developed its offers. Rather than prepare the ground with the Soviets first by sounding them out privately, which would have been an obvious step if the USA was serious about cooperation, the United States always sought to put the Soviet Union on the defensive with some dramatic announcement. As McGeorge Bundy sums it up:

> Eisenhower's personal hope for real agreement and resulting progress on wider issues, with both Atoms for Peace and Open Skies, is beyond doubt. Yet it is equally clear that in both cases his serious purpose was obstructed by his other preferences. He made both proposals publicly, by surprise, in speeches whose first object was immediate popular success at home and abroad.[56]

Actual progress toward cooperation would become possible only when the administration's priorities changed, because the requirements of "popular success at home and abroad" changed to require serious negotiations on an issue where agreement was both possible and meaningful.

[56] Bundy, *Danger and Survival*, p. 303.

5 Eisenhower and the test ban movement

In the mid-1950s, for the first time, a sizable popular campaign addressing nuclear arms issues arose in the United States. This movement's goal was a ban on the testing of nuclear weapons. In this chapter, I demonstrate that this societal activism contributed to an evolution in the Eisenhower administration's arms control agenda in a way that established a US preference for cooperation. As the previous chapter showed, although President Eisenhower favored nuclear arms control in the abstract, through 1957 the overall priorities of his administration kept the United States from acting in a way that demonstrated willingness to cooperate. A possible alternative subject for talks emerged in 1954, when calls for an end to nuclear testing began being aired publicly. But Eisenhower and his advisors initially rejected the idea of immediate negotiations on a test ban, preferring to maintain their existing agenda.

The efforts of the test ban movement, however, in conjunction with certain developments in world affairs, led Eisenhower by mid-1958 to elevate the goal of halting nuclear testing to the top of the US arms control agenda. That summer, Eisenhower decided to impose a temporary moratorium on nuclear testing and enter negotiations on a treaty to make that suspension more permanent. The moratorium and accompanying negotiations were the first concrete manifestation in the Cold War of a US preference for cooperation on nuclear weapons (they were also the most serious steps on arms control to that point for the Soviet Union as well). These talks eventually led to an agreement, the Limited Test Ban Treaty, signed by President Kennedy in 1963.

I begin this chapter by setting a baseline of Eisenhower administration policy, in order to establish that the administration did not view restrictions on testing as a high priority in arms control. Then, after briefly describing the origins and nature of the test ban movement, I examine the potential this movement developed for influencing policy through each of the three pathways laid out in chapter 3. Rather than mobilizing electoral pressures via mechanism 1, I show, the test ban movement, with a significant boost from transboundary connections, worked through mechanisms 2 and 3 to alter the arms control agenda. First, the elite coalition-shift pathway operated together with world opinion to distinguish a test ban from other arms control proposals being considered at the time. Then, the bureaucratic pathway functioned to tilt the balance of opinion within the administration in favor of accepting calls to put a test ban first on the list of items about which to negotiate. This change at the specific level of policy, by separating a test ban from other proposals known to be unacceptable to the Soviets, signaled the development of a willingness to begin cooperation on arms control.

I do not claim that activism was solely responsible for this elevation of the test ban objective at the specific level of policy. Rather, understanding this case will require moving away from a dichotomous view of preferences in favor of a more continuous notion of the propensity for cooperation. In other words, while several factors were increasing the US propensity to seek cooperation in the late 1950s, they still left the country somewhat short of actual willingness to cooperate. Societal activism then added the necessary increment to make willingness greater than the counterpressures. The test ban movement did not alone have sufficient strength to force a halt in testing, but it was a necessary element in the process that changed US preferences to favor pursuing that objective.

Eisenhower policy baseline

During Eisenhower's first term in office, there was little support in the administration for placing restrictions on nuclear testing. As the previous chapter showed, the administration put its emphasis on other proposals instead, especially Atoms for Peace and Open Skies. Because these proposals reflected a significant imprint from Cold War objectives, they did not evince a willingness to cooperate. As it became increasingly clear that the Soviet Union did not see it as worthwhile to seek cooperation on this proposed US agenda, the rise of concern about nuclear testing suggested a possible alternative first-step accord. But the administration continued to give priority to the goals behind its own proposals, leading it to proclaim that a test ban should not be considered until steps to limit nuclear stockpiles and establish inspection had been taken first.

Initial test ban proposals and the US response

Public suggestions for an agreement to halt testing first arose after the initial American test of an operational hydrogen bomb, in March 1954. Code-named Bravo, the detonation at a Pacific test site caused the exposure of hundreds of civilians to radioactive fallout. The United States had to evacuate 236 Marshall Islanders who lived downwind, and a Japanese fishing vessel, the *Lucky Dragon*, was also exposed, resulting in the death of one crewman.[1] The incident demonstrated a new danger that accompanied the advent of the H-bomb – its ability to carry radioactive material high into the atmosphere where it could return to earth miles away and days later. As a result, there were demonstrations in Japan and calls by a number of individuals in the United States and abroad for the superpowers to stop testing. The most prominent of these came from the prime minister of India, Jawaharlal Nehru. On April 2, he proposed an immediate "standstill agreement" by the USSR and the USA.[2]

Eisenhower initially wanted to be responsive to these concerns. On April 19, he told Secretary of State Dulles that the United States should complete its current test series, but then propose "a moratorium on all further experimentation whether with H-bombs or A-bombs." At Dulles' recommendation, the president appointed an interdepartmental committee to study the idea. The committee came back with a unanimous negative recommendation. The strongest counterarguments came from the AEC. Chairman Lewis Strauss and

[1] Higher-than-anticipated yield and fallout, a shift in the wind direction, and an exclusion zone determined more by concerns with secrecy than with safety caused the civilian exposures. See Richard G. Hewlett and Jack M. Holl, *Atoms for Peace and War, 1953–1961: Eisenhower and the Atomic Energy Commission* (Berkeley: University of California Press, 1989), pp. 171–77; Gregg Herken, *Cardinal Choices: Presidential Science Advising from the Atomic Bomb to SDI* (New York: Oxford University Press, 1992), pp. 80–81.

[2] Robert A. Divine, *Blowing on the Wind: The Nuclear Test Ban Debate, 1954–1960* (New York: Oxford University Press, 1978), pp. 18–21; Harold K. Jacobson and Eric Stein, *Diplomats, Scientists, and Politicians: The United States and the Nuclear Test Ban Negotiations* (Ann Arbor: University of Michigan Press, 1966), p. 20. This initial protest soon died down, and no coordinated campaign to ban testing arose at that point in time.

the directors of the weapons labs argued that the Soviets would find a way to cheat and that further American tests were necessary to develop a new anti-aircraft weapon. After the committee presented its report, on June 23, 1954, the NSC formally decided to shelve the test moratorium proposal. The administration made this position public the following February. In response to a reporter's question, Eisenhower announced that the administration had studied the test ban idea and had rejected it.[3]

The question of enforceability requires further comment. Contrary to the AEC position, the prospects for verification should have been a plus for a test ban. Because all testing was in the atmosphere at that point, there was no way to prevent the detection of radiation from a test explosion. Thus, a test halt had the advantage that it could be verified without inspection, which had been a major roadblock in previous negotiations. Nor were administration officials ignorant of this possibility. Indeed, the one dissenting member of the AEC on the test ban question, Thomas Murray, had written to Eisenhower in March to propose a moratorium on tests above 100 kt, hoping that this would forestall H-bomb development. As one of the arguments in favor of his proposal, Murray pointed out that it would bypass the inspection problem. Yet, at the NSC meeting that shelved the moratorium idea, no one pointed out that a moratorium on large-yield tests could in fact be monitored, even according to Strauss' own analysis, which only noted the difficulty of detecting tests below 50 kt. This omission suggests that administration officials in fact preferred to proceed with the development of new weapons that would require megaton-level tests. Hence, they were explicitly not interested in a ban on the high-yield tests for which there was little chance of cheating.[4]

With the USA having publicly rejected the idea, the Soviet Union became the first superpower to endorse a test ban. In May 1955, in conjunction with other proposals, the Soviet delegation formally proposed a test ban at UN disarmament talks in London. The chief US negotiator, Harold Stassen, turned for advice to Ernest Lawrence and

3 Stephen E. Ambrose, *Eisenhower: The President* (New York: Simon and Schuster, 1984), pp. 169–70; Hewlett and Holl, *Atoms for Peace and War*, pp. 223–25, 274–76; Herken, *Cardinal Choices*, pp. 84–85; Divine, *Blowing on the Wind*, p. 62.

4 Hewlett and Holl, *Atoms for Peace and War*, p. 222; Herken, *Cardinal Choices*, p. 83; Memorandum of Discussion at the 203rd Meeting of the National Security Council, June 23, 1954, in *FRUS*, 1952–54, vol. II, pp. 1467–72.

Edward Teller, two Livermore Lab scientists serving as advisors to his delegation. They reiterated the argument that the Soviet Union could cheat undetected. This convinced Stassen not to pursue the idea further.[5]

Stassen ultimately advised Eisenhower that "a moratorium on H-bomb testing would not be in the interest of the US and should not be agreed to except as a part of a comprehensive disarmament agreement." The administration agreed, adopting the policy that a test ban by itself was unacceptable. At a press conference in January 1956, Secretary of State Dulles said a test ban would have to wait until the two sides had first agreed on a comprehensive arms control plan "with proper inspection safeguards." As Eisenhower began his second term, therefore, the administration position was that there could be no discussion of limiting testing until after there had been progress on its own Atoms for Peace and Open Skies proposals.[6] This ranking of priorities forms the policy baseline for this case study.

Overview of the test ban movement

Origins

Between 1954 and 1957, a campaign calling for an end to nuclear testing gradually emerged. Its organizers were interested in arms control more broadly and hoped that an agreement on testing might be the first step toward further disarmament. But for much of the broader public, fallout itself was the major issue. After the Bravo accident created public awareness of possible risks from nuclear testing, collecting and analyzing data on the dangerousness of fallout took time, while the results proved open to differing interpretations. The AEC, starting with a report issued in February 1955, consistently argued that testing did not add sufficiently to natural background radiation to be harmful. But, while some experts agreed, other scientific experts publicly disputed claims that testing posed no serious health hazard.

Without knowing exactly how dangerous it was, many Americans learned that not only foreigners but they themselves were sometimes being exposed to fallout. After the United States began a new series of

[5] Herken, *Cardinal Choices*, p. 94.

[6] Divine, *Blowing on the Wind*, pp. 62, 67, 70.

tests at a site in the Nevada desert in February 1955, a band of radioactive fallout stretching from Nebraska to New York was reported the following month. In fact, it later turned out that even Soviet test series could lead to increases in atmospheric radiation levels across much of the United States. For this reason, the 1950s saw occasional panics about fallout in various regions of the country. One fallout product, strontium-90, caused particular concern because it got into the milk supply and, from there, into people's bones, especially those of growing children. Studies at the end of the decade revealed, moreover, that Sr-90 concentrations were greater on US territory than anywhere else on earth. Even without the mistakes that caused exposure of civilians to fallout in the Bravo test, any detonations of nuclear devices in the atmosphere, Americans learned, could expose people across wide areas of the globe to increased radioactivity.[7]

The resulting public concern made nuclear testing an issue around which advocates of nuclear arms control and disarmament could organize. In April 1957, a number of leading peace activists held a meeting to discuss how to give greater focus to the largely fragmented US peace movement. Those present quickly agreed to a suggestion to target the "nuclear testing issue as the first step toward disarmament." As one organizer put it, "at last we have an issue that the average Joe understands. Let's start with him and move on from there."[8]

Elements of the test ban movement

The test ban movement had three major components: traditional pacifist groups, scientists, and mainstream liberal activists. Established peace groups and scientists who had earlier worked for international control of atomic energy were the first to call for restrictions on test explosions of nuclear devices. However, protest against testing remained fairly limited in scope and amorphous in organization from the Bravo incident until 1957. New organizations and campaigns launched that year, especially the group SANE (Committee for a Sane Nuclear Policy), then brought a number of supporters of liberal causes

[7] Hewlett and Holl, *Atoms for Peace and War*, pp. 286–87, 290; Divine, *Blowing on the Wind*, pp. 42–43, 65, 131–32, 262–67; Howard Ball, *Justice Downwind: America's Atomic Testing Program in the 1950s* (New York: Oxford University Press, 1986), pp. 29–83.

[8] Milton S. Katz, *Ban the Bomb: A History of SANE, the Committee for a Sane Nuclear Policy* (New York: Praeger, 1987; Greenwood Press, 1986), pp. 22, 24.

in general into the test ban coalition and gave the movement a higher profile.

Test ban advocates stressed two lines of argument, one moral and the other more technical and prudential. Peace groups, many with ties to religious denominations, not surprisingly emphasized moral arguments. For example, the religiously based Fellowship of Reconciliation circulated a petition after the Bravo incident that argued "no nation has the right . . . to inflict this horror upon innocent and defenseless multitudes." SANE also stressed this argument. The group focused its initial efforts on public education, using a series of newspaper advertisements. SANE's second advertisement was entitled "No Contamination Without Representation." Appearing in the *New York Herald Tribune* in March 1958, the advertisement contended that it was wrong for the United States to expose people in other countries to fallout when they had not consented to accept that risk.[9]

Pacifist and religious groups often called on the United States to take unilateral action. Citing the "tremendous moral effect" this would have on world opinion, the Women's International League for Peace and Freedom petitioned Eisenhower in spring 1956 to cancel an upcoming US test series. Similarly, in late 1957, an interdenominational group of clergy, including A. J. Muste, the leading figure in Christian pacifism, and Martin Luther King, Jr., sent Eisenhower a telegram that urged him to suspend US nuclear testing. The clergy said that such a step would place a moral obligation on the other nuclear powers, the Soviet Union and Britain, to follow suit.[10]

Scientists who had campaigned for international control of the bomb after World War II formed a second source of test ban advocacy. An organization established in this earlier campaign, FAS, served as the main vehicle through which scientists expressed opposition to testing. Rather than moral arguments, scientists stressed the arms control benefits that initiatives to limit testing could bring about. In various magazine articles, mostly in the *Bulletin of the Atomic Scientists*, these scientists put forward the first public descriptions of fallout and a cogent arms control rationale for a test ban. They pointed out that a test ban might not require inspection, the sticking point of past

[9] Lawrence S. Wittner, *Rebels Against War: The American Peace Movement, 1941–1960* (New York: Columbia University Press, 1969), p. 240; Divine, *Blowing on the Wind*, p. 196.

[10] Divine, *Blowing on the Wind*, pp. 77, 160–61.

negotiations, to be verified; would slow the pace of development of new offensive weapons; and could serve as a first step in breaking the stalemate between East and West in disarmament talks.[11]

As the group seeking to represent mainstream public opinion, SANE adopted the arms control arguments of scientists in addition to the assertions of peace groups concerning the immorality of testing. Its first public statement, a full-page advertisement in the *New York Times* on November 15, 1957, thus used the same first-step argument advanced by scientists. It said that suspension of testing would be "a place to begin on the larger question of armaments control." SANE tried explicitly, moreover, to link concerns about testing and the arms race as a whole. Its inaugural advertisement therefore took note of both "the grave unanswered questions" about the effects of fallout and the larger possibility that nuclear war could "put an end to the life of man on earth."[12]

Mass electoral pressure not a factor

How successful were these arguments in pressuring the administration to change its approach to arms control talks and give a test ban top priority? Chapter 3 outlined three possible pathways or mechanisms through which domestic activism might influence US arms control policy. The first of these requires activist groups to create or take advantage of significant dissatisfaction in the mass public with how the president is balancing the objectives of strength and restraint. If brought to bear, mechanism 1 creates electoral incentives for the administration to alter the degree of urgency it attaches to the goal of arms control, an impact at the general level. In this case, the electoral pathway was not an option for activists before test ban talks began.

Absence of opinion disjunction

The pre-condition for electoral pressure is opinion disjunction, a situation in which the majority position in public opinion assesses the

[11] Ralph E. Lapp, "Civil Defense Faces New Peril," *Bulletin of the Atomic Scientists* (*BAS*), 10 (November 1954), pp. 349–50; David R. Inglis, "H-Bomb Control," *Nation*, July 24, 1954, pp. 67–70; Inglis, "Ban H-Bomb Tests and Favor the Defense," *BAS* 10 (November 1954), pp. 353–56; Inglis, "We Haven't Really Tried," *BAS* 11 (January 1955), pp. 3–4.

[12] *NYT*, November 15, 1957, p. 15.

Table 5.1. *Public opinion on test cessation, 1954–1958*

	United States only			Multilateral		
Date	Percent for	Percent against	Percent no opinion	Percent for	Percent against	Percent no opinion
April 6, 1954	21	72	7			
January 21, 1955	11	84	5			
March 11, 1955	15	80	5	65	28	7
January 26, 1956	12	83	5	62	29	9
October 16, 1956	28	53	19			
November 15, 1956				42	52	6
April 23, 1957				64	28	8
June 25, 1957				64	22	14
January 22, 1958				49	36	15
April 14, 1958	28	61	11			

Source: Eugene J. Rosi, "Public Opinion and National Security Policy: The Nuclear Testing Debate," in Rosi, ed., *American Defense and Detente: Readings in National Security Policy* (New York: Dodd, Mead, 1973), p. 369.

need for initiatives to achieve arms control progress quite differently than does the president. In this case, the possibility of an opinion disjunction sufficient to make electoral pressure a feasible influence route did not develop until after test ban negotiations had begun. From the time of the Bravo incident through the start of test ban negotiations over four years later, US opinion regarding a test ban remained quite stable, with support for such a measure largely dependent on whether the Soviet Union would be required to accept the same constraints as the United States (see table 5.1). When questions specified that all nations, including the Soviet Union, would be included in an accord, a clear majority usually approved of stopping nuclear tests. However, when questions asked only whether the United States should stop, implying a unilateral step, even greater majorities opposed such an action.

Thus, most Americans did not support grassroots groups when they called for a moral initiative, whereby the United States would stop testing on its own and then see what others did. It is less clear whether this data implies that the public actually agreed with Eisenhower, since polls did not ask the public to compare a test ban to the proposals favored by the administration. But the importance the public attached to simultaneous Soviet acceptance of any test halt suggests at least broad agreement with the president about how to balance the risks of potential weakness versus unrestrained arms racing. Combined with the fact that support for even a multilateral agreement never topped 65 percent, this suggests that there was no groundswell of opinion that could form the basis for electoral pressure. But neither was the climate unfavorable to negotiations on a test ban. Consistent majority approval of an agreement that would impose equal restrictions implied that the public would support leaders who worked to bring about talks on the testing issue. There was thus enough support to make conditions favorable for building a larger coalition to advocate test cessation.

The Stevenson campaign

Both the difficulty of exerting electoral pressure and the potential for coalition-building were graphically revealed by the 1956 presidential election. Eisenhower's Democratic challenger, Adlai Stevenson, made the call for a test ban a major focus of his campaign. Stevenson even devoted a national television address to the subject, on October 15. But the issue gave him little if any electoral benefit. In part, this reflected Stevenson's inept handling of the issue. Stevenson first suggested an H-bomb test moratorium in April, during the primaries. But within days, he also charged the administration with being "dangerously dilatory" in the development of ballistic missiles. Eisenhower and much of the press quickly pointed out that it would be contradictory to speed up missile development while at the same time halting the testing necessary to develop warheads for those missiles, making Stevenson look foolish. After winning the Democratic nomination, Stevenson again raised the idea of stopping H-bomb tests, but tended to paint it as a unilateral US initiative. Because Stevenson failed to recognize that the public would favor only a bilateral test halt, Eisenhower and his campaign aides were successfully able to portray the Democrat as being irresponsible on national security.[13]

[13] Divine, *Blowing on the Wind*, pp. 72–75, 86–102; Hewlett and Holl, *Atoms for Peace and War*, pp. 338–39; Emmet John Hughes, *The Ordeal of Power: A Political Memoir of the Eisenhower Years* (New York: Atheneum, 1963), pp. 180, 186–87, 191; Dwight D. Eisenhower, *The White House Years: Waging Peace, 1956–1961* (Garden City, NY: Doubleday & Co., 1965), pp. 18, 475.

First Soviet influence attempt counterproductive

Beyond his various self-inflicted wounds, Stevenson's attempts to promote a test cessation in 1956 were also hurt by a Soviet attempt to use US domestic politics to influence American policy on testing. On October 19, Soviet premier Bulganin sent Eisenhower a letter that referred favorably to "the opinion recently expressed by certain prominent public figures in the United States concerning the necessity . . . of prohibiting atomic weapon tests." After the Soviets made Bulganin's letter public, the White House released the president's sharply worded rejoinder. In his reply, Eisenhower harshly criticized this "interference by a foreign nation in our internal affairs." Vice President Nixon publicly labeled Stevenson a "clay pigeon" for Soviet sharpshooters, a sentiment echoed by most of the press. The USSR's clumsy attempt to take advantage of Stevenson's test ban advocacy thus backfired and actually did significant damage to his campaign.[14]

The Bulganin letter is an example of what two-level game theorists call "negative reverberation." When a country's adversary attempts to appeal to domestic constituencies, Robert Putnam suggests, a public rally in favor of more hard-line policies should be expected.[15] Although this incident fits Putnam's expectations, it is not true that every effort by an adversary to forge cross-level connections with the other side's public need be counterproductive. Despite this unsuccessful effort, potential existed for the Soviet Union to interact positively with the US campaign. To avoid casting suspicion on the test ban movement, however, Soviet gestures would have to involve concrete actions that American test ban supporters could reasonably interpret as promising.

New administration review leaves policy unchanged

Stevenson's advocacy of test suspension in fact came at an awkward time for the administration. President Eisenhower was not in principle

[14] Hewlett and Holl, *Atoms for Peace and War,* pp. 371–73; Eisenhower, *Waging Peace,* pp. 60–62; Divine, *Blowing on the Wind,* pp. 98–100. Some political professionals estimated that Stevenson's test ban proposal, in conjunction with a proposal to end the draft, in the end cost him three million votes, though what proportion of this was due to Soviet interference is not specified (Porter McKeever, *Adlai Stevenson: His Life and Legacy* [New York: William Morrow, 1989], p. 380).

[15] Robert D. Putnam, "Diplomacy and Domestic Politics: The Logic of Two-Level Games," *International Organization* 42 (Summer 1988), p. 456.

opposed to a test ban, provided it would not risk American security, so he periodically asked his advisors to reconsider the administration's position. Eisenhower set in motion one such review just before Stevenson injected his own test halt proposal into the general election campaign. On August 30, Eisenhower asked AEC chair Strauss to meet with him, writing "I have spoken to you several times about my hope that the need for atomic tests would gradually lift and possibly soon disappear."[16]

However, the overall balance of forces in the administration remained firmly opposed to a test ban. In September, Eisenhower met with his advisors to discuss a new plan that disarmament advisor Harold Stassen had submitted. The plan called for a test ban, along with arms reductions and a "cut-off" of fissile materials production. The test ban suggestion met with substantial opposition, though, especially from Strauss and JCS chair Admiral Radford. In response, Eisenhower ordered his advisors to work out a common position, a process that took until after the election.[17]

The new US plan revealed that administration priorities at the specific level had not changed. The administration offered its new proposal at the United Nations in January 1957. The offer was largely a cobbling together of previous US proposals, with the addition of a proposal to place restrictions on the launch of objects into space (a measure intended to address the imminent development of ballistic missiles). The administration plan, for the first time, included an offer to discuss limiting or prohibiting testing. But the concession was more apparent than real, as it was linked to a particular sequencing of arms control steps. The first phase would involve stopping the production of fissionable materials for weapons, under strict international supervision, an idea that basically combined the goals of the earlier Atoms for Peace and Open Skies proposals. Only after a cut-off and inspections were in place would test ban negotiations follow. As Robert Divine points out, "Most observers had seen the test ban as a way to loosen the disarmament logjam. The Eisenhower administration was now proposing just the opposite – holding out a test ban as a reward for Russian agreement on complete nuclear disarmament."[18]

[16] Divine, *Blowing on the Wind*, pp. 85–86; Ambrose, *Eisenhower*, pp. 343–44.

[17] Hewlett and Holl, *Atoms for Peace and War*, pp. 348, 362–64; Ambrose, *Eisenhower*, p. 344.

[18] Hewlett and Holl, *Atoms for Peace and War*, pp. 380–81; *NYT*, January 15, 1957, p. 1; Divine, *Blowing on the Wind*, pp. 113–14.

Expansion of the test ban coalition

Because there was no major opinion disjunction on testing, the test ban movement was unable to exert pressure through the electoral pathway. But, by 1957, the potential developed for activism to exert pressure through the other two pathways I have identified. The movement was able to utilize the elite and bureaucratic pathways, with their impact greatly enhanced by transboundary connections to world and allied opinion. In many ways, these various sources of pressure became fused into a single complex, which successfully promoted a change in US policy at the specific level, making test ban negotiations possible. I begin by describing the part of this process that involved mechanism 2, the elite coalition-shift pathway. This pathway came into play when popular advocacy groups began working with important members of Congress and various scientists, especially biologists, many of whom were not part of the inner circle of atomic scientists who had previously dominated nuclear matters. This coalition-building effort helped activists differentiate a test ban from the proposals on Eisenhower's own arms control agenda and create a political constituency for giving a test ban higher priority.

Role of Stevenson and Humphrey

Mechanism 2 became a factor in this case starting with the Stevenson campaign in 1956. Stevenson's advocacy did two things that were important for subsequent efforts to build a coalition to alter US policy on testing. First, although Stevenson's proposals never put much electoral pressure on Eisenhower, they did reveal the existence of significant public support for finding some way to stop testing. Despite the Democratic nominee's poor handling of the issue, White House mail actually ran heavily in favor of test suspension.[19] His campaign thus indicated that many Americans would support future suggestions to limit testing, making further efforts on behalf of this idea by political elites appear feasible.

Second, the Stevenson campaign helped bring together disparate strands of interest in a test ban, thereby facilitating further coalition-building after the election. In fact, Stevenson's decision to raise the issue in the first place reflected the sort of activist–elite interaction

[19] Ambrose, *Eisenhower*, p. 349.

involved in mechanism 2. Harrison Brown, one of the founders of FAS, was one of the first to urge Stevenson to tackle the test ban issue and also helped draft Stevenson's October 15 television address. Norman Cousins, who later played a major role in the creation of SANE, also helped prompt the Democratic challenger to take up the testing issue. Stevenson's efforts in turn stimulated greater interest in a test ban among scientists. Nearly 200 scientists from major US universities endorsed a test halt, as did FAS, which was the first time that group had advocated any step beyond greater study of fallout effects.[20]

Though the voters kept Stevenson out of office, another elected official, Senator Hubert H. Humphrey (D-MN), took over his advocacy of a nuclear test ban.[21] Humphrey chaired a Disarmament Subcommittee created by the Senate Foreign Relations Committee in late 1955. During its first few years, subcommittee hearings increasingly focused on the test ban question, and Humphrey became a strong advocate of halting nuclear testing. Stevenson's and Humphrey's efforts both contributed to widening the scope of conflict, as the Schattschneiderian logic in mechanism 2 requires. Thus, the Disarmament Subcommittee became an institutional base for alternative views to those of the congressional Joint Committee on Atomic Energy (JCAE), which shared the AEC's coolness toward a test ban. The Humphrey subcommittee also gave citizens' groups that favored a test ban their first access to national government officials. In June 1956, representatives of four such groups testified at a subcommittee hearing in support of test suspension.[22]

Both the scientists and the grassroots groups were necessary. Scientists provided technical arguments that made advocacy of a test ban credible. But, short of finding data that decisively proved that any further testing would be harmful, scientific analysis could not make

[20] Divine, *Blowing on the Wind*, pp. 93–94, 104; Katz, *Ban the Bomb*, p. 15; Hewlett and Holl, *Atoms for Peace and War*, p. 368. For Brown's role in the early activities of FAS, see Alice Kimball Smith, *A Peril and a Hope: The Scientists' Movement in America, 1945–1947* (Cambridge: MIT Press, 1970; Chicago: University of Chicago Press, 1965), pp. 103, 290.

[21] Humphrey credits Stevenson's campaign call for a test halt with paving the way for his subsequent efforts to promote a test ban, stating in his memoirs that "Stevenson made it easier for me to later hold serious senatorial hearings and gain attention for the entire subject" (Hubert H. Humphrey, *The Education of a Public Man: My Life and Politics* [Garden City, NY: Doubleday & Co., 1976], p. 228).

[22] Divine, *Blowing on the Wind*, pp. 71, 74.

test cessation a matter of urgency. Only efforts to mobilize a broader constituency and to provide political or moral arguments for a test ban could do that. Thus, when the scope of protest began to widen, it added another reason for elites to conclude that efforts to achieve a test ban were a *sine qua non* for progress in arms control.

Protest against testing takes off

Over the course of 1957, nuclear testing opponents organized new groups and campaigns that encouraged such a realignment in elite opinion. One campaign, begun in 1957, widened the circle of scientists involved in the test ban movement. In April, biochemist Linus Pauling, a Nobel laureate, began circulating a petition calling for "immediate action . . . to effect an international agreement to stop the testing of all nuclear weapons." In June, he sent a copy signed by 2,000 American scientists to the White House, simultaneously releasing it to the press.[23] Pauling reached out beyond the set of physical scientists active in FAS, tapping a segment of the scientific community (especially in the biological sciences) that was even more strongly opposed to testing. Thanks to this effort, Pauling was later able to add a Nobel peace prize to his earlier award in chemistry.

At about the same time as Pauling launched his petition campaign, leading peace and liberal activists got together and decided to create two new organizations to coordinate anti-testing work. They envisioned that one group would be fairly mainstream and focus on education; the other would use civil disobedience tactics and position itself at the leading edge of opposition to the arms race. At the suggestion of psychologist Erich Fromm, the more mainstream group adopted the name SANE, the Committee for a Sane Nuclear Policy. The more radical group became known as the Committee on Non-Violent Action (CNVA).[24]

In CNVA's first action, timed for the twelfth anniversary of the bombing of Hiroshima, members of the group marched onto the Nevada Test Site to protest weapons tests. Police arrested eleven people, the first time anyone had ever been arrested for protesting at the US test site. At the same time, SANE successfully reached out to a number of prominent citizens. Forty-eight prestigious Americans, including Eleanor Roosevelt, John Hersey, and Oscar Hammerstein,

[23] Katz, *Ban the Bomb*, p. 18. [24] Ibid., pp. 21–24.

signed the group's first newspaper advertisement, in November 1957. SANE also received significant support from ordinary Americans. By the middle of 1958, SANE had grown to 130 chapters around the United States with 25,000 members.[25]

In addition to the efforts of SANE and CNVA, increasing numbers of religious organizations gave support to the test ban movement. Several church organizations, including Lutheran and Methodist governing bodies, called during 1957 for an intensified effort to reach a test ban agreement. Existing peace groups also continued promoting an end to testing. In mid-1957, the American Friends Service Committee (AFSC) started circulating a petition asking the president to cancel a US test series scheduled for the following spring. By March 1958, AFSC had delivered 74,000 signatures in support to the White House.[26] Peace groups also staged rallies against testing in front of the White House and at the UN in New York. In a more colorful action, a Quaker group in Berkeley sent vegetables that had been contaminated with radiation to Eisenhower, Soviet leader Khrushchev, and British prime minister Macmillan. And, in May 1958, protesters affiliated with CNVA staged a sit-in in the lobby of the AEC headquarters, where they launched a hunger strike to dramatize their concern about testing.[27]

The most successful activist effort to focus public attention on the testing issue was another civil disobedience action initiated by members of CNVA. In early 1958, four CNVA activists announced plans to sail a boat into the US Pacific testing area as a protest against testing. Officials arrested the group when they attempted to set sail, in a boat named the *Golden Rule*, from Honolulu in May. But the protest still came off when a family that attended their trial was inspired to complete the voyage for them. As a dramatic illustration of personal concerns with a Hollywood-like plot, the whole affair received regular press coverage, including a picture-filled story in *Life*.[28]

Some test ban advocates also began working directly with political elites. In January 1958, SANE approached Senator Humphrey, who

[25] *NYT*, August 7, 1957, p. 6; Katz, *Ban the Bomb*, pp. 26–28; Divine, *Blowing on the Wind*, p. 168.

[26] *NYT*, June 7, 1957, p. 5; October 27, p. 27; Divine, *Blowing on the Wind*, pp. 160, 196.

[27] *NYT*, November 3, 1957, p. 21; March 30, 1958, p. 30; April 6, 1958, p. 1; Divine, *Blowing on the Wind*, pp. 197, 213–14; Hewlett and Holl, *Atoms for Peace and War*, pp. 484–85.

[28] Wittner, *Rebels Against War*, pp. 247–50; Divine, *Blowing on the Wind*, pp. 197, 215, 220; *Life*, June 16, 1958, p. 38.

promised to hold a new round of hearings in his subcommittee and to give a major speech on the testing issue. On February 4, Humphrey took the Senate floor to urge the administration to break apart its disarmament package and offer a separate accord on testing. SANE then solicited letters endorsing the speech, from members of fifty-five of its local chapters, to their members of Congress. Humphrey subsequently praised SANE on the Senate floor, a sign that activists and elites were finding one another increasingly helpful in the effort to promote a test ban.[29]

Effects of activist–elite interaction

The range of protest against testing and of individuals who supported a test ban made it clear that the administration did not enjoy consensus behind its own arms control priorities. This worried the administration, especially because Eisenhower and his advisors placed a lot of emphasis on the need for public consensus behind US foreign policy. Following discussions with a number of former associates of the president, Kenneth Thompson concluded that Eisenhower viewed consensus in American public opinion "as an ingredient of power" itself. The president's disarmament advisory committee thus noted with concern in early 1956 that "Proposals for cessation of nuclear weapons tests have long had a popular appeal in many quarters of the world, including some quarters within the United States itself." The president shared this dismay. In a June 1957 meeting, Eisenhower said that the difficulty with testing was "that we are witnessing not only intense Soviet propaganda but an actual division of American opinion and other opinion as to the harmful effects of testing."[30]

[29] Katz, *Ban the Bomb*, p. 31; *Congressional Record*, February 4, 1958, vol. 104, pt. 2, 1607–24; June 4, 1958, vol. 104, pt. 7, 10097.

Humphrey's speech also reflected the impact of bureaucratic leaks. After the collapse of disarmament talks the previous year, Harold Stassen and Henry Cabot Lodge had told Humphrey in private that they believed that the USSR would agree to a test ban despite the Soviet government's rejection of the overall US package. Humphrey decided that a speech on his part could give outside reinforcement to the position of those inside the administration who advocated de-linking a test ban from other arms control steps (Carl Solberg, *Hubert Humphrey: A Biography* [New York: W. W. Norton, 1984], pp. 186–87).

[30] Kenneth W. Thompson, "The Strengths and Weaknesses of Eisenhower's Leadership," in Richard A. Melanson and David Mayers, eds., *Reevaluating Eisenhower: American Foreign Policy in the 1950s* (Urbana: University of Illinois Press, 1987), p. 23;

This rise in domestic concern created an important distinction between a test ban and other possible arms control steps. On the positive side, the test ban movement signaled a reservoir of support that a president could mobilize in favor of an agreement to eliminate testing, which would be especially helpful in the Senate ratification process. Other proposals would not necessarily start with such a benefit. On the negative side, the combination of grassroots and elite activism created the possibility that it would grow more difficult to conduct testing in the future unless testing was made acceptable by an international agreement that reduced fallout levels.

This was what caused the greatest consternation for the AEC, the agency in charge of US testing. In normal times, the AEC would surely have been almost invisible to the US public. But in May 1957, the first month of a major new test series at the Nevada Test Site, the agency received nearly 600 letters from citizens concerned about the dangers of testing. In July, a worried Chairman Strauss wrote Eisenhower that the numbers of letters and petitions to the agency supporting cessation of nuclear testing were continuing to grow.[31] Other elements of the US nuclear weapons program faced no such demands that they be stopped and hence did not require immediate attention in arms control talks to legitimate them.

The test ban movement also underlined a second distinction between testing and the items the administration preferred to put first on the agenda. Unlike testing, the superpowers' weapons stockpiles and their unwillingness to permit inspection of them did not have byproducts that might actually be harming people at that moment. Expressing the view subscribed to by activists, one letter-writer to the *New York Times* argued that, "whereas a nuclear attack is an uncertainty, even an improbability, the peril of increasing fall-out is a dead certainty."[32]

By emphasizing these distinctions, activism promoted pursuit of a test ban as a separate measure of arms control, prior to the other items on the administration's existing agenda. The test ban movement explicitly rejected the administration position that a test ban should only be accepted as one element in a comprehensive proposal.

President's Special Committee on Disarmament Problems, "Position Paper on Restrictions on Nuclear Weapons Tests," March 20, 1956, *DDRS*, 1989-1074; Memorandum of Conference with the President, June 24, 1957, *DDRS*, 1977-253C.

31 Hewlett and Holl, *Atoms for Peace and War*, pp. 450, 458.

32 *NYT*, March 28, 1959, p. 16.

Believing that the Soviet Union was unlikely to accept other US arms control demands anytime soon, test ban supporters argued that tying a test ban to agreement on other proposals "may continue to postpone progress indefinitely," as FAS put it in a policy statement in February 1957. Advocates contended that a test ban by itself had the greatest likelihood of leading to a breakthrough arms control agreement. In its policy statement, therefore, FAS urged the administration "to seek worldwide cessation of nuclear weapons tests without making this contingent on achieving more far-reaching goals in arms limitation." Senator Humphrey likewise urged the administration to abandon the policy of linking a test ban to other arms control steps.[33] In all these ways, the interaction of activism and elite opinion in mechanism 2 raised expectations that US arms control policy would have to tackle the problem of nuclear testing.

Administration efforts to defend testing

Through 1957, the Eisenhower administration resisted these calls to seek an agreement on testing as the first step in establishing control over nuclear arms. At first, the administration simply emphasized the necessity of continued US testing. It took a two-pronged approach. The administration tried to "stress . . . the defensive nature of US weapons" and to "emphasize that none of the extensive data collected . . . shows that radioactivity is being concentrated in dangerous amounts anywhere in the world outside the testing area."[34]

The first argument emphasized in particular that continued testing was necessary to bolster the USA's nuclear deterrent. In response, test ban advocates pointed out that there were other possible avenues to war besides an erosion of deterrence, scenarios they claimed were reasons for a test halt. FAS thus noted that a test ban "would slow down the development of even swifter and more easily hidden weapons for devastating surprise attack." By helping preserve what would later be called crisis stability, this meant a test ban might actually lower the risk of nuclear war.[35]

33 "FAS Policy Statement on Arms Limitation, February 3, 1957," reprinted in *BAS* 13 (April 1957), p. 138 (see also *NYT*, February 4, 1957, p. 2); Jacobson and Stein, *Diplomats, Scientists*, p. 26.

34 President's Special Committee on Disarmament, "Position Paper," March 20, 1956, *DDRS*, 1989-1074.

35 *NYT*, April 26, 1957, p. 1; "FAS Policy Statement," in *BAS* 13 (April 1957), p. 138.

As for the government's second defense, the question of how hazardous different levels of radiation are remains a matter of debate to this day. This makes it difficult to evaluate the claim that fallout from testing was not extensive enough to be harmful. But test ban proponents had a strong rejoinder to the main tactic used to dismiss the harm that was potentially being done. Defenders of testing frequently argued that the risks from fallout were "extremely small compared with other risks which persons everywhere take as a normal part of their lives."[36] Eugene Rabinowich, the editor of the *Bulletin of the Atomic Scientists,* objected that comparisons with everyday risks were inappropriate. Rather than a product of individual choice, he noted, risks from fallout resulted from "deliberate government action" and were "inflicted . . . on the whole population of the world" rather than just the people of the countries that chose to test.[37]

In an attempt to respond to and defuse these objections, the administration started justifying continued testing as necessary in order to find ways to reduce the fallout produced by thermonuclear weapons. Describing a 1956 test series involving weapons designed to produce less fallout, Lewis Strauss issued an official statement declaring such tests "produced much of importance . . . from a humanitarian standpoint." The following year, Eisenhower also defended testing as useful because it would help the United States develop a "cleaner" bomb.[38]

This defense did not prove very successful. One opponent of testing labeled it "madness" to "use a word like humanitarian to describe an H-bomb." And the *New Republic* suggested it is no "'cleaner' to be vaporized by H-bomb blast than to be poisoned by H-bomb fallout."[39] These comments reveal once more that it was not just fallout from testing to which test ban supporters objected. Rather, most activists wanted to halt testing as a way to begin reversing the whole buildup of nuclear weapons and reliance upon them for security. As a result,

36 AEC Commissioner Willard Libby, quoted in *NYT,* April 26, 1957, p. 1. In other examples, Edward Teller and Albert L. Latter equated the impact of worldwide fallout to "smoking one cigarette every two months" (*Our Nuclear Future: Facts, Dangers, Opportunities* [New York: Criterion Books, 1958], p. 124), and Strauss compared it to wearing a luminous watch dial (Divine, *Blowing on the Wind,* p. 140).

37 Eugene Rabinowich, "The Nuclear Weapon Test Ban," *BAS* 13 (June 1957), p. 201.

38 Divine, *Blowing on the Wind,* p. 82; *NYT,* June 6, 1957, p. 1.

39 Ralph Lapp, "The 'Humanitarian' H-Bomb," *BAS* 12 (September 1956), p. 264; *New Republic,* July 15, 1957, p. 3.

defenses of testing predicated upon the importance of improving nuclear weapons – because the United States might someday need to use them – were simply not persuasive with that segment of public opinion that favored an accord to stop testing.[40] Acknowledging this, Eisenhower lamented in March 1958 that, "Testing is not evil, but the fact is that people have been brought to believe that it is."[41]

Scientists at the weapons labs still believed fallout to be the main cause of opposition to testing, however, and so decided to see if they could find a way to conduct tests that would not release any radioactivity into the atmosphere.[42] They showed that they could when, in September 1957, the United States detonated a nuclear device deep underground. The test shot, code-named Rainier, created serious complications for the test ban movement. The administration could now try to remove some of the pressures it faced by agreeing to stop testing in the atmosphere, which would eliminate fallout, without necessarily having to negotiate an accord to prohibit all testing, as desired by those who wanted a test ban in order to place a brake on the arms race. Moreover, with the concerns of the president and most Americans about monitoring Soviet compliance, there would be a strong argument for measures limited to atmospheric testing. Precisely because of the radiation they released, explosions above ground could reliably be detected and identified at a great distance. Without the tell-tale radiation, detection of underground blasts, especially of low yield, would prove more uncertain. With the success of Rainier, a comprehensive test ban (CTB), which would now have to include underground tests, would prove a more elusive goal.

At this point, though, the Defense Department and the AEC were unwilling to see even atmospheric testing outlawed. When other arguments failed, they returned to the importance of first making progress on the administration's earlier proposals for reducing the nuclear danger. AEC chair Strauss thus testified before the Humphrey subcommittee in spring 1958:

> A test cessation does nothing to reduce the existing weapon stockpiles . . . It does nothing to curtail the improvement of an aggressor's

[40] Between January 1956 and late June 1957, the period in which Strauss and Eisenhower made their "clean bomb" comments, opposition to a multilateral test suspension actually dropped slightly (see table 5.1).

[41] Memorandum of Conference with President Eisenhower, March 24, 1958, *FRUS*, 1958–60, vol. III, p. 570.

[42] Jacobson and Stein, *Diplomats, Scientists*, p. 58; Divine, *Blowing on the Wind*, p. 158.

> delivery system . . . [T]he emphasis on cessation of testing is . . . a spurious argument from the point of view of its effect on disarmament or the security of the world.
>
> . . . Since we are a defendant nation . . . it would be a tragic mistake in my opinion to cease the development of our defenses unless the whole threat of a surprise attack with atomic weapons were cancelled at the same time.[43]

In short, because testing was more a symptom than a cause of the fears driving the arms race and making war possible, officials argued that the dangers of testing should not be addressed until these other, larger problems were dealt with. This amounted to making the perfect the enemy of the possible. For administration officials knew full well that the Soviets would not agree to US proposals for a weapons production cutoff and extensive inspection system. But the Soviet side had repeatedly expressed an interest in test limitations. By holding to its earlier agenda, the administration maintained a preference not to cooperate unless cooperation meant one-sided Soviet concessions that would eliminate the Soviet threat. Such an outcome was obviously desirable from an American standpoint, but it was not feasible. And by continuing to oppose the feasible, the administration indicated that it still lacked willingness to cooperate.

External pressures bolster test ban movement

While the administration kept trying to defend its own priorities at the specific level, world opinion and initiatives taken by the Soviet Union helped keep arms control debates focused on the test ban idea instead. These external pressures were important on their own account. But they also created positive reverberation with US activism, giving added ammunition to the domestic US campaign.

Superpower competition for world opinion

Testing and fallout elicited genuine concern from a number of world leaders. Indian prime minister Nehru quickly emerged as the leading advocate of a test ban among non-aligned nations. Japan's memory of the atomic bombs used against it also led to special efforts to ensure that no one should again suffer as a result of nuclear detonations. In

[43] Lewis L. Strauss, *Men and Decisions* (Garden City, NY: Doubleday & Co., 1962), p. 424.

spring 1957, for example, Japan dispatched a special emissary to Washington, London, and Moscow to plead for cessation of testing. Even the Pope added his voice to these efforts, calling for a test ban in his 1955 Christmas message.[44]

Both superpowers believed this opinion mattered. As chapter 4 showed, Eisenhower and his aides gave great emphasis to the struggle for propaganda advantage. In a similar fashion, the Soviet Union devoted a lot of energy to trying to get other governments that were critical of testing to endorse its own test ban proposals, though with mixed results.[45] Even so, the administration felt it had to counter any such Soviet efforts. After a Khrushchev speech in February 1956 indicating receptivity to a test ban, the State Department counseled, "in deciding how to meet the new Soviet position, the US must take into account also the great interest expressed by many other UN members in some agreement restricting tests, the Pope's Christmas message favoring such limitations, and [British prime minister] Eden's recent expression of desire for some positive Western approach to restrictions in this area." More and more, the military benefits of further American testing had to be weighed against the potential diplomatic costs. At an August 1957 meeting where he authorized another new test series, Eisenhower acknowledged that "The main dilemma in conducting tests of this magnitude in 1958 . . . is that of planning and carrying out extensive tests on the one hand while professing a readiness to suspend testing in a disarmament program on the other. From much of the world this paradoxical conduct may bring accusations of bad faith."[46]

While the administration worried about world opinion, leaders of the US test ban campaign saw foreign proponents of test cessation as

[44] *NYT*, May 18, 1957, p. 2; May 19, p. 20; May 20, p. 4; Jacobson and Stein, *Diplomats, Scientists*, pp. 20–21; Hewlett and Holl, *Atoms for Peace and War*, p. 304.

[45] In spring 1957, the Soviet Union several times asked Japan to endorse its test ban proposals or issue a joint statement with it. Japan refused (*NYT*, April 21, 1957, p. 1; May 12, p. 2; May 13, p. 4). The Soviet Union also proposed several resolutions on nuclear testing to the UN General Assembly in the late 1950s, but did not gain endorsement of its proposals by that body either (Jacobson and Stein, *Diplomats, Scientists*, pp. 22, 105). On the other hand, the USSR did get occasional support from India. In December 1955, for example, Nehru issued a joint communique with Khrushchev and Bulganin calling for "unconditional prohibition" of the production, use, and testing of nuclear arms (Divine, *Blowing on the Wind*, p. 66).

[46] US Department of State, "US Position on Banning or Limiting Nuclear Weapons Tests," February 15, 1956, *DDRS*, 1991-1836; Memorandum of Conference with the President, August 9, 1957, *DDRS*, 1992-1088.

useful allies. They actively sought not only to make connections with, but to further mobilize, world opinion. A founder of SANE, Norman Cousins, instigated one dramatic international appeal. In 1957, Cousins convinced the widely admired physician Albert Schweitzer to speak out against testing. Schweitzer gave a speech on Radio Oslo in April, under the auspices of the Nobel Prize Committee. In it, he described the health consequences of fallout and called on the superpowers to end testing. He also urged ordinary citizens to apply more pressure. "The real reason" statesmen have not agreed to ban testing, Schweitzer declared, "is that in their own countries there is no public opinion asking for it." AEC chair Strauss later called Schweitzer's appeal "a body blow to the testing program."[47]

Schweitzer's appeal was in turn a major factor in Linus Pauling's decision to initiate his petition campaign. Moreover, after releasing the first 2,000 signatures in June 1957, Pauling also went international. In January 1958, he delivered more than 9,200 signatures from scientists around the world to UN Secretary General Dag Hammarskjöld. The signers included thirty-seven Nobel laureates.[48]

Most expressions of world opinion, of course, were not so tightly interwoven with US-based activism. But many still had their origins in societal concerns, only within other countries' own domestic arenas. Britain, the only other country besides the superpowers engaged in nuclear testing, faced especially strong pressure from domestic protest. By autumn 1958, the British had started putting forward their own test ban proposals without waiting for US approval. In explanation, Foreign Minister Selwyn Lloyd informed Secretary of State Dulles that their action "was primarily motivated by domestic political considerations."[49]

Japan's active efforts for test cessation also reflected societal pressures. In autumn 1957, Japanese foreign minister Fujiyama informed Secretary of State Dulles that the Japanese people were "very sensitive on this question." Fujiyama even forecast that, if his government mishandled the test issue, "the very existence of the [ruling] Liberal-Democratic Party might be endangered. Japan has therefore

[47] Katz, *Ban the Bomb*, pp. 16–17; Lawrence S. Wittner, "Blacklisting Schweitzer," *BAS* 51 (May/June 1995), pp. 55–56; Hewlett and Holl, *Atoms for Peace and War*, pp. 390, 450.

[48] Katz, *Ban the Bomb*, pp. 17–18; Divine, *Blowing on the Wind*, pp. 125–27, 182.

[49] US Department of State, Memorandum of Conversation with Mr. Selwyn Lloyd, October 19, 1958, *DDRS*, 1988-2661.

concluded that it had to make a unilateral proposal for the banning of nuclear tests."[50]

The interaction between, and simple fact of, parallel domestic and foreign protest greatly helped the test ban cause. In fact, US and world opposition were seen as so closely related that Eisenhower generally spoke of them together, as a single problem. Thus, in an autumn 1956 meeting, "The President spoke of the rising concern of people everywhere over the effect of radiation from tests." Similarly, in spring 1958, Eisenhower argued, "we need some basis of hope for our own people and for world opinion . . . [I]t is simply intolerable to remain in a position wherein the United States, seeking peace, . . . is unable to achieve an advantageous impact on world opinion."[51] In short, when articulate spokespeople in other parts of the world and US advocacy groups both argued that nuclear testing was the most important area in which to seek an initial arms control agreement, the message became even harder to ignore.

Test ban gains sympathizers in administration

Growing world opinion and Soviet interest in a test ban, while taken seriously by the administration, were not alone sufficient to bring about US acceptance of an agenda that gave priority to negotiating test limitations. During 1957, bureaucratic politics emerged as the chief impediment to a change in US willingness to cooperate. By year's end, however, the potential developed for mechanism 3, which involves interaction between protest and bureaucratic policy debates, to take effect. Particularly important was appointment of a President's Science Advisory Committee (PSAC) in late 1957, headed by James Killian.

Part of PSAC's impact was independent of the test ban movement and better fits the epistemic communities approach, in which like-minded technical experts gain influence through bureaucratic appointment.[52] In addition, though, the scientists gained leverage by

[50] Memorandum of a Conversation, Secretary Dulles' Office, September 23, 1957, *FRUS*, vol. XXIII, 1955–57, pp. 495–96.

[51] Both quotes are taken from Thomas Risse-Kappen, *Cooperation Among Democracies: The European Influence on US Foreign Policy* (Princeton: Princeton University Press, 1995), p. 110.

[52] For this interpretation of PSAC's role, see Emanuel Adler, "The Emergence of Cooperation: National Epistemic Communities and the International Evolution of the

utilizing windows of opportunity and political arguments made possible by the rise of activism on this issue, in line with mechanism 3. When added to the impact of mechanism 2 and transboundary connections, this process convinced the United States to make testing the focus of its arms control policy, leading to the development of superpower cooperation on this issue by the end of 1958.

Objections of advisors slow policy change

Within the administration, through the latter part of 1957, only disarmament advisor Stassen and UN Ambassador Lodge supported seeking an immediate agreement on testing. In contrast, the Atomic Energy Commission and the Defense Department remained solidly opposed to a test ban, and Secretary of State Dulles tended to side with them against Stassen. Together, they succeeded in blocking a possible change in US policy in 1957. The possibility of an agreement arose when the UN Disarmament Subcommittee began a new round of talks in London in March. As the last chapter showed, these talks had always been fruitless propaganda exercises that the United States never took seriously. In 1957, the opening US position still made any discussion of test limitations contingent on prior agreement on other US proposals. After the first month of talks, however, Stassen felt that the Soviet delegation was showing greater seriousness than in the past. He thus recommended seeking a first-step agreement involving a one-year suspension of both testing and fissile materials production.

In a private meeting with his disarmament advisor, Eisenhower expressed concern about whether the other agencies would accept the idea, and in fact they all responded negatively. In a perverse twist on the bureaucratic utilization pathway, supporters of testing actually used public and world opposition as an argument against offering a temporary test suspension. The AEC, JCS, and US Information Agency all suggested that, once the USA entered a moratorium, public pressure at home and abroad would make it "psychologically impossible" for the United States to resume testing after the twelve-month period ended. In short, a temporary agreement on testing in isolation could easily become permanent, without the United States achieving progress on the other items on its arms control agenda. This

Idea of Nuclear Arms Control," *International Organization* 46 (Winter 1992), pp. 114–18.

argument helped reinforce Eisenhower's inclination to insist on the linkage between a test halt and disarmament, and decline separate action on testing.[53]

But Eisenhower also worried that the United States would suffer serious harm with world opinion if it showed no flexibility on the testing issue.[54] The result was a compromise between his advisors' contrasting recommendations. In May 1957, the president authorized Stassen to offer to accept a brief test suspension if the Soviet Union would agree to certain arms control steps favored by the USA at the same time. The Soviet government responded with two concessions. On June 14, 1957, the chief Soviet negotiator, Valerian Zorin, said the Soviet Union would no longer insist on a permanent test ban. He proposed a two- to three-year test suspension instead. Zorin also said the Soviets would now accept control posts on their soil to help verify a test halt.[55]

After Zorin announced the new proposal, Eisenhower told the press, "I would be perfectly delighted to make some satisfactory arrangement for temporary suspension of tests." This opening did not last long, however. AEC scientists, Secretary of State Dulles, and the British government all worked to prevent a test suspension in 1957. One effort came from scientists at the Livermore Lab. On June 24, Edward Teller, E. O. Lawrence, and Mark Mills visited the White House to make the case for further testing. The Livermore scientists told Eisenhower that, given six to seven years, they could make a "virtually clean" bomb, but a test ban would prevent this. Lawrence also told Eisenhower that failure to clean up weapons that might be used in war would be a "crime against humanity."[56]

Eisenhower told the scientists that "no one could oppose the development program they had described." He again expressed concern about world and US opinion, but also reiterated his commit-

[53] Hewlett and Holl, *Atoms for Peace and War*, pp. 385–89, 395–96; Draft Memorandum from the Joint Chiefs of Staff to the Secretary of Defense, *FRUS*, 1955–57, vol. XX, p. 603.

[54] In his memoirs, Eisenhower writes that, by summer 1957, "I had come to the conclusion that, in view of worldwide apprehensions, we should propose a ban, strictly limited as to time, on the testing of nuclear weapons" (*Waging Peace*, p. 476).

[55] Divine, *Blowing on the Wind*, pp. 145–46; Jacobson and Stein, *Diplomats, Scientists*, p. 15.

[56] Divine, *Blowing on the Wind*, p. 146; Memorandum of Conference with the President, June 24, 1957, *DDRS*, 1977-253C (an edited version appears in *FRUS*, 1955–57, vol. XX, pp. 638–40).

ment to linkage: "We have not thought of stopping tests without some kind of package deal." The meeting's impact became apparent at Eisenhower's next press conference. The president now qualified his previous support for a test ban and instead emphasized that a bomb without any fallout might soon be possible.[57]

Beyond AEC efforts, Secretary of State Dulles and allied governments also intervened to slow US policy change. Dulles was primarily motivated by desire to rein in Harold Stassen. As discussed in the previous chapter, after Eisenhower authorized Stassen to explore a temporary test suspension, the disarmament advisor ignored orders to wait for allied approval and revealed his new negotiating instructions to Zorin before the British and French governments had given their reactions. The British and French, however, had been privately urging the United States not to accept a test halt, as they still wanted to be able to test to further their own weapons programs. British prime minister Harold Macmillan now took several steps to get the US administration to put off any possible test suspension. Because Eisenhower did not want the testing issue to damage NATO harmony, he asked Dulles to take charge of the London negotiations. The Secretary then took special pains to make it clear that hints Stassen had given about a possible separate deal on testing did not reflect US policy. At a press conference on June 25, 1957, Dulles said that the United States would agree to suspend testing only if the Soviet Union accepted a deal involving a cutoff in nuclear weapons production and an adequate inspection system.[58]

With the weapons scientists, Dulles, and the allies all inducing caution, Eisenhower remained unwilling to permit any lengthy test suspension without agreement on other elements of the administration's arms control package. The final American proposal in August offered a test moratorium of one year provided there was an adequate control system, with possible extension to a second year if an

[57] Memorandum of Conference with the President, June 24, 1957; Ambrose, *Eisenhower*, pp. 398–400; Divine, *Blowing on the Wind*, pp. 150–51.

Eisenhower either misunderstood or deliberately exaggerated what Teller and his associates had told him. At the press conference, he said that a completely clean bomb would be possible, which is not true because an atomic-fission device has to be used as the trigger for the fusion-based hydrogen bomb. He also shortened the already unrealistic six- to seven-year estimate he had been given to just four to five years in his public remarks.

[58] Divine, *Blowing on the Wind*, pp. 152–53; Risse-Kappen, *Cooperation Among Democracies*, pp. 112–13; *NYT*, June 26, 1957, p. 1.

agreement to halt nuclear weapons production had been reached. Since it generally took nine or ten months to prepare a new test series anyway, this effectively meant that there would still be no real restriction on testing prior to other arms control measures. Administration officials in fact expected the Soviet Union to reject this offer, and indeed they did so.[59]

Nor did this disappoint Dulles and Strauss, who both responded with relief. Secretary Dulles' own disarmament advisor, Gerard Smith, revealed administration thinking when he briefed members of the Senate Foreign Relations Committee in August. Smith indicated that the administration was more concerned with reassuring nervous NATO allies than with compromising with the Soviet Union. The final US offer, he added, was designed to ensure American freedom to test in the future. The United States' offer at the 1957 disarmament talks thus still did not imply a preference for cooperation.[60]

After the London talks closed in mutual acrimony, the Soviet side made it clear that they wanted a new negotiating forum. If the administration did get serious about negotiating test cessation, this meant, it could signal so by eschewing the UN Disarmament Subcommittee in favor of direct bilateral talks. In December and January, Stassen argued for just such a course and was again overruled after the other agencies objected. Having realized that Stassen was no longer an effective advocate for arms control, in February 1958 Eisenhower asked him to resign as disarmament advisor. Highlighting the importance of the bureaucratic obstacles, Eisenhower even admitted at a meeting in January 1959 that he had let his advisors talk him out of pushing a test ban in 1957:

> The President stated that two years ago he had visualized much propaganda mileage to be gained by a positive stand . . . It had been his belief that the Soviets had no intention of allowing a true agreement on nuclear testing and that we would make many gains by pressing the issue. However, he had given way on this position in the light of resistance on the part of Defense and AEC.[61]

59 Divine, *Blowing on the Wind*, pp. 153–56; Ambrose, *Eisenhower*, p. 404.

60 Ambrose, *Eisenhower*, p. 404; Hewlett and Holl, *Atoms for Peace and War*, pp. 459–61.

61 Hewlett and Holl, *Atoms for Peace and War*, pp. 460–64, 469–71; Divine, *Blowing on the Wind*, pp. 177–78; Memorandum of Conversation with the President, January 19, 1959, *DDRS*, 1986-3473.

Divine speculates that one reason the president asked Stassen to step down was so he could later order a shift in policy without appearing to overrule Dulles in favor of

Advisors favorable to test ban brought in

Despite the fact that US–Soviet talks in summer 1957 saw elements of progress, prospects for a test ban dimmed again after a Soviet rocket boosted a satellite into space on October 4. The launch of Sputnik implied that the Soviet Union had mastered the technology for an ICBM before the USA had, leading to fears that the United States had fallen behind in the arms race and a drop off in demands for arms control. But Sputnik also caused a development that over the longer run tilted US policy in favor of pursuing a test ban. President Eisenhower decided that the best response to Sputnik would be to emphasize improving US science and technology. To help in this task, in November 1957, Eisenhower appointed James Killian to the newly created post of White House science advisor. Killian brought members of a Pentagon science committee with him into the White House, reconstituted as PSAC.

The new committee gave Eisenhower exposure to scientific opinion on the testing issue that contrasted with what he had previously heard. Most PSAC members were more favorable to talks with the USSR than were Teller and the other AEC scientists from whom Eisenhower had been getting advice so far. In fact, several PSAC members had been affiliated with FAS.[62] They now introduced that group's perspective on arms control into the administration debate. Moreover, there is evidence that the president wanted them to be a counterweight to his other advisors. According to Herbert York, at a meeting shortly before he appointed them to PSAC, Eisenhower asked several of the scientists, "Why don't you fellows help with this nuclear test ban? Everybody in the Pentagon is against it."[63]

Through the science committee, arguments developed by outside test ban advocates would now be transmitted to the president; in turn, continuing indications of public consternation about testing would strengthen PSAC's hand in arguing for a test ban. This is the process I have labeled mechanism 3. In fact, this bureaucratic pathway proved

Stassen. With Stassen gone, Dulles could also become more receptive to a test ban without appearing to lose face to a rival.

[62] At least six of the twenty-three original members and consultants of PSAC had been activists in FAS (based on how many of the people listed in James R. Killian, Jr., *Sputnik, Scientists, and Eisenhower* [Cambridge: MIT Press, 1977], app. 2, appear in Alice Kimball Smith's history of the early years of FAS, *A Peril and a Hope*).

[63] Gregg Herken, *Counsels of War*, expanded edn. (New York: Oxford University Press, 1987), p. 118.

important almost immediately. The president's new science advisor was present at an NSC meeting in January 1958 that shot down one last test ban proposal by Stassen. In the course of the discussion, Secretary of State Dulles and President Eisenhower both expressed concern that "world public opinion . . . [was] steadily growing stronger and insisting on results," meaning that there would be ever greater criticism in the UN and elsewhere of further American testing. Yet Dulles and Eisenhower also both argued that the United States should not at that time propose any modifications to its proposal of the previous August, in part because doing so might damage NATO. Killian then interjected that the United States also should not make any new proposals because it needed to update its technical assessments. He read from a PSAC report that questioned the adequacy of previous, skeptical scientific assessments, and indicated that PSAC's initial studies suggested that verification of a test ban was potentially feasible. Killian's intervention created an opening to do something new and positive while shelving Stassen's proposals. Dulles and Eisenhower responded favorably, and the meeting ended with an NSC decision to have PSAC oversee a new technical study of the key issues in a test ban.[64]

This is a classic example of the "garbage can" logic involved in mechanism 3. Within the bureaucracy, PSAC was looking for a chance to promote arms control as a solution, but needed a favorable problem. Administration concern over how public and world opinion would react to further US testing provided the problem. Since both the problem and the idea for the solution had first arisen outside the government, this was not a purely internal administration process. Rather, it involved interaction between outside activism and internal bureaucratic politics, as mechanism 3 suggests.

Killian appointed a panel chaired by Hans Bethe to conduct the test ban study. The panel concluded that monitoring of a test ban would be feasible and that such an agreement would also leave the United States ahead militarily. These conclusions were critical because they addressed Eisenhower's main concerns about a possible test ban accord. Since this technical analysis was not shaped by the public demands of the test ban movement, PSAC's influence was also partly independent of the pressures exerted by citizen activism.

64 Killian, *Sputnik, Scientists*, p. 154; Jacobson and Stein, *Diplomats, Scientists*, pp. 46–47; Memorandum of Discussion at the 350th Meeting of the National Security Council, January 6, 1958, *FRUS*, 1958–60, vol. III, pp. 537–42, 544–47.

However, PSAC's input was not wholly technical. When PSAC met as a whole on April 8–10, 1958, to review the Bethe Panel's findings, Killian reminded them that the Pentagon and the AEC still strongly opposed cessation of testing. Another PSAC member, Herbert Scoville, went even further, suggesting that bureaucratic positions were now so entrenched that no amount of scientific evidence would change anyone's mind. The implication was that the PSAC could not simply report its technical judgments, confident these would lead the administration to change its policy. As a result, the science board decided to go beyond its mandate and make an explicit policy recommendation. PSAC voted to recommend that the United States de-link a test ban from a weapons manufacturing halt and seek technical talks with the Soviet Union on the sole question of devising a system to monitor a test ban. In meetings with Dulles and Eisenhower to report PSAC's conclusions, Killian also urged that the USA make an immediate public proposal to suspend testing after the completion of its upcoming test series.[65]

In taking these steps, moreover, the scientists were aware that they were giving voice to a perspective they shared more with outside activists than with the rest of the Eisenhower administration. Killian's memoirs thus introduce this whole episode by recalling that PSAC members desired, "[a]long with many others" outside the administration, to promote "more fundamental achievements in arms limitation." Furthering the mechanism 3 dynamic, once they had adopted these positions, PSAC members also sought to use societal concerns as an additional argument for seeking a test ban. Killian's argument for the advantage of making an early public proposal for test cessation was clearly addressed to the administration's problems with public opinion, not the technical feasibility of a test ban. Similarly, representing PSAC at a meeting of the AEC's general advisory committee, James Fisk also promoted a test ban as a way to calm public fears about fallout. In short, the existence of protest created an important

[65] Killian, *Sputnik, Scientists*, pp. 156–57; Hewlett and Holl, *Atoms for Peace and War*, pp. 475–77; Herken, *Cardinal Choices*, p. 109; Herbert F. York, *Making Weapons, Talking Peace: A Physicist's Odyssey from Hiroshima to Geneva* (New York: Basic Books, 1987), p. 118; Memorandum of Conversation, Report on Disarmament and Inspection by President's Science Advisory Committee, April 11, 1958, *FRUS*, 1958–60, vol. III, pp. 597–98; Memorandum of Conference with President Eisenhower, April 17, 1958, *FRUS*, 1958–60, vol. III, pp. 603–04.

argument that administration arms control supporters could use in the ongoing bureaucratic debate.[66]

Soviet moratorium triggers US policy shift

PSAC's report could not have come at a better time for test ban supporters. On March 31, 1958, a week before PSAC met to review the Bethe Panel report, the Soviets announced a unilateral halt in testing and called on other nations to follow suit. Because of the pressures being channeled through the elite and bureaucratic pathways, this event provided the catalyst for a change in US policy. Indeed, the impact of public pressure is especially apparent here, because it is clear that, left to its own devices, the administration would simply have rejected the Soviet moratorium.

US officials believed that the USSR had hurried its most recent test series in order to complete it before the scheduled start of the next American test series. They thus thought that the Soviet Union wanted only to pressure the United States to abandon its next test series during a period when the Soviets would not be testing anyway. More recent information from Soviet sources suggests that the moratorium was instead Khrushchev's personal initiative and was not coordinated with those in charge of the Soviet weapons program, meaning the US imputation of cynical timing was possibly mistaken.[67] Given what they believed, though, US officials were not at all receptive. In press conferences right after the Soviet announcement, Dulles described why the administration took its timing to be purely propagandistic, while Eisenhower called the Soviet moratorium "a gimmick."[68]

Despite its initial public dismissal of the Soviet move, however, by the end of April the administration decided to propose a new series of

[66] Killian, *Sputnik, Scientists*, pp. 153–54; Hewlett and Holl, *Atoms for Peace and War*, p. 486.

[67] Andrei Sakharov, *Memoirs* (New York: Alfred A. Knopf, 1990), pp. 206–07; Sergei Khrushchev, *Nikita Khrushchev: krizisy i rakety* (Moscow: Novosti, 1994), vol. I, p. 358, as cited in Matthew Evangelista, "Taming the Bear: Transnational Relations and the Demise of the Soviet Threat" typescript, Cornell University (1997); Arkady N. Shevchenko, *Breaking with Moscow* (New York: Alfred A. Knopf, 1985), pp. 86–87. Sakharov was a high-ranking scientist in the Soviet nuclear program at the time, while Sergei Khrushchev was the son of the Soviet leader, so both were in a position to have first-hand information about the moratorium decision. I thank Matt Evangelista for bringing these sources to my attention.

[68] Divine, *Blowing on the Wind*, pp. 198–201.

talks devoted solely to the possibility of an accord on nuclear testing. How did this come about? Since the administration made what seemed a fair argument that the timing of the Soviet announcement suggested an intent to hamstring the US defense effort, officials should have been able to refuse to cancel the upcoming American test series and leave it at that, confident of public support. However, the two mechanisms activated by the test ban movement made it necessary for the administration to offer a new initiative on testing instead.

Domestic activism did not alone dictate making some positive reply to the Soviet gesture. Primarily because of world opinion, the president and the secretary of state felt that the USA had to make a response of some kind. At the first NSC meeting after the Soviet announcement, Eisenhower contended that because of the "tension which is gripping the Free World . . . we were facing a psychological erosion of our position with respect to nuclear testing, and that we must take this fact into account." Dulles agreed. As he later explained, "Wholly apart from the true merits of the argument, the Russians were winning world opinion and we were losing it."[69]

Seeking to strengthen the president's hand, the secretary of state met with a small group of private advisors whom Eisenhower respected about how to respond to the Soviet moratorium. After their discussion, Dulles reported to the president: "There was a consensus that steps must be taken to put clearly before the world the US devotion to peace . . . [T]he slight military gains [from continued testing] appear to be outweighed by the political losses, which may well culminate in the moral isolation of the United States in the coming years." Eisenhower agreed that world opinion required "some positive action."[70] But this did not dictate the shape of the US response. Besides proposing negotiations on a possible test ban, there were other ways to show a devotion to peace and responsiveness to world concerns. The administration could instead have modified one of its earlier proposals, while taking unilateral steps to reduce the fallout caused by US testing.

This was the approach the AEC favored. To buy acceptance of some testing, in the period just before and after the Soviet moratorium announcement, the AEC tried out several alternatives. Strauss first

[69] Memorandum of Discussion at the 361st NSC Meeting, April 3, 1958, *DDRS*, 1990-334; Divine, *Blowing on the Wind*, p. 212.

[70] John Foster Dulles, Memorandum for the President, April 30, 1958, *DDRS*, 1989-712; Divine, *Blowing on the Wind*, pp. 210–12.

proposed a three-year moratorium on testing and fissile materials production, during which time the superpowers would cannibalize existing weapons to make contributions for peaceful uses. He then pushed for a new emphasis on clean weapons. And the AEC finally proposed limiting atmospheric testing to 1 mt per year while moving all other testing underground.[71]

If he had seen it as realistic, it is likely that Eisenhower would have preferred to make a response of this kind. His own priorities at the specific level had not changed. So, if an announcement of new steps to limit fallout would have enabled the president to return the focus to his previous proposals, he would have found it an attractive option. However, in part because of the US test ban movement, the administration no longer enjoyed complete freedom to define the arms control agenda. When the administration reviewed its options, it concluded that it could not afford to address the concerns of world opinion in any way other than negotiations specifically on test cessation. The key reason was the reaction to the Soviet moratorium in the domestic political arena. There, a broad coalition argued for responding in a way that could lead to an end to testing. In contrast to the USSR's clumsy intervention in the 1956 Stevenson campaign, this time the Soviets took concrete action. While mere rhetoric provoked negative reverberation, a proposal backed by substantive restraint interacted positively with domestic activism. Test ban proponents accepted administration assertions about the cynical nature of its timing, but argued that the opportunity for progress the Soviet moratorium represented outweighed its propagandistic elements.

The domestic response

The Soviet moratorium thus triggered renewed activity by the test ban movement, plus a broadening of the test ban coalition. A. J. Muste, a prominent member of CNVA, called on the United States to join the moratorium. SANE likewise took out a new full-page advertisement that declared "WE *MUST* POSTPONE OUR COMING TESTS." SANE also broadened its tactics, sponsoring its first rally ever. In addition, on April 4, eighteen people, including Linus Pauling, philosopher Bertrand Russell, and socialist leader Norman Thomas, filed a suit in

[71] Hewlett and Holl, *Atoms for Peace and War*, pp. 476, 485, 543; Ambrose, *Eisenhower*, p. 448; Herken, *Cardinal Choices*, p. 108.

federal court to enjoin the United States from holding its upcoming test series.[72]

Upset at the lack of a more positive administration response to the Soviet moratorium, Hubert Humphrey gave a five-minute speech in the Senate each day of the week following the Soviet government's announcement (he refrained from calling on the administration to cancel the next US test series, however, suggesting instead the United States offer to negotiate a test suspension). Now that the Soviets had suspended testing, support for reciprocal American action spread to new organizations not normally involved in peace activism as well. In May, Americans for Democratic Action approved a resolution urging the United States to halt its tests immediately.[73] These advocacy efforts did two things that limited the administration's options. First, they made it less likely that the public would rally behind the administration if it flatly rejected all Soviet demands for a test halt. Second, activism created expectations that testing would be the focus of any new talks.

On the first point, the US public could easily have interpreted the Soviet moratorium and ensuing world criticism of US refusal to join as a case of outside nations ganging up on the United States. This in turn could have resulted in a classic "rally around the flag" response if there had not been groups, with the support of prominent individuals like Humphrey and Pauling, calling for a favorable reply. Research on foreign policy events that have hurt a president's popularity suggests that the key reason the public fails to rally behind the president in such cases is the willingness of some elites to criticize the president. The implication is that the well-known "rally effect" occurs in other cases because an absence of criticism by elites deprives the rest of the public of cues or license to express disapproval, so that they follow opinion leaders in supporting the president.[74] In this case, activist calls for a positive reply to the moratorium meant that the

[72] *NYT*, April 1, 1958, p. 13; April 5, 1958, p. 1; Katz, *Ban the Bomb*, pp. 32–33.
A judge dismissed the suit at the end of July, removing any possibility that the courts would serve as an avenue of change on US policy. Activists who filed the suit presumably expected this result and meant their action more to gain additional publicity for the test ban cause.

[73] Solberg, *Humphrey*, pp. 187–88; *NYT*, April 4, 1958, p. 1; May 18, 1958, p. 24.

[74] Richard A. Brody and Catherine R. Shapiro, "A Reconsideration of the Rally Phenomenon in Public Opinion," in Samuel Long, ed., *Political Behavior Annual*, vol. II (Boulder: Westview Press, 1989).

administration would not benefit from increased public support if it insisted on continuing to test indefinitely.[75]

In addition, activism created expectations that the US response would involve possible test ban discussions. Indeed, it raised the possibility of growing opposition to administration policies if the president did not indicate openness to test ban talks. In their deliberations about how to respond to the pressures created by the Soviet moratorium, Dulles and his disarmament advisors considered possible new initiatives on each of the administration's past proposals. To demonstrate an administration commitment to achieving progress on disarmament, though, Dulles concluded, "action on nuclear testing was the only real possibility in the areas . . . reviewed." As he explained to British officials that summer, "in the face of public pressure," the United States "would have to suspend tests."[76]

Once talks were underway, the president also acknowledged that the growing domestic coalition against testing was a major motivation. At a meeting with his advisors in May 1959, Eisenhower "said that we were going to be forced by public opinion in the United States to stop tests unilaterally." To avoid this undesirable outcome, he continued, "We must find a reasonable and decent way to do this by agreement if possible, even if the arrangement is not necessarily a perfect one." Even test ban opponents acknowledged the logic at work. "Test cessation and nuclear disarmament became equated" because of the test ban movement, Lewis Strauss later lamented, meaning that initiatives in other areas would be seen merely as attempts to evade the issue rather than indications of seriousness about arms control.[77]

Persuaded of the need to offer a new initiative focused on testing, Eisenhower adopted PSAC's recommendation, which was helped because it matched an earlier suggestion by the British foreign minister. On April 28, 1958, the president wrote Khrushchev to

[75] Brody and Shapiro do not include the Soviet moratorium in their list of potential rally events. Yet the moratorium announcement would seem to fit the three criteria developed by John E. Mueller in the classic work in this field, *War, Presidents, and Public Opinion* (New York: John Wiley, 1973), pp. 209–10. It was international, involved the United States directly, and was "specific, dramatic, and sharply focused." Thus, the absence of a rally needs to be explained.

[76] Memorandum of Conversation, "Meeting with Disarmament Advisors – April 26, 1958," *DDRS*, 1989-711; Wittner, "Blacklisting Schweitzer," p. 59.

[77] Department of State, Memorandum of Conversation, May 5, 1959, *DDRS*, 1990-1894; Strauss, *Men and Decisions*, p. 421.

suggest a technical conference to study inspection. In contrast to past US proposals on inspection, which had been general, Eisenhower limited this proposal specifically to the question of a system to detect testing. The president's letter implied further that the United States would enter negotiations on a test ban if the outcome of the technical conference was satisfactory. The key phrase, drafted by Dulles, read: "Studies of this kind are the necessary preliminaries to putting political decisions actually into effect." Khrushchev wrote back on May 9 accepting Eisenhower's proposal.[78]

Test ban talks get underway

The technical talks on detection of tests began in Geneva on July 1, 1958. By the third week of August, Western and Soviet scientists had agreed on a monitoring system for a nuclear test ban they could each recommend to their governments.[79] Although the Department of Defense (DOD), the JCS, and the AEC still objected to separating the testing issue from the administration's existing arms control package, the president was now ready to overrule them. Besides the pressures from domestic and world opinion, a shift in US policy was also facilitated by an easing of alliance constraints. The British had now advised the US government that they would be willing to suspend testing that autumn, once they had completed their H-bomb tests.[80]

On August 22, therefore, Eisenhower proposed beginning formal test ban negotiations on October 31, a date chosen because it would let Britain and the United States finish their current test series. The president also suggested that the United States, Britain, and the Soviet Union suspend testing for a year, starting at the outset of the talks. The US announcement made it clear that talks would take place in a new forum limited to the three nuclear powers. Taking the testing issue out of the UN Disarmament Subcommittee talks was a clear sign of US seriousness. The president made one concession, though, to

[78] Risse-Kappen, *Cooperation Among Democracies*, p. 114; Divine, *Blowing on the Wind*, pp. 210–11; Jacobson and Stein, *Diplomats, Scientists*, pp. 49–50.

[79] Jacobson and Stein, *Diplomats, Scientists*, pp. 64–80; Divine, *Blowing on the Wind*, pp. 215–16, 225–27. The system would use 170 monitoring posts on land and up to 10 on ships, and be supplemented by on-site inspections in cases of suspicious seismic signals. The scientists left vague certain details that would become contentious later, including the criteria for ordering an on-site inspection and how control posts on each country's soil would be staffed.

[80] Risse-Kappen, *Cooperation Among Democracies*, p. 114.

Defense and AEC desire to maintain some linkage between testing and other arms control measures. Eisenhower offered to renew the informal test moratorium after a year – but only if an inspection system had been developed and there had been progress on other elements of disarmament.[81]

Khrushchev agreed to start talks on October 31, but in the interim the USSR resumed its own testing since the Western powers were continuing to test. The Soviet Union even conducted two tests in the first three days of November, but after that point adhered to the moratorium Eisenhower had proposed. According to the chief US negotiator, James Wadsworth, the talks in the next few months were the most productive of the postwar period to that point. For the first time, the United States and USSR were seriously seeking cooperation on nuclear arms.[82]

Alternative explanations inadequate

One might question whether activism was really an important cause of the shift in Eisenhower's test ban policy at this time. Several factors besides activism obviously contributed to the new American initiative on testing in spring 1958. I here consider two sets of potential alternative explanations. First, I examine the factors most commonly associated with success in arms control in general. Then I look at the factors most often emphasized in accounts of the US policy change in 1958 specifically.

The limits of arms control theory

As discussed in chapter 2, most studies of arms control associate three variables with success: military parity, improvement in political relations, and presidential leadership. These variables have only a weak relationship with the development of US willingness to pursue cooperation on restricting nuclear testing. First, the role of the military balance does not fit the standard account. Although the two sides were moving closer, they were still a long way from nuclear parity. The United States held a commanding lead in nuclear warheads; it

[81] Jacobson and Stein, *Diplomats, Scientists*, pp. 89–92; Divine, *Blowing on the Wind*, pp. 228–29.

[82] Divine, *Blowing on the Wind*, pp. 229, 233–38; James J. Wadsworth, *The Price of Peace* (New York: Frederick A. Praeger, 1962), pp. 63–64.

had also conducted far more tests than the USSR.[83] The idea that a test ban would preserve an essentially equal nuclear balance is not accurate, nor does it appear in any of the US documents of the time.

In fact, some administration advocates of test cessation were attracted to it because they knew it would favor the United States militarily. Desire to freeze a US lead would certainly fit a national interest explanation and would thus be consistent with the underlying orientation of traditional accounts of arms cooperation. The problem is that the United States let several opportunities go by to lock in what would have been larger advantages before it finally shifted policy. In October 1957, for example, I. I. Rabi informed the president that Hans Bethe had discovered a weakness in Soviet H-bomb design that could make Soviet weapons vulnerable to an ABM. But he forecast that the Soviets would likely discover the problem in their next test series, meaning that immediate test cessation would favor the United States.[84]

However, other key advisors never accepted this line of analysis, and they kept the president from acting in such a way as to maximize US military advantage. Discussing Rabi's recommendation with Strauss, "The President recalled that he had many times thought that if in fact we are ahead in the types of atomic weapons we have, we should stop testing at once in order to 'freeze' our lead." But Strauss replied that AEC scientists disagreed with Rabi. Unsure of whom to believe, Eisenhower simply referred the matter for further study, thus enabling the Soviets to proceed with their next test series unhindered.[85] Given the fact that the United States did not act when objective circumstances were most favorable, nuclear balance considerations cannot by themselves do much to explain this case.

Nor does this case favor the idea that some prior political detente is a key to arms control. To be sure, some of the chill in US–Soviet relations lifted after the death of Stalin in 1953, with a further boost from the "spirit of Geneva" following the 1955 summit. But relations had begun to harden again by the time talks began in 1958. There had been crises over the Suez and Hungary in 1956. The 1957 disarmament

[83] As of the end of 1957, the US arsenal contained 5,543 warheads, of which 2,460 were strategic. The Soviets had only 650 warheads, of which only 102 were strategic. As for tests, the United States had conducted 117, the USSR 49. Data from tables in *BAS* 50 (November/December 1994), p. 59; 51 (May/June 1995), p. 71.

[84] Ambrose, *Eisenhower*, pp. 431–32; Herken, *Cardinal Choices*, pp. 102–03.

[85] Ambrose, *Eisenhower*, p. 432; Herken, *Cardinal Choices*, pp. 103–04.

talks broke off with vitriolic Soviet denunciations of the West, and the launch of Sputnik soon after did nothing to improve matters. Finally, at a time when US officials still perceived a monolithic Communist bloc, the second showdown with China over its shelling of islands in the Formosa straits erupted in August 1958, on the eve of test ban talks. There is thus no basis for concluding that cooperation on testing had been made more likely, let alone redundant, by a prior warming of political relations.

Of the three factors stressed by arms control theory, the third – presidential leadership – would appear to be the most important. Eisenhower's personal desire for progress in arms control is undeniable. In March 1958, the president wrote his secretary of state that the effort to achieve "reliable agreements" on arms reduction "transcends all other objectives we can have."[86] Moreover, as this chapter has shown, Eisenhower remained open to considering a possible test ban from the time the issue first arose in 1954.

The question is not just interest, though, but leadership. Existing arms control theory looks to the president as the only actor who can bring about national political will to cooperate. Yet, in this case, leadership is distinctly lacking in Eisenhower's performance. Over and over, the president asked whether the United States needed to continue testing. And in every case, he accepted the answer of someone like AEC chair Strauss, who described various new weapons on the drawing board that required testing, while emphasizing the impossibility of obtaining Soviet compliance. The ease with which Eisenhower let himself be talked out of offering test ban talks suggests that the president was more a follower of his advisors on this issue than a leader. Indeed, the most comprehensive study of Eisenhower's policymaking on nuclear testing identifies this as the single greatest problem in US pursuit of a test ban. Robert Divine concludes that Eisenhower's ultimate failure to negotiate a test ban treaty was "due primarily to his own lack of leadership" in allowing "a difference of opinion" among his advisors "to paralyze" US policy for such a long time.[87]

In sum, the three factors arms control theorists normally invoke to explain successful cooperation take us only a short distance in this case. Looking at state leaders' calculations of interest does help

86 Thomas F. Soapes, "A Cold Warrior Seeks Peace: Eisenhower's Strategy for Nuclear Disarmament," *Diplomatic History* 4 (Winter 1980), p. 67.

87 Divine, *Blowing on the Wind*, p. 314.

explain why Eisenhower felt motivated to do something about the arms race. But it cannot explain when or on what issue US willingness to cooperate actually developed.

Societal sources in context

Even if the variables emphasized by arms control theory do not satisfactorily explain this case, other factors besides activism are clearly relevant. Most existing accounts of the origins of the test ban talks stress two other factors: (1) the introduction into policy deliberations of an alternative source of technical advice, following the appointment of PSAC, and (2) criticism of testing by world leaders and allied publics.[88] It might appear that one could leave domestic concerns out of the picture and account for the change in US policy purely in terms of these two factors.

The importance of these other factors should not be underestimated. Eisenhower's own testimony on the role of world opinion is eloquent. On August 12, 1958, Edward Teller and AEC officials made a last-ditch appeal to the president not to halt testing, pointing to potential weapons developments that would thereby be precluded. In reply, Eisenhower said he "recognized that the new thermonuclear weapons are tremendously powerful; however, they are not, in many ways, as powerful as is world opinion today in obliging the United States to follow certain lines of policy." Likewise, most observers endorse Killian's view that "the work of PSAC . . . was crucial in starting the long last lap to the successful consummation of the atmospheric test-ban treaty." By showing that a test ban could be monitored adequately and would not be militarily disadvantageous, PSAC's studies addressed Eisenhower's most important reservations about proceeding.[89]

However, the evidence presented above shows that these other variables are not alone sufficient to explain increased administration willingness to enter test ban negotiations in spring 1958. The test ban movement was also integral to the process of policy change. The rise of protest was important in part because it made the question of whether to move a test ban to the top of the arms control agenda a

[88] See, e.g., ibid., pp. 211–12.

[89] Memorandum of Conference with the President, August 12, 1958, *DDRS*, 1982-1289; Killian, *Sputnik, Scientists*, p. 151.

serious topic of debate well before the other factors listed above came to a head in early 1958, thus setting the stage for them to alter the balance of forces in the administration. More importantly, PSAC and world opinion themselves gained part of their force because of the way they interacted with citizen activism. American test ban advocates actually increased the pressure arising from world opinion both by helping stimulate some cases of it and by drawing greater attention to it. Furthermore, by portraying the concerns of external actors and the Soviet unilateral test halt of spring 1958 as reasons for changing US policy and an opportunity for arms control progress, activist groups made it less likely that the administration could rally public support for continuation of testing in the face of these foreign pressures. Similarly, it was only because activism created a public opinion problem for the administration that Killian gained the window of opportunity to propose the PSAC study that finally paved the way for policy change. Thereafter, the ability of the scientists' proposals to address popular protest became a recurring argument PSAC members put forward for taking action on testing, as the bureaucratic utilization pathway suggests.

One could perhaps respond that PSAC would simply have found some other way to put its ideas before the president. If PSAC's analyses were the key factor, this would make the explanation of cooperative preferences primarily cognitive. As noted above, stressing the new source of scientific advice does fit well with the epistemic communities approach, an approach that emphasizes changing cognitions. Following this approach, one could argue that, once Eisenhower learned that the scientists' technical analyses showed a test ban to be in US interests, his beliefs changed, causing him to overrule the defense establishment.

The problem with this explanation is that, while PSAC helped address some negative arguments against a test ban, Eisenhower never accepted the scientists' positive case for making a test ban a priority. Despite their claim that a test ban could help prevent destabilizing technological breakthroughs, the president never saw arms control benefits in a test ban in and of itself. Even as he was moving to accept the idea of talks focused solely on testing, Eisenhower emphasized, "Our position is that we want to look on testing as a symptom rather than a disease." In his memoirs, Eisenhower wrote likewise that the test ban effort "was not an integral part of disarmament," describing it instead as something that unfortunately became a necessary "preliminary to – even though not a definite part of – attaining any worthwhile disarmament agreement."[90]

Because the president never did come to value a test ban for its intrinsic arms control merits, US policy change cannot be attributed to Eisenhower's own cognitive evolution. This chapter has shown that, as long as the president felt free to act on his own cognitions, he tried to use greater Soviet interest in a test ban as bait to get the Soviet government to accept his own preferred proposals for stopping fissile materials production and instituting an inspection regime. In the absence of domestic protest, therefore, Eisenhower would have tried to deflect outside pressures and satisfied administration arms control supporters with initiatives that advanced his own, quite different, arms control preferences. Overall, while pushing in the direction of some change in policy, the other explanatory variables besides US citizen activism did not require the administration to increase its receptivity to a test ban specifically. For this reason, domestic activism, as channeled through the elite and bureaucratic pathways, was a necessary part of the process leading the United States in 1958 to place test cessation first on the arms control agenda.

If asked to weigh the three factors overall, I would still assign a greater impact to world opinion and the new scientific advice than to domestic activism. But, with respect to the larger interest of this study – whether society is an important source of preferences for co-operation – the three should not be so sharply distinguished. As indicated above, much of the foreign government opposition to testing reflected domestic concerns within those countries. Moreover, the key discussions of early 1958 repeatedly show that Eisenhower and Dulles were keenly aware of this fact.[91] Hence, world opinion might better be viewed as another component of societal pressures, rather than an alternative explanation to US domestic activism.

Likewise, it is also not clear exactly where the boundary between the epistemic community and societal activism lies. Several PSAC members had previously been active in FAS, one of the groups that helped trigger the test ban movement. They had thus developed their interest in a test ban as private citizens involved in earlier advocacy efforts. Hence, they can also in part be seen as representing societal

90 Ambrose, *Eisenhower*, p. 452; Eisenhower, *Waging Peace*, pp. 474, 480.

91 Memorandum of Discussion at the 350th NSC Meeting, January 6, 1958, *FRUS*, 1958–60, vol. III, pp. 539, 541; Memorandum of Conversation, Meeting with the Disarmament Advisors, April 8, 1958, *FRUS*, 1958–60, vol. III, pp. 591, 593, 596.

support for the test ban movement in the counsels of government. Moreover, PSAC members were not the only scientists who played an important role. Biologists like Linus Pauling were not part of the epistemic community among nuclear physicists, and these other scientists worked through public advocacy rather than bureaucratic channels. Scientists were thus both respected experts and citizen activists, and their efforts in the second role contributed to their actions and effectiveness in the first role. Because PSAC's technical analyses were also clearly important, the explanation in this case is not purely bottom-up. But even less does this case fit traditional top-down conventions. Much more of the impetus for cooperation came from below, in a reflection of the hopes and fears of ordinary individuals, than came from above, in the form of statesmen's pursuit of power and interest.

Aftermath

Test ban talks and the moratorium continued for the rest of Eisenhower's term, but did not produce a formal agreement before he left office. Instead, the test ban talks bogged down in early 1959 over several disputes related to verification.[92] From this point on, activism had only a minor impact at the specific level on the evolution of the American negotiating position. Rather than peace groups, several governmental actors took the initiatives that most helped the test ban cause with respect to the details of policy.[93] Their efforts were responsible for getting Eisenhower to offer several compromises in an effort to keep the negotiations going and maintain the objective of as comprehensive a test ban as possible. As a result, in early 1960, the prospects for a compromise agreement began to look favorable, until the U-2 incident intervened.[94] After the U-2 affair, the Soviet bargain-

[92] Jacobson and Stein, *Diplomats, Scientists*, pp. 133–66; Divine, *Blowing on the Wind*, pp. 243–54.

[93] Three sets of actors were especially important: a transgovernmental alliance of officials in the US State Department and British Foreign Office; Senator Humphrey; and members of PSAC. On the transgovernmental alliance, see Risse-Kappen, *Co-operation Among Democracies*, pp. 116–25; on Humphrey and PSAC, and the degree to which their efforts still interacted with those of the test ban movement, see Jeffrey W. Knopf, "Domestic Politics, Citizen Activism, and US Nuclear Arms Control Policy," Ph.D. dissertation, Stanford University (1991), pp. 174–95.

[94] On May 1, 1960, the Soviets shot down an American U-2 plane on a reconnaissance mission over Soviet soil. Not knowing that the pilot had parachuted to safety and

ing position hardened again, dashing hopes for a test ban agreement before the end of Eisenhower's term.[95]

Even though once talks were underway activism had little impact at the specific level, it did have some effect at the general level, helping ensure that arms restraint would remain a priority. Once a test moratorium was in operation, public support for continuing it reached such levels that advocacy groups were, for the first time, able to benefit from the possibility of mobilizing electoral pressure. The potential to engage mechanism 1 helped keep the United States from breaking off talks or ending the moratorium during Eisenhower's last year in office.[96] By helping maintain US willingness to cooperate, activism made it possible for John F. Kennedy to continue the negotiations when he entered office.

After Kennedy became president, prospects for a test ban dimmed further at first, when the Soviets resumed testing and the United States followed suit. But the Cuban Missile Crisis convinced both sides to renew their efforts to reach some agreement on nuclear arms. In 1963, they concluded an LTBT. It outlawed testing in the atmosphere, underwater, and in outer space, but not underground, as activists had hoped. Individuals in the test ban movement did help the two sides overcome some of the last obstacles to agreement, however, and the citizens' campaign also made an important contribution to securing Senate ratification of the treaty.[97]

Even though the test ban movement did not get the CTB it sought, by placing and keeping the testing issue on the agenda, activism did make possible an agreement that had important benefits nonetheless. The LTBT, by stopping atmospheric testing by the first three nuclear

had been captured, the US government initially claimed that the U-2 was a weather plane that had strayed off course. The Soviet Union then produced the pilot, forcing the United States to admit that it had been lying. When Eisenhower defended the necessity of such spy flights and refused to apologize, Khrushchev walked out of a Paris summit meeting where it had been hoped that a test ban deal might be finalized.

95 George B. Kistiakowsky, *A Scientist at the White House* (Cambridge, MA: Harvard University Press, 1976), pp. 197–98, 210–12, 281–82, 311–14; Jacobson and Stein, *Diplomats, Scientists*, chap. 7; Divine, *Blowing on the Wind*, pp. 294–302, 310–14.

The impact of the U-2 incident is consistent with the traditional explanation of arms control. It is an example of how events that worsen other aspects of the relationship can undermine efforts to cooperate on limiting arms as well.

96 Knopf, "Domestic Politics, Citizen Activism," pp. 181–88.

97 Ibid., chap. 3.

states, greatly reduced radioactive fallout and the attendant health risks. Because it was the first-ever arms control treaty between the United States and USSR, it was also important symbolically, in that it showed agreement with the Soviet Union was really possible. In the years after this treaty was signed, activists periodically returned their attention to the testing issue, helping make possible eventual agreement on a CTB in 1996.

Conclusions

Influence mechanisms play role

Two of the potential pathways for activist influence outlined in chapter 3 had an important effect in the development of willingness to cooperate in this case. Mechanism 3, where arguments connected with the rise of a citizens' movement are used by actors inside an administration, had the greatest direct impact. When Eisenhower brought a science advisory committee into the White House, its arguments for the feasibility and desirability of a separate test ban agreement successfully countered arguments that scientists associated with the AEC had used to prevent a serious US effort to negotiate test limitations. Some of the influence of this science advice arose from technical expertise PSAC brought to bear irrespective of domestic activism. However, PSAC's opportunity for influence was greatly assisted by activism because the problems created by the test ban campaign let Killian get approval for the key PSAC study in the first place. Moreover, the scientists' *political* recommendations reflected a viewpoint PSAC shared with the test ban movement, in part because many members of PSAC had previously worked with arms control advocacy groups.

Mechanism 2, in which the efforts of activist groups interact with those of elites, had an important stage-setting effect in this case. The contacts between activists and major political figures like Stevenson and Humphrey, and the ability of groups like SANE to mobilize well-known figures from other walks of life behind the test ban objective, made testing an object of ongoing political and media attention that distinguished it from other possible subjects of arms control talks. Dramatic protest actions furthered this distinction by placing a moral stigma on testing compared to other elements of the superpowers' nuclear arms competition. Overall, mechanism 2 created certain expectations that the administration had to meet to prevent loss of both public and elite support.

Transboundary connections helped the domestic US campaign by reinforcing the effects of mechanisms 2 and 3. Moreover, though world opinion and Soviet initiatives were, like the administration's science advice, to some extent independent variables, they were not wholly separable from domestic activism. The US test ban movement itself arranged some important expressions of world opinion, such as the Schweitzer appeal. And activism made it less likely the administration would be able to secure public support for a policy of simply dismissing the Soviet moratorium. Together, mechanisms 2 and 3, as amplified by transboundary connections, promoted a US decision to break apart its disarmament package and elevate a test ban to the top of the arms control agenda. Because this was an agenda in which the Soviets had already indicated an interest, this shift in priorities at the specific level signaled a new level of US willingness to cooperate, paving the way for formal test ban negotiations and a multilateral moratorium to get underway in autumn 1958.

Lessons of the Eisenhower years as a whole

When this case is compared with Eisenhower's first term, two broader insights emerge. One has to do with how to conceptualize the nature of societal influence on state preferences. The other concerns the symbolic aspects of activism. First, although game theoretic analysis has gained powerful insights by representing preferences dichotomously, it has long been understood that preferences in reality are often more complex. This is apparent in the first two cases, as it is clear that at no point did the Eisenhower administration have an absolute preference for either cooperation or defection, leading it to dismiss altogether the opposed competitive or cooperative concerns. When both impulses may be mixed together, but at different levels, it may be more helpful to think of preferences as a continuum reflecting an underlying propensity to cooperate. The best way to describe activism's impact would then be in terms of how it affects this underlying propensity.

This conceptualization certainly works well for the Eisenhower years. In the first two cases, there was always some propensity to cooperate, in large part because of the president's personal horror at the thought of nuclear war. But, through 1957, this propensity remained less than needed to generate a preference for cooperation, in the sense that the United States never became willing to seek cooperation on an agenda that would be acceptable to the Soviet Union as well. What the rise of activism did was move the propensity to cooperate somewhere above the necessary threshold to get the USA to seek an agenda on which serious arms talks would become possible. But the propensity to cooperate still never became absolute, as there were countervailing pressures that slowed the search for agreement once the test ban talks began.

Some continuum representing the propensity to cooperate seems likely to exist because preferences are not the product of only a simple yes-or-no question about whether cooperation is desirable. Decisions to seek cooperation must also compete against other foreign policy objectives. At various points, especially in Eisenhower's first term, the goals of bolstering deterrence, reassuring allies, or scoring propaganda points with world opinion took precedence over the desire to control the arms race. In short, cooperation is also a matter of priorities. At times, state leaders may express an interest in cooperation, but still assign it lower priority than other objectives.

Changing priorities was thus the key to the test ban movement's influence. Activism did not change Eisenhower's image of the Soviet Union or his perception of the desirability of cooperation to control arms. What it did change was administration priorities. Taking action to address popular opposition to testing came to be a greater priority than other goals Eisenhower had previously put higher on his arms control agenda. Though not solely responsible for changing US policy, activism added another increment to the US propensity to cooperate, and this addition was critical in shifting the US position on arms control. Taking societal activism into account is therefore necessary if one is to explain how cooperation to limit nuclear testing emerged.

But why did entering a test suspension and test ban talks serve so well to signal a US interest in cooperation to slow the arms race? Here, it appears that activism was partly important for symbolic reasons. The decision to separate a test ban from other US objectives conveyed a lot about US preferences precisely because the test ban idea did not originate with the superpowers. Proposals incubated inside the Kremlin or the White House were in some sense automatically tainted by their origins. At the height of the Cold War, each side viewed any proposal by the other with the utmost suspicion, expecting it to contain some hidden trap. An agenda that they could both agree provided a possible basis for cooperation therefore almost had to come from outside.

And the impetus for a test ban mostly did not come from the governments of the United States or the Soviet Union. The governments of India and Japan first put it on the international agenda. Then the efforts of respected doctors and scientists like Schweitzer and Pauling, and thousands of ordinary citizens who joined SANE or CNVA or their counterparts in other countries, helped ensure that the test ban did not become too closely associated with the foreign policy goals of either superpower. It was precisely the availability of an issue that did not come out of the self-serving machinations of either superpower that made testing a useful focus for the effort to begin seeking arms control in earnest. Hence, to some extent, activism on testing was important simply because it existed. Just by existing, the test ban movement established an issue that could serve as a focal point for cooperation.

6 The decision to begin SALT

Of all the cases in this study, the US decision to enter the Strategic Arms Limitation Talks (SALT) should be the least susceptible to an explanation in terms of domestic stimuli. SALT is the only set of major arms control talks during the Cold War that began at a time when there was no sizable citizen protest against nuclear weapons. Indeed, in the statistical analysis in chapter 2, SALT is the only negotiation whose initiation was not predicted by the level of domestic activism. In addition, the traditional explanation of arms control was to a large extent developed by studies of the rise and fall of SALT. Because SALT figured so prominently in the development of arms control theory, one would expect that its origins would be explained fairly well by that theory. A finding that domestic pressures were nonetheless important in this case would therefore greatly strengthen the hypothesis that grassroots concerns can be a major source of state preferences for cooperation. In fact, I will argue, the decision to get SALT underway does owe much to societal interest in arms restraint.

This chapter begins by discussing how the concept of SALT first emerged in the Johnson administration. While this period fits the conventional wisdom on arms control fairly well, talks did not actually get underway before Johnson left office. The bulk of this chapter therefore focuses on the early part of Nixon's first term. It will show how controversy over proposed ABM deployment triggered some societal activism. Although protest against ABMs was initially quite localized, its emergence at the height of the anti-Vietnam War movement created a possibility that activism for nuclear restraint might expand rapidly. This helped ensure that societal activism on ABMs would become connected to elite divisions on arms control, thereby engaging the coalition-shift pathway. Because this led the White House to fear that its political opponents would be able to capitalize on the nuclear issue, this mechanism 2 process persuaded the administration to give up on an initial policy of postponing talks, thereby restoring US willingness to cooperate.

Compared to the test ban and START cases, the role of elites is greater in this case, so I do not argue that the impulse to seek cooperation arose fully from the bottom up. Instead, this chapter will show that it is not possible to explain the initiation of SALT without recognizing the impact of the nascent domestic protest campaign. Thus, once again the interest in cooperation cannot be accurately accounted for by traditional top-down perspectives, and the role of societal inputs must also be acknowledged.

Johnson puts SALT on the agenda

The SALT talks began during the presidency of Richard M. Nixon, most directly as a result of a decision in June 1969 to ask the Soviet Union to set a date for initiating such talks. However, the idea of SALT and initial feelers to the USSR developed while Lyndon B. Johnson occupied the White House. For this reason, I begin this chapter by reviewing why Johnson proposed these talks and why they nonetheless did not get started while he was still in office. At the outset, it must be acknowledged that the Johnson period conforms rather closely to the traditional account of arms control. Domestic factors still formed part of the picture, but citizen activism was a relatively unimportant part of the domestic equation. Strategic concerns and White House efforts to deflect congressional pressures for new military programs instead accounted for most of the interest in SALT, while international political developments were the main reason why talks did not come to pass.

Johnson came to office shortly after the conclusion of the LTBT, produced by the talks whose initiation formed the subject of chapter 5. Johnson did not immediately follow this up with any serious strategic arms control proposals, though he did enter talks on preventing nuclear proliferation to other countries. Signs of change in the strategic balance, however, made Johnson officials begin to think more seriously about arms control. At about this time, partly in response to their humiliation in the Cuban Missile Crisis, the USSR began a massive missile buildup that would pull them equal with the United

States by the end of the decade. The Soviets also began deploying new defense systems, including an ABM system around Moscow.[1]

Due to technical limitations of proposed US ABM systems, Robert McNamara, who served as secretary of defense to Kennedy and Johnson, chose not to ask for funds to deploy an ABM in response, only for research money. McNamara was also coming to accept what would become the standard arms control argument against any ABM deployment, namely that it would provoke offensive buildups that would overwhelm any possible defense, ultimately leaving both sides worse off. However, most military officials disagreed, and so did Congress. In 1966, although McNamara had not requested it, Congress added money to the defense budget for procurement of ABM components. This led the defense secretary to make a last-ditch effort to forestall deployment. In December 1966, McNamara proposed that the administration put funds for building ABMs in its next budget request, but hold off on spending the money or choosing a particular ABM system while making an effort to negotiate with the Soviet Union to limit or ban ballistic missile defense.[2]

Johnson's acceptance of this recommendation signaled the development of US willingness to cooperate on strategic arms limitation. His decision also fits standard arms control theory fairly well. It was motivated by approaching nuclear parity. It came at a time when political relations had improved slightly due to signing of the LTBT. And it involved an exercise of presidential leadership to overrule the interest of other domestic actors in simple arms racing behavior. But SALT talks did not get underway while Johnson was still in office. The initial problem was that the Soviets had not yet developed willingness to cooperate in this area. In early 1967, they tentatively agreed to talks, provided that limitations on offensive systems were discussed at the same time as defensive limitations. But the Soviet government then dragged its feet when the United States pressed it to set a date, while

[1] Lloyd Jensen, *Bargaining for National Security: The Postwar Disarmament Negotiations* (Columbia, SC: University of South Carolina Press, 1988), p. 157; John Newhouse, *Cold Dawn: The Story of SALT* (New York: Holt, Rinehart, and Winston, 1973), pp. 69–71; Fen Osler Hampson, "Headed for the Table: United States Approaches to Arms Control Prenegotiation," in Janice Gross Stein, ed., *Getting to the Table: The Processes of International Prenegotiation* (Baltimore: Johns Hopkins University Press, 1989), pp. 150–51.

[2] Newhouse, *Cold Dawn*, pp. 83–86; Michael Charlton, *From Deterrence to Defense: The Inside Story of Strategic Policy* (Cambridge, MA: Harvard University Press, 1987), p. 4.

Soviet premier Kosygin defended Soviet ABM efforts at a summit meeting in June 1967.

At the same time, the Republican National Committee and prospective presidential candidates like Richard Nixon made clear their intent to make an "ABM gap" a major issue in the 1968 election. Unable to hold off pro-ABM forces any longer, in September 1967 the administration announced plans to deploy a new ABM system. In announcing the decision, McNamara painted the system, named Sentinel, as a "thin" population defense system directed against China's emerging arsenal and possible accidental launches, rather than as an anti-Soviet system.[3]

Finally, in May 1968, the Soviets signaled that they were ready to begin strategic arms talks. Johnson used the signing of the Non-Proliferation Treaty (NPT) on July 1 to announce that the two sides had agreed to enter talks soon. But at this point, one of the factors emphasized in the conventional approach – the impact of international behavior on political relations – intervened to derail the process. On August 20, Soviet tanks rolled into Czechoslovakia. In response, the United States canceled plans to hold a summit meeting on September 30 at which it had been agreed that SALT would begin.[4]

Citizen activism for arms control may be significant in the Johnson case only because of the fact it was largely non-existent. This meant there was nothing that could restore US willingness to pursue cooperation after the Soviet invasion of Czechoslovakia changed US policy back to a position that this was not the time to offer a cooperative move. This is potentially relevant, because the administration did not actually want the Soviet action to prevent the initiation of SALT. Johnson officials thus began signaling almost immediately after the invasion that they still hoped to get a dialogue going on strategic arms limitation. In November, Johnson even began trying again to arrange a summit meeting before he left office. When Soviet officials and Johnson aides broached the idea with President-Elect Nixon and his aides, however, Nixon's advisors informed them that the new

[3] Newhouse, *Cold Dawn*, pp. 89–91, 94–96; Gregg Herken, *Counsels of War*, expanded edn. (New York: Oxford University Press, 1987), pp. 196–98; Ernest J. Yanarella, *The Missile Defense Controversy* (Lexington: University Press of Kentucky, 1977), chap. 7; Joel Primack and Frank Von Hippel, *Advice and Dissent: Scientists in the Political Arena* (New York: New American Library, 1974), p. 63.

[4] Newhouse, *Cold Dawn*, pp. 102–04, 130.

president would not be bound by any commitments made by his predecessor, effectively quashing the summit idea.[5]

Even under the best of circumstances, it would have been hard for a lame-duck president to commit a successor from the other party, less than two months from his inauguration, to an agenda for new negotiations. The only way Johnson might have succeeded would have been if he had had an obvious base of domestic support for such a step. The absence of any widespread advocacy for arms control left Johnson with no basis to bind Nixon to accept his SALT agenda. The situation of the Johnson administration in late 1968 thus resembles that of Eisenhower's first term. Though the president had a personal interest in arms control and the military balance had grown more favorable, this was not enough to bring about the successful beginning of talks. Without greater societal interest in arms control, the US willingness to cooperate was not strong enough to overcome unfavorable international political developments. Although Johnson's initial invitation to talks reflects almost perfectly the factors emphasized by arms control theory, these factors did not prove sufficient actually to get the USA to the table.

Nixon policy baseline

To an unusual degree, Richard Nixon and his national security advisor, Henry Kissinger, sought to maintain near-total control over foreign policymaking. The administration's policy baseline can thus be set by looking at the views of those two men. With respect to arms control, the attitude of both was neither especially favorable nor especially hostile. In 1963, for example, Nixon endorsed ratification of the test ban treaty. Yet he also warned that if the treaty lessened people's sense of the communist threat, it would mark "the beginning of the most dangerous period of the cold war since it began." Kissinger had a similarly ambivalent attitude. In a 1962 book, he wrote "our willingness to negotiate" with the USSR should be "taken for granted," and not made contingent on changes in Soviet society. But he saw no intrinsic value in arms control. The arms race was a reflection, not a cause, of tensions, Kissinger believed. He thus felt

[5] *NYT*, August 22, 1968, p. 19; Newhouse, *Cold Dawn*, pp. 134–37; Henry Kissinger, *White House Years* (Boston: Little, Brown, and Company, 1979), pp. 49–50.

that negotiations should focus on resolving political differences rather than simply on arms limitations.[6]

Accompanying this lukewarm attitude about the merits of arms control was a more active antipathy to those regarded as "arms controllers." Officials with arms control responsibilities soon learned that both the president and his national security advisor were wary or even contemptuous of those who they thought placed too much value on the search for agreement.[7] Despite this attitude, though, Nixon and Kissinger accepted the idea that the United States would enter SALT talks at some point. For one thing, the Soviets made it clear that this was a basis on which they were willing to pursue cooperation. On January 20, the day of Nixon's inauguration, the Foreign Ministry issued a statement expressing Soviet desire for strategic arms limitations, adding, "when the Nixon administration is ready to sit down at the negotiating table, we are ready to do so, too."[8]

Given this general acceptance of SALT, arms control proponents did not have to reverse initial White House preferences completely. Instead of whether talks would happen, the real questions in US policy were when and for what purpose. These were questions, respectively, about the priority the administration would give to arms restraint at the general level and the objectives they would emphasize at the specific level. And, because of the answers Nixon and Kissinger gave to these questions, to get cooperation underway would still require some changes in policy.

To start with the general level, in January 1969, arms control clearly took a back seat to Vietnam. As Raymond Garthoff observes:

> The dominant foreign policy preoccupation of Nixon and Kissinger in 1969, and indeed for the entire period through 1972, was not a detente summit meeting with Moscow, but finding an honorable exit

[6] Stephen E. Ambrose, *Nixon: The Triumph of a Politician, 1962–1972* (New York: Simon and Schuster, 1989), p. 23; Deborah Welch Larson, "Learning in US–Soviet Relations: The Nixon–Kissinger Structure of Peace," in George W. Breslauer and Philip E. Tetlock, eds., *Learning in US and Soviet Foreign Policy* (Boulder: Westview Press, 1991), pp. 353–55, 357.

[7] Seymour M. Hersh, *The Price of Power: Kissinger in the Nixon White House* (New York: Summit Books, 1983), pp. 147, 153; William Safire, *Before the Fall: An Inside View of the Pre-Watergate White House* (Garden City, NY: Doubleday & Company, 1975), p. 139; Gerard Smith, *Doubletalk: The Story of SALT I* (Lanham, MD: University Press of America, 1985), p. 164.

[8] Gerard Smith, *Doubletalk*, p. 21; Raymond L. Garthoff, *Detente and Confrontation* (Washington, DC: The Brookings Institution, 1985), p. 127; Newhouse, *Cold Dawn*, p. 140.

> from Vietnam. Improvement of relations with the Soviet Union, and a possible parallel rapprochement with China, were at that time seen as much as means to that end as they were ends in themselves.[9]

Various decisions in the first few months of 1969 make it clear that getting talks underway was not an administration priority. During the transition, Nixon requested that Johnson delay asking for Senate ratification of the NPT, which was understood to be a pre-requisite to SALT. The new president subsequently requested ratification on February 5. But the administration then used that process as a pretext to defer missile talks, saying it did not want to enter such talks until it had tested domestic attitudes toward the Soviet Union by seeing how the NPT fared in the Senate. In fact, the White House did not even ask the bureaucracy to begin preparing possible SALT proposals until March 13, when it issued National Security Study Memorandum (NSSM) 28. These directives reflected administration priorities, indicating that Nixon and Kissinger put twenty-seven other foreign policy problems ahead of arms control.[10]

Nixon gave a clear statement of his goals at both the general and the specific level in his first press conference, on January 27. This session put two new terms into the public eye: "linkage" and "sufficiency." The latter is a good summary of Nixon's views at the general level with regard to the balance between strength and restraint. During the 1968 campaign, Nixon had called for military superiority. But, as president, Nixon drew back from this position, while still trying to avoid committing himself to the acceptance of parity, as McNamara had during the Johnson years. He thus told reporters, "I think 'sufficiency' is a better term, actually, than either 'superiority' or 'parity.'"[11]

"Sufficiency" was an elastic term that could be stretched to support either military buildup or acceptance of equal limits. But, in practice, Nixon had reason to believe that the latter was the best he could hope for. Given projected deployment rates for the next several years, the administration's top concern was actually to keep the Soviet side from

[9] Garthoff, *Detente and Confrontation*, pp. 69–70.

[10] Ibid., pp. 74, 128; *NYT*, February 4, 1969, p. 1; Newhouse, *Cold Dawn*, pp. 146, 159.
The Senate ratified the NPT on March 13 by eighty-three to fifteen. The administration's top foreign policy priorities were revealed by the first three NSSMs, issued the day after the inauguration. They dealt with Vietnam, the Middle East, and the US military posture.

[11] Newhouse, *Cold Dawn*, pp. 140–41; Larson, "Learning," p. 358.

gaining the lead. Thus, Nixon's first foreign policy report to Congress described sufficiency as the capacity "to deny other countries the ability to impose their will on the United States and its allies under the weight of strategic military superiority."[12]

Though some have for this reason seen sufficiency as indicating tacit acceptance of the outgoing administration's views on parity,[13] the evidence suggests otherwise. The term "parity," as used by Johnson officials, connoted acceptance of the idea that deterrence required only a retaliatory second-strike capability. Nixon, in contrast, believed adherence to the notion of security through what would soon be labeled mutual assured destruction (MAD) had made the Democrats too relaxed about US defense needs. His attack on parity was based on the idea that it had kept the Democrats from responding vigorously enough to the Soviet nuclear buildup. Ernest Yanarella's conclusion, that sufficiency indicated a goal "lying somewhere between decisive military superiority and assured destruction," is thus more accurate.[14]

This point is important because the intellectual case for arms control was closely tied to the notions of parity and assured destruction. This approach held that functional equality in the ability to destroy each other was the surest path to security, which meant that arms control gained an important role. It could ensure that neither side did anything to undermine the other side's confidence in its retaliatory capabilities or foolishly waste resources in unnecessary buildups – the goals of crisis and arms race stability. But if Nixon did not buy into this conceptual framework – and I can find no evidence that he did so, at least not fully, at the time he took office – then arms control would enjoy much less importance at the general level.

The rejection of superiority in favor of sufficiency meant that arms control was not ruled out. But arms control was also not seen as a goal in itself. Instead, sufficiency implied that the administration would use a mix of buildup and negotiated restraint to maintain at least equality with the USSR. Without an overriding commitment to one or the other, the emphasis at the general level would go to whatever tool

12 Larson, "Learning," p. 359; Ambrose, *Nixon*, p. 289; Kissinger, *White House Years*, p. 124; Gerard Smith, *Doubletalk*, p. 23; Yanarella, *Missile Defense Controversy*, p. 175.

13 Ambrose, *Nixon*, pp. 203, 253; Steve Weber, *Cooperation and Discord in US–Soviet Arms Control* (Princeton: Princeton University Press, 1991), p. 160.

14 Yanarella, *Missile Defense Controversy*, p. 175.

ended up receiving the greatest domestic support. Only if the pursuit of strength proved impossible or arms limitation wildly popular would restraint become the clear priority.

By leaving open the possibility of going either way, Nixon's approach at the general level was fairly centrist, if weakly held. His agenda at the specific level was more unusual. He accepted the SALT agenda inherited from Johnson, that talks would focus on offensive and defensive missile systems. But achieving restraint on such systems *per se* was not his chief specific objective. Rather, Nixon hoped to use arms control as a lever to change Soviet behavior in other areas and achieve a broader political settlement, an approach quickly dubbed "linkage."

Nixon took pains to make it clear from the outset that linkage was now US policy. Thus, at his first press conference, Nixon purposely announced, "What I want to do is see to it that we have strategic arms talks in a way and at a time that will promote, if possible, progress on outstanding political problems at the same time." What Nixon said in public matched the instructions he gave in private. On February 4, the president wrote to his secretaries of state and defense and to the CIA director:

> [With respect to] the proposed talks on strategic weapons[,] I believe our decision on when and how to proceed does not depend exclusively on our review of the purely military and technical issues . . . The decision should also be taken in the light of the prevailing political context and, in particular, in light of progress toward stabilizing the explosive Middle East situation, and in light of the Paris talks [on Vietnam] . . . This may, in fact, mean delay beyond that required for our review of the technical issues. Indeed, it means that we should – at least in our public position – keep open the option that there may be no talks at all.[15]

Nixon also stressed this message at his first meeting with the Soviet ambassador to the United States, Anatoly Dobrynin, on February 17. When Dobrynin indicated Soviet willingness to negotiate on a broad range of issues simultaneously, Nixon and Kissinger decided that their linkage strategy was working. In a memo to the president analyzing this first discussion with Dobrynin, the national security advisor concluded:

> I believe the current Soviet . . . interest in negotiations, especially on

[15] Richard Nixon, *RN: The Memoirs of Richard Nixon* (New York: Warner Books, 1978), vol. I, p. 428; Kissinger, *White House Years*, pp. 126–29, 135–36.

arms control . . . stems in large measure from their uncertainty about the plans of this Administration . . . Some would argue that regardless of motive, we should not let this moment of Soviet interest pass . . . My own view is that we should seek to utilize this Soviet interest . . . to induce them to come to grips with the real sources of tension, notably in the Middle East, but also in Vietnam.[16]

Changing domestic context

What ultimately forced the administration to abandon linkage and agree to nuclear arms talks was changing conditions in the domestic environment. Activism for arms control itself was not widespread, but other developments created fertile conditions in which such activism might take off. First and foremost was protest against the Vietnam War. By the time Nixon took office, the rise of the anti-war movement had made it clear that support for presidential foreign policy goals could no longer be assumed, and that a president could even lose his job when his foreign policy became widely unpopular.[17]

In addition, Vietnam changed the climate in which new military programs would be received. Different survey organizations provide slightly different pictures of public opinion, but by 1969 the trend toward a plurality in favor of cutting the defense budget was clear. A Gallup poll in July 1969 even found that 57 percent of the public thought the United States was spending "too much" on defense, and only 9 percent "too little." Such changing attitudes would make it much harder for the Nixon administration to pursue a nuclear buildup as part of its route to maintaining sufficiency.[18]

Finally, opposition to Vietnam also created a reservoir of activists who could potentially be mobilized for other foreign policy protests. Now that American policy was being questioned, it was not hard to imagine that protest against Vietnam could spill over into a campaign for nuclear weapons restraint. This was especially true because some traditional arms control groups like SANE had joined the campaign to

16 Kissinger, *White House Years*, pp. 143–44; Nixon, *RN*, pp. 456–57.

17 A good summary of the growth and impact of anti-war protest in this period is Melvin Small, *Johnson, Nixon, and the Doves* (New Brunswick, NJ: Rutgers University Press, 1988), chaps. 5–6.

18 Thomas Hartley and Bruce Russett, "Public Opinion and the Common Defense," *American Political Science Review* 86 (December 1992), p. 909, tab. 1; Benjamin I. Page and Robert Y. Shapiro, *The Rational Public: Fifty Years of Trends in Americans' Policy Preferences* (Chicago: University of Chicago Press, 1992), p. 240.

end the war, without entirely abandoning their concern about nuclear weapons.[19] If a group like SANE were to become aroused over nuclear arms policy, it might be able to draw new support from other activists and organizations in the anti-war movement.

Thus, even though protest against nuclear weapons never became very widespread, having Vietnam in the background greatly amplified the message of the activism that did emerge. The main stirrings in 1968–69 concerned the ABM system that the United States was beginning to build. In addition, there were also some efforts, primarily at a more elite level, to prevent the development of MIRVs (multiple independently targetable reentry vehicles). This program to put multiple warheads on nuclear missiles was at a critical juncture, and many experts were predicting (correctly) that proceeding to deployment would end up eroding confidence in the stability of the nuclear balance.

Domestic activism never developed to such an extent that it could generate electoral pressures via mechanism 1 on Nixon arms policy. However, with the breakdown of the Cold War foreign policy consensus, it was possible for activism to exert leverage through mechanism 2, by helping shift elite coalitions. This process gained its greatest effect in this case by arousing administration fears that its future political opponents would seek to capitalize on the arms control issue. There also turned out to be internal divisions within the administration on arms control, enabling activism to have an impact through mechanism 3, the bureaucratic utilization pathway, as well. In this case, the bureaucratic pathway mostly reinforced the elite pathway. Together, these processes defeated the attempt to place linkage at the top of the specific-level agenda, and restored the emphasis on seeking immediate limitations on defensive and offensive missiles.

The ABM campaign

The most significant campaign on nuclear weapons in this period arose over ABMs. After McNamara's Sentinel announcement, the Army announced the first ten sites for the new ABM program in November 1967. Eight of them turned out to be in or near large cities.

19 Milton S. Katz, *Ban the Bomb: A History of SANE, the Committee for a Sane Nuclear Policy* (New York: Praeger, 1987; Greenwood Press, 1986), chap. 5; *NYT*, January 26, 1969, p. 30.

This was not required by the stated purposes of the program – a thin defense against a future Chinese threat or accidental launch. It was also not required by existing technology, since the Spartan missile that formed the heart of the proposed system had a range of 400 miles. Instead, in a classic case of bureaucratic politics, the Pentagon officials in charge designed the initial deployment to facilitate a possible later decision to expand the program into a "heavy" population defense against Soviet missiles.[20]

Several features of the proposed deployments aroused concern in the metropolitan areas scheduled to get Sentinel sites. First, the ABM systems would be prime Soviet targets. Despite the fact they were supposed to defend cities, therefore, many felt that ABM systems would actually make their city more likely to be destroyed in a nuclear war. Second, the interceptor missiles in the system would themselves carry a high-yield nuclear explosive. Because ABMs would have to be ready to go on a moment's notice, some scientists argued that there was a real danger of nuclear accident with these weapons. Finally, there was, as journalist Elizabeth Drew observed, "good old American feelings about real estate."[21]

Over the course of 1968, opposition to Sentinel grew in several of the proposed deployment areas. Boston, Chicago, and Seattle had the largest campaigns; significant opposition also emerged in Honolulu and Detroit. In each of these cities, a coalition developed comprising local officials, ordinary citizens, and scientists from local universities or research centers. In most locales, these scientists were not those elite members of the profession who had served on government advisory boards. Many were, however, members of FAS, the arms control advocacy group established by atomic scientists after World War II.[22]

In a localized version of mechanism 1, many of the campaigns convinced local authorities to reject plans to build Sentinel sites in their communities. In the Chicago suburbs, starting in December 1968, various village boards, community associations, and township super-

[20] Primack and Von Hippel, *Advice and Dissent*, pp. 179–80.

[21] Ibid., pp. 182–87; George Rathjens, "The ABM Debate," in Bernard Brodie, Michael D. Intriligator, and Roman Kolkowicz, eds., *National Security and International Stability* (Cambridge, MA: Oelgeschlager, Gunn, & Hain, 1983), p. 382; Anne Hessing Cahn, "American Scientists and the ABM," in Albert H. Teich, ed., *Scientists and Public Affairs* (Cambridge, MA: MIT Press, 1974), p. 57.

[22] Cahn, "American Scientists"; Primack and Von Hippel, *Advice and Dissent*, chap. 13.

visors voted to oppose ABM sites. In the Boston area, local organizing against the proposed ABM site culminated in January 1969 with a hearing in Reading, a suburb proposed as a Sentinel site. A former DOD official who attended the meeting sent his analysis of it to the director of defense research and engineering. He found the audience of over 2,000 people to be "extremely well informed," and predicted that, if the reaction in Reading was typical, "there is a very good chance that the Congress would have to act to cancel the system."[23]

In fact, several important members of Congress did react to constituent concerns about Sentinel. Massachusetts senator Edward Kennedy responded to the Reading meeting by writing the incoming defense secretary, Melvin Laird, with a request to stop Sentinel deployment and hold a thorough review. Washington senator Henry Jackson, normally a staunch pro-defense Democrat, was convinced to pressure the Army to move the Seattle site to outside the city. Heavy mail, or proposed sites near their own homes, also prompted several other legislators to speak out against proceeding with ABM plans.[24]

The local ABM protests were largely driven by "not in my backyard" (NIMBY) concerns. For many of the participants, this did not lead to activism on the broader objective of restraining the nuclear arms race. Indeed, because the campaign was so NIMBY-oriented, it was mostly limited to the designated deployment areas. No nationwide grassroots protest against ABMs emerged at this time. Thus, although individual members of Congress were clearly reacting to electoral incentives in pushing for changes in Sentinel, this is not truly a case of mechanism 1. Activism did not reflect an underlying opinion that not enough was being done to limit or end the arms race. Nor was it sufficiently national in scope to create electoral incentives for Congress as a whole, or for future presidential candidates, to scramble to get on some anti-ABM bandwagon.

This locally based opposition was enough to force changes in the program, however. Bowing to the congressional pressure that community opposition had engendered, Secretary Laird ordered a stop in further Sentinel deployment on February 6, pending an administra-

[23] Cahn, "American Scientists," pp. 67–68; Roger W. Cobb and Charles D. Elder, *Participation in American Politics: The Dynamics of Agenda-Building*, 2nd edn. (Baltimore: Johns Hopkins University Press, 1983), pp. 72–73; Primack and Von Hippel, *Advice and Dissent*, pp. 185–88.

[24] Primack and Von Hippel, *Advice and Dissent*, p. 188; Cobb and Elder, *Participation in American Politics*, pp. 73–74; Yanarella, *Missile Defense Controversy*, p. 152.

tion review of the issue. President Nixon appointed the deputy secretary of defense, David Packard, to chair an interagency review of the ABM program.[25] Thus, by early 1969, the ABM issue had emerged as the prime fulcrum with which domestic supporters of arms restraint might gain leverage. But the ability of advocacy groups to exert leverage would ultimately depend on whether the necessary pre-conditions for any of the three influence mechanisms were in place. The evidence will reveal that mechanism 1, the electoral pathway, would not be available, but that potential did exist to affect policy through mechanisms 2 and 3, the elite and bureaucratic pathways.

Mechanism 1 not a factor

As discussed in chapter 3, the necessary pre-condition for the electoral pathway is an opinion disjunction between the administration and the public. In this case, an opinion disjunction never developed. This was not because of a lack of support for SALT. A Harris poll released in February 1969 found that the public favored by two to one trying to reach an arms control deal with the Soviet Union. This did not lead to opinion disjunction, however, because there was not much intensity behind this support. In Gallup polls in 1969, the public named Vietnam as the country's most important problem, followed by civil rights and domestic unrest. Arms control was not a high enough priority to create electoral incentives for a change in policy.[26]

Moreover, on the key dispute between the administration and arms control advocates, the public largely sided with the president. Repeated polls during the 1960s and early 1970s found that more people favored building an ABM system than opposed it. This included one private poll conducted for the Nixon administration in spring 1969, which revealed roughly 80 percent support for building an ABM system. Because this implied that grassroots opposition was largely limited to the proposed deployment cities, the administration knew it had no reason to fear electoral retribution on ABMs.[27]

25 Newhouse, *Cold Dawn*, p. 151; Yanarella, *Missile Defense Controversy*, p. 154; Kissinger, *White House Years*, p. 205, acknowledges that congressional pressure triggered the review.

26 *NYT*, February 4, 1969, p. 18; Tom W. Smith, "The Polls: America's Most Important Problems," *Public Opinion Quarterly* 49 (Summer 1985), p. 272.

27 Thomas W. Graham, "The Politics of Failure: Strategic Nuclear Arms Control, Public

Potential for mechanism 2 develops

Even if there was no widespread public clamor for arms control, the administration quickly found itself facing sizable elite pressure for arms talks. These divisions among the elite created a possibility that activism could affect policy through the coalition-shift pathway. That the administration took elite opposition seriously is indicated by the amount of attention Kissinger devotes in his memoirs to various elite sources that called for arms control in Nixon's first few months. He takes note of reports issued by the Council on Foreign Relations and the United Nations Association that labeled an early SALT agreement "imperative" and "urgent," respectively. Kissinger also cites editorials in the *New York Times*, the *Washington Post*, *Business Week*, and other newspapers and magazines calling on Nixon to start negotiations right away and abandon the idea of linkage.[28]

Former Johnson administration officials and high-ranking congressional Democrats also took up the call. They argued that it was a rare moment of opportunity for arms control, which might slip away if Nixon continued to delay. In February, Clark Clifford, who had replaced McNamara as secretary of defense in LBJ's final year, called on the Nixon administration to enter missile talks right away without linking them to progress on political issues. Clifford argued, "we may never again expect to be in as favorable a position as we now enjoy for entry into talks." Former vice president Hubert Humphrey and Senators Frank Church (D-ID), Albert Gore (D-TN), and Mike Mansfield (D-MT) sounded similar alarms about the need to begin talks, before further development of ABM and MIRV systems made arms limitation more difficult to achieve.[29]

Though some legislators were clearly responding to the concerns of local residents on the ABM question, elite fissures on this issue had actually begun developing prior to the rise of grassroots opposition. The origins of elite-level opposition to ABMs lie with scientists within what Adler has labeled the arms control "epistemic community."

Opinion, and Domestic Politics in the United States, 1945–1980," Ph.D. dissertation, MIT (1989), pp. 246–48, 251–52, 445–50; Memorandum for the President from Ken BeLieu, June 2, 1969, White House Special Files (WHSF): Confidential Files (CF): Box 43: "Weapons–Ordnance–Munitions" (WOM), Nixon Presidential Materials, National Archives at College Park, MD.

28 Kissinger, *White House Years*, pp. 130–34.

29 *NYT*, February 18, 1969, p. 10; April 13, 1969, p. 61; Kissinger, *White House Years*, pp. 134, 206; Larson, "Learning," p. 365.

Though criticisms of ballistic missile defense had developed in this group in the early 1960s, the scientists' objections to ABMs did not spill into the public eye until after McNamara's announcement of the Sentinel program in autumn 1967. This decision showed White House and Pentagon science advisors that they had lost the internal administration debate. Following the Schattschneiderian logic of mechanism 2, the losers in this round sought to overturn the decision by widening the circle of debate. The opening salvo in the experts' attack on the ABM program came the following March, when physicists Richard Garwin and Hans Bethe published an article in *Scientific American* outlining the technical arguments against ABMs.[30]

The first signs of opposition in Congress also appeared at this time, where it proved to be bipartisan. The initiator of the first serious challenge was in fact a Republican, Senator John Sherman Cooper of Kentucky. In 1968, Cooper offered three amendments, the last two co-sponsored with Michigan Democrat Philip Hart, to delay or delete funds for Sentinel deployment. Although the amendments fell short, with grassroots protest arising that winter, anti-ABM senators, including some Republicans, felt encouraged to continue the fight after Nixon became president.[31]

There also proved to be bipartisan opposition to the president on the MIRV issue. Flight-testing of MIRVs had begun in 1968, but a second round of tests considered necessary for deployment was scheduled to begin in May 1969. Critics thus regarded it as vital to postpone the tests, in order to give SALT a chance to ban MIRVs before they became operational. A Republican senator from Massachusetts, Edward Brooke, took the lead in this effort. On June 17, he sponsored a sense-of-the-Senate resolution calling for "mutual suspension of MIRV flight tests." Brooke's resolution gained forty co-sponsors, while a similar measure in the House obtained over 100 sponsors. The *Wall Street Journal*, the *New York Times*, the *Washington Post*, and the *Boston Globe* all endorsed the idea of a MIRV test moratorium.[32]

30 Emanuel Adler, "The Emergence of Cooperation: National Epistemic Communities and the International Evolution of the Idea of Nuclear Arms Control," *International Organization* 46 (Winter 1992), pp. 101–45; Herken, *Counsels of War*, pp. 187–98, 230–32; Cahn, "American Scientists," pp. 47–81; Primack and Von Hippel, *Advice and Dissent*, pp. 63–64.

31 Yanarella, *Missile Defense Controversy*, pp. 149–54.

32 Gregg Herken, *Cardinal Choices: Presidential Science Advising from the Atomic Bomb to SDI* (New York: Oxford University Press, 1992), p. 271; Kissinger, *White House Years*,

These efforts to slow the ABM and MIRV programs, and to promote talks that might ban such weapons, signaled the existence of serious divisions among political and national security elites. The key demands revolved around specific-level goals. Critics of the Nixon approach wanted to see limits on ABMs and MIRVs accorded greater prominence on the arms control agenda, while diminishing the priority given to linkage by the administration. Development of this elite-level split indicated that the administration might have problems with Congress regardless of grassroots opinion. However, it also created the necessary pre-condition for mechanism 2, efforts to alter the winning elite coalition, meaning that activism could potentially gain input at the specific level as well. Grassroots groups did not cause these elite fissures and for the most part followed the lead set by elite arms control supporters. However, to the extent that elites reached out for societal support and needed it to succeed, it would not be correct to see state preferences purely as a function of developments at the top. If the balance of societal activism determines the outcome of elite debates, then preferences in a very real sense are a reflection of the concerns of non-elites.

Potential for mechanism 3 also develops

Though Nixon and Kissinger sought to maintain firm White House control over arms limitation policy, their effort encountered considerable resistance elsewhere in the executive branch. Many officials, especially in the State Department and ACDA, held views similar to those of the administration's congressional critics. Their reluctance to go along with linkage created bureaucratic divisions, opening a possibility for activist influence through mechanism 3.

Nixon and Kissinger heard almost immediately from bureaucratic advisors who wanted more rapid progress on SALT. Llewellyn Thompson, the dean of State Department Soviet experts, urged the new president to respond positively to Soviet overtures on SALT. Thompson warned that delay might tilt the balance in the Soviet leadership toward hard-liners. Gerard Smith, appointed director of ACDA, meaning that he would head any SALT delegation, and Secretary of State William Rogers also refused to toe the line on

pp. 210–12; John Newhouse, *War and Peace in the Nuclear Age* (New York: Vintage Books, 1990; Alfred A. Knopf, 1988), pp. 206–07.

linkage. On March 19, Smith told a Soviet disarmament negotiator that the start of SALT "need not be tied, in some sort of package formula, to the settlement of specific international problems." Similarly, on April 7, Rogers told reporters, "there is nothing that stands in the way [of SALT talks], and they can go forward soon." Thereafter, various leaks to the press kept implying that the United States would soon set a date to start talks, probably that summer.[33]

These statements revealed disagreements within the administration on the advisability of withholding SALT as a source of leverage. Which side would prevail would depend on outside support. To convince the president and the national security advisor to back off from linkage, diplomatic officials would have to have their concerns resonate elsewhere in the American body politic. In this situation, there was potential for activism to contribute to policy change through the bureaucratic utilization pathway.

The ABM debate as prelude

The first major conflict over Nixon's nuclear arms policy involved the ABM program. The way this battle developed, though, ultimately limited the administration's freedom of action on SALT. During winter 1968–69, scientists and members of Congress who opposed ABMs joined forces. By starting to work together, outside experts and legislators expanded their coalition, creating a possibility of shifting the winning coalition at the elite level. Moreover, though they were not the prime instigators, advocacy groups helped facilitate this process, creating an impact through mechanism 2. Two organizations that had represented scientists in the campaign for a test ban took up the ABM issue in 1968. In April, FAS urged President Johnson to suspend any further work toward ABM deployment. Then, once the Senate began consideration of the Cooper–Hart amendment, FAS and the Council for a Livable World (CLW) arranged briefings by prominent scientists for selected senators and their aides.[34]

Cooperation between anti-ABM scientists and senators took a big step forward the following year. Prominent scientists who publicly

[33] Kissinger, *White House Years*, pp. 135–37.

[34] *NYT*, April 26, 1968, p. 87; Cahn, "American Scientists," p. 72. CLW was founded in the early 1960s by Leo Szilard, an atomic scientist who had played an important role in convincing FDR to launch the Manhattan Project. CLW's main purpose was to lobby Congress for arms control.

opposed the ABM program had never been asked to testify at Armed Services Committee hearings. They gained access in 1969, when J. William Fulbright (D-AR), the Senate Foreign Relations Committee chair, created a new disarmament subcommittee, chaired by Al Gore (the father of Clinton's vice president). The Gore subcommittee began hearings on the ABM program on March 6, 1969, while the administration's review of Sentinel was still underway. While the subcommittee took care to hear witnesses on both sides of the issue, a number of prestigious scientists testified against ABMs, including all previous presidential science advisors. Thereafter, the Senate Armed Services Committee invited many of the same scientists to testify, as did the House Foreign Affairs and Armed Services Committees.[35]

Besides arranging congressional testimony, ABM opponents took several other steps in early 1969 to broaden their coalition. One was reaching out to other elements of the traditional Democratic coalition, such as organized labor. Thus, in February, the United Auto Workers came out against the ABM program. To a limited extent, anti-ABM forces also tried to create positive reverberation through transnational connections. For example, FAS endorsed a call by the dissident Soviet physicist Andrei Sakharov for a moratorium on further ABM development, thus highlighting that some Soviet scientists shared the concerns of their American counterparts.[36]

Elites who were critical of ABM systems also made a conscious effort to enlist broader public support. At the end of February, Hubert Humphrey announced a nationwide campaign to stir public opposition to Sentinel deployment. Likewise, Senator Kennedy commissioned former JFK advisors Jerome Wiesner and Abram Chayes to organize a report on ABMs that could be released publicly as a counterpoint to the Defense Department review already underway. And students and scientists at MIT organized a one-day strike in early March to protest the misuse of science and technology. This action generated letters and telegrams to the president and members of Congress opposing ABM deployment.[37]

[35] Cahn, "American Scientists," pp. 70–75, 92–93; Primack and Von Hippel, *Advice and Dissent*, p. 64.

[36] *NYT*, February 23, 1969, p. 51; February 15, 1969, p. 30.

[37] *NYT*, February 26, 1969, p. 21; February 20, 1969, p. 11; Yanarella, *Missile Defense Controversy*, pp. 144–45.

The Safeguard decision

On March 14, Nixon announced the outcome of the administration's ABM review. System-level considerations ensured that the ABM program would not be canceled. Because the president believed that something needed to be done to improve the strategic balance in light of the Soviet missile buildup, he ruled out any options that did not involve some form of ABM deployment.[38] But a combination of strategic considerations and domestic politics also led to a decision to abandon Johnson's Sentinel program. The president thus announced a new ABM program, called Safeguard.

Safeguard did not involve a change of hardware; it would use the same components as Sentinel. But the deployment plans and avowed purpose of the program were different. The emphasis in Safeguard would be on defense of US ICBM sites, not cities, while deployment would take place in phases, starting with building ABMs around two ICBM bases. But later phases still envisioned building a "thin" population defense with the same purposes as Sentinel. Even though the differences from Sentinel were not great, the administration hoped that they would lay to rest all of the concerns that had generated controversy on ABMs.

Nixon's public explanation of the change suggested acceptance of some of the arms controllers' arguments, especially regarding the destabilizing effects of national defenses. As the president put it in his announcement, "a massive city defense system . . . tends to be more provocative in terms of making credible a first strike capability against the Soviet Union. I want no provocation which might deter arms talks."[39] However, most evidence suggests that the shift to Safeguard was driven less by this strategic logic than by desire to defuse domestic opposition. The administration's goal was to ensure support for ABMs by designing a program that would get around local concerns and the experts' objections.

For one thing, the administration did not alter the proposed ABM system in ways commensurate with the avowed new goal of protecting missile silos. The Sentinel hardware was designed for area defense and had serious technical liabilities as a system for point defense.[40] Yet the administration did not seek to develop and procure new

[38] Yanarella, *Missile Defense Controversy*, pp. 171–73.

[39] *NYT*, March 15, 1969, p. 16. [40] Rathjens, "The ABM Debate," pp. 389–91.

components more appropriate for the job of defending missiles. This suggests that it did not find the strategic logic for the shift all that compelling. Moreover, contributors to the Defense Department review explicitly pointed out that moving deployment away from cities might solve the administration's problems with the public on ABMs. An analysis by Harold Agnew at the Los Alamos Lab noted that putting the ABM sites on missile bases would have the effect of "minimizing problems presently being posed by citizens worried over safety matters." David Packard made the same observation when he presented his final recommendations to the NSC on March 5.[41]

In fact, the administration's adoption of arguments favored by arms controllers does not appear to have represented actual conversion to such logic at all. Discussing the downgrading of city defense in his memoirs, Kissinger writes, "Thinning out the defense of the population was a purely political decision; it was designed to reassure arms control advocates." This dismissal of the arms control logic for avoiding population defenses creates a problem for any attempt to attribute Nixon policy directly to epistemic community influence, as it suggests that Nixon and Kissinger never underwent the cognitive evolution that approach sees as the main element in the re-definition of state interests. Because Kissinger instead saw the Safeguard decision as a way to quiet the objections of the scientists who had opposed the ABM program, he "complained of being personally betrayed when their opposition to missile defense continued," Gregg Herken reports.[42]

The campaign against Safeguard and MIRVs

In fact, opposition to the ABM program did continue after the Safeguard announcement. In part, the administration seems to have misjudged the source of its problems. The administration acted as though pressure was mainly being channeled through mechanism 1, when in reality mechanism 2 dynamics were more pronounced. To the extent that electoral pressures were an issue in the proposed Sentinel cities, the Safeguard decision did address that problem. After Nixon's announcement, the administration was no longer plagued by resolutions against ABM deployment from local community associations. By

41 Cahn, "American Scientists," pp. 110–11; Yanarella, *Missile Defense Controversy*, p. 172.

42 Kissinger, *White House Years*, p. 208; Herken, *Counsels of War*, p. 233.

this time, however, a national campaign fueled by arms control concerns had also taken shape. This anti-ABM coalition remained unconvinced that the Nixon decision represented a true commitment to the goal of mutual restraint. Such concerns were only reinforced by Nixon's decision to allow a new round of MIRV flight-tests to proceed as scheduled starting in late May.[43] Thus, the elite coalition-shift process continued unabated after the switch from Sentinel to Safeguard. It continued to focus mainly on ABMs, but expanded to include some efforts to stop the MIRV program as well.

For example, a campaign to get members of the National Academy of Sciences to sign a statement against the ABM program, which began before the Safeguard decision, was not slowed in the least by the program change. By two weeks after Nixon's announcement, organizers had transmitted the signatures of 276 Academy members to the president.[44] ABM opponents also took advantage of a meeting of the American Physical Society in Washington later that spring to circulate another petition. They then marched from the convention to the White House to present the petition to Presidential Science Advisor Lee DuBridge. The scientists also took their case to the halls of Congress. FAS and CLW organized a "how to lobby" briefing during the Physical Society meeting for over 300 interested physicists, who then met with fifty-three senators or their aides.[45]

Because the role of scientists has been stressed in the epistemic communities approach, this activity may appear to be just another case of the power of technical elites to change decisionmakers' ideas about an issue. However, most of these scientists were not those members of the profession who had been appointed to government advisory boards because of their recognized weapons expertise. By signing petitions, marching, and lobbying, they were engaging in the traditional tactics of citizen activism. Scientists who lacked the inside access stressed in standard accounts of epistemic communities had to take an outside route, trying to educate the public and its representatives on the case against ABMs. Still, it is clear that much of the

43 Ambrose, *Nixon*, pp. 276–77; Hersh, *Price of Power*, p. 160.

44 *NYT*, March 14, 1969, p. 20; Letters to President Nixon from Bruno Rossi and George Wald, March 19 and 25, 1969, White House Staff Member and Office Files (SMOF): David, Dr. Edward E.: Box 4. A handwritten notation on one of the letters initialed by Nixon indicates that the president did actually see the petition.

45 Letter to Lee DuBridge from David Nygren, Thomas Kirk, and John Peoples, April 23, 1969, SMOF: David: Box 4; Cahn, "American Scientists," pp. 78, 80.

impetus for opposition to ABM development came from scientists and other elites. It would thus be a mistake to dismiss the role of the epistemic community. The key point is simply that the scientists had to reach out to and work with other groups in order to gain leverage on administration policy.

Some of these groups also involved other individuals who had a certain social prestige. Scientists were joined by other academics in an open letter to Nixon in which 3,200 scholars asked the president to cancel Safeguard. Two former aides to President Kennedy organized a non-partisan "coalition of eminent citizens" to foster and coordinate opposition to Safeguard. A conference of congressional Democrats, former officials of previous administrations, and academics, held in Washington in late March, concluded by urging the administration to defer both ABM deployment and further MIRV flight-testing until those weapon systems could be addressed in arms talks. Religious leaders also got involved. In late April, twenty-six prominent clergy announced the formation of a National Religious Committee Opposing ABM. Then, in June, the Central Conference of American Rabbis urged halting both the ABM and the MIRV programs.[46]

In an important development, elite initiatives were increasingly matched by support from below, as peace movement organizations also began redirecting part of their focus from Vietnam to the ABM and MIRV battles. Twenty-five peace and liberal groups met in late February to develop a coordinated campaign to mobilize opposition to ABMs, to be headed by the executive director of SANE. SANE also had its members lobby their senators directly against ABM funding. And on June 7, SANE adopted a resolution calling on the United States to halt the ABM and MIRV programs while seeking a moratorium on these systems.

However, SANE's most effective gambit was a newspaper advertisement it sponsored. Drawn by satirical cartoonist Edward Sorel, it depicted a group of generals huddled excitedly around a small missile. The advertisement's headline read, "From the people who brought you Vietnam: The anti-ballistic missile system." The advertisement first appeared in the *New York Times* on March 24, 1969, and was reprinted twelve more times in various newspapers, mostly in the states of undecided senators. The advertisement was also featured

[46] *NYT*, March 23, 1969, p. 35; March 30, 1969, pp. 2, 26; April 30, 1969, p. 9; June 18, 1969, p. 54; Yanarella, *Missile Defense Controversy*, pp. 156–57.

in stories in *Time* and the *Wall Street Journal* and was turned into a poster that became a popular item in college dorm rooms.[47]

The advertisement made overt what was underlying much of the unease about ABM proposals – distrust of the Pentagon's word as a result of Vietnam. For this reason, the advertisement drew blood. Henry Kissinger even mentions it in his memoirs as one of the things that made it harder to get approval for defense spending. Together with the less widespread but growing opposition to MIRVs, the anti-ABM effort was clearly fostering an ever-larger elite and advocacy group coalition in favor of immediate steps to restrain the nuclear arms race.[48]

Administration priorities revisited

In the face of this growing opposition, winning on the ABM issue became the administration's top priority in national security policy. President Nixon later called it "the biggest congressional battle of the first term." As historian Stephen Ambrose observes, "Nixon put more effort, and more of his prestige, into ABM than any other issue in his first year in office." In memos, moreover, the president instructed aides to allow "*no* talk of Compromise on Safeguard." Thus, when some Republican senators said they were considering proposing an immediate strategic arms moratorium, the president asked Kissinger for ideas about how to "contain this kind of nonsense." The president also went on the attack in a graduation speech at the Air Force Academy on June 4, in which he implied that the critics of ABM and MIRV development were "new isolationists" who favored "unilateral disarmament."[49]

It is thus clear that the president had no intention of compromising on his approach to nuclear arms talks. He wanted approval of the ABM program – and Soviet help on Vietnam – before he would consider beginning SALT. Yet it didn't work out that way.

47 *NYT*, March 30, 1969, p. 26; Katz, *Ban the Bomb*, pp. 129–32.

48 Kissinger, *White House Years*, pp. 199, 204–12.

49 Nixon, *RN*, p. 516; Ambrose, *Nixon*, pp. 289, 276–77 (emphasis in original); Memo for Henry Kissinger from Alexander Butterfield, April 25, 1969, WHSF: SMOF: Haldeman: Box 50: "Kissinger, April 69"; Yanarella, *Missile Defense Controversy*, pp. 177–78.

SALT gets a green light

By June, Nixon and Kissinger had to give up on their initial policy on arms talks and agree to seek a date for SALT. All of the factors introduced above converged to produce this policy change. Domestic concerns gained leverage primarily through the elite coalition-shift pathway, but these pressures were reinforced by the bureaucratic utilization pathway.

Probably the most important factor in this policy shift was the ABM fight. The Safeguard announcement did not succeed in quelling the rising opposition to the ABM program in the Senate, as the administration had hoped. To win ABM funding, therefore, the administration needed a new argument that could appeal to arms control supporters. Increasingly, the administration turned to the claim that the ABM program would be a vital bargaining chip in arms talks with the USSR. This argument was not insincere, given an administration philosophy of negotiating from strength, but stressing the bargaining chip argument was misleading. It suggested that the administration wanted ABMs only for arms control purposes, when in fact its pursuit of an ABM system was mostly due to other motivations and the administration was in practice still trying to keep out of SALT talks until the Soviet side made concessions in other areas.

After the Safeguard announcement, though, all the other arguments for ABM deployment, such as its potential contribution to improving the nuclear balance or value against a future Chinese threat, took a back seat. The administration decided the bargaining chip argument was also its best bargaining chip with Congress. But making this argument credible required the administration to pledge its commitment to arms talks where the chip might be cashed in. Thus, in April, Vice President Spiro Agnew declared one purpose of Safeguard was to increase US bargaining power to secure disarmament. Likewise, in testimony before the Gore subcommittee, Defense Secretary Laird proclaimed that Safeguard "offered the Soviet Union added incentive for productive arms control talks." As the Senate ABM vote approached, Nixon reiterated to his chief lobbyist, Bryce Harlow, that he should be "getting across the idea that a no vote would weaken our SALT negotiating position."[50]

[50] *NYT*, April 23, 1969, p. 44; Weber, *Cooperation and Discord*, p. 126; Ambrose, *Nixon*, p. 290.

Though this argument did not reflect the president's true feelings about the urgency of SALT, it is true that the administration was not actively against negotiating limits on ABMs. Nixon was more cynical on MIRVs. On this issue, he suggested willingness to seek a deal on MIRVs, when in fact the administration had already studied and rejected the possibility of a MIRV ban.[51] Nonetheless, the administration's suggestions that ABMs and MIRVs would serve as bargaining chips proved critical with Congress. On August 6, 1969, a Senate amendment to delete funding for Safeguard failed on a 50–50 tie, with Vice President Agnew adding his "no" vote so that the administration could claim that supporters of ABM deployment outnumbered opponents. Accounts at the time suggested the bargaining chip argument was a major factor in convincing the requisite number of senators to approve funding for deployment. As for MIRVs, the relevant House and Senate committees decided not to report out proposed legislation in 1969. Several considerations were involved, including desire not to divert energy from the ABM contest, but the feeling that the administration would address the issue in upcoming talks also played a role.[52]

However, for the implied promise to use the ABM and MIRV programs as bargaining chips in talks to carry weight, there actually had to be talks. As SALT negotiator Gerard Smith later explained, "I think Nixon as a politician realized that his chances of getting large appropriations for weapons systems depended, substantially, on offering to *control* arms."[53] The key thing to recognize, though, is that this is not something the president and national security advisor actually wanted to pursue yet. Throughout the spring and early summer, as the opposition to the administration's ABM and MIRV plans was growing, Nixon and Kissinger kept trying to hold out

[51] Bureaucratic constraints played a role, as Kissinger is widely believed to have concluded by spring 1969 that DOD and JCS insistence on proceeding with MIRVs would make it impossible to pursue limits on both ABMs and MIRVs. Ted Greenwood, *Making the MIRV* (Cambridge, MA: Ballinger Publishing, 1975), pp. 130–31; Weber, *Cooperation and Discord*, pp. 177–78; Kissinger, *White House Years*, pp. 211–12; Memorandum for the President from Henry Kissinger, June 26, 1969, WHSF: CF: Box 43: "WOM"; Hersh, *Price of Power*, pp. 155, 160; Garthoff, *Detente and Confrontation*, p. 135; Gerard Smith, *Doubletalk*, pp. 119, 175.

[52] Yanarella, *Missile Defense Controversy*, p. 158; Nathan Miller, "The Making of a Majority: Safeguard and the Senate," *Washington Monthly*, October 1969, p. 60, as cited in Primack and Von Hippel, *Advice and Dissent*, p. 190; Weber, *Cooperation and Discord*, p. 178.

[53] Charlton, *From Deterrence to Defense*, p. 32 (emphasis in original).

against the demands for talks. They were still interested in pursuing linkage and had not yet gotten any of the help they wanted from the USSR on Vietnam.

Thus, in various memos, the president pleaded for "complete and absolute backing from everybody in the Administration," ordering officials to refrain from any further leaks or lobbying that would give momentum to demands for SALT or for an ABM or MIRV moratorium. Evidence is also available of Kissinger's continuing desire to postpone arms talks, as a result of wiretaps ordered by the president in an effort to discover sources of disloyalty in the bureaucracy. Morton Halperin, a Kissinger aide in the NSC, is one who had his phone tapped. A transcript of a Halperin phone conversation in late May reveals Kissinger's thinking at the time. Asked what was happening with arms talks, Halperin replied that the administration was still "waiting for the propitious international climate." Turning to the subject of MIRVs, Halperin added, "I had a meeting with Hal [Sonnenfeldt] and Larry [Lynn, two other NSC officials] and those guys are convinced and have convinced Henry there is absolutely no strategic rationale for an arms control view." There was thus clearly no belief at the top of the administration that the time was right for arms control.[54]

Yet, on June 11, just two weeks after Halperin's conversation, Nixon authorized Secretary of State Rogers to inform the Soviet Union that the United States was now ready to start SALT. At a press conference on June 19, Nixon announced his decision and conveyed a desire to get talks underway quickly. He told reporters that he believed that talks could begin "between July 31 and August 15." The fact that this is also when the Senate was scheduled to vote on the ABM system can hardly be a coincidence.[55]

As it turns out, the USSR now decided to stall. It seems likely they were motivated in part by desire to see whether the absence of talks would sway the Senate against ABMs. However, the Soviets also expressed anger at an announcement that Nixon would visit Romania and may have been returning tit for tat given Johnson's earlier decision to delay SALT over the Soviet invasion of Czechoslovakia.

[54] Memorandum to the Secretary of State, Secretary of Defense, Ambassador Bunker, Ambassador Lodge, and Henry Kissinger, from the President, April 14, 1969, WHSF: President's Personal Files (PPF): Box 5: "ABM"; Gerard Smith, *Doubletalk*, p. 163; Hersh, *Price of Power*, p. 153.

[55] Kissinger, *White House Years*, p. 138; Newhouse, *Cold Dawn*, p. 162.

Finally, the Soviet government was also preoccupied by border clashes with China in 1969. Only after China agreed, on October 20, to talks on the border issue did the Soviet Union express willingness to set a date for SALT. On October 25, a joint announcement by the two superpowers indicated that SALT would begin on November 17, 1969.[56]

Explaining the decision

It is perhaps best to begin with Kissinger's own account of what precipitated the sudden announcement of willingness to begin arms talks. In his memoirs, Kissinger devotes roughly equal space to congressional calls to enter talks and leaks from the bureaucracy declaring that the USA would soon set a date for SALT. "The cumulative impact of all the bureaucratic indiscipline, with media and Congressional pressures added, was that we had to abandon our attempt to use the opening of SALT talks as a lever for other negotiations." The main previous study of US decisions to enter arms talks, by Fen Hampson, concurs: "As pressures in Congress grew, and a manipulative bureaucracy helped accelerate the timetable for talks, the administration found itself headed to the negotiating table earlier than it expected."[57]

I do not dispute this conclusion. Instead, I ask what made this congressional and bureaucratic interest in arms talks effective. The US foreign policy literature concerning both bureaucratic politics and executive–legislative relations suggests that, when presidents really care about an issue and are determined to get their way, they usually succeed.[58] Thus, Nixon's failure to prevail on SALT should be considered something of a puzzle. Moreover, in this case, Nixon had obvious reservoirs of support on which he could have drawn. It was only a short time since Congress had voted to *add* funds to the defense budget for the ABM program; surely there were still many legislators

[56] Kissinger, *White House Years*, pp. 145, 161; Garthoff, *Detente and Confrontation*, pp. 73, 132; Newhouse, *Cold Dawn*, pp. 163–65.

[57] Kissinger, *White House Years*, p. 138; Hampson, "Headed for the Table," p. 160.

[58] Stephen D. Krasner, "Are Bureaucracies Important? (Or Allison Wonderland)," *Foreign Policy* 7 (Summer 1972), pp. 159–79; Terry Sullivan, "A Matter of Fact: The 'Two Presidencies' Thesis Revitalized," in Steven A. Shull, ed., *The Two Presidencies: A Quarter Century Assessment* (Chicago: Nelson-Hall, 1991); Barbara Hinckley, *Less than Meets the Eye: Foreign Policymaking and the Myth of the Assertive Congress* (Chicago: University of Chicago Press, 1994).

who could have been rallied in support of Nixon's agenda. Likewise, in the bureaucracy, the military was strongly against limiting new US strategic weapons. Since the Joint Chiefs in particular are usually viewed as having a *de facto* veto over any arms deal they dislike, it should have been possible for Nixon to use them as a counterweight to bureaucratic advocates of arms talks. Thus, it is necessary to go beneath the surface of the Kissinger/Hampson thesis and ask why the White House could not more effectively resist congressional and bureaucratic pressures.

The administration's strategic objectives, combined with its reading of US public opinion, provide one possible answer. Nixon and Kissinger both feared that the USSR was about to pull ahead of the USA in nuclear strength. However, it eventually became clear that, given changing public attitudes about defense spending due to Vietnam, Congress would not readily be willing to provide the funds to match the Soviet buildup. Later testimony by administration officials gives great weight to this calculation. As Kissinger explained in one interview, "SALT, paradoxically, was the only way to *preserve* our military programs. Without SALT the Congress would have continued to cut."[59]

This explanation is more relevant to the outcome of talks than their initiation, however. This calculation certainly helps explain why the administration, and especially the Defense Department, accepted the SALT I deal that was ultimately negotiated in 1972. In congressional testimony, for example, Defense Secretary Laird said he went along with the ABM treaty because he was convinced after annual battles with Congress that the administration would never get approval for full deployment of Safeguard.[60] But there is little evidence or reason to believe that the administration felt its options to be so severely limited in June 1969, less than five months after taking office. Even on Vietnam, where the visible opposition was much greater, Nixon did not believe he had to give in to demands to negotiate an immediate US withdrawal. When the protests began to grow in autumn 1969, Nixon responded by calling on a "silent majority" to make known its support for his Vietnam policies.[61] While promising arms talks did help win ABM funding, given Nixon's combativeness on other foreign policy issues, along with poll data suggesting that a silent majority

[59] Charlton, *From Deterrence to Defense*, p. 41 (emphasis in original).

[60] Primack and Von Hippel, *Advice and Dissent*, p. 191.

[61] Ambrose, *Nixon*, pp. 305–13.

really did support ABMs, it is surprising that Nixon abandoned his resistance to early initiation of arms talks so easily.

In fact, all of the statements linking SALT to administration difficulties in getting public and congressional support for a strategic buildup come from after SALT I was signed, and documents from the time indicate that the reluctance in summer 1969 to buck the proponents of SALT stems rather from a different set of political calculations. The Nixon White House saw the ABM program as a seed that might give rise to a new opposition coalition that could compete effectively with it for political power. The president and his political aides primarily feared a larger change in elite-level coalitions that might result from the ABM fight, and the popular support that new elite coalition might be able to rally. Shifting elite coalitions are at the heart of mechanism 2, suggesting that this was the key pathway in changing US policy. Mechanism 3 reinforced this process because bureaucratic leaks provided extra ammunition for a potential counter-coalition on arms control.

Administration concerns about the anti-ABM coalition were partly idiosyncratic. They focused heavily on Senator Edward Kennedy, reflecting an obsession with the Kennedys Nixon had felt ever since his narrow defeat by JFK in 1960. But many people saw Ted Kennedy as a potential presidential candidate, so it still made sense for the administration to pay attention to those issues the Massachusetts senator might adopt. Kennedy's decision to take up the ABM cause was thus the initial source of administration concern. The personal diary of Chief of Staff H. R. Haldeman conveys how strongly White House political aides felt threatened by the senator's role in the ABM fight. His entry for April 8, 1969, records, "All on staff feel . . . this is first battle of '72, vs. Teddy Kennedy, and we *must* win."[62]

White House aides devoted several memos in spring 1969 to Kennedy's association with anti-ABM efforts. The main analyses came from Nixon's chief speechwriters, Pat Buchanan and William Safire, with whom the president worked closely on matters of political strategy.[63] In March, Buchanan proposed that the administration take available defense intelligence and "use it in this ABM battle with EMK [Edward M. Kennedy]" to make it appear that Kennedy's proposals would harm national security. If the release of information

[62] H. R. Haldeman, *The Haldeman Diaries* (New York: G. P. Putnam's Sons, 1994), p. 48 (emphasis in original).

[63] See Ambrose, *Nixon*, p. 67.

was timed correctly, "We can not only win this fight; we can visit some permanent damage on our opponents for the future."[64]

Although Buchanan's proposal does not appear to have been implemented, it is nonetheless indicative of what Nixon's inner circle saw as the stakes in the ABM fight. This sense that Kennedy's role in the ABM battle could pose future political problems for the administration is even more pronounced in a William Safire analysis of late May 1969. Safire's memo asked, "Since public opinion usually follows a president on matters of national security, why should Teddy Kennedy seize the ABM issue now?" Safire's analysis ran through seven steps – the first two and the last convey the essential elements:

> 1. When the Vietnam war starts to end, the liberal establishment will be all dressed up with no place to go. The anti-war amalgam will vanish, and the New Left is too far out.
> 2. To fill this vacuum and find a cause, they must make their central issue the mis-direction of Federal funds. The anti-Vietnam crowd is a ready market for an attack on military spending . . .
> 7. The peaceniks will become the arms controlniks; they will picture themselves as for disarmament, and you against it, or ineffectual about it. Your attempts to link arms control with a broad strategy of peace will be twisted into "He threw away the chance for arms control by using it as a tool in the old containment policy."[65]

The available internal documents of the time – which are admittedly incomplete – do not reveal any great concern in mid-1969 with whether Congress would support adequate defense spending to let the United States keep pace with the USSR. Rather, they suggest that the administration viewed the main stakes in the ABM and arms control debates as lying in the arena of domestic politics. These were seen as prime issues for Nixon's opponents, who would presumably be led by Ted Kennedy, to build a new liberal electoral coalition with which to challenge Nixon's hold on the White House. The ABM debate would serve in this process as a lightning rod to deflect the anti-Vietnam movement into a larger critique of military spending. And linkage would come back to haunt the administration in the form of charges it led to a missed opportunity for arms control. The decision in June 1969 to seek SALT talks was thus a pre-emptive strike

[64] Memorandum to the President from Patrick J. Buchanan, March 19, 1969, WHSF: CF: Box 43: "WOM".

[65] Memorandum for the President from Bill Safire, May 21, 1969, WHSF: CF: Box 43: "WOM".

against the anticipated future political opponents of the administration.

Though electoral calculations were involved, this was not a mechanism 1 process. Public opinion was not yet demanding arms control, and the administration knew that a majority favored defenses against Soviet missiles (see above, p. 171), so it did not abandon the fight for the ABM program. This was rather a question of what issues might provide the means for an opposition coalition to expand its base of support, creating problems for the administration in Congress in the short term, but perhaps also with the voting public down the road. Grassroots activists were not the main initiators of this process, but the support they gave to anti-ABM elites was the key ingredient in making the administration fear the possible outcome of coalition-shift dynamics.

The development of citizen activism on ABMs and arms control provided the main evidence that this could be a real area of administration vulnerability. It involved groups like SANE, which were already active opposing the war in Vietnam, thus ensuring a direct link between the two movements. Yet it also involved other groups and individuals – ranging from nuclear scientists to local community associations – many of whom were not part of the anti-Vietnam crowd. This suggested that arms control advocacy had the potential to spread to an even wider segment of the American public. Finally, even the first stirrings of local protest against ABM deployment triggered significant activity in Congress, while a number of prominent Democrats started working to arouse still greater public opposition to Nixon's arms control priorities. This combination gave the administration ample reason to fear that an elite countercoalition could gain majority status by attacking Nixon arms policy. Largely through a process of anticipated reactions, then, the administration decided to take this issue away from its opponents by changing its own priorities at the specific level. Linkage receded from view; Nixon now promised to seek limits on ABMs and offensive missiles as a high priority.

This political context also explains why bureaucratic arms control advocates were able to defy Nixon's and Kissinger's efforts to impose linkage. They could use leaks to reinforce mechanism 2 dynamics. If their leaks led to media reports suggesting talks would begin soon and still no talks got underway, this would just be further fuel for elite efforts to build an opposition coalition around nuclear weapons issues. Since the White House saw arms control as an issue that could pose political problems, bureaucratic supporters of SALT could then argue that giving up on linkage and starting talks promptly was the best solution to that problem – a mechanism 3 process. But this bureaucratic utilization process would only work if there was a plausible political problem to start with. Hence, the main contribution of bureaucratic politics was simply to further the mechanism 2 process of shifting elite coalitions.

Alternative explanations not adequate

A number of studies discuss why the 1972 SALT I treaty became possible, but only a few have tried to account for the decision to seek talks in 1969. These studies suggest three possible lines of explanation, but none adequately account for the development of US willingness to cooperate. The first line of analysis is that developed by Kissinger and Hampson, which I have dealt with above. To reiterate the main point, I do not deny the importance of congressional and bureaucratic pressures, but I argue that they gained much of their effectiveness from larger societal concerns that were becoming increasingly apparent. Without various expressions of societal opposition to continued reliance on military power, the administration would not have been so worried that rival elites could mobilize substantial public support for pursuing arms control if the administration failed to move on the issue first.

A second possible alternative is more consistent with the traditional explanation for arms control. Since the standard variables did account for Johnson's interest in SALT, one could argue that Nixon's decision simply followed from the same factors that persuaded Johnson to seek talks. Such an explanation sees a basic continuity in US policy. It argues that Nixon always accepted the need for SALT, so that there is no puzzle in the June 1969 decision to seek a date for talks.

Steve Weber's study of the ABM and MIRV cases, though designed for a different purpose, presents a sophisticated version of this kind of reasoning. Weber explores why different cases that match the prisoner's dilemma (PD) game have different outcomes. Given this goal, Weber combines the Johnson and Nixon administrations in his analysis, arguing that both confronted PD payoffs on the ABM issue. Thus, once the Sentinel program had apparently led the Soviets, in 1968, to agree to SALT, "The problem for the incoming [Nixon] administration was established as one of maintaining the new momentum toward cooperation that Sentinel had presumably triggered."[66]

But an assumption that objective conditions at the international level made the effort to seek an ABM accord inevitable simply cannot be sustained. The new administration did not see its task "as one of maintaining . . . momentum." As everything in this chapter has made clear, Nixon and Kissinger sought desperately to slow the momentum toward SALT talks. And they did so because they did not share the exact same preferences as the outgoing Johnson administration. It is plausible that both saw the basic situation as prisoner's dilemma. But, if so, that imparted a much greater willingness to seek cooperation to Johnson than it did to Nixon. Johnson, swayed by McNamara, wanted to stop the arms race. Nixon, with his goal of sufficiency, wanted to match Soviet power. Nixon therefore gave priority to convincing Congress to fund new strategic weapons, not to getting into talks to forestall their development. Compared to its predecessor, the Nixon administration clearly had a lower willingness to seek immediate talks.

One might respond that the delay in SALT was only tactical. Because the president seemed to accept that SALT would happen at some point, one might assume Nixon was merely waiting until he had secured ABM funding from Congress and completed MIRV flight-testing so that he could enter talks with extra bargaining chips, meaning the move to begin SALT would have occurred at about the same time regardless of the domestic context. But the notion that the administration was merely waiting until it had new bargaining chips to enter talks does not fit the facts of this case. First, the timing is off. Nixon's announcement of the decision to seek a date for SALT and the target date he set for beginning talks both fell *before* the Senate ABM vote or the completion of MIRV testing. More importantly, the president in 1969 was not seeking an ABM system primarily in order to use it as a bargaining chip in the literal sense of trading Safeguard for reductions in Soviet ABMs or other weapons. If one reviews the quotes from administration arguments concerning the importance of Safeguard for arms talks, it is apparent that the administration never actually promised to give up ABMs. Rather, officials always spoke more broadly in terms of achieving a favorable bargaining position, without specifying what they wanted to bargain for.

[66] Weber, *Cooperation and Discord*, pp. 111, 123.

This is because Nixon in spring 1969 sought ABM deployment for other purposes and did not especially want to trade away the US ABM system. In particular, the president wanted ABMs to improve the nuclear balance so that the United States could engage the USSR in talks on other subjects without being forced into a disadvantageous agreement. The records of internal deliberations make it clear that Nixon subscribed to a strongly realist view of diplomacy, in which the side with greater military power overall would force the other side to make political concessions. On March 20, Nixon and Laird briefed the Cabinet on the Safeguard decision. Haldeman's diary entry that day indicates the president stated his desire for "military superiority and defense as a base for negotiations." While this may sound like a bargaining chip argument, the very next sentence suggests a somewhat different goal. "P [Haldeman's abbreviation for the president] stated flatly that war will be over by next year." This suggests that Nixon saw the ABM program in the context of his linkage policy, as another source of leverage to get the USSR to put pressure on Hanoi.[67]

In an April 14 memo to Rogers, Laird, and Kissinger, the president laid out his thinking in more detail. This document, in which he refers to himself in the third person, is the most complete record of Nixon's priorities at this time:

> The President, after thorough consideration of all the options – building more Polaris submarines, hardening Minuteman sites, etc., has determined that the least provocative and the most effective action we can take is to go forward on a limited system (which the Soviet Union already has) which will accomplish two purposes – an area defense which covers any possibility of a Chinese Communist or other mini-nuclear power threat for the next 10 years and the protection of some of our Minuteman sites against a possible Soviet attack . . .
>
> What is most important is that we take a consistent affirmative line – brooking no compromise on the fundamental issue: we are going forward with this system as the best possible way to see to it that the United States, at a time the Soviet Union has widened the conventional gap and has closed the strategic gap, does not [allow the USSR to] move into a pre-eminent position and thereby leave the United States in the position of being basically a second-class power as far as overall nuclear capability is concerned . . . [T]he great fundamental issue involved is very simply whether during this Administration we

67 Haldeman, *Diaries*, p. 42.

> allow the Soviet Union to pass the United States in overall nuclear capability and thereby leave us in a second-rate position. From a diplomatic standpoint this would be devastating to our policies all over the world . . .
>
> With regard to the question as to whether we would be willing to discard our [S]afeguard system, provided the Soviet Union agreed to do so in arms talks, we should come back to the fundamental point that I made in my press conference – with the Soviet Union now turning its radars toward the threat from Communist China could either of the major nuclear powers leave itself naked against a potential Communist Chinese attack?[68]

This memo makes several things clear. First, Nixon was partially swayed by the logic of arms controllers – he thus describes Safeguard as less provocative. But the memo also reveals that this was not the primary consideration. Between more destabilizing area defense and less provocative point defense, Nixon in private still gives greater emphasis to area defense, especially against Chinese weapons. But even this goal gets less consideration than larger concerns about the nuclear balance. These are not, however, related to the goals of nuclear deterrence or strategic stability, but to US political standing in the world. For Nixon, an ABM program was first a way to neutralize Soviet gains in the global balance of power and second a hedge against China.

Neither goal lends itself to giving up ABMs. Because the administration did not view the ABM system primarily as a bargaining chip to use in arms talks, the argument that Nixon was only waiting until he had ABMs and MIRVs in his arsenal to enter talks is incorrect. Since Nixon was not being driven by desire to trade these weapons for Soviet arms limitations, there was no reason to think he would enter talks automatically the moment some new bargaining chips became available. In fact, understanding Nixon's priorities at the specific level makes it clear that the administration did not expect to enter arms talks as soon as it had won ABM funding. At this point, the administration's top goal at the specific level was still linkage. Nixon and Kissinger wanted to heighten Soviet interest in arms talks, not in order to get a SALT treaty, but to force a settlement of other political issues, especially Vietnam.

[68] Memorandum to the Secretary of State et al. from the President, April 14, 1969, WHSF: PPF: Box 5: "ABM".

Weber does not discuss linkage at all, treating the ABM issue as self-contained. But the degree of preference for cooperation cannot be established by looking at the arms issue in isolation. It is once again a matter of priorities. Because Nixon and Kissinger wanted to see outstanding political disputes addressed first, they did not enter office with a willingness to cooperate immediately on limiting arms. Although Nixon and Kissinger were not actively against discussing ABM limitations, it was not a priority item on their agenda at the specific level. Hence, a US preference for cooperation had to be re-established, as a result of other developments in the first six months of 1969. Only under the weight of domestic pressures did the administration agree the time had come to seek talks on the possibility of limiting ABMs. It is thus not correct to see Nixon's decision to enter SALT as simply a case of continuity in preferences established in the Johnson years. Because different presidents assessed the correct response to the Soviet achievement of parity differently, which priorities prevailed was determined by which could form the basis for the greater level of societal mobilization.

A final alternative explanation accepts that the SALT decision was the product of a change in Nixon policy, but attributes that change to learning, thus reflecting a more general approach that attributes cooperation to cognitive evolution. In this view, the reason Nixon downgraded linkage and restored priority at the specific level to missile limitation is because the administration had to adapt to signals from the international environment which showed that the USSR either would not or could not give the USA what it wanted elsewhere, meaning that linkage would not work. Deborah Larson is one proponent of a learning explanation. As she puts it: "By 1972 Nixon had learned that he could not expect simultaneous progress on the major issues at stake in US–Soviet relations. In order to move toward negotiations with the Soviets, Nixon learned to decouple difficult issues from more manageable problems . . . In short, he abandoned linkage."[69]

69 Larson, "Learning," p. 386. Though I cite Larson on learning from the international environment, as that constitutes a clearly alternative explanation to mine, her version of the learning explanation is not in fact fully systemic. It is thus also partially complementary to the domestic politics argument of this chapter, as she argues that Nixon learned more from congressional opposition than from Soviet behavior ("Learning," p. 390). For further discussion of how the administration progressively abandoned linkage, see Newhouse, *War and Peace*, pp. 220, 232.

Larson is correct that the administration had to learn to downplay linkage in order to reach a SALT agreement in 1972. But this learning argument does not work as an explanation for why the administration initially decided to seek talks in summer 1969. In the first months of 1969, Nixon and Kissinger still thought linkage was working. When the president met Soviet ambassador Dobrynin in February, Dobrynin gave him a note expressing Soviet willingness to move forward on a range of topics. In his memoirs, Nixon writes, "This note seemed to augur well for our policy of linkage." And Kissinger's way of putting the decision to enter SALT – "we had to *abandon* our attempt to use the opening of SALT talks as a lever" – is not the phrasing of someone who has learned that leverage will not work anyway.[70] Instead, what the administration really learned is that, if they did not move to make arms control a priority, rival political elites would do so, and there was plenty of evidence that a sizable segment of society would follow. The administration acted to get SALT underway before this mechanism 2 process of building a new winning coalition could get out of hand.

Conclusions

SALT is the only case of serious arms talks during the Cold War in which a major surge in citizen activism did not predate the start of talks. A closer examination reveals that even in this case, however, domestic factors were a significant source of the US preference for cooperation. Mechanism 2 was the primary process at work. A coalition among scientists, activist groups, and members of Congress to oppose ABM deployment created the possibility that rival political elites could damage President Nixon on the arms control issue. Mechanism 3 reinforced this process. Bureaucratic leaks to the media raised expectations that arms talks would begin soon, thereby accentuating the president's potential problem with an elite countercoalition. In these circumstances, the administration had to adjust its priorities at the specific level. In place of linkage, the administration moved control of ABMs and offensive weapons to the top of the arms control agenda, de-linking missile control from other political issues.

Mechanism 1, the electoral pathway, did not factor in the decision to enter SALT. Though the administration was to some extent motivated

[70] Nixon, *RN*, p. 457; Kissinger, *White House Years*, p. 138 (emphasis added).

by electoral calculations, it was not responding to an existing protest movement for arms restraint. Rather, Nixon and his aides took their cues primarily from the actions of rival political elites, especially Ted Kennedy's decision to take on the ABM issue. With the anti-Vietnam movement and changing attitudes about military spending in the background, the administration worried that delaying arms control would create a potent issue around which its opponents could build a new majority liberal coalition.

Although domestic pressure is significant in this case, its impact differs in an important way from that exerted by the test ban and freeze movements. In chapter 1, I argued that most empirical studies of cooperation treat domestic factors only as constraints on state action, and I contended that domestic politics can just as easily serve as a stimulus to cooperative preferences instead. As I have shown in the test ban case and as we will see in the freeze case, those two periods strongly support the notion that societal concerns can be one of the main sources of interest in cooperation. But in the SALT case, it is probably more accurate to view domestic politics as a constraint. There was no major push from below driving the government into arms talks. When Nixon and Kissinger entered office, they had already accepted the idea that SALT would be a tool of US policy – but they wanted to be able to control that tool. They wanted to delay SALT in order to exert leverage on Soviet behavior in other areas and they wanted to get congressional support for new US strategic programs so as to improve the nuclear balance.

But the domestic system did not give the administration what it needed to carry out this plan of action. Congress refused to fund as much of a strategic buildup as the administration desired. And to get any funding at all, Nixon had to promise to use ABMs and MIRVs as bargaining chips in SALT. This made it impossible for the administration to carry out its preferred linkage policy. Domestic society was not telling the administration what it should do so much as preventing the administration from doing certain other things it wanted to do. It was through a process of running up against these domestic constraints that Nixon and Kissinger were convinced to get SALT underway. Thus, although domestic factors are quite important in this case, the nature of their influence comes closer to matching the conventional view of the domestic arena as a source of constraints.

This should not obscure the fundamental conclusion of this chapter, however. In order to understand when the United States actually manifested a willingness to seek cooperation, by inviting the Soviets to set a date for SALT, it is still vital to take the level of societal interest in military restraint into account. Though elites played a greater role in initiating pressure in this case, they gained much of their leverage from the existence of a wider peace movement that was starting to show an interest in nuclear weapons issues. Thus, even in this case, chosen because it appeared unfavorable to societal sources of preferences for cooperation, part of the explanation involves inputs arising from the bottom up. Grassroots activists did not do it alone, but to ignore them would be to miss a factor necessary to explain when the United States decided to enter SALT.

Aftermath

The SALT talks that began in November 1969 produced an agreement at a Moscow summit in May 1972. Due to bureaucratic constraints and limited domestic interest in the anti-MIRV campaign, MIRVs were not restricted in this agreement at all. Because Congress had continued to cut the administration's ABM requests, however, the administration made ABMs a centerpiece of the SALT negotiations, trying only to ensure a final deal would link defensive limitations with some level of offensive limitations. The resulting SALT I treaty thus had two components. The ABM treaty limited both sides to just two ABM sites (later reduced to one), and the Interim Offensive Agreement simply froze the number of ballistic missile launchers on both sides at their existing level.[71]

The United States and USSR began SALT II negotiations immediately upon the conclusion of SALT I, suggesting willingness to cooperate carried past the first treaty. Concluding a second treaty proved much more difficult however. Once both sides brought MIRVs on line, certain weaknesses of the SALT I deal quickly became apparent. SALT I allowed the Soviet Union to retain a larger number of ICBMs than the United States, in return for American advantages in other areas. When this was combined with the fact that Soviet ICBMs were also larger than US missiles, meaning they could carry more warheads, worries arose that US land-based missiles were approaching a "window of vulnerability" to a Soviet first strike. Political

[71] For details of the evolution of the US negotiating position during the talks, see Newhouse, *Cold Dawn*, or Gerard Smith, *Doubletalk*.

relations between the two sides also worsened, as the Soviets became more active in Third World conflicts.

These complications delayed completion of SALT II until 1979. In the meantime, an activist coalition opposing SALT developed in the United States. Former government officials in the Committee on the Present Danger led the domestic opposition to SALT II, with support from conservative advocacy groups with sizable grassroots memberships. Societal preferences regarding cooperation had now reversed, it appeared, with SALT II enjoying little active popular support. Facing what would already be a difficult battle in the Senate, after the Soviet invasion of Afghanistan in December, President Jimmy Carter simply withdrew the SALT II treaty from Senate consideration.[72] As the 1980s began, the United States had changed its preference again, deciding that it should for the time being no longer pursue cooperation with the USSR on controlling nuclear arms. This is the situation in which a new citizens' movement on behalf of restraint would arise.

[72] For a general overview, see Dan Caldwell, *The Dynamics of Domestic Politics and Arms Control: The SALT II Treaty Ratification Debate* (Columbia, SC: University of South Carolina Press, 1991). Accounts of the opposition that stress the connections between elite critics and mass-based conservative groups are Jerry W. Sanders, *Peddlers of Crisis: The Committee on the Present Danger and the Politics of Containment* (Boston: South End Press, 1983); David Skidmore, "The Politics of National Security Policy: Interest Groups, Coalitions, and the SALT II Debate," in Skidmore and Valerie M. Hudson, eds., *The Limits of State Autonomy* (Boulder: Westview Press, 1993).

7 Reagan and the freeze movement

The early 1980s witnessed the most extensive citizens' campaign on nuclear arms issues to date in the United States. Participation in this movement was roughly an order of magnitude larger than the protest against nuclear testing in the 1950s, and perhaps two orders of magnitude greater than the anti-ABM protest of the late 1960s. Though diverse in objectives and tactics, this movement had at its core an effort to get the US government to propose to the Soviet Union a bilateral nuclear weapons freeze. The drafters of the freeze proposal believed that the danger of nuclear war was being greatly increased by an ongoing technological arms race, leading them to suggest that the superpowers immediately halt all testing, production, and deployment of nuclear weapons.

Of all of the movements in the United States that have addressed nuclear arms control, the freeze movement was, from one perspective, in the best position to exert an influence on policy. The necessary precondition was clearly present in this case for each of the three potential influence mechanisms defined in chapter 3. From another perspective, though, the freeze movement also faced the toughest opposition of any of the campaigns examined here. President Ronald Reagan and his aides vehemently opposed the nuclear freeze proposal and wanted to defer arms control in any form for several years.

This makes the present case different from the others studied in this book. In the other cases, there is not much doubt that arms talks, if and when they got underway, revealed US willingness to seek

An earlier version of some of the material in this chapter appeared in "The Nuclear Freeze Movement's Effect on Policy," by Jeffrey W. Knopf, in Thomas R. Rochon and David S. Meyer's edited work, *Coalitions and Political Movements: The Lessons of the Nuclear Freeze*.

cooperation. There is, however, considerable doubt in the Reagan years. The SALT talks, the origins of which formed the subject of the previous chapter, collapsed in the opening days of 1980, when Jimmy Carter withdrew the SALT II treaty from Senate consideration. In the presidential campaign that year, candidate Reagan labeled the treaty "fatally flawed" and made it clear he had no interest in reviving the SALT agenda. Yet, in May 1982, President Reagan invited the Soviets to begin a new set of talks on long-range weapons, which the United States designated START (Strategic Arms Reductions Talks). In one sense, this decision represents the clearest case of societal concerns leading to talks, as there is no doubt the beginning of START was almost entirely due to the rise of the freeze movement. But many people, including the leaders of the freeze campaign, expressed great skepticism that this decision signaled actual willingness to cooperate. Reagan's opening proposal was widely seen as being so one-sided as to be non-negotiable, making it far from clear that the start of START re-established a US preference for cooperation.

As a result, this case study extends past the actual opening of talks to the 1984 election. Activist pressure continued throughout this period and helped produce a series of further adjustments to the administration position that indicated ever greater willingness to cooperate. The presence in the administration of hard-line opponents of US–Soviet arms control meant that the government continued to send mixed signals. But, I will argue, an overall US preference for cooperation had definitely emerged by 1984, in large part due to domestic activism.

In particular, I will show that the nuclear freeze movement had a significant impact at the general level, where the importance of nuclear issues on the national agenda and the balance between the goals of strength and restraint are set. This result obtained because of the influence pathways the freeze movement successfully activated. This citizens' campaign most strongly engaged mechanism 1, a mobilization of public opinion that alters the electoral incentives of government officials. It also activated mechanism 2, a shifting of elite coalition patterns, in this case at the general level, thereby reinforcing mechanism 1's influence. These pressures led the Reagan administration to respond as expected. The administration formulated a strategic arms control plan and entered talks earlier than it otherwise would have. Thereafter, it steadily increased the emphasis it gave to making progress toward strategic arms reductions. Finally, Reagan also came to give greater declaratory emphasis to avoiding nuclear war and to proclaim reductions in nuclear weapons *per se* as a major goal of strategic policy.

Reflecting the nature of the pathways it activated, though, with regard to the specific details of arms control policy, the freeze movement had only limited impact. Despite some potential for its operation, mechanism 3 – the bureaucratic pathway – came into play hardly at all, while the pressures arising through mechanism 2 were all directed at the general level. Lacking leverage at the specific level, the freeze never got its own proposal adopted as an official objective of arms control policy.

I begin this chapter by describing the origins and nature of the nuclear freeze movement. To be able to show how the freeze changed policy, I then establish a policy baseline for the Reagan administration. Subsequent sections then demonstrate the influence mechanisms engaged by the freeze movement and their impact on US policy.

Overview of the freeze movement

A note on terminology

It is important to distinguish between two aspects of what has become known as the freeze movement. Construed narrowly, the freeze was a specific policy proposal that was promoted by a national organization, the Nuclear Weapons Freeze Campaign. But this campaign was just one aspect of a larger and broader anti-nuclear weapons movement, involving a number of other organizations and approaches to dealing with the nuclear issue. For purposes of clarity, I use the term "freeze movement," with lower-case letters, to refer to the full range of anti-nuclear weapons protest in this period. I reserve the term "Freeze Campaign," starting with capital letters, for the organizations set up to promote the nuclear weapons freeze proposal itself.

Emergence of the freeze movement

The nuclear freeze proposal and arrangements to launch a national campaign around it were put together between 1979 and 1981. Once it emerged, the freeze movement became a national phenomenon with unusual rapidity, only to subside from sight nearly as quickly. In 1982, the freeze became a focus of legislation in Congress, a massive political demonstration, and numerous state and local ballot initiatives. The House passed a freeze resolution in May 1983, but no further freeze legislation ever passed either chamber of Congress. After failing in efforts to elect a pro-freeze president in 1984, the freeze largely disappeared from the national scene. In 1987, the national campaign organization merged with SANE, signaling the end of the freeze as an independent peace initiative. Before its demise, though, the freeze had a significant impact on US arms control policy.

Although the freeze came to be seen as an expression of opposition to the arms policies of the Reagan administration, the movement was a product of trends and organizing that occurred before Ronald Reagan moved into the White House.[1] One source of the freeze movement was protest during the 1970s against commercial nuclear energy production, which sensitized some activists to the dangers of nuclear weapons as well. For example, Dr. Helen Caldicott, a prominent figure in the anti-nuclear power movement, helped revive Physicians for Social Responsibility (PSR), an organization that had been set up in the earlier battle over nuclear testing. PSR developed lectures and films that graphically described the effects of a one mt nuclear bomb, an effort that did a great deal to raise concerns about the danger of nuclear war.

The efforts of traditional peace groups formed another strand in the emergence of the freeze movement. A number of groups came together in the mid-1970s in a campaign to stop the B-1 bomber. Those involved found the effort to stop the arms race one weapon at a time highly frustrating and decided to seek a more comprehensive proposal. Various groups started gathering signatures in 1979 on petitions proposing a moratorium on building nuclear weapons (and, in some versions, nuclear power plants as well) and calling for the abolition of such arms.

At this stage, the woman most often credited with being the "author" of the freeze, Randall Forsberg, entered the scene. At a meeting in December 1979, Forsberg convinced activists involved in the moratorium effort to allow her to re-work existing moratorium proposals into a new vehicle that could appeal to "the majority of middle class, middle-of-the-road citizens."[2] In April 1980, Forsberg

1 Pam Solo in particular stresses the amount of local organizing that took place to lay the groundwork for the freeze movement (*From Protest to Policy: Beyond the Freeze to Common Security* [Cambridge, MA: Ballinger Publishing Co., 1988], pp. 18–50).

2 Forsberg interview in Robert Leavitt, "Freezing the Arms Race: The Genesis of a Mass

completed the draft of her "Call to Halt the Nuclear Arms Race." In an effort to increase the appeal of the moratorium idea, Forsberg made it bilateral rather than call on only the United States to stop nuclear weapons work. And she limited it to call only for "a mutual freeze on the testing, production, and deployment of nuclear weapons and [their delivery vehicles]," not the abolition of nuclear weapons or nuclear power.[3]

Some fairly straightforward assumptions lay behind the freeze. Forsberg and other supporters of a freeze believed that a condition of parity existed in US and Soviet nuclear arsenals, because either side would have enough weapons in reserve to destroy its opponent after suffering any first-strike blow. This contrasted with the view of the Reagan administration and other conservatives that the Soviet Union had an edge in MIRVed ICBMs that put the United States at risk of nuclear blackmail – an outlook captured by the concept of a "window of vulnerability." Instead of vulnerability, freeze backers saw the primary danger of the next several years elsewhere, in the development of new, more accurate weapons with counterforce potential, meaning that they could potentially take out the other side's nuclear weapons. In the words of the "Call":

> The weapon programs of the next decade, if not stopped, will pull the nuclear tripwire tighter. Counterforce and other "nuclear war-fighting" systems will improve the ability of the USA and USSR to attack the opponent's nuclear forces and other military targets. This will increase the pressure on both sides to use their nuclear weapons in a crisis, rather than risk losing them in a first strike.[4]

Because, in this view, the chief danger lay in new qualitative developments, the surest way to preserve the peace would be simply to stop all new weapons.

While Forsberg was producing the "Call" in Boston, another set of events established what became the basic organizing approach of the Freeze Campaign. Former anti-Vietnam War activist Randall Kehler and several associates at the Traprock Center in western Massachusetts launched a petition drive to get referenda calling for a nuclear

Movement," pp. 12–13, Case Study C14-83-557, written for the Case Program, John F. Kennedy School of Government, Harvard University, 1983.

3 [Randall Forsberg], "Call to Halt the Nuclear Arms Race: Proposal for a Mutual US–Soviet Nuclear Weapons Freeze," pamphlet, April 1982 (St. Louis: Nuclear Weapons Freeze Campaign, 1982), p. 1.

4 Ibid.

freeze placed on the 1980 ballot in three state senatorial districts. The referendum proved a smashing success. The freeze passed in fifty-nine of the sixty-two towns in which it was on the ballot, by an overall margin of 59 to 41 percent. Most significantly, of thirty-three towns that went for Ronald Reagan, thirty of them also approved the freeze. Seeing this outcome, activists decided that the Reagan administration's nuclear buildup could be successfully opposed. In March 1981, peace activists from around the country met at a National Freeze Conference in Washington, DC, in order to launch a national campaign. They took the western Massachusetts referenda campaign as a model for their organizing strategy and appointed Randy Kehler the first national coordinator of the Freeze Campaign.[5]

Besides the Freeze, other efforts arose, both more moderate and more radical. Some initiatives were purely educational, designed to increase public awareness of the nuclear danger. For example, one new organization, called Ground Zero (the technical term for the spot where a nuclear weapon explodes), sponsored a week of educational events in some 760 towns and cities in April 1982. Though not intended to be pro-freeze, these events produced a further surge in volunteers for the freeze movement.[6] At the other extreme, the most radical wing of the movement tried to take on the military-industrial complex directly. In a series of loosely related actions, activists engaged in civil disobedience at defense plants, tried to block Trident submarine launchings, and protested along the route of the government "white train" that carried nuclear warhead components. A small group of "Plowshares" activists even tried to disable nuclear missiles at their site of manufacture or in their silos.

Reagan policy baseline

Though the freeze movement began to take off before Ronald Reagan entered the White House, the policies of his administration became the movement's chief target. To show how much of a shift this

[5] Solo, *Protest to Policy*, p. 49; Douglas C. Waller, *Congress and the Nuclear Freeze: An Inside Look at the Politics of a Mass Movement* (Amherst: University of Massachusetts Press, 1987), p. 35; Leavitt, "Freezing the Arms Race: Genesis," pp. 22–24.

[6] Interview with Roger Molander, founder of Ground Zero (June 8, 1989); David S. Meyer, *A Winter of Discontent: The Nuclear Freeze and American Politics* (New York: Praeger, 1990), p. 184.

campaign brought about requires establishing a baseline of the administration's own intentions prior to the influence of the freeze. Fortunately, the basic outline of the administration's initial arms control policy is quite clear.[7] Arms control enjoyed very low priority at the general level, while at the specific level the chief objectives were to force cuts in Soviet land-based warheads while allowing US modernization programs to proceed.

To start with the general level, the administration saw no urgency in getting arms talks underway. For one thing, the president and his advisors felt it was a mistake to try to focus on too many issues at once. They gave top priority to domestic economic issues and a major defense buildup, and according to David Gergen, White House communications director until early 1984, "deliberately de-emphasized" everything else.[8] With respect to arms control, this meant that a military buildup took precedence over talks. Reagan and his aides argued that the SALT negotiations had allowed the Soviets to gain an advantage in land-based missiles with multiple warheads, creating a potential "window of vulnerability" to threats of a Soviet first strike. The administration felt that the USA would have to reverse this situation before entering new talks. In the words of Robert Linhard, senior director of arms control policy in the NSC, the administration

7 Most of the internal decisionmaking documents of the Reagan administration are not yet publicly available. I have thus relied on other sources of information. In spring 1989, I interviewed twenty-three government officials who worked on arms control under Reagan, representing all the relevant agencies (I also interviewed seven members of Congress and congressional staff, and people who worked for advocacy groups that concerned themselves with the freeze, either for or against).

Some officials asked that all or part of what they told me not be attributed to them by name. In these cases, I identify the source at most only by the agency in which the official worked. Despite the inconsistency that results, in order to allow others to verify my findings, I have attributed quotes by name when I had permission to do so. Any footnotes citing an interview without giving a name indicate that those comments were made on a not-for-attribution basis.

I have also drawn from contemporary press accounts of the period under study. While scholars often regard the mass media as a source of dubious quality, many former Reagan officials have described press reports on administration policymaking as generally reliable. See Alexander M. Haig, Jr., *Caveat: Realism, Reagan, and Foreign Policy* (New York: Macmillan Publishing Co., 1984), pp. 17–19; and Donald T. Regan, *For the Record* (New York: St. Martin's Press, 1988), pp. 280–83.

8 Interview with David Gergen (May 22, 1989). See also Martin Anderson, *Revolution: The Reagan Legacy*, rev. edn. (Stanford, CA: Hoover Institution Press, 1990), pp. 57, 283–84; Edwin Meese, *With Reagan* (Washington, DC: Regnery Gateway, 1992), p. 73.

"had a serious concept of negotiating from strength, which meant we had to pursue the military buildup first."[9]

Moreover, according to a source familiar with Pentagon deliberations, Defense Department officials believed that the United States "could outspend and out-tech" the Soviets on defense and thereby force internal reform on them. This strategy for dealing with the USSR would require delaying arms talks so as not to alleviate the pressure on the Soviet government, and was apparently shared by the president.[10] At the extreme, therefore, some officials like Defense Secretary Weinberger suggested that it might take eight years before the United States was ready to get serious about arms talks. Even if not all officials shared this timeline, given the administration's priorities, "no one in the new administration was too keen to get [arms negotiations] under way, at least before the Reagan economic program and military buildup were begun," observed Kenneth Adelman.[11]

At the specific level of policy, administration objectives followed from the proposition that there was an imbalance in counterforce capabilities favoring the Soviet Union, meaning that the chief goal was to get the Soviets to cut their ICBM warheads down to a level where they would be equal with American forces.[12] Developing an actual plan for achieving its objectives took a long time, however. Beyond the fact that the administration placed a military buildup ahead of arms negotiations, formulation of an arms control position also proceeded slowly because officials disagreed sharply about how to translate Reagan's specific-level objectives into an actual US offer. Reflecting the low priority given to arms talks, the administration initially placed responsibility for arms control policy at a relatively low level, in interagency groups chaired by officials at the assistant secretary level or below. Since no one department was given final authority over the interagency process, splits at these lower levels prevented progress in formulating an arms control plan. The main

[9] Interview with Robert Linhard (May 31, 1989).

[10] Interview by author; Meese, *With Reagan*, pp. 166–67.

[11] David Cortright, *Peace Works: The Citizen's Role in Ending the Cold War* (Boulder: Westview Press, 1993), p. 8; Kenneth L. Adelman, *The Great Universal Embrace: Arms Summitry – A Skeptic's Account* (New York: Simon and Schuster, 1989), p. 260. Adelman was an assistant to Jeanne Kirkpatrick at the UN at the time, and later became director of ACDA.

[12] For a sympathetic treatment of the administration's approach to strategic policy and arms control, see Adam M. Garfinkle, *The Politics of the Nuclear Freeze* (Philadelphia: Foreign Policy Research Institute, 1984), pp. 160–69.

split was between relatively moderate officials in the State Department, led by Richard Burt, and conservatives in the Office of the Secretary of Defense, who had Richard Perle as their chief spokesperson. The conservatives wanted the US proposal to cover only ballistic missile warheads initially, while the moderates argued that it would have to include other items where the United States had an advantage if the administration's proposals were to have a realistic chance of interesting the Soviet Union.[13]

Only when outside forces intervened did the administration overcome its internal divisions and move forward. This happened first in the area of intermediate-range nuclear forces (INF), where the administration inherited a commitment to a "dual track" policy adopted by NATO in 1979. One track, which fit well with Reagan's overall plans, involved developing cruise and Pershing II missiles to deploy in Europe as a response to recent Soviet deployments of a new missile, the SS-20. The other track, however, called for negotiations to limit INF weapons. After demonstrations against the planned new NATO weapons began sweeping Europe in 1981, European governments pressured the US government to make good on its inherited commitment to the arms control track, leading the administration reluctantly to open INF talks at the end of November.[14]

Until the development of equivalent pressures to reach closure on strategic arms control, disagreements at the Burt–Perle level and below created deadlock in the administration about what to propose in a strategic arms plan. Nor did the president intervene to force his system to move forward more quickly. According to Robert Dean, an aide to Burt at the State Department, "If Ronald Reagan had asked for an arms control proposal, he would have gotten it. But there was no leadership from the White House on [strategic] arms control." Reagan did not even get his first briefing on the various options being considered by his bureaucracy until late April 1982, fifteen months after he took office.[15]

When the United States finally announced its opening START offer

13 Strobe Talbott, *Deadly Gambits: The Reagan Administration and the Stalemate in Nuclear Arms Control* (New York: Vintage Books, 1985; Alfred A. Knopf, 1984).

14 Talbott, *Deadly Gambits*, chaps. 3–5; Richard C. Eichenberg, "Dual Track and Double Trouble: The Two-Level Politics of INF," in Peter B. Evans, Harold K. Jacobson, and Robert D. Putnam, eds., *Double-Edged Diplomacy: International Bargaining and Domestic Politics* (Berkeley: University of California Press, 1993).

15 Interview with Robert Dean (June 6, 1989); Talbott, *Deadly Gambits*, p. 248.

the following month, it was closer to the position favored by the Perle faction. The plan envisioned that arms control would proceed in two phases. The first phase would require the Soviet Union to make sharp cuts in their ballistic missile warheads, resulting in an equal ceiling for the two sides. The US proposal would not restrict planned American deployments of the new MX or Trident II ballistic missiles, designed to increase American counterforce capability, nor allow discussion of cruise missiles, a major Soviet concern, until a second phase of the talks.[16] This proposal certainly addressed the top American concern about the nuclear balance, but provided nothing that could give the Soviet Union an incentive to agree. In contrast to the test ban and SALT talks invitations, therefore, the initial START offer was not generally seen as signaling development of US willingness to co-operate. With arms restraint given low priority at the general level and an agenda at the specific level that seemed designed to frustrate progress, societal activism continued to grow.

Opinion disjunction develops

Administration rhetoric adds to problems

An opinion disjunction, the pre-condition for the electoral pathway, developed quickly once Reagan policies became clear. Besides the low priority they assigned to arms restraint, administration officials aroused public concern with a number of casual pronouncements about nuclear war. Perhaps the most infamous statement came from T. K. Jones, a deputy undersecretary of defense. Discussing the potential of civil defense, Jones told an interviewer, "Dig a hole, cover it with a couple of doors, and then throw three feet of dirt on top . . . It's the dirt that does it . . . [I]f there are enough shovels to go around, everybody's going to make it." Even the president himself added to public worries. Reagan told journalists in October 1981, "I could see where you could have the exchange of tactical weapons against troops in the field without bringing either one of the major powers to pushing the button."[17]

[16] Talbott, *Deadly Gambits*, chap. 14.

[17] Both quotes in Robert Scheer, *With Enough Shovels: Reagan, Bush, and Nuclear War*, updated edn. (New York: Vintage Books, 1983), back cover, p. 131. For other statements that worried critics, see Waller, *Congress and the Freeze*, p. 19; Solo, *Protest to Policy*, pp. 70–71.

Such statements made the administration's nuclear strategy appear especially ominous. Reagan officials believed that the Soviet Union was preparing to fight, if necessary, a nuclear war, in the belief that the USSR could survive and win such a war. To bolster deterrence, they thought that the USA should seek comparable capabilities for fighting at the nuclear level. As a Pentagon defense guidance leaked to the press in 1982 put it, "Should deterrence fail . . . the United States must prevail and be able to force the Soviet Union to seek earliest termination of hostilities on terms favorable to the United States."[18] Administration officials denied, with some justice, that their thinking about nuclear weapons was especially inconsistent with that of past administrations. Even though administration strategy involved less a significant break with the past than a further development of trends already underway,[19] what the public mostly responded to was the tone and higher public profile of US proclamations on nuclear strategy. What many people saw was an administration able to contemplate and plan a nuclear war in an entirely cold-blooded way.

When such rhetoric was added to the administration's apparent dismissal of arms control as a goal, this combination proved quite troubling to the American public. Evidence soon emerged of a divergence between majority public preferences and the administration's approach to nuclear arms. The difference was wide enough to create the potential for activism, through mechanism 1, to generate electoral incentives for a change in policy.

Evidence of opinion disjunction

The most direct evidence for this opinion disjunction comes from public opinion polls. The percentage believing that the United States should "get tough" with the USSR dropped from 74 percent in January 1980 to 40 percent by May 1982. More directly, when asked whether the administration's arms limitation effort was adequate, in five separate surveys in 1982 and 1983, either a plurality or an outright majority always said no. And in July 1983, 68 percent said the administration was "going too far" in its buildup of nuclear

[18] *NYT*, May 30, 1982, p. 1.

[19] Robert W. Tucker, "The Nuclear Debate," *Foreign Affairs* 63 (Fall 1984), pp. 1–32; Scott D. Sagan, *Moving Targets: Nuclear Strategy and National Security* (Princeton: Princeton University Press, 1989), chap. 1.

weapons.[20] These polls are a clear sign of divergence between public preferences and the administration's approach, meaning that the precondition for activating the electoral pathway was present.

To engage mechanism 1, however, it is also necessary for activism to interact with this broader current in public opinion. One significant indication of such interaction is a focus in opinion polls on the freeze itself. Between 1981 and 1984, all the major polling operations asked about public support for a nuclear freeze. Moreover, the freeze was just the tip of the iceberg. In fact, in 1982, survey takers asked far more questions about nuclear issues in general than they had in any year since the nuclear age began. Why did pollsters decide to focus on the public's feelings about nuclear arms issues? During the decade of SALT negotiations, when arms control was a subject of high-level government attention and serious elite-level debates, survey organizations asked fewer questions about arms control than they did after the Reagan administration came into office and put arms control on the back burner. No crisis or other world event suddenly put nuclear weapons in the spotlight, and the freeze was not a proposal made by the US government or some other world leader. Hence, pollsters' sudden interest can only be due to the rise of activism on behalf of a freeze. Indeed, before the formation of the Freeze Campaign, survey organizations had never queried the public about whether they would support a freeze.[21]

Just as importantly, surveys also consistently showed large majorities in favor of the freeze proposal. After autumn 1983, in fact, the polls rarely found less than 80 percent approval for a bilateral nuclear freeze. Even when asked to compare the freeze directly with the administration's basic approach, a sizable majority preferred a freeze. In a *New York Times*/CBS poll in April 1983, the public in fact preferred seeking an immediate freeze by a 64–25 margin over building up US forces in order to stimulate reductions.[22] This pattern

[20] Robert Y. Shapiro and Benjamin I. Page, "Foreign Policy and the Rational Public," *Journal of Conflict Resolution* 32 (June 1988), p. 243; Leavitt, "Freezing the Arms Race: Public Opinion" (supplement), p. 4, written for the Case Program, Kennedy School of Government, 1983.

[21] Bernard M. Kramer, S. Michael Kalick, and Michael A. Milburn, "Attitudes Toward Nuclear Weapons and Nuclear War, 1945–1982," *Journal of Social Issues* 39 (1983), pp. 9–11, 14.

[22] Michael A. Milburn, Paul Y. Watanabe, and Bernard M. Kramer, "The Nature and Sources of Attitudes Toward a Nuclear Freeze," *Political Psychology* 7 (December 1986), p. 664; *NYT*, April 15, 1983, p. 1.

of survey data clearly indicates that activist efforts were interacting with concern in the wider public, as required to engage the electoral pathway.

Support for the freeze, however, did prove sensitive to changes in question wording. Approval of the freeze fell dramatically if the question specified that a freeze would leave the Soviet Union ahead, that it would be a unilateral US action, or that Soviet cheating could not be detected.[23] This suggests the high public approval in other formats was not primarily a product of attraction specifically to the nuclear freeze proposal. Instead, it indicates that the freeze gained support mainly by tapping into unease at the general level about the nuclear arms race and how the Reagan administration was handling it. Indeed, in a survey that asked respondents about their reasons for favoring or opposing a freeze, by far the majority of freeze supporters cited fear of nuclear war or concern for the future of their children or grandchildren, i.e., worries in general rather than attributes of the freeze idea itself.[24]

The extent of concern at the general level is indicated by a 1984 Gallup survey, in which 25 percent named nuclear weapons and the arms race the most important problem facing the country, a greater number than selected any other issue. This contrasted sharply with the period from 1973 to 1979, when defense and foreign policy issues as a whole were rarely cited by more than 10 percent of the public. The combination in public opinion of a high level of concern and a clear differentiation between the freeze and the administration's approach means that nuclear arms control had achieved the conditions under which issue voting is likely.[25]

Beyond survey data, the speed with which anti-nuclear weapons

Similarly, in a 1984 Public Agenda Foundation survey, 62 percent rejected building more dangerous nuclear weapons to get the Soviet Union to make concessions on arms control, the approach advocated by the Reagan administration, while only 31 percent favored this approach (Daniel Yankelovich and John Doble, "The Public Mood: Nuclear Weapons and the USSR," *Foreign Affairs* 63 [Fall 1984], p. 44).

23 Support dropped off most sharply when the question specified that cheating could not be detected. Under these circumstances, only 18 percent still favored a freeze while 71 percent now rejected the idea (*NYT*, May 30, 1982, pp. 1, 22).

24 Milburn et al., "Nature and Sources," p. 670.

25 John H. Aldrich, John L. Sullivan, and Eugene Borgida, "Foreign Affairs and Issue Voting: Do Presidential Candidates 'Waltz Before a Blind Audience?,'" *American Political Science Review* 83 (March 1989), pp. 123–41, esp. 129–31.

protest grew and spread is further evidence of the two requirements for engaging mechanism 1: opinion disjunction and interaction between activism and public opinion. Repeated victories at the polls provide one additional sign of public attraction to the Freeze Campaign's message. In the autumn 1982 elections, voters approved freeze referenda in eight of nine states and thirty-six of thirty-eight cities and counties where they were on the ballot. The freeze also became the focal point of the largest political demonstration in American history. Between 700,000 and 1,000,000 Americans (depending on whose estimate one accepts) converged on New York's Central Park for a rally on June 12, 1982, most drawn by the demonstration's call for a freeze.[26]

The creation and growth of support for other organizations besides the Freeze provides yet another indicator of disjunction and interaction. First, activists launched many new groups with the idea of reaching out to and mobilizing some constituency in public opinion, such as women or business executives. In particular, a number of occupation-specific organizations modeled on PSR sprang up, such as the Lawyers' Alliance for Nuclear Arms Control, Educators for Social Responsibility, and High-Tech Professionals for Peace. Second, many existing public interest groups also decided for the first time to address nuclear weapons issues, including the nation's largest public interest group, Common Cause.[27] Finally, established arms control groups also saw their memberships increase as much as ten-fold.[28] The fact that activism grew so much across the board in the early 1980s again suggests that the movement took off more because it was tapping into concern about Reagan's views on the appropriate balance between buildup and restraint than because of the technical merits of the freeze idea itself.

[26] Waller, *Congress and the Freeze*, pp. 107–08, 164–65; Leavitt, "Freezing the Arms Race: The Campaign in Washington" (supplement), p. 4.

[27] Leavitt, "Freezing the Arms Race: Genesis," pp. 30–31; Daniel Wirls, *Buildup: The Politics of Defense in the Reagan Era* (Ithaca: Cornell University Press, 1992), pp. 72–74.

[28] The Center for Defense Information's mailing list grew from 14,000 at the beginning of 1981 to 105,000 five years later (interview with Eugene Carroll, deputy director, Center for Defense Information, May 10, 1989). Membership in CLW similarly increased, from roughly 7,500 in 1979 to between 80,000 and 100,000 at its peak (interview with John Isaacs, legislative director, CLW, May 12, 1989). And SANE saw its membership quadruple, to 80,000, between 1980 and 1984 (Wirls, *Buildup*, p. 73).

Activism communicates a general-level message

This was apparent also in the message communicated by advocacy groups, which mostly emphasized desire for change in the general direction of US policy. Even the Freeze Campaign, which sought change at the specific level of arms control policy to favor the freeze proposal, also explicitly played to the opinion disjunction between the administration and the public. The basic slogan of the Freeze, found on brochures and bumper stickers produced by the Campaign, said simply, "The Freeze: Because Nobody Wants a Nuclear War." The messages of other advocacy groups also tended to emphasize the general feeling that President Reagan was not doing enough to avoid precipitating nuclear war, rather than substantive aspects of the freeze proposal itself. For example, a Common Cause solicitation for donations to support work on the freeze and disarmament said that the group's aim was to raise the subject of the nuclear arms race to the top of the national agenda.[29]

Worries at the general level are also what official Washington perceived as being behind popular support for the freeze. Congressional staffer Bob Sherman, who was active in maneuvering the freeze through the House, argues that support for the freeze in public opinion polls "was really for nuclear restraint, a black box with a label 'nuclear restraint' but no specific content." Administration officials had a similar reading. Thomas Graham, who handled public affairs for the Arms Control and Disarmament Agency in the early 1980s, reported that in ACDA's analysis the freeze movement "represented peoples' fear, not desire for that proposal *per se*." In short, to politicians, the freeze movement served to dramatize a feeling among much of the US public that pursuit of arms control should have a higher place on the national agenda than it was being accorded by the Reagan administration.[30]

Elite concerns reinforce general-level pressures

Many of the general-level issues motivating public support for the freeze were also a concern to members of the liberal foreign policy

[29] Frances B. McCrea and Gerald E. Markle, *Minutes to Midnight: Nuclear Weapons Protest in America* (Newbury Park, CA: Sage Publications, 1989), p. 110.

[30] Interview with Bob Sherman (May 12, 1989); interview with Thomas Graham (May 10, 1989).

establishment, who came to see the citizens' campaign as a potential ally in altering Reagan arms policy. Indications that important segments of the elite disapproved of the administration's approach to arms control began proliferating in early 1982. Two articles published then drew particular attention: a Jonathan Schell series in the *New Yorker*, later released as a book, suggesting that "The Fate of the Earth" now hung in the balance; and a piece in *Foreign Affairs* by four former high-ranking national security officials – Robert McNamara, McGeorge Bundy, George Kennan, and Gerard Smith – that called on the United States to adopt a policy of "no first use" with regard to nuclear arms.[31]

Many Democratic politicians also came to see the freeze as one of their best hopes for defeating President Reagan or other members of his party at the polls. For all these reasons, Dan Wirls observes, the whole left–liberal "new politics" coalition ultimately rallied around the freeze as the most promising vehicle available by which they might rebuild themselves into a force that could wrest power from Reagan's conservative coalition.[32] When popular activism and the efforts of political elites began interacting, this engaged mechanism 2, the coalition-shift pathway. Because most elites were motivated by desire to reverse Reagan's apparent dismissal of arms control as an objective, rather than by strong support for the freeze proposal itself, the elite pathway came into operation at the general level, reinforcing the pressures generated by the electoral pathway.

The single most important step in this process was the response of Congress. In March 1982, Senators Edward Kennedy (D-MA) and Mark Hatfield (R-OR) introduced a bill calling for superpower negotiations to establish a freeze, with House sponsorship by Edward Markey (D-MA), Jonathan Bingham (D-NY), and Silvio Conte (R-MA). From the outset, the actions of Congress reflected a mix of both mechanisms 1 and 2.

Mechanism 1, the electoral pathway, created the promise of significant benefits to those politicians who could first get themselves identified with the freeze. This helped trigger the initial decisions by Kennedy and Markey to sponsor a freeze bill. Kennedy was considering another run for the presidency in 1984. Insiders suggest that the

31 Jonathan Schell, *The Fate of the Earth* (New York: Alfred A. Knopf, 1982); McGeorge Bundy, George F. Kennan, Robert S. McNamara, and Gerard Smith, "Nuclear Weapons and the Atlantic Alliance," *Foreign Affairs* 60 (Spring 1982), pp. 753–68.

32 Wirls, *Buildup*.

senator was attracted to the freeze because it was a new national cause, appropriate to his reputation as a leading liberal, that he could champion. Similarly, Douglas Waller, a former legislative assistant in Markey's office, relates how the congressman's administrative assistant, Peter Franchot, convinced them to introduce freeze legislation: "'The freeze is going to sweep the country,' he told us time and again in those early days. 'I can feel it in my bones. And there's no reason why we shouldn't be in the middle of it.'"[33]

Because many other members of Congress also shared the public's concerns about the general direction of Reagan arms policy, however, the electoral pathway was not the only mechanism that operated in the congressional debate. Many members became interested in using the legislative process to pull US policy back to a more centrist position on the arms buildup versus arms restraint spectrum. They began to see working with public advocacy groups to promote freeze legislation as the best way to pressure the administration to make this policy change, bringing mechanism 2, the elite coalition-shift pathway, into action as well.

Using the freeze to pressure Reagan

Most legislators did not share the specific-level objectives of the Freeze Campaign, however, so not all of those desiring to act on arms control immediately rallied around the freeze. Many members introduced their own personal arms control resolutions instead. By the end of 1982, over thirty arms control resolutions had been introduced in Congress. Among Democratic leaders in the House, initial interest focused especially on ideas for salvaging SALT II.[34] But SALT II and all of the other resolutions introduced suffered from one important flaw. They did not have the same grassroots backing as the freeze. As a result, many foreign policy elites who objected to Reagan's arms policies came to see working with the Freeze and its public interest

33 Interviews; Wirls, *Buildup*, pp. 102–03; Waller, *Congress and the Freeze*, p. 47.

The fact that initial sponsors like Markey and Kennedy were convinced that they could gain significant benefits does not mean they acted out of cynicism. Unless they were martyrs, congressional freeze supporters could not risk taking up the proposal unless they knew they had the electoral security to become active on such a sensitive national security issue.

34 Waller, *Congress and the Freeze*, pp. 86–89, 113; Edward F. Feighan, "The Freeze in Congress," in Paul M. Cole and William J. Taylor, eds., *The Nuclear Freeze Debate: Arms Control Issues for the 1980s* (Boulder: Westview Press, 1983), p. 33.

group allies as the best way to get the administration to restore the emphasis given to arms control by its predecessors. Thus, many former government officials and other prominent national figures endorsed the Kennedy–Hatfield freeze resolution. In terms of ability to legitimate the freeze for moderates and conservatives, former CIA director William Colby was probably the most important of these "defectors" to the freeze cause.[35]

As the freeze movement continued to gain grassroots momentum and elite endorsements, more and more members of Congress also decided to rally around the freeze, bringing mechanism 2 into play. In mid-1982, for example, House Foreign Affairs Committee Chairman Clem Zablocki (D-WI) and other prominent Democratic representatives, including Les Aspin (D-WI) and Al Gore (D-TN), decided to stop promoting other alternatives they had initially favored. They all signed on as co-sponsors of the freeze instead. As all the other proposals that had been made dropped out of sight, *Congressional Digest* labeled the freeze the "current vehicle for debate over nuclear weapons policy."[36]

Despite the initiating role of Senators Kennedy and Hatfield, it early on became clear that the freeze would face an uphill climb in the Republican-controlled Senate. The chances for victory, while by no means certain, appeared better in the House. But the House had not traditionally played a role in arms control matters. To promote a freeze, therefore, required the House to become active in a new area. Pressures being generated through the electoral and elite pathways thus caused an evolution in the House's role on arms control. After extensive interviews with members of Congress and congressional staff, Barry Blechman concluded:

> As the antinuclear tide grew stronger in 1982 and 1983, politicians, especially Democrats, many of whom shared their constituents' concerns, also began to see personal rewards in associating themselves with the cause. Political incentives favoring arms control operated at two related levels. On the national level, the nuclear issue appeared to be one of Ronald Reagan's two vulnerabilities (the other being the economic recession) . . . On the state and local level, the antinuclear movement appeared to have a direct effect on candidates' electoral prospects . . . The new participation of the

[35] Waller, *Congress and the Freeze*, p. 67; interview with Chris Paine, staffer for FAS and Senator Kennedy (June 6, 1989).

[36] Waller, *Congress and the Freeze*, pp. 123–24, 130–35; Meyer, *Winter of Discontent*, p. 227.

> House of Representatives in arms control issues . . . is the direct result of these considerations.[37]

In short, a combination of electoral and elite concerns made many legislators interested in working with the freeze. This brought about operation of mechanism 2, in this case at the general level of policy rather than the specific. Instead of seeking to impose an immediate, across-the-board halt on all nuclear activities, many congressional sponsors wanted to use the freeze as a tool to prod Reagan into doing more about controlling the arms race. Thus, in urging his colleagues to vote for the freeze during floor debate in August 1982, Aspin argued, "If we had a President who was genuinely interested in arms control, perhaps [the freeze resolution] would not be necessary. If we had a President . . . who would negotiate in good faith . . . we would need no resolution at all." Even some of the freeze's strongest supporters saw the resolution as chiefly symbolic. Senator Hatfield says he felt that "the geo-politics of US–Soviet relations called for some kind of . . . a pause, a breather [in the arms race] . . . We needed to cool the environment . . . and let the diplomats come up with a plan." To do this, he noted, "we had to have a rallying point, a vehicle for public feelings."[38]

The fact that both influence mechanisms operating in the congressional debate involved pressure to change the general direction of policy, rather than to impose a specific ordering on the arms control agenda, affected the form that the freeze resolution took. The Kennedy–Hatfield bill, as it went through a series of modifications, never took a form that could legally compel the president to offer a freeze to the Soviet Union. It was hence largely symbolic.[39]

[37] Barry M. Blechman, "The New Congressional Role in Arms Control," in Thomas E. Mann, ed., *A Question of Balance: The President, the Congress, and Foreign Policy* (Washington, DC: The Brookings Institution, 1990), pp. 137–38.

Bob Huber of the House Foreign Affairs Committee staff concurs that "House votes repudiating administration arms control policy wouldn't have been possible without the freeze." The freeze, Huber says, "made national security policy and debates about it legitimate business for the Hill, [which] it wasn't before" (interview by author, June 6, 1989).

[38] Aspin quoted in Waller, *Congress and the Freeze*, p. 153; interview with Mark Hatfield (June 16, 1989).

[39] Specifically, freeze sponsors introduced a joint resolution, which if passed by both chambers is sent to the president's desk for his signature into law. This gave it more teeth than a concurrent resolution, which merely expresses the sense of Congress, because passage of a joint resolution could force a presidential veto. Nonetheless, the

Freeze passes despite countermobilization

Its symbolic nature notwithstanding, top administration officials took a combative stance toward the freeze resolution. In doing so, they suggested that the non-binding measure would be taken as a vote of confidence in the administration's existing course on arms issues. This also meant the proposal would not be allowed to sail through Congress without opposition. Secretary of State Al Haig set the tone for the administration on the very day Kennedy and Hatfield introduced their freeze resolution. Appearing at a Senate hearing, Haig said the freeze was "not only bad defense and security policy, it's bad arms control policy as well." Administration officials stressed two arguments against a freeze. First, they argued that it would, as one Reagan letter to Congress put it, leave "dangerous asymmetries in the nuclear balance." Secondly, they asserted that passage of the resolution would undercut the US position in arms negotiations by removing any incentive for the USSR to negotiate.[40]

On the first point, freeze advocates contended that existing numerical imbalances were not sufficient to take the superpowers' arsenals out of a condition of rough parity, so that it would actually be more dangerous to allow continued development and deployment of highly accurate new weapons. As for the second argument, according to Markey aide Douglas Waller, "because the Reagan plan was so lopsidedly stacked against the Soviets many congressmen privately felt there were no negotiations to undercut."[41]

Neither side expected the freeze to win the first time the House voted on it. However, constituent pressure was sufficiently high that many members of the president's party wanted to vote for the resolution as long as their vote would not affect the outcome. As a result, Republicans had to convince two of their number to switch their votes at the last second to prevent their substitute measure, which endorsed the president's approach, from losing to the freeze. The final vote, on August 5, 1982, sustained the president's position by just 204 to 202.[42] Given this close vote, passage the following year seemed assured after the Democrats picked up twenty-six seats in the

bill was purely advisory, stating that the president "should," rather than "shall," make a freeze his goal.

40 Waller, *Congress and the Freeze*, pp. 76, 139; Feighan, "Freeze in Congress," p. 36.

41 Waller, *Congress and the Freeze*, p. 140.

42 Ibid., pp. 157–58; Feighan, "Freeze in Congress," p. 39.

House in the November election. But countermobilization by freeze opponents made progress for the freeze resolution difficult in 1983. The most important opposition came from within Congress, but the administration and conservative advocacy groups also helped slow down the freeze movement's momentum.

Studies of interest groups and foreign policy have stressed the balance of groups on the two sides of an issue as an important determinant of influence.[43] The freeze coalition initially had the field to itself, as the rapidity with which the movement grew took interest groups on the other side of the issue by surprise. Only in late 1982 did pro-defense advocacy groups decide that they should do something to check the momentum of the freeze. Overall, though, their impact was limited. Those who worked against the freeze generally agreed that conservative interest groups lacked much influence because they "got onto the issue late and were not effectively organized nationwide." The one development for which conservative groups take credit is stimulating an amendment by Rep. Mark Siljander (R-MI) that first revealed softness in congressional support for the freeze resolution.[44] Among societal actors, though, the balance still remained clearly favorable to the freeze, if not as exclusively as the year before.

Adding to the opposition in 1983, however, the administration also "went all out to defeat the freeze in the House." President Reagan reportedly even threatened some Republicans that if they voted for the freeze he would not support them in their next re-election campaign. Reagan also invited groups of undecided members from both parties to the White House for what presidential spokesman Larry Speakes referred to in one case as an "arm-twisting" session.

43 Mitchell Geoffrey Bard, "The Influence of Ethnic Interest Groups on American Middle East Policy," in Eugene R. Wittkopf, ed., *The Domestic Sources of American Foreign Policy*, 2nd edn. (New York: St. Martin's Press, 1994); David Skidmore, "The Politics of National Security Policy: Interest Groups, Coalitions, and the SALT II Debate," in Skidmore and Valerie M. Hudson, eds., *The Limits of State Autonomy* (Boulder: Westview Press, 1993).

44 Congressional and administration interviews by author (the quote is from an administration official); interview with Don Todd, executive director of the American Conservative Union (June 7, 1989); interview with Paul Weyrich, chairperson of the Stanton Group, an umbrella group for conservative interest group efforts on defense (June 23, 1989).

The Siljander amendment would have given Reagan the option of a freeze or reductions, which was taken to be a buzzword for his existing START proposal. The amendment fell short of passing by a mere six votes, a much narrower margin of solid support for the freeze than its sponsors thought they had.

And Reagan sought to sway the public at large, denouncing the freeze proposal in three different major speeches during the month of March.[45]

However, the most troublesome opposition for the freeze came from the measure's opponents in Congress itself. They offered amendment after amendment to the freeze resolution in an attempt to wear down its supporters. Freeze sponsors accepted those they thought were harmless, and successfully neutralized or defeated all but one of those they opposed, an amendment proposed by Elliot Levitas (D-GA). The Levitas amendment said that a freeze should be followed by reductions "within a reasonable, specified period of time," implying that the United States could call off a freeze if reductions did not soon follow.[46]

Support for the freeze still proved stronger than the opposition, however, as the House passed the final freeze resolution on May 4, 1983, by 278 to 149. Though the bill was much amended, according to Reuben McCornack, the chief lobbyist for the Freeze Campaign, "the nut of the freeze was preserved."[47] Most importantly, the resolution preserved the sequence that held that a freeze should be the first priority in arms talks and a prelude to reductions, rather than allowing Reagan the option to pursue his existing reductions plan first. The final bill also called for a comprehensive freeze, with no nuclear weapons systems exempted. In fact, the Reagan administration still criticized the amended freeze resolution, indicating that it still saw the final bill as a vote against administration policy.[48]

The sizable margin of victory, which included sixty Republicans, thus reflects the amount of constituent pressure the freeze movement brought to bear. McCornack reports, "The Campaign could get 200 calls to a member of Congress in twenty-four hours. This made the difference in a lot of cases." Administration officials also acknowledge that electoral pressure was the main reason many members of Congress voted for the freeze. An administration official who lobbied against the freeze said a leading House sponsor told him the bill would pass because "'there aren't 535 profiles in courage in Con-

[45] Interviews with administration officials; Feighan, "Freeze in Congress," p. 47; *NYT*, March 16, 1983, p. 23; April 13, 1983, p. 21; *Washington Post*, April 13, 1983, p. 3.

[46] Waller, *Congress and the Freeze*, chaps. 7–8.

[47] Interview with Reuben McCornack (June 16, 1989). For a contrasting view, see Meyer, *Winter of Discontent*, pp. 230–31.

[48] Waller, *Congress and the Freeze*, p. 286.

gress.''' This aide added, "I had probably fifty conversations with members of Congress. They'd . . . say they had to vote for it or get creamed on Main Street."[49] Despite the opposition's efforts, therefore, a combination of public pressure and coalition-building between activists and elites, i.e., of mechanisms 1 and 2, prompted the House to signal to the administration its support for the freeze movement's interest in seeing more done to end the arms race.

While the freeze won the House debate in terms of the final vote outcome, it was still a mixed outcome for the movement as a whole. Since the bill would not itself actually halt the arms race, the fact the battle in the House went on much longer than had been expected drained a lot of the movement's momentum. Many activists were further demoralized when, only a few weeks later, the House voted to approve funding for the MX missile.[50] Finally, the Freeze Campaign and other arms control groups that worked on the resolution had never developed an agreed strategy for where to go after the House vote, meaning that their efforts diffused considerably once the resolution passed. For all these reasons, the freeze movement achieved no more victories in Congress over the next couple of years.

Policy impact of the freeze

For activists, though, moving legislation through Congress was not a goal in itself. It was a means to an end – changing US policy. And, in response to the general-level pressures generated through the electoral and elite coalition-shift pathways, the Reagan administration made policy changes of exactly the sort expected with these mechanisms. First, the administration got START talks underway and then sought to make progress in these talks. Second, the administration toned down and eventually reversed the thrust of its rhetoric about nuclear war. Taken together, these shifts indicate an increase in the priority assigned to arms restraint as a national objective.

49 Interview with Reuben McCornack (June 16, 1989); interview with administration official.

50 Freeze activists especially felt betrayed by freeze resolution supporters who then voted for the MX. However, congressional freeze sponsors had repeatedly argued during the debate in Congress that, because the proposal was bilateral, nothing would be frozen until both sides agreed to freeze. Until a freeze was in place, then, there was nothing strictly contradictory about supporting the freeze resolution and also voting for the MX. Since grassroots activists thought differently, though, the MX vote reduced their willingness to rely on Congress.

Pressures felt by the administration

The administration came to realize that it had problems with both constituent opinion and congressional opposition. As mechanism 1 requires, interaction between the freeze movement and public opinion made arms control and US–Soviet relations into significant enough issues that key officials felt that the administration could potentially be hurt by them electorally. Indeed, the freeze emerged as a major issue in the 1982 congressional mid-term election. Rep. Edward Feighan (D-OH) observed, "On every talk show, and in every forum in which candidates sought to get their message across, they [found they] had to have a position on the nuclear weapons freeze." In a Harris poll, 56 percent of the voters that year even said that they would vote against any congressional candidate who did not support a freeze.[51]

The freeze remained important into the next electoral campaign. In spring 1984, pollster Peter Hart concluded that the freeze was the one issue that might induce Reagan supporters to split their ticket and vote for a Democratic congressional candidate that autumn, as he found most voters still felt that the president had not done enough on arms control. Democratic presidential hopefuls that year also embraced the freeze. In fact, the freeze movement succeeded in making support for arms control a prerequisite for success in the 1984 Democratic primary race, and also in making support for the freeze itself the litmus test of such support. Seven of the eight Democrats running for their party's presidential nomination thus endorsed a nuclear freeze, including the two front-runners. At one point, eventual nominee Walter Mondale even tried to hold off the rising challenge of Gary Hart by accusing him, not of opposing the freeze, but only of endorsing the proposal later than Mondale had.[52]

The Reagan White House watched these developments closely. Public affairs director Michael Baroody reports, "There was growing awareness in the White House of the nuclear issue, particularly the nuclear freeze question." As a result, during Reagan's first few years in office, David Gergen says, White House staff asked Reagan's pollster, Richard Wirthlin, for "lots and lots" of surveys on domestic arms control opinion. Even the president felt concern. According to

51 Feighan, "Freeze in Congress," p. 29; Meyer, *Winter of Discontent*, p. 88.

52 Garfinkle, *Politics of the Freeze*, p. 219; Cortright, *Peace Works*, p. 82; Waller, *Congress and the Freeze*, p. 295.

Strobe Talbott, Reagan frequently commented to his aides during the freeze movement's rise that they could not afford to subject themselves to the charge that they weren't "serious about wanting an agreement." Going into the 1984 campaign, Reagan's closest political advisor, Michael Deaver, likewise felt that the nuclear issue was a "big negative" and that Reagan was "vulnerable on war and peace issues."[53]

In contrast, a number of other administration officials I interviewed denied that they had any worries the freeze might cost them the 1984 election. Many of these officials cited as the reason they lacked concern, however, polls in autumn 1984 which indicated that the arms control issue would not cost Reagan votes. As I will explain below, these poll results reflected adjustments the administration had already made in response to public pressure, so that a lack of worry as of autumn 1984 does not mean that the freeze failed to generate electoral pressure on the administration.[54] In other words, by signaling the possibility of electoral consequences, the freeze got forward-looking administration officials to press for action on arms control before matters could get sufficiently out of hand to put Reagan's re-election in doubt.

It was not only the loss of support in the opinion polls that got the administration to begin this adjustment process. The taking up by Congress of the freeze created even greater pressures on the administration to respond to anti-nuclear weapons activism. If Congress passed a freeze resolution, many officials felt, it might create an impression that Congress could vote against Reagan's defense programs with impunity or lessen administration leverage to extract arms concessions from the USSR. Thus, Thomas Graham reported, "there was a lot of consternation in ACDA over . . . the danger of the

[53] Baroody and Deaver interviews in Cortright, *Peace Works*, p. 90; interview with David Gergen (May 22, 1989); Talbott, *Deadly Gambits*, p. 267.

In interviews I conducted, administration officials who admit at least some worry that the arms control issue could hurt Reagan in 1984 include David Gergen; Fred Ikle, the undersecretary of defense for policy (phone interview, May 17, 1989); and Thomas Graham of ACDA.

[54] It is true though that the freeze failed to bring about any national swing in congressional outcomes or the defeat of President Reagan. But there is evidence that the freeze helped determine the outcome of a number of individual congressional races in 1982 and 1984 (see Feighan, "Freeze in Congress," p. 41; Waller, *Congress and the Freeze*, pp. 165, 296–97; Carla B. Johnston, *Reversing the Nuclear Arms Race* [Cambridge, MA: Schenkman Books, 1986], pp. 122, 131–32).

wrong resolution from Congress." A State Department official said that he and his colleagues worried in particular about whether the freeze would have spillover effects on "congressional funding of the strategic modernization program." White House Communications Director David Gergen summed up these concerns, declaring that "there was a widespread view in the administration that the freeze was a dagger pointed at the heart of the administration's defense program."[55]

In short, both electoral incentives and coalition dynamics triggered by the freeze created pressure on the administration to make changes at the general level of policy. As one would expect, therefore, the Reagan administration began trying to move forward more quickly in arms control and changed its public description of its goals to give greater emphasis to disarmament.

Shifts in policy

The freeze speeds things up

As one reaction to activism, the administration increased the priority attached to achieving progress on arms control. The administration had no desire to propose a freeze. But by early 1982 administration officials realized they had to be seen to be doing something on arms control. First and foremost, this required developing a proposal of their own and getting talks underway.

As the policy baseline section indicated, in its first year in office the administration did all it could to delay talks as long as possible. For example, in their first two meetings with Reagan's first secretary of state, Al Haig, Soviet diplomats asked the United States to resume arms talks. These requests were turned down.[56] Thus, entering its second year in office, the only decision the administration had made on strategic arms control was on a name for the effort, START, for Strategic Arms Reductions Talks.[57] On substance, though, there was

[55] Interview with Thomas Graham (May 10, 1989); interview with State Department official; interview with David Gergen (May 22, 1989).

[56] Haig, *Caveat*, pp. 104–08.

[57] The name was adopted because President Reagan liked the emphasis it gave to achieving reductions rather than mere limitations, as well as the acronym's connotation that the administration's approach represented a new start. These were both ways to differentiate the effort from SALT, which the administration had condemned (Talbott, *Deadly Gambits*, pp. 222–23).

still no agreed position on what the administration should propose, let alone when its opening START proposal should be offered.

Moreover, there was little push within the administration to resolve the remaining bureaucratic disagreements and get a final proposal on the table. The freeze provided that push. Robert McFarlane, as a deputy in the NSC, decided in early 1982 that it was necessary to "blast apart the logjam in the bureaucracy." McFarlane and National Security Advisor William Clark thus engineered an NSC directive at the end of February that gave the rest of the executive branch two months to complete work on a START proposal. McFarlane explained, "I felt the President was vulnerable to allied pressures to take a bad position, or Congress would impose one, if the administration did not develop a position of its own." And domestic pressure arising from the freeze gave him grounds to rein in centrifugal forces in the bureaucracy, he said.[58]

Other highly placed officials concur that the freeze movement brought "some pressure on the administration to get back into a dialogue with the Soviet Union. It might have taken longer otherwise." Further confirmation comes from background briefings given shortly before Reagan first invited the Soviet Union to begin START talks and announced his opening proposal, in a May 1982 speech at his alma mater, Eureka College. At that time, the *New York Times* reported that "The administration's main concern, according to the officials [present at an NSC meeting to discuss START], is to go on record quickly with a simple and comprehensible plan to show that the Reagan team is for peace, thus taking some of the steam out of the nuclear freeze movements in Europe and the United States."[59] Even Defense Secretary Caspar Weinberger has also since acknowledged that pressures generated by the freeze had at least "something" to do with the timing of the decision to open START talks.[60]

After the Soviet Union accepted Reagan's invitation to begin START talks, negotiations got underway in Geneva on June 29. The story does

58 Ibid., p. 247; interview with Robert McFarlane (June 1, 1989).

59 In other discussions with reporters, senior administration officials "described the speech, as well as several others the President [was] planning to make in the next few weeks, as an effort to turn public attention away from the antinuclear movements in the United States and Western Europe." *NYT*, May 2, 1982, p. 16; May 8, 1982, p. 7.

60 Interview with administration official; Weinberger interview in Cortright, *Peace Works*, pp. 104–05. Tom Graham of ACDA also said that the freeze movement "helped propel the US into negotiations somewhat earlier than we otherwise would have entered them" (interview by author, May 10, 1989).

not end here, however. In the test ban and SALT cases, there was little doubt that, when they entered the talks, the Eisenhower and Nixon administrations really wanted an agreement to result. This had the effect, especially in the test ban case, of shifting citizen activism from a demand to a support role. No such shift occurred in this case. Because the initial US START offer asked the Soviets to make deep cuts in their most advanced ICBMs, while offering almost nothing in return, critics thought Reagan's opening proposal was designed solely to prevent agreement. Freeze coordinator Randy Kehler thus charged, "The Reagan negotiations are simply smoke screens for achieving military superiority over the Soviet Union."[61] As indicated above, congressional freeze sponsors also doubted the Reagan administration was serious about a START deal. The start of negotiations thus did nothing to slow the activism on behalf of a freeze.

Beyond getting the administration to enter strategic arms control negotiations earlier than it had planned, therefore, the freeze movement also made it necessary for the administration to keep moving forward. Assessing the impact of the freeze overall, McFarlane believes that "it accelerated the pace" of government arms control policymaking. David Gergen gives a similar assessment, saying "The peace movement accelerated the move towards an agreement, [and] prodded the administration to act more swiftly . . . I know all of us felt we had to move [on arms control]."[62]

Because continuing deadlock at lower levels made reaching decisions about how to move forward very difficult, White House officials became ever more involved in making arms control policy. Chief of Staff James Baker now began to put his input into NSC meetings at which arms control was discussed. As David Gergen describes it, "Baker's would be the voice saying we've got a domestic political problem as well as a problem with the Soviets on this, and . . . we need a substantive idea of our own." According to Strobe Talbott, "Baker was particularly worried in the face of the pro-freeze movement" that sticking to a highly inflexible approach would land the president in trouble by creating a START proposal that failed to be "reasonable-looking."[63]

[61] Quoted in Garfinkle, *Politics of the Freeze*, p. 173.

[62] Interview with Robert McFarlane (June 1, 1989); interview with David Gergen (June 21, 1989).

[63] Interview with David Gergen (June 21, 1989); Talbott, *Deadly Gambits*, p. 267.

Those with substantive responsibilities did not always appreciate this pressure

In July 1983, the administration formally assigned responsibility for arms control policy to a new committee chaired by the national security advisor. The impetus to move control of arms control policy to this more senior level came from Robert McFarlane, who was still deputy national security advisor at the time. McFarlane says he got his superiors to make this change by convincing them that "the one issue on which the President [was] most vulnerable . . . was arms control."[64] The effort to maintain momentum in arms control policy-making continued even after the 1984 election. In a meeting shortly after the election, which White House staff intended to signal the direction Reagan would take, Secretary of State George Shultz told the president he would have to overrule the opponents of arms control because the public and Congress would not support his weapons plans "without meaningful negotiations."[65]

Changes in declaratory policy

In addition to speeding up the pace at which the administration sought to move forward in START, another aspect of policy at the general level that the freeze affected was how officials, in their public statements, described their concerns and objectives. For, beyond the absence of talks, administration rhetoric about nuclear arms had also helped stimulate the freeze movement. The administration recognized this, leading to an end to the earlier loose talk about the winnability of nuclear war. Lumping this together with the other effects already discussed, one official who played an important role in administration public affairs efforts said the main effects of the freeze were "with respect to speed, urgency, tone, how things [were] packaged."[66]

Because public statements about nuclear arms constitute a form of policy – i.e., declaratory policy – administration pronouncements on the issue came to entail another shift at the general level. In the areas of tone and packaging, in fact, the administration did more than just

from the White House. One delegate to the arms negotiations expressed resentment at the fact that Baker and other White House political operatives "were involved in arms control policy discussions," because they cared too much about "the President's popularity or how to increase Republican electoral chances" (interview by author).

64 Interview with Robert McFarlane (June 1, 1989).

65 George P. Shultz, *Turmoil and Triumph: My Years as Secretary of State* (New York: Charles Scribner's Sons, 1993), pp. 496–97.

66 Interview with administration official. For acknowledgment by other officials that the freeze brought about a conscious decision to moderate administration rhetoric, see Cortright, *Peace Works*, pp. 94, 104.

clamp down on its war-fighting rhetoric. The president, in his own statements, began to replace such talk with indications that he doubted the utility of nuclear weapons. This may even have reflected the president's personal feelings. Most former administration officials I interviewed contend that Reagan wanted sharp reductions in nuclear weapons from day one. And Reagan himself claims that, soon after he took office, as he learned the number of fatalities that a nuclear war would cause, "My dream, then, became a world free of nuclear weapons."[67]

However, no sign of the president's feelings in this regard escaped into the public realm in his first year or more in office. Indeed, Reagan's rhetoric was every bit as harsh as that of his most hard-line assistants. At his first press conference, the president claimed "So far detente's been a one-way street that the Soviet Union has used to pursue its own aims . . . They reserve unto themselves the right to commit any crime, to lie, to cheat." Reagan also consistently argued that the USA needed to modernize all three legs of the strategic nuclear triad, and even talked about the possibility of a nuclear war limited to battlefield exchange of tactical weapons.[68] Given the available evidence, therefore, no one outside the administration had any reason to think that Ronald Reagan harbored a deep distaste for nuclear weapons.

The president began to express more anti-nuclear views, however, in spring 1982. The decision to speak out in this way at that point in time, when Reagan still primarily wanted to build up US strength and focus on issues other than arms control, was due entirely to pressures arising from the freeze movement. One source familiar with discussions of the administration's private polling data reported that their polls at that time indicated that Reagan was being hurt by the nuclear arms control issue. This source said that the poll results made the administration decide to give more attention to the nuclear issue in its public statements.[69]

The president made one statement around this time, which he later repeated many times, whose connotations were especially significant. According to one source, the president first made this comment at the

[67] Ronald Reagan, *An American Life* (New York: Simon and Schuster, 1990), p. 550. See also the memoirs of Anderson, *Revolution*, pp. xxxii, xxxvi; George P. Shultz, *Turmoil and Triumph*, pp. 360, 376; and Adelman, *Great Universal Embrace*, p. 20.

[68] Talbott, *Deadly Gambits*, p. 227; Solo, *Protest to Policy*, p. 70.

[69] Interview with administration official.

suggestion of an NSC aide, including it in a telegram he sent to a meeting of the International Physicians for the Prevention of Nuclear War. In it, Reagan said he believed that "a nuclear war cannot be won, and must never be fought." The president also used this line in his weekly radio address on April 17, 1982. He said his goal was to reassure "those who protest against nuclear war . . . [that] I'm with you." While claiming these statements reflected the president's true opinions, the above-cited aide acknowledged that the main reason his advisors urged the president to express these views was the criticism of administration policy coming from the freeze.[70] In response to societal protest, this means, the president in effect publicly disowned an important premise of his administration's nuclear strategy, that the United States could plan to prevail in a nuclear conflict.

Reagan's change in rhetoric did not imply acceptance of the freeze proposal itself, though. Because the administration maintained a stance of unswerving opposition to the movement's specific demands, the administration had to convince the public that its own arms control program could achieve the goals motivating support for the freeze proposal. As a result, the administration changed not only its rhetoric concerning nuclear war but also its description of its objectives in arms control. Rather than linger on the need to establish equality in the US and Soviet arsenals or close a window of vulnerability, the administration began to emphasize the goal of reductions *per se*. This enabled it to argue against the freeze by saying, in essence, "we can do better than a freeze."[71]

The first opportunity for the administration to highlight a desire for arms reductions came with Reagan's Eureka College address in May 1982. A year before, George Kennan had caused a stir by calling for 50 percent cuts in nuclear arsenals. James Goodby, designated to be the State Department representative at the START talks, drafted the section of the Eureka speech outlining the numbers in Reagan's opening proposal. He recalled:

> I was very conscious of Kennan's calls for 50 percent reductions. So I calculated what the reductions would be under our START proposal. They turned out to be about 35 percent [if ballistic missile warheads were taken as the unit of account]. I wrote it in Kennanesque

70 Interview with administration official; *NYT*, April 18, 1982, p. 35.

71 In his very first public comment on the freeze, in fact, President Reagan departed from the text of a speech on income tax cuts to say "A freeze simply isn't good enough because it doesn't go far enough" (*NYT*, March 16, 1982, p. 21).

> language so it would have the same public appeal. I wanted it to look like the President was paying attention to public concern.[72]

Reflecting on the administration's attempts to address public concerns, another official with arms control duties contends that the freeze "increased support for bold steps, like the zero option and deep reductions . . . The public debate drove people in the administration to adopt a more disarmament type focus rather than [return to more] traditional arms control."[73] Once Reagan began to speak out on his desire for arms reductions, moreover, his political aides learned that such a stance actually increased his public standing.[74] As ACDA official Tom Graham put it, the freeze movement demonstrated that "arms control was good politics. The White House operatives did not appreciate that at first."[75]

Once they learned that lesson, however, his aides sought to ensure that all Reagan's subsequent pronouncements on US–Soviet relations included some pro-peace rhetoric. Before Reagan's 1983 State of the Union address, for example, the administration released a statement in his name that declared "We have no higher priority" than arms control. Such a statement represented quite a change from the administration's initial emphasis on its economic program and military buildup. It reflected recognition of what the freeze movement had shown, namely that the American people wanted arms restraint moved to a higher place on the national agenda. White House officials thus told reporters in spring 1983 that "voter sentiment" was "a factor in persuading Mr. Reagan to couple every appeal for military preparedness with an equally fervent appeal for peace."[76]

By making all of the above policy shifts, the administration forestalled any possibility that the arms issue would cost Reagan the 1984 election or that the public would pressure Congress to impose a freeze. Because the opinion disjunction that opened up in the early 1980s primarily reflected concerns at the general level, rather than a widespread conviction that all new nuclear weapons programs must

[72] Interview with James Goodby (May 15, 1989).

[73] Interview with State Department official.

[74] The *New York Times* reported in July 1982 that "The President's polltaker, Richard Wirthlin, says he has found a sharp rise, since April, in the percentage of Americans who think Mr. Reagan [really] wants to reduce arms . . . The shifts followed Mr. Wirthlin's advice to Mr. Reagan to begin speaking out on arms control" (July 6, 1982, p. 13).

[75] Interview with Thomas Graham (May 10, 1989).

[76] *NYT*, January 22, 1983, p. 4; April 6, 1983, p. B8.

immediately be stopped, the administration did not necessarily have to propose a freeze to the USSR to lessen public concerns. It merely had to adjust its policy at the general level in a way that indicated a commitment to continue negotiating with the Soviet Union for arms control. Thus, in response to the signals conveyed by the freeze, the administration stopped claiming publicly that the United States should seek the ability to prevail in the event deterrence failed and proclaimed the goal of reducing nuclear weapons as a national priority instead. And the administration moved forward earlier and more quickly on strategic arms control than it had intended to.

These steps apparently convinced many Americans that Ronald Reagan would seriously seek arms control. A September 1984 poll found that 60 percent of the public believed Reagan would "make a real effort" to negotiate an arms control deal with the Soviet Union if he were re-elected, a figure that increased to 69 percent right after the election. Richard Wirthlin says his polls for the administration likewise found the public, in a turnaround from their earlier discomfort, "at ease with Reagan's positions" on nuclear arms as the election approached.[77]

Freeze paves way for a centrist compromise

Although the pressures arising from the freeze movement were mostly felt at the general level of policy, this does not mean that the specific level remained unaffected. As administration officials came to feel they had to be able to demonstrate progress toward an agreement, they made several changes in the US START offer designed to make it more negotiable.[78] The most significant change was not a direct product of freeze pressure, but was made possible indirectly by the effects of protest. Though the Freeze Campaign proved unable to use the elite coalition-shift pathway to get its own proposal placed at the top of the arms control agenda, the larger process of coalition formation it brought about helped enable a different coalition to alter Reagan's policy at the specific level. By contributing to the need for the administration to negotiate with a new centrist coalition in Congress, activism helped bring about a decision by the administra-

[77] *NYT*, September 19, 1984, p. B9; November 19, 1984, p. 1; interview with Richard Wirthlin (June 2, 1989).

[78] See *NYT*, June 8, 1983, p. 1; July 14, 1983, p. 1; August 6, 1983, p. 1; Talbott, *Deadly Gambits*, pp. 311–13, 325–26.

tion to drop its attempt to obtain reductions in ballistic missiles as a separate and prior step to other nuclear arms limitations.

This occurred because, alongside the freeze effort, arms control and disarmament groups in the early 1980s maintained a second major campaign, directed at stopping the MX missile. The rise of the freeze movement helped boost the anti-MX campaign and, combined with the Reagan administration's inability to come up with a convincing basing scheme, this effort put continued funding of the MX in serious doubt. The administration responded by creating a bipartisan outside commission, chaired by Brent Scowcroft, to propose a basing scheme for the MX. A small group of legislators from both chambers of Congress then worked behind the scenes with the Scowcroft Commission to get certain other commitments from the president included in Scowcroft's recommendations. The senators, led by William Cohen (R-ME) and Sam Nunn (D-GA), were interested in promoting a nuclear "build-down" proposal. This proposal would require that, for whatever new weapons either side deployed, they retire a greater number of older weapons.[79] The senators were joined by representatives, led by Aspin and Gore, who wanted to promote rapid transition to a force of single-warhead ICBMs, dubbed the "Midgetman."[80]

By helping create an opposition to the MX that held nearly a majority in Congress, the anti-nuclear weapons movement enabled these moderate members to threaten to vote with the opposition if the administration did not make concessions to their more limited concerns. By playing this bargaining chip over the course of several close MX votes in 1983, the centrist coalition extracted commitments from the administration to proceed with Midgetman development, offer a build-down proposal, and – most significantly from the perspective of the freeze movement – make its START proposal more realistic.[81] The centrists acknowledge that citizen activism created the situation that forced the administration to listen to them. Aspin told David Cort-

[79] Freeze leaders opposed build-down because they feared that it could lead to a destabilizing situation as the superpowers replaced older, less accurate weapons with newer, more accurate ones. Markey thus likened build-down to "trading in two crossbows for one artillery piece" (quoted in Waller, *Congress and the Freeze*, p. 243).

[80] Cortright, *Peace Works*, pp. 144–48; Robert C. Gray, "Congress, Arms Control, and Weapons Modernization," in US House of Representatives, Committee on Foreign Affairs, *Congress and Foreign Policy, 1983*, a Congressional Research Service report (Washington, DC: Government Printing Office, 1984), pp. 86–94; Talbott, *Deadly Gambits*, pp. 300–07.

[81] Robert C. Gray, "Congress, Arms Control," pp. 97–99.

right, "The citizens and grassroots organizations did come up very big time against the MX. That clearly had an impact on forcing the administration to deal with the moderates in the House." Likewise, Al Gore wrote at the time:

> Because Congress proposed to choose between . . . [Reagan's] conduct of arms control and the audacious freeze, it was imperative for him to make his conduct in arms control and arms planning more persuasive. That led him to expand the charter of the Scowcroft Commission to encompass arms control, and to embrace its recommendations, even though they are in many ways contrary to his original goals.[82]

Though the build-down idea itself went nowhere in the end,[83] the administration negotiations with the congressional build-down coalition brought about another change in the US START position that was more consequential. As I have noted, the administration initially sought a two-phase approach in START, asking for sharp reductions to equal levels in ballistic missiles as a prior step to any other nuclear arms limitations. Freeze and build-down supporters both saw the focus on ICBMs as unrealistically one-sided. They pointed out that, while the United States had its nuclear weapons fairly evenly distributed across the three legs of the triad (land-, air-, and sea-based), the great majority of Soviet weapons, and those they regarded as most reliable, were exactly the land-based missiles targeted by the Reagan plan.

When he approved the initial START offer, however, the president was unaware of this difference between US and Soviet deployment patterns.[84] This changed only when Reagan and Secretary of State Shultz were forced, by the precarious situation of the MX and inability of lower-level officials to close a deal, to meet personally with the congressional centrists to work out a compromise. In these meetings, months after his May 1982 Eureka speech, the president finally learned that his proposal to impose deep cuts in Soviet land-based

82 Cortright, *Peace Works*, p. 145; Albert Gore, Jr., "Beyond the Freeze," *Washington Post*, May 9, 1983, p. 11.

83 For explanation, see Talbott, *Deadly Gambits*, pp. 341–42.

84 Lacking much understanding of the technical details involved in arms control, Reagan generally relied on some simple rules of thumb in making arms decisions. One of these was that "fast flyers," like ballistic missiles, were bad, while "slow flyers," like bombers and cruise missiles, were good, a rule of thumb that had led him to approve a plan targeted exclusively on ballistic missiles (Talbott, *Deadly Gambits*, pp. 132, 241).

missiles without compensating cuts in areas of US advantage was bound to appear one-sided. Brent Scowcroft convinced Shultz of the corollary, that asymmetries in the two arsenals meant that the USA could trade its bombers and cruise missiles against Soviet ballistic missiles. Shultz in turn convinced Reagan to give up the idea of treating ballistic missiles separately from other systems. The administration now promised the centrist coalition that it would seek to "negotiate trade-offs" between each side's areas of relative advantage.[85]

This decision marked the end of the two-phase approach in START. From the perspective of making cooperation a real possibility, it was the most important adjustment the administration made in its first term in the specific details of the START proposal. Asked later how he could have been ignorant of the differences in the US and Soviet arsenals, Reagan replied "I never heard any one of our negotiators or any of our military people or anyone else bring up that particular point."[86] This suggests that, if the freeze movement had not created a situation that forced the president to discuss arms control with figures outside his administration, it would have been much later, if at all, before he gained the insight that enabled him to make the US approach more realistic.

Though the adjustments in the START package did not involve movement toward a freeze, they were changes in the details of US policy that improved the prospects for an eventual START agreement. In this way, they indicate the development of greater willingness to cooperate. And activism contributed significantly to this development. The freeze movement's activation of mechanisms 1 and 2 made the administration feel it had to show flexibility on arms control to the public. These pathways also set up the situation that required the administration to bargain with more moderate members of Congress. Together, these developments pushed the administration to move away from the most unrealistic elements of its opening proposal.

Nor were these changes just part of the normal give-and-take in negotiations. Administration conservatives wanted arms control to do one thing and only that one thing: to force the Soviets to reduce their counterforce capabilities to a level equal to the USA's. They thus opposed any plan that would treat other weapons as a threat equal to

[85] Ibid., pp. 337–39; Robert C. Gray, "Congress, Arms Control," pp. 102–04.
[86] Quoted in Talbott, *Deadly Gambits*, p. 263, n.

the Soviet advantage in ballistic missile warheads.[87] As a result, conservatives tried to forestall any changes in the US position whose main purpose was to generate progress in the arms talks. Thus, just as the administration was altering its START proposal in response to threats by the build-down coalition to scuttle the MX, Richard Perle, in congressional testimony, asked rhetorically:

> Is the ease with which we abandon our objectives and make "progress" toward an agreement – any agreement – a sign of seriousness? . . . Demand too much restraint on the part of the Soviets . . . and you are not serious . . . Seriousness resides with those who don't worry too much about the terms of an agreement as long as something gets signed. That is, needless to say, not our view of what constitutes being serious about arms control.[88]

But the pressures to show progress arising from the freeze made it impossible for the administration to maintain the most unrealistic provisions of its initial START offer. In the words of a senior official, "we wanted it to appear that a real effort was being made, and therefore a real effort had to be made."[89] One key part of making a real effort was allowing other items on the table besides deep cuts in ballistic missile warheads. Reagan's compromise with the build-down coalition still left policy at the specific level far from what the freeze movement sought, however. It is therefore important also to recognize the limitations on freeze movement influence.

Limitations on influence

This chapter has shown that the freeze had a major impact with respect to arms control's place on the national agenda. However, the movement did not succeed in altering the arms control agenda itself in the way its organizers had hoped. This is in part a function of the influence pathways engaged by the freeze. By its nature, any electoral pressure generated by a citizens' campaign is felt on the broad dimension involving the balance between buildup and restraint. To

87 For example, in reference to congressional critics of the administration approach, ACDA head Kenneth Adelman reportedly told colleagues, "We're just going to have to bear this cross of all these little congressmen with . . . their political-psychological hangups about how it's somehow immoral to try to reduce the Soviet threat by the measure in which it's most threatening" (quoted in Talbott, *Deadly Gambits*, p. 308).

88 Quoted in Garfinkle, *Politics of the Freeze*, p. 174.

89 Interview with administration official.

get the government to pursue a freeze itself, therefore, advocates would have had to engage one of the other influence mechanisms in a way that altered policy at the specific level.

As indicated above, though, foreign policy elites who worked with the freeze movement, activating mechanism 2, mostly did not share the specific-level objectives of the Freeze Campaign. Influence through the coalition-shift pathway was therefore also exerted mainly at the general level, or else used by congressional centrists for purposes not fully consonant with freeze objectives. The only remaining mechanism by which the citizens' campaign could have brought the arms control agenda more into conformity with its preferences is the bureaucratic pathway. But mechanism 3 was never activated by the freeze in a way that could advance the movement's proposals.

Barriers to engaging the bureaucratic pathway

Earlier sections have shown that a bureaucratic division, which is the pre-condition for mechanism 3, clearly existed. For mechanism 3 to take effect, however, there must be some interaction between the bureaucratic debate and arguments arising from the outside citizens' movement. Such interaction never occurred. Despite the deep divisions on arms control within the administration, both factions in the internal debate rejected the nuclear freeze proposal, believing that it would leave the Soviet Union with a meaningful lead in ICBMs. Hence, neither side saw in the proposals of the US anti-nuclear weapons movement anything that could serve as a solution to the problems with which they were concerned.

Though they rejected the freeze proposal, both factions in the internal debate did try to make the political problem posed by rise of the citizens' movement itself an argument in favor of their own proposals. However, as Robert Dean, an assistant to Richard Burt, observed, in debating whose position would better meet public concerns, "the arguments cut either way. They didn't necessarily favor one position over another." Thus, the State Department argued that its more traditional options could more plausibly be seen containing the basis for an agreement and would therefore, as one official who supported those options put it, convince "the public . . . [that] the administration [was] serious on arms control."[90] Richard Perle

[90] Interview with Robert Dean (June 6, 1989); interview with administration official.

and his allies had a rejoinder, however. They argued that the Pentagon's more radical proposals would have greater public appeal because they were simpler and more in tune with sentiment for disarmament.[91] Neither side emerged as a clear winner in this debate. As a result, there was no interaction between the freeze movement and internal bureaucratic struggles of a sort that could affect which specific proposals moved up on the arms control agenda.

Transboundary connections aid freeze little

The only other way in which freeze influence might have been enhanced was through transnational connections that magnified the impact of those influence mechanisms the freeze activated. In chapter 3, I suggested that the domestic influence mechanisms engaged by activism can be affected, either positively or negatively, by interaction with Soviet foreign policy or with expressions of world concern or protest elsewhere. In the early 1980s, the US anti-nuclear movement received a mild boost from interaction with European expressions of concern. This was probably outweighed, though, by the adverse consequences for the movement of Soviet arms diplomacy.

Turning first to the European peace movement, it is clear that European protests helped encourage and draw media attention to US activism in the early stages of the freeze. Massive demonstrations against nuclear weapons swept across Europe during 1981, triggered mainly by NATO plans to deploy new US intermediate-range nuclear forces. After the European protests took off, the US media started looking for signs of anything similar in the United States, leading to a boost in media coverage for the initial stirrings of activism there.[92] European and US activist groups also coordinated some of their activities directly so as to increase the visibility and leverage enjoyed by both.

However, the transnational alliance that developed remained quite

[91] Talbott, *Deadly Gambits*, p. 156. Although conservatives argued that their proposals would better assuage public concerns, this was clearly an attempt to make a virtue out of necessity. Administration hard-liners in fact tried strenuously to keep arms control from being raised in importance on the administration agenda. Perle, for example, regularly argued the administration should not let itself "be stampeded" into an agreement (Talbott, *Deadly Gambits*, pp. 135, 294). This is not an argument someone would use if he saw citizen activism providing an opportunity to advance his own favored proposals.

[92] McCrea and Markle, *Minutes to Midnight*, p. 108.

limited. The main reason is that the two movements focused mostly on different proposals at the specific level. European energies were aroused by the impending deployment of Pershing and cruise missiles. Activists in Europe were less enthusiastic about the freeze proposal, because it would still leave the superpowers with large arsenals of weapons designed for possible use in the European theater. In contrast, while more radical groups in the US movement made Euromissiles their main focus, the Freeze and many of the larger advocacy groups in the United States downplayed or eschewed work on the INF issue. More moderate freeze supporters believed that Soviet SS-20 deployments, which had prompted the NATO INF decision, had created an imbalance in the European theater that would make it hard to win a debate limited to tactical weapons. They also feared that opposition to cruise and Pershing deployment would be taken as a sign of "unilateralism," weakening the message that a freeze should be bilateral. Since strong transnational connections were not established, the freeze movement's ability to boost its leverage by pointing to European concerns was limited.[93]

Soviet diplomacy hurts freeze

While transnational connections with the European peace movement still benefited the freeze movement somewhat, this was more than offset by the negative consequences of interaction with Soviet diplomacy. When the US and European nuclear weapons protests arose, the Soviet government made some obvious attempts to exploit their criticisms of the Reagan administration. However, Soviet efforts contained little that could elicit a sympathetic response from Western activists. In fact, the Soviet Union ultimately ended up hindering freeze efforts through its negotiating behavior.

The Soviet Union certainly tried to take advantage of the growing citizens' movements in Europe and the United States.[94] Starting soon

[93] Solo, *Protest to Policy*, pp. 111–14, 119–21; Meyer, *Winter of Discontent*, pp. 74–76, 180, 189, 228–29; Sam Marullo, "US Grass-Roots Opposition to the Euromissile Deployment," in Bert Klandermans, ed., *International Social Movement Research*, vol. III (Greenwich, CT: JAI Press, 1991), pp. 283–310.

[94] This led to charges of Soviet penetration of the freeze movement in *Reader's Digest* and several right-wing periodicals. And President Reagan, in several speeches in late 1982, claimed that "some who want the weakening of America" were "manipulating" the freeze movement. Asked to investigate these charges, the FBI concluded, in contrast, that the USSR did not "have . . . a dominant role in the US peace and

after Reagan took office, the USSR made several proposals for some form of nuclear freeze. But these proposals differed in important ways from what the US campaign had in mind, rendering them unattractive to US freeze backers. For example, soon after Reagan's May 1982 Eureka speech, Leonid Brezhnev proposed that as soon as the START talks got underway "the strategic armament of the USSR and the USA be . . . frozen quantitatively – and that modernization be limited to the utmost." Because it appeared that this proposal would not halt testing or fully stop production, Senators Kennedy and Hatfield refused to endorse Brezhnev's proposal. They said it was "not the kind of freeze that we favor." The Soviet government also made several proposals for a freeze or moratorium that covered only the European theater. Such attempts to use the popularity of the freeze slogan to keep its SS-20s in Europe while preventing US INF deployments further harmed the credibility of Soviet claims to support a freeze.[95]

In sum, the Soviets took no concrete actions that offered a promise of mutual advantage, limiting themselves instead to rhetorical endorsements transparently meant to serve purely Soviet interests. They thus gave freeze activists nothing that could invite a positive response and generated little, if any, pressure on the US government. In fact, Soviet behavior in the Euromissile dispute actually ended up undercutting the US freeze movement. When deliveries of new US intermediate-range weapons began in late 1983, Soviet negotiators walked out of both the INF and START talks. This action ultimately reduced the freeze movement's leverage through the electoral pathway. According to Kenneth Adelman, director of ACDA at the time, "their walkout helped a lot to prevent the administration from being hurt on arms control in the election." As one State Department official pointed out, President Reagan could then say he was still willing to negotiate and blame the Soviets for quitting the talks.[96]

Though activists lacked the leverage to get their own preferred

nuclear freeze movements, or . . . control or manipulate the movement." Solo, *Protest to Policy*, pp. 94, 99; Meyer, *Winter of Discontent*, pp. 213–15; *NYT*, March 26, 1983, pp. 1, 7.

95 Brezhnev quoted in Talbott, *Deadly Gambits*, p. 279; see also pp. 40–42, 86; Kennedy and Hatfield quoted in *NYT*, May 19, 1982, p. 10.

96 Interview with Kenneth Adelman (May 23, 1989); interview with State Department official.

Other Soviet actions, like shooting down a Korean airliner in August 1983 and deciding to send Foreign Minister Gromyko to a meeting at the White House right before the 1984 election, also made it harder for freeze activists and the candidate

proposals adopted, previous sections nonetheless suggest that Reagan's arms control policy would not have developed the same way without the freeze. To make this case satisfactorily, though, requires considering possible alternative explanations for the policy developments I have attributed to the freeze.

Other factors do not explain policy shifts

Two broad types of alternative explanation might account for Reagan administration policy. Given the president's preferences, one could argue that the administration would have eventually taken the same steps even without outside pressures. Such an alternative would be largely consistent with the traditional explanation of arms control. Or one could argue that other sources of outside pressure would have induced the shifts described above even without the existence of the freeze movement.

The first alternative line of argument suggests that policy ultimately reflected what the president wanted, so that Reagan's own preferences explain that policy. Long-time Reagan advisor Martin Anderson advances this claim, reporting that Reagan told him "I came in with a plan" for dealing with the Soviet Union and simply followed that plan all along. This plan involved setting out and sticking to an ambitious set of arms control objectives, then using a massive military buildup to lever the Soviets into accepting the sharp cuts in their forces called for in the opening US proposal. Besides Anderson, several other former Reagan aides have argued that the administration's own initial game plan was the main source of Reagan's Soviet policy.[97]

This alternative emphasizes two of the three factors in traditional arms control theory – the military balance and presidential leadership. It accepts the Reagan premise that the USSR had pulled ahead in nuclear capability, so that a buildup to restore parity or even superiority had to precede talks. And it points to Reagan's own leadership in formulating and implementing a plan to make successful negotiations possible. This alternative does not explicitly address the third factor in conventional wisdom, the state of political relations. But it

they supported, Walter Mondale, to blame the administration for an absence of dialogue with the Soviet Union or a lack of progress on arms control.

[97] Anderson, *Revolution*, pp. xxxi, 72–78; Meese, *With Reagan*, pp. 164–71; Richard Pipes, "Misinterpreting the Cold War," *Foreign Affairs* 74 (January/February 1995), pp. 154–60.

implies that the United States would not have moved toward agreement if Soviet behavior remained unfavorable. Early administration actions fit this expectation, as officials pointed to the crackdown on Solidarity and imposition of martial law in Poland in late 1981 as reasons to continue deferring arms talks.[98]

The problem with this explanation is that Reagan made achievement of an arms reduction pact a high priority before the United States was in a position to implement his plan. Moreover, adverse Soviet behavior did nothing to slow this process. When Reagan announced his decision to begin START in May 1982, the situation in Poland had not changed from that which a few months earlier was held to make talks impossible. Nor did the Soviet shootdown of a Korean Air Lines flight on August 31, 1983, change the US position on START. Although Reagan denounced the callous Soviet action and imposed sanctions, he took pains in a televised speech to say that the incident would not affect US efforts to achieve an arms control agreement.[99]

More importantly, Reagan began trying to demonstrate a commitment to arms control well before the US defense buildup had borne fruit. Efforts to proclaim a willingness to cooperate on arms control reached a new peak in early 1984. Despite the fact that Soviet negotiators had walked out of arms talks less than two months earlier, Reagan decided, in January 1984, to make a major speech expressing his readiness to compromise to reach a pact on arms control. Because there were obvious election year motivations, the US media did not give much weight to the speech at the time. Yet a number of separate sources have indicated that the administration also intended the speech and various follow-up actions as a serious signal of willingness to cooperate so as to achieve arms control.[100]

In the speech, the president argued that the buildup of US military forces had placed the United States "in its strongest position in years," so that the US government could now afford to be forthcoming in arms control talks.[101] By any objective measure of the strategic

98 Interviews with administration officials; John Newhouse, *War and Peace in the Nuclear Age* (New York: Vintage Books, 1990; Alfred A. Knopf, 1988), p. 345.

99 *NYT*, September 6, 1983, p. 14; Talbott, *Deadly Gambits*, p. 193.

100 Interview with David Gergen (June 21, 1989); Newhouse, *War and Peace*, p. 369; *NYT*, February 24, 1984, p. 14; George P. Shultz, *Turmoil and Triumph*, pp. 465–67; Cortright, *Peace Works*, p. 97.

101 *NYT*, January 16, 1984, p. 8. For more on the speech, see Talbott, *Deadly Gambits*, p. 344.

balance, however, the United States had not improved much on its position of 1980, meaning that the USA did not yet have the kind of additional leverage Reagan now claimed. Two DOD officials in fact noted in 1984 that the Soviets had opened up a big lead in ICBM re-entry vehicles. They argued, "The effects of the Reagan defense program are only beginning to be reflected in . . . improved readiness and . . . it will be several years before . . . [efforts] to modernize are translated into [equipment ready for use]." A report for the Congressional Research Service, comparing the strategic balance in 1985 with that in 1980, concluded similarly that the "Soviet posture nevertheless continues to improve in relative terms."[102]

Other administration officials pointed out that the new weapons called for in strategic modernization plans – the MX, B-1, and Trident II – had won funding, and noted that Reagan's Strategic Defense Initiative clearly worried the Soviet Union. But none of the new offensive systems had begun to be deployed yet in 1984, while any prospects for deployment of defensive systems were decades in the future at best. Given how often administration officials had argued the Soviets would never get serious in INF talks until US cruise and Pershing II missiles were deployed, one would have expected them to apply the same logic to START. When one also recalls their earlier pessimistic assessments of Soviet intentions and the military balance, as well as skeptical comments about arms control, it is clear that one would normally have expected the administration to wait for more concrete forms of progress in the US military buildup before trying to make progress toward a strategic arms control treaty.[103]

Moreover, it was not the hard-liners in the administration who advanced the argument that Reagan had successfully followed through on their game plan and could now accept a deal. Rather, officials credit Robert McFarlane with first suggesting that the United States could now claim to be negotiating from a restored position of equality. Along with Secretary of State Shultz, McFarlane had joined political operatives Baker and Deaver in trying to overcome conserva-

102 Lawrence J. Korb and Linda P. Brady, "Rearming America: The Reagan Administration Defense Program," *International Security* 9 (Winter 1984/85), pp. 3–18; John M. Collins, *US–Soviet Military Balance, 1980–1985* (Washington, DC: Pergamon-Brassey's, 1985), p. 60.

103 I am setting aside the INF area, where deployment was in the process of going through, since such deployments had little effect on the strategic balance and strategic arms were being negotiated separately from intermediate-range forces.

tive resistance to renewing arms control efforts. Reports were that this group was motivated by fear that ongoing hostility between the superpowers might turn voters against Reagan.[104]

In a different domestic climate, therefore, Reagan would probably have chosen to defer until much later any seriousness about START talks in order to give the buildup time to produce results. But the public and congressional criticisms being channeled through the freeze movement served, as one official put it, as "a useful reminder of the need for concrete achievements, the need to show something out of the policy review process, of the political reality that you have to . . . engage in arms control." In this way, Bud McFarlane observed, the freeze "helped counter pressure from the Right to do nothing."[105] In short, the president had strong motivations by 1984 to suggest that the conditions for progress on arms control had improved, motivations he would not have had in the absence of outside pressure.

But was the freeze movement necessary, or could other sources of pressure outside the administration have brought about the same effects? Perhaps centrists in Congress could have elicited the same adjustments in administration policy without the presence of a citizens' movement. Or maybe pressure from the USA's European allies would have been sufficient in the absence of domestic US activism.

Though administration officials expressed their greatest worries about the possible actions Congress would take, I have shown that congressional action would not have taken the same course nor exerted as much leverage without the freeze movement. It was the rise of the freeze that first encouraged many members, especially in the House, to take up arms control. In contrast to the freeze resolution, moreover, SALT II, the alternative initially favored by leading Democrats, simply lacked grassroots support and was tarnished among many elites as well, while build-down came on the scene later than the freeze and never attracted much interest in the general public. In addition, the build-down coalition only gained leverage because grassroots lobbying against the MX put them in a position to control the fate of the program. Congress thus did not have much impact on administration policy independent of that made possible by its interaction with the freeze movement.

104 Cortright, *Peace Works*, p. 97; *NYT*, February 24, 1984, p. 14.

105 Interview with administration official; interview with Robert McFarlane (June 1, 1989).

A push from allied governments and publics is the most credible alternative to the freeze as an outside source of policy change. While the Europeans clearly exerted pressure, the administration perceived it as being driven by different priorities from those of US activists. In interviews, Reagan officials mostly discussed the Europeans in connection with the INF issue, not strategic arms. As a result, the pressures the administration felt from US allies were reflected primarily in the zero option proposal for theater forces.[106] In contrast, Reagan and his aides saw strategic arms control as a dominating concern only for US actors.

Allied governments, believing that INF talks could not succeed in the absence of START progress, did press their US counterpart to push ahead with strategic arms talks. However, the allies did not have as concrete a form of leverage on START as they did on INF. On INF, the United States needed the continued support of European governments and publics to be able to deploy cruise and Pershing II missiles there. But only domestic US actors actually had the power to pull the plug on the administration's strategic modernization plans. The fact that US priorities regarding strategic arms changed as much as they did between 1981 and 1984, therefore, must be attributed more to the freeze movement than European pressure. Given the larger thesis of this study, though, perhaps the most important point is that European pressures themselves resulted primarily from societal activism. Because allied governments were reacting in large part to their own peace movements, just as congressional action was shaped in large measure by the US freeze movement, it is clear that social protest was the single most important cause of the increases in US willingness to cooperate over Reagan's first term.

Conclusion

The anti-nuclear weapons movement of the early 1980s activated, in a mutually reinforcing way, the first two influence pathways identified in chapter 3. The freeze engaged mechanism 1 by interacting with broader public concerns in a way that created electoral incentives for raising the place of arms restraint on the national agenda. The freeze also interacted with divisions among political elites, bringing mech-

[106] Jeffrey W. Knopf, "Beyond Two-Level Games: Domestic–International Interaction in the Intermediate-Range Nuclear Forces Negotiations," *International Organization* 47 (Autumn 1993), pp. 599–628.

anism 2 into play in a way that also promoted congressional efforts to get Reagan to give less emphasis to increasing US strength and more to achieving mutual restraint.

Together, the mass electoral pressure and elite coalition shifts brought about by the freeze movement produced the expected outcome – a change in arms control policy at the general level. The administration accelerated the pace of policy formulation in this area, moving more quickly to enter strategic arms talks and to signal willingness to compromise in the search for an accord. By making it necessary for the administration to show it could move forward, the general-level pressures arising from the freeze also contributed to decisions to be more flexible about those details of Reagan's initial proposal most likely to frustrate progress. Finally, in response to the freeze, the president and his advisors also changed their tone, giving more emphasis to the need to avoid nuclear war and achieve arms reductions. By taking all these steps, the administration showed that the United States had once again developed a preference for co-operation on arms restraint.

Though it had a major impact on arms control's place on the national agenda, the freeze did not succeed in altering policy at the specific level to get its own proposal placed on the negotiating agenda. This is in part a function of the influence mechanisms the freeze activated. The electoral pathway typically affects only the general priority attached to arms restraint, while the overlap between elite and grassroots opponents of the administration that activated the coalition-shift pathway also involved only general-level objectives. Finally, there was simply no productive interaction between outside activism and internal debates, meaning that the bureaucratic pathway also did not provide the freeze with a mechanism to alter policy at the specific level in conformity with its wishes.

This does not mean the changes at the general level lacked significance, though. Several recent studies have argued that the peace movement helped end the Cold War.[107] As part of their case, they claim that activism got the Reagan administration to signal to the Soviet Union, before Gorbachev took power, that the United States was committed to arms control and not just a relentless nuclear

[107] Cortright, *Peace Works*; David S. Meyer and Sam Marullo, "Grassroots Mobilization and International Politics: Peace Protest and the End of the Cold War," in Louis Kriesberg and David R. Segal, eds., *Research in Social Movements, Conflicts, and Change*, vol. XIV (Greenwich, CT: JAI Press, 1992), pp. 99–140.

buildup. This in turn, they argue, created necessary political space for Gorbachev's concessions in arms talks and attempt to pursue domestic reform.

This chapter has shown that the freeze movement really did have the impact on Reagan policy ascribed to it by those who credit activism with helping end the Cold War, thereby supporting one of the key contentions necessary to make that argument persuasive. In contrast, the claim of former Reagan aides that the president deserves the credit for ending the Cold War must be modified in light of the fact the administration did not actually follow its original script, due to modifications in US policy brought about by the freeze. From getting talks underway, to making a rhetorical commitment to serious negotiations, to altering the opening START proposal in a way that made serious negotiations possible, the administration moved faster because of citizen activism. This was not its original game plan. More clearly than in any other case in this study, a US preference for cooperation developed in the early Reagan years because of a push from below provided by societal activism.

Conclusions

This study has investigated the extent to which domestic society has been a source of US preferences for cooperation to limit strategic arms. Traditionally, arms control has been explained in terms of international circumstances and the leadership exercised by heads of state. When domestic politics is considered, it is most often treated as a constraint, or perhaps an indirect cause of cooperative initiatives designed to deflect attention from other issues. This study has questioned whether this is the whole story and there is nothing ordinary citizens can do directly to promote an interest in cooperation. Several important conclusions have emerged. I begin by summarizing the main findings, then turn to some thoughts about their implications for a range of questions beyond arms control.

Research findings

Peace movement impact

The most basic empirical conclusion of this study is that citizen activism on behalf of arms control and disarmament had an impact. Peace movements *can* make a difference. This finding emerged from both statistical and case study analysis. In a quantitative analysis that controlled for the variables stressed in existing arms control theory, the amount of protest activity proved statistically significant. In fact, protest by itself was capable of predicting US decisions to enter two of the three major sets of strategic arms talks in the Cold War era.

In-depth case studies confirmed this result. They showed that there were causal connections behind the correlations observed in the quantitative analysis. Moreover, not only did the case studies corroborate the statistical finding that activism had an impact on US decisions to begin the test ban and START negotiations, they showed that societal activism played a role in the decision to begin SALT talks as well. Even when the case studies took into account the other factors that have been used to explain cooperation and arms control, they found that grassroots protest also played an important role.

Sources of state preferences

These empirical results have several theoretical implications. The most important is that state preferences for cooperation can arise in a relatively bottom-up manner. Grassroots-based campaigns can be a direct stimulus to decisions to seek cooperation. This possibility adds another alternative to the most common ways of conceptualizing the relation between domestic politics and cooperation. Most studies of cooperation or state preference formation adopt a fairly top-down perspective, falling into one of three categories. Some derive preferences solely from system-level factors, meaning that they treat the domestic arena only as a source of constraints. Others adopt a statesman-centered perspective, in which domestic conditions can be an indirect stimulus to international action intended to help the statesman gain his or her own objectives in some domestic game. Finally, some focus on societal inputs, but emphasize dominant economic interests or technical elites.

In the cases I examined, all of these patterns can sometimes be observed. The three top-down perspectives are not wrong; they are merely incomplete. In the two Eisenhower cases, there were both constraints and a direct stimulus. Bureaucratic actors, primarily the military and the atomic weapons complex, served as a constraint across both Eisenhower terms. From a more radical perspective, these actors could also be viewed as representatives of a societal elite. From this perspective, one would say that preferences for arms racing arose via a direct stimulus from the military-industrial-scientific complex. At the same time, though, Eisenhower's second term saw a shift toward a preference for cooperation, arising in part through a direct stimulus from below, so Eisenhower policy cannot be understood without incorporating this role of domestic society as well.

In the Nixon case, in contrast, domestic actors, both at the grassroots and the elite level, probably are best characterized as a constraint. SALT had been placed on the agenda in the Johnson years, largely in response to international developments, but such developments also caused it to be taken back off again. When Nixon then tried to postpone talks further to gain leverage on the USSR, domestic constraints frustrated this objective and forced Nixon to return to the earlier arms control agenda. Grassroots actors still mattered, but more in restoring an earlier preference for cooperation than in triggering it in the first place. There was also an element of indirect stimulus in this case, as the Nixon White House was thinking partly in terms of what action would help it win a possible election battle against Ted Kennedy in 1972.

Finally, the Reagan years provide the best example of a direct stimulus from the grassroots. The nuclear freeze movement swept the country like a wildfire. Never had the message that the American public wanted efforts to achieve arms control been so clear. The decision to seek cooperation thus emerged mainly from the bottom up. This pattern across the cases suggests that the different views of the role of domestic politics are not mutually exclusive. Different relations between domestic actors and state preferences may be observed at different times, and more than one type of relationship may be operating at any given point in time.

The three prevailing perspectives each arose from the laudable ambition to find some master key that would unlock the secrets of state action in all situations. Unfortunately, empirical reality will not cooperate with this ambition to have a single grand theory of state preferences. If our theories are to help us understand why world politics unfolds as it does, they must respect the range of roles that domestic factors can play in reality. We need to add to our theoretical arsenal recognition of the possibility that state preferences can arise through a direct stimulus from below.

Building on domestic structure: three influence pathways

In looking for a way to assess the impact of activism on arms control preferences, I found the most suggestive work in the foreign policy field to be the research on domestic structure. Some of this work has even started to examine the role of public opinion and other societal actors on security issues.[1] For the most part, as befits an emphasis on

[1] Thomas Risse-Kappen, "Public Opinion, Domestic Structure, and Foreign Policy in Liberal Democracies," *World Politics* 43 (July 1991), pp. 479–512; Peter J. Katzenstein and Nobuo Okawara, *Japan's National Security: Structures, Norms, and Policy Responses*

structure, the focus of this work has been comparative. The goal has been to explain variations in the typical influence of societal actors across countries, or across issue-areas or regime changes within a country.

This work suggests, quite reasonably, that some countries or issues permit greater access to grassroots actors, thereby giving them greater impact on average. But, beyond knowing the average or maximum possible influence domestic actors will enjoy across a number of cases, it would also be worthwhile to be able to explain how much impact a societal actor will have in a given individual case. When will a citizens' campaign be able to take full advantage of the access points hypothetically available to it? While existing conceptions of domestic structure provide a useful starting point for addressing this question, they are not fully enough specified to permit a precise answer.

I thus sought to build on the insights of domestic structure by adding a more detailed understanding of process as well. I began by identifying specific institutions in the US system that could provide grassroots actors with access to arms control policymaking. The three I identified were national elections, an independent legislature, and a large federal bureaucracy. I then drew on existing research on the impact of public opinion and interest groups in domestic policymaking to identify when and how peace movements could utilize these institutions to affect arms policy. Taking process-oriented models that are well-established in the study of domestic politics proved a fruitful way to supplement the state structure approach. The resulting framework identified specific conditions under which activist influence would be possible, specified the form of interaction which would be necessary to take advantage of those conditions, and indicated the type of policy impact that would result. This framework made it possible to engage in process tracing in the case studies in a way that greatly strengthened the resulting inferences. This suggests that marrying the domestic structure approach with models of the

in a Changing World (Ithaca: Cornell University East Asia Program, 1993); Matthew Evangelista, "The Paradox of State Strength: Transnational Relations, Domestic Structures, and Security Policy in Russia and the Soviet Union," *International Organization* 49 (Winter 1995), pp. 1–38; Risse-Kappen, ed., *Bringing Transnational Relations Back In: Non-State Actors, Domestic Structures, and International Institutions* (Cambridge: Cambridge University Press, 1995); Susan Peterson, *Crisis Bargaining and the State: The Domestic Politics of International Conflict* (Ann Arbor: University of Michigan Press, 1996).

domestic policymaking process in a country might be a useful technique for explaining individual cases more generally.

One key insight that emerged from this process is that there is more than one potential pathway for activist influence in the United States. In fact, the theoretical framework laid out in chapter 3 identified three possible influence mechanisms. Moreover, all three played a role in at least one case. Studies that assume or focus on just one potential route to influence, such as elections or lobbying the legislature, are therefore likely to underestimate the impact of societal actors.

A closer review of the cases suggests, however, that, while all three mechanisms were important, they were not equally important. Mechanism 1 identifies circumstances under which activism could interact with public opinion to produce electoral pressures. This pathway played a central role in the START case, giving the freeze movement its main leverage on Reagan arms policy. There were also some electoral calculations involved in Nixon's decision to enter SALT, but they had a different source than the process identified by mechanism 1. In the Eisenhower years, finally, the electoral pathway played no role prior to the start of test ban talks. An assumption that electoral pressure is the main mechanism by which the public affects US security policy would therefore miss much of the influence that occurs.

Mechanism 3 is perhaps the most unusual pathway. It combines insights from a "garbage can model" of agenda setting with the bureaucratic politics approach to foreign policy. This bureaucratic utilization pathway was quite important in the test ban case, and also played a subsidiary role in the SALT case. It thus suggests a concrete process by which ideas and their carriers, such as epistemic communities, might gain influence.

However, of the three pathways, mechanism 2, the elite coalition-shift pathway, was clearly the most important. Interaction between grassroots activism and political or national security elites, especially in relation to congressional action, played a role in all three cases. Mechanism 2 was the key process in the Nixon case, and had a substantial impact in the Eisenhower and Reagan years as well. The importance of this pathway suggests that popular protest will not make a difference unless there is some overlap and connection between the goals and efforts of activists and elites.

This conclusion is entirely consistent with what studies of social movements on domestic issues have found. The social movement literature argues that access to part of the state is often a requirement for influence. Divisions among elites appear to be a pre-condition for having an impact, and forming a coalition with elites a critical component of the influence process.[2] The starting assumption of the theoretical framework, that activism on arms control would gain influence through the same channels that allow societal actors to affect domestic policy, was thus borne out. Peace movement efforts to influence foreign policy ultimately work in much the same way as domestic social movements.

Bottom-up versus top-down reconsidered

This study posed the question of the relation between domestic politics and interstate cooperation in terms of the difference between bottom-up and top-down conceptions. The fact that grassroots actors were important in every case where arms talks got underway supports the argument that analysis should not focus only on actors at the top. But the fact that divisions among and access to elites proved crucial also suggests that any image of a purely bottom-up process would be misleading. In none of the cases did citizens' movements produce efforts to seek cooperation solely on their own. The protest campaigns in this study always needed help from other actors, most often prestigious scientists and members of Congress, before they could change US policy.

Given the importance of elite coalition partners, one might reasonably ask whether citizen activism need be part of the explanation for arms control at all. If Congress always plays a role, why not, in the name of parsimony, leave out grassroots protest? At the very least, given the prominent role of the scientific epistemic community and senators like Hubert Humphrey and Ted Kennedy, why not conclude that the cases come closer to fitting the traditional top-down perspective? Here is one reason why the theoretical framework for this study stressed the importance of interaction. Just as protest movements cannot succeed without help, the same is often true of elites. The interaction goes two ways and is often vital to explaining the congressional role.

2 Leo W. Huberts, "The Influence of Social Movements on Government Policy," in Bert Klandermans, ed., *International Social Movement Research*, vol. II (Greenwich, CT: JAI Press, 1989); Thomas R. Rochon, "Political Movements and State Authority in Liberal Democracies," *World Politics* 42 (January 1990), pp. 299–313.

In all of the cases where talks began, the rise of citizen activism gave important encouragement to elites who favored arms control. Many of their decisions to take up the advocacy of arms restraint owed a great deal to their learning through protest of constituent interest, and many decisions to continue were made easier by supporting messages from activists. This was true for Stevenson's and Humphrey's efforts for a test ban, for several senators on the ABM issue, and for the House as a whole in the early 1980s. Especially for Ted Kennedy, decisions to take an active role in anti-ABM and pro-freeze efforts came only after the senator saw the high level of interest in those causes in his home state.[3]

Moreover, societal activism was also a critical resource for these elites. The possibility that the public would demand a unilateral halt to atmospheric testing or that grassroots lobbying would get Congress to vote against the MX created a concrete source of leverage for elites trying to engineer a change in US preferences. Political elites would not have undertaken the same actions, nor been nearly as successful, without such societal concerns lurking in the background, or, more accurately, the foreground. Interaction is important, for both grassroots actors and elites.

An inclination to dismiss the impact of societal activism because of the prominent role of scientific experts or Ted Kennedy would simply reveal an elitist bias. One would not similarly dismiss PSAC, even though these science advisors were in a position to make their key recommendations only because protest against testing had already made it an issue of concern for Eisenhower. Likewise, one would not minimize Nixon's and Kennedy's jockeying for an advantage in the 1972 campaign just because Kennedy's decision to make the ABM issue his focus was only made potent by the rising public opposition to military spending. Yet, many analysts would be inclined to downplay citizens' groups if their effectiveness depended on following the cues of technical experts or presidential hopefuls. If the fact that grassroots protest needs elite allies confirms a top-down approach, why would not elites' need for there to be social protest confirm a bottom-up approach? It merely shows an elitist bias to assume that a top-down explanation is best whenever elites are part of the story.

[3] Joel Primack and Frank Von Hippel, *Advice and Dissent: Scientists in the Political Arena* (New York: New American Library, 1974), p. 188; Douglas C. Waller, *Congress and the Nuclear Freeze: An Inside Look at the Politics of a Mass Movement* (Amherst: University of Massachusetts Press, 1987), p. 59.

My goal here is not to substitute the reverse bias and assume all cases with protest are bottom-up. But the interests and ideas of those near the top do not necessarily explain preferences just because certain elites have a role in mobilizing societal opposition. The question is what level of the domestic arena ultimately determines which preferences are reflected in policy. Top-down approaches assume the answer lies no lower than bureaucratic or intra-elite debates. Yet, PSAC could not have prevailed over the Pentagon and the AEC without outside help. Likewise, Ted Kennedy could not have won a contest on the ABM program with Richard Nixon if it had boiled down to their personal prestige or expertise on national security. Perhaps most clearly, no debate limited to recognized arms control specialists would have endorsed the nuclear freeze proposal.

To understand whose views prevailed, it is necessary to examine the balance of organized opinion in domestic society. US preferences did not always reflect the balance of opinion (or power) among elites taken in isolation. Instead, the preference being actively expressed by, and forming the basis for organizing efforts at, the grassroots level is the one that became policy. The idea of cooperation may not arise at the bottom, but if the decision to pursue that idea depends on its receiving active support from non-elites, then preferences will more accurately be predicted by the balance of concerns being expressed at the grassroots than by the balance among elites. Because citizens' campaigns need elite allies, though, the meaning of a bottom-up explanation has to be carefully delineated. It does not mean that societal activism single-handedly imposes its will on all elites. It means only that popular protest is a necessary part of the explanation because policy would not have turned out as it did had certain elite actions not been initiated in response to and benefited from mobilized societal support.

The results of this study are thus consistent with an observation that has emerged from other discussions of domestic structure. Some of the initial studies in this research program framed the question as one of state-centered versus society-centered explanations.[4] In many

[4] Stephen D. Krasner, *Defending the National Interest: Raw Materials Investments and US Foreign Policy* (Princeton: Princeton University Press, 1978); Peter B. Evans, Dietrich Rueschemeyer, and Theda Skocpol, eds., *Bringing the State Back In* (Cambridge: Cambridge University Press, 1985); G. John Ikenberry, David A. Lake, and Michael Mastanduno, eds., *The State and American Foreign Economic Policy* (Ithaca: Cornell University Press, 1988).

cases, though, one is more likely to see parts of society allied with parts of the state, in a contest with coalitions of other state and societal actors.[5] That was certainly the most common pattern in the cases this book examined.

Measurement of preferences

These observations have important implications for how we measure state preferences. Top-down approaches, especially those that are statesman-centered, tend to identify preferences with what national leaders state as their personal preferences, especially in internal communications that are not for public consumption. To the question of what state preferences are, this approach assumes they are whatever the president tells his advisors they are.[6]

This assumption, which is often only implicit, quickly runs into a problem. US policy does not always match the preferences expressed by the president. This often leads back to the notion of domestic politics as a constraint – the United States would have pursued its interests if only domestic opinion hadn't gotten in the way. However, if a president wants to stay out of arms talks, but 75 percent of the public and a majority of Congress say they want talks and they prevail, does it any longer make sense to say the United States has a preference *not* to pursue arms control? While the president remains the single most important actor in setting US foreign policy, because other actors also have influence, preferences should not always be identified with what the president says they are. As this study makes clear, preferences are really produced by the domestic system as a whole.

Sometimes, moreover, social protest is a decisive factor in which preference wins out. To reiterate, this does not mean that activism has to be the sole cause of a decision to seek cooperation. Because of other actors or developments, there may already be some propensity to cooperate. However, the case studies made it clear that arms control always had to compete against other Cold War and domestic policy

[5] Jeff Frieden, "Sectoral Conflict and US Foreign Economic Policy, 1914–1940," in Ikenberry et al., *The State and American Foreign Economic Policy*; Thomas Risse-Kappen, "Structures of Governance and Transnational Relations: What Have We Learned?" in Risse-Kappen, *Bringing Transnational Relations Back In*.

[6] For an explicit example, see G. John Ikenberry, *Reasons of State: Oil, Politics, and the Capacities of American Government* (Ithaca: Cornell University Press, 1988), p. 15, n. 26.

priorities. This means the desirability of cooperation on this issue taken in isolation did not always determine preferences. Unless the propensity to act on cooperative interests was great enough, it did not necessarily result in willingness to cooperate in practice. But when favorable international circumstances or other domestic actors created some degree of interest in cooperation that still fell short of generating willingness to act, the rise of societal activism consistently tipped the balance in favor of pursuing cooperation. In this sense, it served as a direct stimulus to the development of what would have to be considered a US preference for cooperation, even in some situations where the president did not privately hold the same preference.

One could perhaps argue that the distinction made in this study between society as a stimulus and society as a constraint is merely semantic. If the president prefers not to do something and domestic pressures force him to anyway, one could still say the president was constrained to act. But this again represents a choice to see things from the president's point of view, as activists would not be likely to consider themselves a constraint. Given the term's connotations, labeling all domestic efforts to change the president's policies as constraints could create an implication that domestic forces are in every case keeping the president from acting in the national interest. Yet, the majority of analysts believe nuclear arms control was consistent with the national interest. Thus, adopting the president's perspective and calling any form of domestic pressure a constraint could bias our inferences in favor of assuming the president is always right. This is a matter that is better judged on a case-by-case basis. When it takes a policy change to lead to new talks, it makes more sense to call the cause of that change a stimulus, which will also avoid automatically privileging the president's perspective.

Beyond the Cold War

Now that the Cold War has ended, barring a resurgence of Russian militarism, the issue of strategic arms control is unlikely to be a focus of activism in coming years. But there are many other international issues that might be affected by social protest. The framework developed here could potentially be generalized to cover other cases, meaning that the modified domestic structure approach used in this study could prove useful in exploring the ability of other citizens' movements to influence world politics. What must be generalized is the underlying approach, however, as certain details of the theoretical framework used here may have to be modified in other contexts.

Other countries

One potential direction of generalization is to other countries. This book has focused on protest's impact on US foreign policy, but the policies of many other countries have also been objects of protest. Indeed, the two largest campaigns studied in this book, the test ban and freeze movements, both had sizable counterparts overseas, especially in Western Europe. The impact of these other movements could certainly be studied using a framework similar to the one developed here. Whether the three influence mechanisms identified here would all apply or operate in the same way, however, will depend on the domestic political institutions in the country in question.

The influence pathway that is perhaps most likely to translate into other contexts without much modification may be mechanism 3. All modern countries now have sizable bureaucracies, typically divided into multiple ministries, more than one of which will usually be involved in foreign policymaking. In these circumstances, factions seeking to win a bureaucratic debate will be interested in possible outside sources of support, and they may find the problems or proposals raised by an activist campaign useful in that effort. A possible example, though one initiated by transgovernmental connections rather than domestic activism, is the Japanese use of *gaiatsu*, a term for foreign pressure. Japanese ministries seeking trade liberalization have sometimes explicitly invited US government pressure as a way to mobilize public opinion to overcome the domestic opponents of liberalization.[7] This practice seems to be a good example of the bureaucratic utilization pathway.

Any country with popular elections would also seem to be open to some form of mechanism 1, but the electoral pathway developed here will not hold universally. Rather, it will depend on the nature of election laws. Countries whose electoral systems favor two-party competition will create pressures on the two major parties to adopt policies near the center of voter opinion. But countries with propor-

[7] Leonard J. Schoppa, "Two-Level Games and Bargaining Outcomes: Why *Gaiatsu* Succeeds in Japan in Some Cases, But Not Others," *International Organization* 47 (Summer 1993), pp. 353–86.

tional representation or some other voting system that tends to support multiple parties will not necessarily experience median voter dynamics. On balance, an electoral route to influence on policy is probably made harder in multiparty systems, as major policy change will almost necessarily entail some larger process of coalition-building more akin to mechanism 2 than mechanism 1.

The operation of mechanism 2 as described in the cases in this book is nearly unique to the United States, however, because it depends on an independent legislature. In parliamentary systems where the prime minister is the head of the majority party, seeking to promote legislative opposition will usually not be a feasible option for advocacy groups. But working to build winning coalitions with elites in some form is likely to be necessary. In parliamentary systems, instead of working with congressional committees or individual legislators as in mechanism 2, activists will probably have to work with the political parties. Obtaining party platforms and slates that support activist positions will be the key, and working to build multiparty coalitions may also be necessary. The need to gain the support of whole parties will make influence harder to achieve than in the more entrepreneurial US system, but it may also make influence more long-lasting, as policy changes, once adopted, will tend to be institutionalized.[8]

The foregoing examples all concern democratic countries. The influence mechanisms identified in this study are less likely to translate easily into non-democratic settings. Societal influence will obviously be harder to achieve in most cases and, unlike the pathways in this study, the processes required may not involve gaining access to elites through existing institutions at all. Rather, more oppositional tactics, perhaps involving threats of disruption or even insurrection, may be necessary for grassroots actors seeking to change their government's stance on an international issue.

Other issues

While nuclear weapons protest seems unlikely to be widespread in the near future, it is certainly possible to predict societal activism on a range of other global issues. One way to assess the likely impact of such activism is to consider its potential to take advantage of influence pathways like the ones identified in this study. The most likely focus

[8] Risse-Kappen, "Public Opinion, Domestic Structure."

of extensive activism at the turn of the century is probably environmental issues. In an important way, environmental groups have channels for influence that were not as relevant for arms control and disarmament advocates. Those concerned about the nuclear arms race had to have the concurrence of superpower governments to do anything about it. Environmental groups, in contrast, can also make progress toward their objectives by changing individual lifestyles and corporate practices.[9]

Some environmental goals, however, will likely require changing government policies, especially to bring about international collaboration. Because scientific expertise is even more important in environmental policy than in arms control, a mechanism 3 process is likely to be central. Government scientists who favor environmental measures will often need support from outside scientists and grassroots groups to change state preferences to favor environmental cooperation. The other influence pathways are also likely to play a role, though. It is certainly hard not to suspect that electoral and congressional pressures were the main reason President Bush decided to attend the 1992 Earth Summit in Rio de Janeiro. This is also an issue where the balance of social pressures remains important, though, as it appears that economic interest groups played a major role in Bush's decision not to sign the biodiversity treaty that came out of the summit.[10]

Another issue where there is a well-established network of groups at work is human rights. Because such groups are often trying to target the policies of other states, rather than their own governments, obtaining influence becomes trickier. The cases in this book found that outside actors often gained leverage because of transnational connections with like-minded actors in the United States. This suggests that entering into transnational alliances with domestic human rights groups in the countries where abuses are happening may be especially important. If there is any opening for groups in such countries to petition their own governments, the visible support of the international community will be one of their most important resources.[11]

[9] Paul Wapner, "Politics Beyond the State: Environmental Activism and World Civic Politics," *World Politics* 47 (April 1995), pp. 311–40.

[10] *Los Angeles Times*, April 22, 1992, p. 8; May 30, 1992, pp. 1, 6, 19; *NYT*, May 7, 1992, p. 17; June 14, 1992, section IV, p. 1.

[11] Alison Brysk, "From Above and Below: Social Movements, the International System, and Human Rights in Argentina," *Comparative Political Studies* 26 (October 1993), pp. 259–85; Kathryn Sikkink, "Human Rights, Principled Issue-Networks, and Sovereignty in Latin America," *International Organization* 47 (Summer 1993), pp. 411–41.

In short, the role of transboundary connections is likely to be much greater in the human rights area.

Finally, much of the protest in coming decades may not be on the traditional liberal agenda at all, but may instead be in response to the adverse effects of globalization. Developing countries that have opened their markets to foreign imports may experience a domestic backlash against what traditionalists will see as the promotion of Western images and values. This may lead to demands for "cultural protectionism" that counter the trend toward liberalization of the global economy.[12] Before predicting success for such efforts, however, it will be important to identify the institutional access points for groups making these demands, in order to trace how much influence they can really exert.

In the United States, campaigns to restrict immigration, both legal and illegal, may be an equivalent form of backlash. Such protests need to be taken seriously, as they seem to have the potential to utilize both the electoral and coalition-shift pathways. Indeed, the domestic structure approach developed in this study indicates that anti-immigrant campaigns may have more impact than standard political economy approaches would lead one to expect. Such approaches emphasize the balance of economic interests. Since the firms who benefit from international free trade currently outnumber those who are hurt by it, such approaches imply a coalition in favor of liberalization will continue to be dominant.[13] But this is an area where reducing everything to strictly economic interests is likely to be misleading. Many of those who oppose immigration, greater free trade, and so forth are responding to issues of identity. They are concerned about whether white Americans will continue to be in the majority and familiar cultural patterns will be maintained or overwhelmed. It would be better to trace their efforts to alter the direction of American policy through the influence pathways this study has identified, rather than assume *a priori* that such efforts will fail because they do not reflect the balance of economic interests.

12 This question is the focus of a forthcoming Ph.D. dissertation by Brian K. Dennehy at the University of Southern California.

13 Frieden, "Sectoral Conflict"; Helen Milner, *Resisting Protectionism* (Princeton: Princeton University Press, 1988).

Final thoughts

The findings of this study make it possible to conclude on what I regard as a hopeful note. Ordinary citizens can make a difference in world politics. Grassroots movements played a role in fostering all of the major strategic arms talks of the Cold War. Moreover, this finding probably understates their overall impact. This book has focused on activism's effects on policy at the time. Yet, many observers have noted that social movements can also have a long-run impact on the attitudes prevalent within a culture; movements with a transnational dimension might even be shaping a global civil society.[14]

The longer-run effects of anti-nuclear weapons protest were dramatically illustrated in late 1996. At that time, General George Lee Butler, a former commander of the Strategic Air Command, the main wing of the United States' nuclear arsenal, gave a speech calling for eventual nuclear disarmament. An interview with Butler in the *New York Times* reported:

> The impetus for his anti-nuclear sentiments came from watching worldwide protests against France's testing of nuclear weapons in the South Pacific in the fall of 1995. "Governments lag behind the public in these questions," General Butler said of the protests. "The underlying message was: 'Look, the nuclear era is over. Don't bring it back. Let's get on with it.'"[15]

While important, the observation that citizens' movements can affect social values over the long run was, I suspect, motivated in part by a sense they cannot do much about policy choices at the time. The present study has taken on this area where people may be less inclined to expect influence and shown activism can affect the policies of the moment, even on the rather hard case of nuclear weapons policy. Some important caveats come with this conclusion, though. For one thing, peace movements did not get exactly the outcomes they wanted. None of the arms talks whose initiation I examined in this study produced agreements containing everything advocacy groups sought. The test ban talks did not produce a comprehensive test ban, instead exempting underground testing, a significant loophole. SALT I placed no restrictions on MIRVs, a failure that later produced serious

[14] Joseph Gusfield, "Social Movements and Social Change: Perspectives on Linearity and Fluidity," in Louis Kriesberg, ed., *Research in Social Movements, Conflicts, and Change*, vol. IV (Greenwich, CT: JAI Press, 1981); Wapner, "Politics Beyond the State."

[15] *NYT*, January 8, 1997, p. 12.

problems. And President Reagan never proposed a nuclear freeze, instead taking START talks in a different direction.

This is thus another case of whether the glass is half-full or half-empty. In my research for this study, I found most of the emphasis in the past has been on the limitations of peace movement influence.[16] Those limitations are real, but it is important also to recognize what grassroots campaigns can accomplish. They helped place three sets of arms talks on the agenda, each of which produced treaty agreements and follow-on talks. Even though advocacy groups could not determine the terms of the agreements that resulted, the initial effort to cooperate, which is also very important, owed much in these cases to impulses arising from domestic society.

While citizen activism was significant in these cases, the research in this book also suggests that influence is by no means automatic. It depends on whether other circumstances are favorable. However, the framework developed here did a good job identifying those circumstances for US domestic activism on behalf of arms restraint. Overall, this means that citizen activism is indeed a useful, and usable, variable. It does sometimes make a difference, and it is possible to anticipate when it will have an impact and what kind.

Not everyone favors what the protest movements examined in this study tried to accomplish. For better or for worse, though, these movements had a real impact. It would be a shame, therefore, to rely on theories whose assumptions either do not allow for, or simply do not consider, this possibility. If all explanations for state preferences regarding cooperation retain a top-down perspective, this might send a signal to average individuals that they should not even bother trying to participate in foreign policy debates. It might also imply to national leaders that they can ignore the hopes and fears of ordinary citizens. These conclusions would be a mistake. It is therefore necessary to broaden the ways we think about domestic politics in future research on international cooperation.

16 A thoughtful example is David S. Meyer, *A Winter of Discontent: The Nuclear Freeze and American Politics* (New York: Praeger, 1990).

Bibliography

Memoirs and diaries

Adams, Sherman. *Firsthand Report: The Story of the Eisenhower Administration.* New York: Harper and Bros., 1961.

Adelman, Kenneth L. *The Great Universal Embrace: Arms Summitry – A Skeptic's Account.* New York: Simon and Schuster, 1989.

Anderson, Martin. *Revolution: The Reagan Legacy,* rev. edn. Stanford, CA: Hoover Institution Press, 1990.

Eisenhower, Dwight D. *The White House Years: Mandate for Change, 1953–1956.* Garden City, NY: Doubleday & Co., 1963.

The White House Years: Waging Peace, 1956–1961. Garden City, NY: Doubleday & Co., 1965.

Ferrell, Robert H., ed. *The Eisenhower Diaries.* New York: W. W. Norton & Co., 1981.

Haig, Alexander M., Jr. *Caveat: Realism, Reagan, and Foreign Policy.* New York: Macmillan, 1984.

Haldeman, H. R. *The Haldeman Diaries.* New York: G. P. Putnam's Sons, 1994.

Hughes, Emmet John. *The Ordeal of Power: A Political Memoir of the Eisenhower Years.* New York: Atheneum, 1963.

Humphrey, Hubert H. *The Education of a Public Man: My Life and Politics.* Garden City, NY: Doubleday & Co., 1976.

Killian, James R., Jr. *Sputnik, Scientists, and Eisenhower.* Cambridge: MIT Press, 1977.

Kissinger, Henry. *White House Years.* Boston: Little, Brown, and Company, 1979.

Kistiakowsky, George B. *A Scientist at the White House.* Cambridge, MA: Harvard University Press, 1976.

Meese, Edwin. *With Reagan.* Washington, DC: Regnery Gateway, 1992.

Nixon, Richard. *RN: The Memoirs of Richard Nixon.* New York: Warner Books, 1978.

Reagan, Ronald. *An American Life.* New York: Simon and Schuster, 1990.

Regan, Donald T. *For the Record.* New York: St. Martin's Press, 1988.

Safire, William. *Before the Fall: An Inside View of the Pre-Watergate White House.* Garden City, NY: Doubleday & Co., 1975.

Sakharov, Andrei. *Memoirs.* New York: Alfred A. Knopf, 1990.

Shevchenko, Arkady N. *Breaking with Moscow.* New York: Alfred A. Knopf, 1985.

Shultz, George P. *Turmoil and Triumph: My Years as Secretary of State.* New York: Charles Scribner's Sons, 1993.

Smith, Gerard. *Doubletalk: The Story of SALT I.* Lanham, MD: University Press of America, 1985.

Stassen, Harold, and Marshall Houts. *Eisenhower: Turning the World Toward Peace.* St. Paul, MN: Merrill/Magnus Publishing Corp., 1990.

Strauss, Lewis L. *Men and Decisions.* Garden City, NY: Doubleday & Co., 1962.

Wadsworth, James J. *The Price of Peace.* New York: Frederick A. Praeger, 1962.

York, Herbert F. *Making Weapons, Talking Peace: A Physicist's Odyssey from Hiroshima to Geneva.* New York: Basic Books, 1987.

Interviews (conducted by author, May–August 1989)

Kenneth Adelman
Jim Bodner
Richard Burt
Eugene Carroll
Steve Daggett
Robert Dean
Paula Dobriansky
Nancy Donaldson
Kenneth Duberstein
Robert Einhorn
Bill Fite
David Gergen
James Goodby
Thomas Graham
Pat Harmon
Mark Hatfield
William Hoehn
Sally Horn
Bob Huber
Fred Ikle
John Isaacs
Randall Kehler
Sven Kraemer
Christopher Lehman
Robert Linhard
Reuben McCornack
Robert McFarlane
Carrie McMillen

Judith Mandel
Mike Mawby
Roger Molander
Paul Nitze
Christopher Paine
Richard Pipes
Richard Rolf
Eugene Rostow
Bob Sherman
George Shultz
James Timbie
Don Todd
Paul Weyrich
Richard Wirthlin

Government documents

Branyan, Robert L., and Lawrence H. Larsen, eds. *The Eisenhower Administration, 1953–1961: A Documentary History*. New York: Random House, 1971.

Congressional Record.

Declassified Documents Reference System (DDRS). Woodbridge, CT: Research Publications.

Department of State Bulletin.

Foreign Relations of the United States (FRUS).

Gray, Robert C. "Congress, Arms Control, and Weapons Modernization," in US House of Representatives, Committee on Foreign Affairs, *Congress and Foreign Policy, 1983*, a Congressional Research Service report. Washington, DC: Government Printing Office, 1984.

Nixon Presidential Materials, National Archives at College Park, MD.

US Department of Commerce, Bureau of Economic Analysis. *Handbook of Cyclical Indicators*. Washington, DC: Government Printing Office, 1984.

US Department of State, Historical Office, Bureau of Public Affairs. *Documents on Disarmament*, vol. I, 1945–56. Washington, DC: Government Printing Office, 1960.

Secondary sources

Adler, Emanuel. "The Emergence of Cooperation: National Epistemic Communities and the International Evolution of the Idea of Nuclear Arms Control," *International Organization* 46 (Winter 1992), pp. 101–45.

Adler, Emanuel, and Peter M. Haas. "Conclusion: Epistemic Communities, World Order, and the Creation of a Reflective Research Program," *International Organization* 46 (Winter 1992), pp. 367–90.

Aggarwal, Vinod K., and Pierre Allan. "The Origin of Games: A Theory of the Formation of Ordinal Preferences and Games," in Michael D. Intriligator and Urs Luterbacher, eds., *Cooperative Models in International Relations Research*. Boston: Kluwer Academic Publishers, 1994.

Aldrich, John H., and Forrest D. Nelson. *Linear Probability, Logit, and Probit Models*. Beverly Hills: Sage Publications, 1984.

Aldrich, John H., John L. Sullivan, and Eugene Borgida. "Foreign Affairs and Issue Voting: Do Presidential Candidates 'Waltz Before a Blind Audience'?," *American Political Science Review* 83 (March 1989), pp. 123–41.

Allison, Graham T. *Essence of Decision: Explaining the Cuban Missile Crisis*. Boston: Little, Brown, 1971.

Almond, Gabriel A. *The American People and Foreign Policy*. New York: Frederick A. Praeger, 1960.

Ambrose, Stephen E. *Eisenhower: The President*. New York: Simon and Schuster, 1984.

Nixon: The Triumph of a Politician, 1962–1972. New York: Simon and Schuster, 1989.

Art, Robert J. "Bureaucratic Politics and American Foreign Policy: A Critique," *Policy Sciences* 4 (December 1973), pp. 467–90.

Axelrod, Robert. *The Evolution of Cooperation*. New York: Basic Books, 1984.

Axelrod, Robert, and Robert O. Keohane. "Achieving Cooperation Under Anarchy: Strategies and Institutions," in Oye, *Cooperation Under Anarchy*.

Ayanian, Robert. "Nuclear Consequences of the Welfare State," *Public Choice* 49 (1986), pp. 201–22.

Ball, Howard. *Justice Downwind: America's Atomic Testing Program in the 1950s*. New York: Oxford University Press, 1986.

Bard, Mitchell Geoffrey. "The Influence of Ethnic Interest Groups on American Middle East Policy," in Eugene R. Wittkopf, ed., *The Domestic Sources of American Foreign Policy*, 2nd edn. New York: St. Martin's Press, 1994.

Bauer, Raymond A., Ithiel de Sola Pool, and Lewis Anthony Dexter. *American Business and Public Policy: The Politics of Foreign Trade*, 2nd edn. Chicago: Aldine-Atherton, 1972.

Baumgartner, Frank R., and Bryan D. Jones. *Agendas and Instability in American Politics*. Chicago: University of Chicago Press, 1993.

Blechman, Barry M. "The New Congressional Role in Arms Control," in Thomas E. Mann, ed., *A Question of Balance: The President, the Congress, and Foreign Policy*. Washington, DC: The Brookings Institution, 1990.

Bowie, Robert R. "Eisenhower, Atomic Weapons, and Atoms for Peace," in Pilat, et al., *Atoms for Peace*.

Brody, Richard A., and Catherine R. Shapiro. "A Reconsideration of the Rally Phenomenon in Public Opinion," in Samuel Long, ed., *Political Behavior Annual*, vol. II. Boulder: Westview Press, 1989.

Brysk, Alison. "From Above and Below: Social Movements, the International System, and Human Rights in Argentina," *Comparative Political Studies* 26 (October 1993), pp. 259–85.

Bundy, McGeorge. *Danger and Survival: Choices About the Bomb in the First Fifty Years*. New York: Vintage Books, 1988.

Bundy, McGeorge, George F. Kennan, Robert S. McNamara, and Gerard

Smith. "Nuclear Weapons and the Atlantic Alliance," *Foreign Affairs* 60 (Spring 1982), pp. 753–68.

Burgin, Eileen. "The Influence of Constituents," in Randall B. Ripley and James M. Lindsay, eds., *Congress Resurgent: Foreign and Defense Policy on Capitol Hill*. Ann Arbor: University of Michigan Press, 1993.

Cahn, Anne Hessing. "American Scientists and the ABM," in Albert H. Teich, ed., *Scientists and Public Affairs*. Cambridge, MA: MIT Press, 1974.

Caldwell, Dan. *The Dynamics of Domestic Politics and Arms Control: The SALT II Treaty Ratification Debate*. Columbia, SC: University of South Carolina Press, 1991.

Carnesale, Albert, and Richard N. Haass, eds. *Superpower Arms Control: Setting the Record Straight*. Cambridge, MA: Ballinger, 1987.

Carter, April. *Success and Failure in Arms Control Negotiations*. Oxford: Oxford University Press, 1989.

Chappell, Henry W., Jr., and William R. Keech. "Policy Motivation and Party Differences in a Dynamic Spatial Model of Party Competition," *American Political Science Review* 80 (September 1986), pp. 881–99.

Charlton, Michael. *From Deterrence to Defense: The Inside Story of Strategic Policy*. Cambridge, MA: Harvard University Press, 1987.

Checkel, Jeffrey T. "Ideas, Institutions, and the Gorbachev Foreign Policy Revolution," *World Politics* 45 (January 1993), pp. 271–300.

Ideas and International Politics: Soviet/Russian Behavior and the End of the Cold War. New Haven: Yale University Press, 1997.

Cobb, Roger W., and Charles D. Elder. *Participation in American Politics: The Dynamics of Agenda-Building*, 2nd edn. Baltimore: Johns Hopkins University Press, 1983.

Cohen, Michael D., James G. March, and Johan P. Olsen. "A Garbage Can Model of Organizational Choice," *Administrative Science Quarterly* 17 (March 1972), pp. 1–25.

Collins, John M. *US–Soviet Military Balance, 1980–1985*. Washington, DC: Pergamon-Brassey's, 1985.

Conybeare, John. "Trade Wars," in Oye, *Cooperation Under Anarchy*.

Cortright, David. *Peace Works: The Citizen's Role in Ending the Cold War*. Boulder: Westview Press, 1993.

Coughlin, Peter J. "Candidate Uncertainty and Electoral Equilibria," in Enelow and Hinich, *Advances in the Spatial Theory*.

Crumm, Eileen. "The Value of Economic Incentives in International Politics," *Journal of Peace Research* 32 (August 1995), pp. 313–30.

Daalder, Ivo H. "The Limited Test Ban Treaty," in Carnesale and Haass, *Superpower Arms Control*.

Deese, David A., ed., *The New Politics of American Foreign Policy*. New York: St. Martin's Press, 1994.

Derthick, Martha, and Paul J. Quirk. *The Politics of Deregulation*. Washington, DC: The Brookings Institution, 1985.

Divine, Robert A. *Blowing on the Wind: The Nuclear Test Ban Debate, 1954–1960.* New York: Oxford University Press, 1978.

Downs, Anthony. *An Economic Theory of Democracy.* New York: Harper & Row, 1957.

Downs, George W., and David M. Rocke. *Tacit Bargaining, Arms Races, and Arms Control.* Ann Arbor: University of Michigan Press, 1990.

Eckstein, Harry. "Case Studies in Political Science," in Nelson Polsby and Fred I. Greenstein, eds., *Handbook of Political Science,* vol. VII. Reading, MA: Addison-Wesley, 1975.

Eichenberg, Richard C. "Dual Track and Double Trouble: The Two-Level Politics of INF," in Evans, Jacobson, and Putnam, *Double-Edged Diplomacy.*

Enelow, James M., James W. Endersby, and Michael C. Munger. "A Revised Probabilistic Spatial Model of Elections: Theory and Evidence," in Grofman, *Information, Participation, and Choice.*

Enelow, James M., and Melvin J. Hinich, eds., *Advances in the Spatial Theory of Voting.* Cambridge: Cambridge University Press, 1990.

Evangelista, Matthew. "Issue-Area and Foreign Policy Revisited," *International Organization* 43 (Winter 1989), pp. 147–71.

"Cooperation Theory and Disarmament Negotiations in the 1950s," *World Politics* 42 (July 1990), pp. 502–28.

"Sources of Moderation in Soviet Security Policy," in Philip E. Tetlock, Jo L. Husbands, Robert Jervis, Paul C. Stern, and Charles Tilly, eds., *Behavior, Society, and Nuclear War,* vol. II. New York: Oxford University Press, 1991.

"The Paradox of State Strength: Transnational Relations, Domestic Structures, and Security Policy in Russia and the Soviet Union," *International Organization* 49 (Winter 1995), pp. 1–38.

"Taming the Bear: Transnational Relations and the Demise of the Soviet Threat." Typescript, Cornell University, 1997.

Evans, Peter B. "Building an Integrative Approach to International and Domestic Politics," in Evans, Jacobson, and Putnam, *Double-Edged Diplomacy.*

Evans, Peter B., Harold K. Jacobson, and Robert D. Putnam, eds. *Double-Edged Diplomacy: International Bargaining and Domestic Politics.* Berkeley: University of California Press, 1993.

Evans, Peter B., Dietrich Rueschemeyer, and Theda Skocpol, eds. *Bringing the State Back In.* Cambridge: Cambridge University Press, 1985.

Farley, Philip J. "Strategic Arms Control, 1967–1987," in George, Farley, and Dallin, *US–Soviet Security Cooperation.*

Feighan, Edward F. "The Freeze in Congress," in Paul M. Cole and William J. Taylor, eds., *The Nuclear Freeze Debate: Arms Control Issues for the 1980s.* Boulder: Westview Press, 1983.

Fenno, Richard F. *Congressmen in Committees.* Boston: Little, Brown, 1973.

Ferejohn, John. "The Spatial Model and Elections," in Grofman, *Information, Participation, and Choice.*

Finnemore, Martha. *National Interests in International Society.* Ithaca: Cornell University Press, 1996.

[Forsberg, Randall]. "Call to Halt the Nuclear Arms Race: Proposal for a Mutual US–Soviet Nuclear Weapons Freeze," pamphlet, April 1982 (St. Louis: Nuclear Weapons Freeze Campaign, 1982).

Frieden, Jeff. "Sectoral Conflict and US Foreign Economic Policy, 1914–1940," in Ikenberry, et al., *The State and American Foreign Economic Policy.*

Gaddis, John Lewis. *Strategies of Containment*. New York: Oxford University Press, 1982.

Gais, Thomas L., Mark A. Peterson, and Jack L. Walker. "Interest Groups, Iron Triangles, and Representative Institutions in American National Government," *British Journal of Political Science* 14 (April 1984), pp. 161–85.

Gamson, William A. *The Strategy of Social Protest*, rev. edn. Belmont, CA: Wadsworth Press, 1990.

Garfinkle, Adam M. *The Politics of the Nuclear Freeze*. Philadelphia: Foreign Policy Research Institute, 1984.

Garthoff, Raymond L. *Detente and Confrontation*. Washington, DC: The Brookings Institution, 1985.

George, Alexander L. "Case Studies and Theory Development," in Paul Gordon Lauren, ed., *Diplomacy: New Approaches*. New York: Free Press, 1979.

"Domestic Constraints on Regime Change in US Foreign Policy: The Need for Policy Legitimacy," in Ole R. Holsti, Randolph M. Siverson, and Alexander L. George, eds., *Change in the International System*. Boulder: Westview Press, 1980.

"Factors Influencing Security Cooperation," in George, Farley, and Dallin, *US–Soviet Security Cooperation*.

"Strategies for Facilitating Cooperation," in George, Farley, and Dallin, *US–Soviet Security Cooperation*.

George, Alexander L., Philip J. Farley, and Alexander Dallin, eds., *US–Soviet Security Cooperation: Achievements, Failures, Lessons*. New York: Oxford University Press, 1988.

George, Alexander L., and Timothy J. McKeown. "Case Studies and Theories of Organizational Decision Making," in *Advances in Information Processing in Organizations*, vol. II. Greenwich, CT: JAI Press, 1985.

Gilpin, Robert. "The Politics of Transnational Economic Relations," in Keohane and Nye, *Transnational Relations and World Politics*.

Glaser, Charles L. "Realists as Optimists: Cooperation as Self-Help," *International Security* 19 (Winter 1994/95), pp. 50–90.

Goldstein, Joshua S., and John R. Freeman. *Three-Way Street: Strategic Reciprocity in World Politics*. Chicago: University of Chicago Press, 1990.

Goldstein, Judith, and Robert O. Keohane, eds. *Ideas and Foreign Policy: Beliefs, Institutions, and Political Change*. Ithaca: Cornell University Press, 1993.

Gourevitch, Peter. "The Second Image Reversed: The International Sources of Domestic Politics," *International Organization* 32 (Autumn 1978), pp. 881–912.

Politics in Hard Times: Comparative Responses to International Economic Crisis. Ithaca: Cornell University Press, 1986.

Gowa, Joanne. "Anarchy, Egoism, and Third Images: *The Evolution of Cooperation* and International Relations," *International Organization* 40 (Winter 1986), pp. 167–86.

Graham, Thomas W. "The Politics of Failure: Strategic Nuclear Arms Control, Public Opinion, and Domestic Politics in the United States, 1945–1980," Ph.D. dissertation, MIT, 1989.

"Public Opinion and US Foreign Policy Decision Making," in Deese, *The New Politics of American Foreign Policy.*

Gray, Colin S. *House of Cards: Why Arms Control Must Fail.* Ithaca: Cornell University Press, 1992.

Greenwood, Ted. *Making the MIRV.* Cambridge, MA: Ballinger Publishing, 1975.

Grieco, Joseph. *Cooperation Among Nations: Europe, America, and Non-Tariff Barriers to Trade.* Ithaca: Cornell University Press, 1990.

Griffiths, Franklyn. "The Soviet Experience of Arms Control," in Stein, *Getting to the Table.*

Grofman, Bernard, ed., *Information, Participation, and Choice: "An Economic Theory of Democracy" in Perspective.* Ann Arbor: University of Michigan Press, 1993.

Gusfield, Joseph. "Social Movements and Social Change: Perspectives on Linearity and Fluidity," in Louis Kriesberg, ed., *Research in Social Movements, Conflicts, and Change*, vol. IV. Greenwich, CT: JAI Press, 1981.

Haas, Ernst B. "Why Collaborate? Issue-Linkage and International Regimes," *World Politics* 32 (April 1980), pp. 357–405.

Haas, Peter M. "Introduction: Epistemic Communities and International Policy Coordination," *International Organization* 46 (Winter 1992), pp. 1–35.

Haggard, Stephan, and Beth A. Simmons. "Theories of International Regimes," *International Organization* 41 (Summer 1987), pp. 491–517.

Halperin, Morton H., with the assistance of Priscilla Clapp and Arnold Kanter. *Bureaucratic Politics and Foreign Policy.* Washington, DC: The Brookings Institution, 1974.

Hampson, Fen Osler. "Headed for the Table: United States Approaches to Arms Control Prenegotiation," in Stein, *Getting to the Table.*

Hartley, Thomas, and Bruce Russett. "Public Opinion and the Common Defense," *American Political Science Review* 86 (December 1992), pp. 905–15.

Heclo, Hugh. "Issue Networks and the Executive Establishment," in Anthony King, ed., *The New American Political System.* Washington, DC: American Enterprise Institute, 1978.

Herken, Gregg. *The Winning Weapon: The Atomic Bomb in the Cold War, 1945–1950.* New York: Alfred A. Knopf, 1981.

Counsels of War, expanded edn. New York: Oxford University Press, 1987.

Cardinal Choices: Presidential Science Advising from the Atomic Bomb to SDI. New York: Oxford University Press, 1992.

Hersh, Seymour M. *The Price of Power: Kissinger in the Nixon White House.* New York: Summit Books, 1983.

Hewlett, Richard G. "From Proposal to Program," in Pilat, et al., *Atoms for Peace.*

Hewlett, Richard G., and Jack M. Holl. *Atoms for Peace and War, 1953–1961: Eisenhower and the Atomic Energy Commission*. Berkeley: University of California Press, 1989.

Hinckley, Barbara. *Less than Meets the Eye: Foreign Policymaking and the Myth of the Assertive Congress*. Chicago: University of Chicago Press, 1994.

Holsti, Ole R. "Public Opinion and Containment," in Terry L. Deibel and John Lewis Gaddis, eds., *Containing the Soviet Union: A Critique of US Policy.* Washington, DC: Pergamon-Brassey's, 1987.

Hosmer, David W., and Stanley Lemeshow. *Applied Logistic Regression*. New York: John Wiley & Sons, 1989.

Huberts, Leo W. "The Influence of Social Movements on Government Policy," in Bert Klandermans, ed., *International Social Movement Research*, vol. II. Greenwich, CT: JAI Press, 1989.

Ikenberry, G. John. "The Irony of State Strength: Comparative Responses to the Oil Shocks in the 1970s," *International Organization* 40 (Winter 1986), pp. 105–37.

Reasons of State: Oil, Politics, and the Capacities of American Government. Ithaca: Cornell University Press, 1988.

Ikenberry, G. John, David A. Lake, and Michael Mastanduno, eds. *The State and American Foreign Economic Policy.* Ithaca: Cornell University Press, 1988.

Jacobsen, John Kurt. "Much Ado About Ideas: The Cognitive Factor in Economic Policy," *World Politics* 47 (January 1995), pp. 283–310.

Jacobson, Harold K., and Eric Stein. *Diplomats, Scientists, and Politicians: The United States and the Nuclear Test Ban Negotiations*. Ann Arbor: University of Michigan Press, 1966.

James, Patrick, and John R. Oneal. "The Influence of Domestic and International Politics on the President's Use of Force," *Journal of Conflict Resolution* 35 (June 1991), pp. 307–32.

Jensen, Lloyd. *Bargaining for National Security: The Postwar Disarmament Negotiations*. Columbia, SC: University of South Carolina Press, 1988.

Jepperson, Ronald L., Alexander Wendt, and Peter J. Katzenstein. "Norms, Identity, and Culture in National Security," in Katzenstein, *Culture of National Security.*

Jervis, Robert. "Security Regimes," in Stephen D. Krasner, ed., *International Regimes*. Ithaca: Cornell University Press, 1983.

"From Balance to Concert," in Oye, *Cooperation Under Anarchy.*

"Realism, Game Theory, and Cooperation," *World Politics* 40 (April 1988), pp. 317–49.

The Meaning of the Nuclear Revolution. Ithaca: Cornell University Press, 1989.

Johnston, Carla B. *Reversing the Nuclear Arms Race*. Cambridge, MA: Schenkman Books, 1986.

Jönsson, Christer. *Superpower: Comparing American and Soviet Foreign Policy.* London: Frances Pinter, 1984.

Katz, Milton S. *Ban the Bomb: A History of SANE, the Committee for a Sane Nuclear Policy.* New York: Praeger, 1987; Greenwood Press, 1986.

Katzenstein, Peter J. "Introduction: Domestic and International Forces and Strategies of Foreign Economic Policy," in Katzenstein, *Between Power and Plenty.*

Katzenstein, Peter J., ed. *Between Power and Plenty: Foreign Economic Policies of Advanced Industrial States.* Madison: University of Wisconsin Press, 1978.

The Culture of National Security: Norms and Identity in World Politics. New York: Columbia University Press, 1996.

Katzenstein, Peter J., and Nobuo Okawara. *Japan's National Security: Structures, Norms, and Policy Responses in a Changing World.* Ithaca: Cornell University East Asia Program, 1993.

Keohane, Robert O. *After Hegemony: Cooperation and Discord in the World Political Economy.* Princeton: Princeton University Press, 1984.

"The World Political Economy and the Crisis of Embedded Liberalism," in John H. Goldthorpe, ed., *Order and Conflict in Contemporary Capitalism.* Oxford: Clarendon Press, 1984.

"Institutional Theory and the Realist Challenge After the Cold War," in David A. Baldwin, ed., *Neorealism and Neoliberalism: The Contemporary Debate.* New York: Columbia University Press, 1993.

Keohane, Robert O., and Joseph S. Nye, Jr. "Transgovernmental Relations and International Organizations," *World Politics* 27 (October 1974), pp. 39–62.

Keohane, Robert O., and Joseph S. Nye, Jr., eds. *Transnational Relations and World Politics.* Cambridge, MA: Harvard University Press, 1972.

Khrushchev, Sergei. *Nikita Khrushchev: krizisy i rakety.* Moscow: Novosti, 1994.

King, Gary, Robert O. Keohane, and Sidney Verba. *Designing Social Inquiry: Scientific Inference in Qualitative Research.* Princeton: Princeton University Press, 1994.

Kingdon, John W. *Agendas, Alternatives, and Public Policies.* Boston: Little, Brown, 1984.

Kitschelt, Herbert. "Political Opportunity Structures and Political Protest: Anti-Nuclear Movements in Four Democracies," *British Journal of Political Science* 16 (January 1986), pp. 57–85.

Kleidman, Robert. *Organizing for Peace: Neutrality, the Test Ban, and the Freeze.* Syracuse: Syracuse University Press, 1993.

Klotz, Audie. *Norms in International Relations: The Struggle Against Apartheid.* Ithaca: Cornell University Press, 1995.

Knopf, Jeffrey W. "Domestic Politics, Citizen Activism, and US Nuclear Arms Control Policy," Ph.D. dissertation, Stanford University, 1991.

"Beyond Two-Level Games: Domestic–International Interaction in the Intermediate-Range Nuclear Forces Negotiations," *International Organization* 47 (Autumn 1993), pp. 599–628.

"Domestic Sources of Preferences for Cooperation in Arms Control: The Impact of Protest on US Decisions to Enter Arms Talks," paper presented at the annual meeting of the American Political Science Association, Chicago, August 31–September 3, 1995.

"The Nuclear Freeze Movement's Effect on Policy," in Rochon and Meyer, *Coalitions and Political Movements*.

Kollman, Ken, John H. Miller, and Scott E. Page. "Adaptive Parties in Spatial Elections," *American Political Science Review* 86 (December 1992), pp. 929–37.

Korb, Lawrence J., and Linda P. Brady. "Rearming America: The Reagan Administration Defense Program," *International Security* 9 (Winter 1984/85), pp. 3–18.

Kowert, Paul, and Jeffrey Legro. "Norms, Identity, and Their Limits: A Theoretical Reprise," in Katzenstein, *Culture of National Security*.

Kramer, Bernard M., S. Michael Kalick, and Michael A. Milburn. "Attitudes Toward Nuclear Weapons and Nuclear War, 1945–1982," *Journal of Social Issues* 39 (1983), pp. 7–24.

Krasner, Stephen D. "Are Bureaucracies Important? (Or Allison Wonderland)," *Foreign Policy* 7 (Summer 1972), pp. 159–79.

Defending the National Interest: Raw Materials Investments and US Foreign Policy. Princeton: Princeton University Press, 1978.

Kruzel, Joseph. "From Rush–Bagot to START: The Lessons of Arms Control," *Orbis* 30 (Spring 1986), pp. 193–216.

Larson, Deborah Welch. "Crisis Prevention and the Austrian State Treaty," *International Organization* 41 (Winter 1987), pp. 27–60.

"Learning in US–Soviet Relations: The Nixon–Kissinger Structure of Peace," in George W. Breslauer and Philip E. Tetlock, eds., *Learning in US and Soviet Foreign Policy*. Boulder: Westview Press, 1991.

Leavitt, Robert. "Freezing the Arms Race: The Genesis of a Mass Movement," and supplements, Case Study C14-83-557, written for the Case Program, John F. Kennedy School of Government, Harvard University, 1983.

Legro, Jeffrey W. "Culture and Preferences in the International Cooperation Two-Step," *American Political Science Review* 90 (March 1996), pp. 118–37.

Lepper, Mary Milling. *Foreign Policy Formulation: A Case Study of the Nuclear Test Ban Treaty of 1963*. Columbus, OH: Charles E. Merrill, 1971.

Levy, Jack S. "The Diversionary Theory of War: A Critique," in Manus I. Midlarsky, ed., *Handbook of War Studies*. Boston: Unwin Hyman, 1989.

Light, Paul C. *The President's Agenda: Domestic Policy Choice from Kennedy to Reagan*, rev. edn. Baltimore: Johns Hopkins University Press, 1991.

Lipson, Charles. "International Cooperation in Economic and Security Affairs," *World Politics* 37 (October 1984), pp. 1–23.

McCrea, Frances B., and Gerald E. Markle. *Minutes to Midnight: Nuclear Weapons Protest in America*. Newbury Park, CA: Sage Publications, 1989.

McGinnis, Michael D., and John T. Williams. "Change and Stability in

Superpower Rivalry," *American Political Science Review* 83 (December 1989), pp. 1101–23.

McKeever, Porter. *Adlai Stevenson: His Life and Legacy.* New York: William Morrow, 1989.

Mandelbaum, Michael. *The Nuclear Question: The United States and Nuclear Weapons, 1946–1976.* New York: Cambridge University Press, 1979.

Mansbridge, Jane J. "A Deliberative Theory of Interest Representation," in Petracca, *Politics of Interests.*

Marra, Robin F., Charles W. Ostrom, Jr., and Dennis M. Simon. "Foreign Policy and Presidential Popularity," *Journal of Conflict Resolution* 34 (December 1990), pp. 588–623.

Martin, Lisa L. *Coercive Cooperation: Explaining Multilateral Economic Sanctions.* Princeton: Princeton University Press, 1992.

Marullo, Sam. "US Grass-Roots Opposition to the Euromissile Deployment," in Bert Klandermans, ed., *International Social Movement Research,* vol. III. Greenwich, CT: JAI Press, 1991.

Mastanduno, Michael. *Economic Containment: CoCom and the Politics of East–West Trade.* Ithaca: Cornell University Press, 1992.

Mastanduno, Michael, David A. Lake, and G. John Ikenberry. "Toward a Realist Theory of State Action," *International Studies Quarterly* 33 (December 1989), pp. 457–74.

Melanson, Richard A. "The Foundations of Eisenhower's Foreign Policy: Continuity, Community, and Consensus," in Melanson and Mayers, *Reevaluating Eisenhower.*

Melanson, Richard A., and David Mayers, eds., *Reevaluating Eisenhower: American Foreign Policy in the 1950s.* Urbana: University of Illinois Press, 1987.

Mendelson, Sarah E. "Internal Battles and External Wars: Politics, Learning, and the Soviet Withdrawal from Afghanistan," *World Politics* 45 (April 1993), pp. 327–60.

Meyer, David S. *A Winter of Discontent: The Nuclear Freeze and American Politics.* New York: Praeger, 1990.

Meyer, David S., and Sam Marullo. "Grassroots Mobilization and International Politics: Peace Protest and the End of the Cold War," in Louis Kriesberg and David R. Segal, eds., *Research in Social Movements, Conflicts, and Change,* vol. XIV. Greenwich, CT: JAI Press, 1992.

Milburn, Michael A., Paul Y. Watanabe, and Bernard M. Kramer. "The Nature and Sources of Attitudes Toward a Nuclear Freeze," *Political Psychology* 7 (December 1986), pp. 661–73.

Miller, Steven E. "Politics over Promise: Domestic Impediments to Arms Control," *International Security* 8 (Spring 1984), pp. 67–90.

Milner, Helen. *Resisting Protectionism.* Princeton: Princeton University Press, 1988.

"International Theories of Cooperation Among Nations: Strengths and Weaknesses," *World Politics* 44 (April 1992), pp. 466–96.

Mlyn, Eric. *The State, Society, and Limited Nuclear War.* Albany: State University of New York Press, 1995.

Mo, Jongryn. "Two-Level Games with Endogenous Domestic Coalitions," *Journal of Conflict Resolution* 38 (September 1994), pp. 402–22.

Moravcsik, Andrew. "Introduction: Integrating International and Domestic Theories of International Bargaining," in Evans, Jacobson, and Putnam, *Double-Edged Diplomacy.*

Morris, Irwin L. "Issue Voting and the Coexistence of Directional and Proximity Voters," paper presented at the annual meeting of the American Political Science Association, Washington, DC, September 2–5, 1993.

Morrow, James D. "Electoral and Congressional Incentives and Arms Control," *Journal of Conflict Resolution* 35 (June 1991), pp. 245–65.

Most, Benjamin A., and Harvey Starr. *Inquiry, Logic, and International Politics.* Columbia, SC: University of South Carolina Press, 1989.

Mueller, Dennis C. *Public Choice II.* Cambridge: Cambridge University Press, 1989.

Mueller, John E. *War, Presidents, and Public Opinion.* New York: John Wiley, 1973.

Myrdal, Alva. *The Game of Disarmament*, rev. and updated edn. New York: Pantheon Books, 1982.

Nacht, Michael. *The Age of Vulnerability: Threats to the Nuclear Stalemate.* Washington, DC: The Brookings Institution, 1985.

Newhouse, John. *Cold Dawn: The Story of SALT.* New York: Holt, Rinehart, and Winston, 1973.

War and Peace in the Nuclear Age. New York: Vintage Books, 1990; Alfred A. Knopf, 1988.

Nincic, Miroslav. "The United States, the Soviet Union, and the Politics of Opposites," *World Politics* 40 (July 1988), pp. 452–75.

Nincic, Miroslav, and Barbara Hinckley. "Foreign Policy and the Evaluation of Presidential Candidates," *Journal of Conflict Resolution* 35 (June 1991), pp. 333–55.

Nye, Joseph S., Jr. "Nuclear Learning and US–Soviet Security Regimes," *International Organization* 41 (Summer 1987), pp. 371–402.

O'Heffernan, Patrick. *Mass Media and American Foreign Policy.* Norwood, NJ: Ablex Publishing, 1991.

Ordeshook, Peter C. *Game Theory and Political Theory: An Introduction.* Cambridge: Cambridge University Press, 1986.

Ornstein, Norman J., and Shirley Elder. *Interest Groups, Lobbying, and Policymaking.* Washington, DC: Congressional Quarterly Press, 1978.

Ostrom, Charles W., Jr., and Dennis M. Simon. "The President and the Politics of Military Force," in Joseph R. Goldman, ed., *American Security in a Changing World.* Lanham, MD: University Press of America, 1987.

Owen, John M. "How Liberalism Produces Democratic Peace," *International Security* 19 (Fall 1994), pp. 87–125.

Oye, Kenneth A., ed. *Cooperation Under Anarchy*. Princeton: Princeton University Press, 1986.

Page, Benjamin I., and Robert Y. Shapiro. "Effects of Public Opinion on Policy," *American Political Science Review* 77 (March 1983), pp. 175–90.

The Rational Public: Fifty Years of Trends in Americans' Policy Preferences. Chicago: University of Chicago Press, 1992.

Peterson, Susan. "How Democracies Differ: Public Opinion, State Structure, and the Lessons of the Fashoda Crisis," *Security Studies* 5 (Autumn 1995), pp. 3–37.

Crisis Bargaining and the State: The Domestic Politics of International Conflict. Ann Arbor: University of Michigan Press, 1996.

Petracca, Mark P. "The Rediscovery of Interest Group Politics," in Petracca, *Politics of Interests*.

Petracca, Mark P., ed. *The Politics of Interests: Interest Groups Transformed*. Boulder: Westview Press, 1992.

Pierce, Roy. "Directional Versus Proximity Models: A Second Opinion," paper presented at the annual meeting of the American Political Science Association, Washington, DC, September 2–5, 1993.

Pilat, Joseph F., Robert E. Pendley, and Charles K. Ebinger, eds., *Atoms for Peace: An Analysis After Thirty Years*. Boulder: Westview Press, 1985.

Pipes, Richard. "Misinterpreting the Cold War," *Foreign Affairs* 74 (January/February 1995), pp. 154–60.

Plott, Glenn, Keith T. Poole, and Howard Rosenthal. "Directional and Euclidean Theories of Voting Behavior: A Legislative Comparison," *Legislative Studies Quarterly* 17 (1992), pp. 561–72.

Primack, Joel, and Frank Von Hippel. *Advice and Dissent: Scientists in the Political Arena*. New York: New American Library, 1974.

Pringle, Peter, and James Spigelman. *The Nuclear Barons*. New York: Holt, Rinehart, and Winston, 1981.

Putnam, Robert D. "Diplomacy and Domestic Politics: The Logic of Two-Level Games," *International Organization* 42 (Summer 1988), pp. 427–60.

Rabinowitz, George, and Stuart Elaine Macdonald. "A Directional Theory of Issue Voting," *American Political Science Review* 83 (March 1989), pp. 93–121.

Rathjens, George. "The ABM Debate," in Bernard Brodie, Michael D. Intriligator, and Roman Kolkowicz, eds., *National Security and International Stability*. Cambridge, MA: Oelgeschlager, Gunn, & Hain, 1983.

Rhodes, Edward. "Do Bureaucratic Politics Matter? Some Disconfirming Findings from the Case of the US Navy," *World Politics* 47 (October 1994), pp. 1–41.

Risse-Kappen, Thomas. "Public Opinion, Domestic Structure, and Foreign Policy in Liberal Democracies," *World Politics* 43 (July 1991), pp. 479–512.

"Ideas Do Not Float Freely: Transnational Coalitions, Domestic Structures, and the End of the Cold War," *International Organization* 48 (Spring 1994), pp. 185–214.

Cooperation Among Democracies: The European Influence on US Foreign Policy. Princeton: Princeton University Press, 1995.

Risse-Kappen, Thomas, ed. *Bringing Transnational Relations Back In: Non-State Actors, Domestic Structures, and International Institutions.* Cambridge: Cambridge University Press, 1995.

Rivers, Douglas, and Nancy L. Rose. "Passing the President's Program: Public Opinion and Presidential Influence in Congress," *American Journal of Political Science* 29 (May 1985), pp. 183–96.

Rochon, Thomas R. "Political Movements and State Authority in Liberal Democracies," *World Politics* 42 (January 1990), pp. 299–313.

Rochon, Thomas R., and David S. Meyer, eds. *Coalitions and Political Movements: The Lessons of the Nuclear Freeze.* Boulder: Lynne Rienner Publishers, 1997.

Rogowski, Ronald. *Commerce and Coalitions.* Princeton: Princeton University Press, 1989.

Rosenau, James N. *Public Opinion and Foreign Policy.* New York: Random House, 1961.

Rosi, Eugene J. "Public Opinion and National Security Policy: The Nuclear Testing Debate," in Rosi, ed., *American Defense and Detente: Readings in National Security Policy.* New York: Dodd, Mead, 1973.

Rostow, W. W. *Open Skies: Eisenhower's Proposal of July 21, 1955.* Austin: University of Texas Press, 1982.

Russett, Bruce M. *Grasping the Democratic Peace: Principles for a Post-Cold War World.* Princeton: Princeton University Press, 1993.

Sagan, Scott D. *Moving Targets: Nuclear Strategy and National Security.* Princeton: Princeton University Press, 1989.

Salisbury, Robert H. "The Paradox of Interest Groups in Washington – More Groups, Less Clout," in Anthony King, ed., *The New American Political System,* 2nd ver. Washington, DC: AEI Press, 1990.

Sanders, Jerry W. *Peddlers of Crisis: The Committee on the Present Danger and the Politics of Containment.* Boston: South End Press, 1983.

Schattschneider, E. E. *The Semisovereign People: A Realist's View of Democracy in America.* New York: Holt, Rinehart, and Winston, 1960.

Scheer, Robert. *With Enough Shovels: Reagan, Bush, and Nuclear War,* updated edn. New York: Vintage Books, 1983.

Schell, Jonathan. *The Fate of the Earth.* New York: Alfred A. Knopf, 1982.

Schlozman, Kay Lehman, and John T. Tierney. *Organized Interests and American Democracy.* New York: Harper and Row, 1986.

Schneider, William. "Public Opinion," in Joseph S. Nye, Jr., ed., *The Making of America's Soviet Policy.* New Haven: Yale University Press, 1984.

Schoppa, Leonard J. "Two-Level Games and Bargaining Outcomes: Why *Gaiatsu* Succeeds in Japan in Some Cases, But Not Others," *International Organization* 47 (Summer 1993), pp. 353–86.

Shapiro, Robert Y., and Benjamin I. Page, "Foreign Policy and the Rational Public," *Journal of Conflict Resolution* 32 (June 1988), pp. 211–47.

"Foreign Policy and Public Opinion," in Deese, *The New Politics of American Foreign Policy.*

Shultz, Richard H., and Roy Godson. *Dezinformatsia: Active Measures in Soviet Strategy.* Washington, DC: Pergamon-Brassey's, 1984.

Sigal, Leon V. *Nuclear Forces in Europe: Enduring Dilemmas, Present Prospects.* Washington, DC: The Brookings Institute, 1984.

Sikkink, Kathryn. "Human Rights, Principled Issue-Networks, and Sovereignty in Latin America," *International Organization* 47 (Summer 1993), pp. 411–41.

Simmons, Beth A. *Who Adjusts? Domestic Sources of Foreign Economic Policy During the Interwar Years.* Princeton: Princeton University Press, 1994.

Skidmore, David. "The Politics of National Security Policy: Interest Groups, Coalitions, and the SALT II Debate," in Skidmore and Valerie M. Hudson, eds., *The Limits of State Autonomy.* Boulder: Westview Press, 1993.

Sleeper, Raymond S., ed. *Mesmerized by the Bear: The Soviet Strategy of Deception.* New York: Dodd, Mead, 1987.

Small, Melvin. *Johnson, Nixon, and the Doves.* New Brunswick, NJ: Rutgers University Press, 1988.

Smith, Alice Kimball. *A Peril and a Hope: The Scientists' Movement in America, 1945–1947.* Cambridge: MIT Press, 1970; Chicago: University of Chicago Press, 1965.

Smith, Richard A. "Advocacy, Interpretation, and Influence in the US Congress," *American Political Science Review* 78 (March 1984), pp. 44–63.

Smith, Tom W. "The Polls: America's Most Important Problems," *Public Opinion Quarterly* 49 (Summer 1985), pp. 264–74.

Snidal, Duncan. "The Game *Theory* of International Politics," in Oye, *Cooperation Under Anarchy.*

Snyder, Jack. *Myths of Empire: Domestic Politics and International Ambition.* Ithaca: Cornell University Press, 1991.

Soapes, Thomas F. "A Cold Warrior Seeks Peace: Eisenhower's Strategy for Nuclear Disarmament," *Diplomatic History* 4 (Winter 1980), pp. 57–71.

Sokolski, Henry. "The Arms Control Connection," in Pilat, et al., *Atoms for Peace.*

Solberg, Carl. *Hubert Humphrey: A Biography.* New York: W. W. Norton, 1984.

Solingen, Etel. "The Political Economy of Nuclear Restraint," *International Security* 19 (Fall 1994), pp. 126–69.

Solo, Pam. *From Protest to Policy: Beyond the Freeze to Common Security.* Cambridge, MA: Ballinger Publishing Co., 1988.

Stein, Janice Gross, ed., *Getting to the Table: The Processes of International Prenegotiation.* Baltimore: Johns Hopkins University Press, 1989.

Stone, Deborah A. "Causal Stories and the Formation of Policy Agendas," *Political Science Quarterly* 104 (Summer 1989), pp. 281–300.

Strong, Robert A. "Eisenhower and Arms Control," in Melanson and Mayers, *Reevaluating Eisenhower.*

Sullivan, Terry. "A Matter of Fact: The 'Two Presidencies' Thesis Revitalized," in Steven A. Shull, ed., *The Two Presidencies: A Quarter Century Assessment*. Chicago: Nelson-Hall, 1991.

Talbott, Strobe. *Deadly Gambits: The Reagan Administration and the Stalemate in Nuclear Arms Control*. New York: Vintage Books, 1985; Alfred A. Knopf, 1984.

Tarrow, Sidney. *Power in Movement: Social Movements, Collective Action, and Politics*. Cambridge: Cambridge University Press, 1994.

Teller, Edward, and Albert L. Latter. *Our Nuclear Future: Facts, Dangers, Opportunities*. New York: Criterion Books, 1958.

Thompson, Kenneth W. "The Strengths and Weaknesses of Eisenhower's Leadership," in Melanson and Mayers, *Reevaluating Eisenhower*.

Tierney, John T. "Organized Interests and the Nation's Capitol," in Petracca, *Politics of Interests*.

Tucker, Robert W. "The Nuclear Debate," *Foreign Affairs* 63 (Fall 1984), pp. 1–32.

Van Evera, Stephen. "Why Cooperation Failed in 1914," in Oye, *Cooperation Under Anarchy*.

Walker, Jack L., Jr. "Setting the Agenda in the US Senate: A Theory of Problem Selection," *British Journal of Political Science* 7 (October 1977), pp. 423–45.

"The Diffusion of Knowledge, Policy Communities, and Agenda Setting," in John E. Tropman, Milan J. Dluhy, and Roger M. Lind, eds., *New Strategic Perspectives on Social Policy*. New York: Pergamon Press, 1981.

Mobilizing Interest Groups in America: Patrons, Professions, and Social Movements. Ann Arbor: University of Michigan Press, 1991.

Waller, Douglas C. *Congress and the Nuclear Freeze: An Inside Look at the Politics of a Mass Movement*. Amherst: University of Massachusetts Press, 1987.

Waltz, Kenneth N. *Foreign Policy and Democratic Politics: The American and British Experience*. Boston: Little, Brown, 1967.

Theory of International Politics. Reading, MA: Addison-Wesley, 1979.

"Reflections on *Theory of International Politics*: A Response to My Critics," in Robert O. Keohane, ed., *Neorealism and Its Critics*. New York: Columbia University Press, 1986.

Wapner, Paul. "Politics Beyond the State: Environmental Activism and World Civic Politics," *World Politics* 47 (April 1995), pp. 311–40.

Ward, Michael D. "The Political Economy of Arms Races and International Tensions," *Conflict Management and Peace Science* 7 (Spring 1984), pp. 1–23.

Ward, Michael D., and David R. Davis. "Risky Business: US–Soviet Competition and Corporate Profits," in Alex Mintz, ed., *The Political Economy of Military Spending in the United States*. London: Routledge, 1992.

Weber, Steve. *Cooperation and Discord in US–Soviet Arms Control*. Princeton: Princeton University Press, 1991.

Wirls, Daniel. *Buildup: The Politics of Defense in the Reagan Era*. Ithaca: Cornell University Press, 1992.

Wittman, Donald. "Spatial Strategies When Candidates Have Policy Preferences," in Enelow and Hinich, *Advances in the Spatial Theory.*

Wittner, Lawrence S. *Rebels Against War: The American Peace Movement, 1941–1960*. New York: Columbia University Press, 1969.

"Blacklisting Schweitzer," *Bulletin of the Atomic Scientists* 51 (May/June 1995), pp. 55–61.

Yanarella, Ernest J. *The Missile Defense Controversy.* Lexington: University Press of Kentucky, 1977.

Yankelovich, Daniel, and John Doble. "The Public Mood: Nuclear Weapons and the USSR," *Foreign Affairs* 63 (Fall 1984), pp. 33–46.

Young, Oran. *International Cooperation: Building Regimes for Natural Resources and the Environment*. Ithaca: Cornell University Press, 1989.

Zimmerman, William. "Issue Area and Foreign-Policy Process: A Research Note in Search of a General Theory," *American Political Science Review* 67 (December 1973), pp. 1204–12.

Zisk, Kimberly Marten. *Engaging the Enemy: Organization Theory and Soviet Military Innovation*. Princeton: Princeton University Press, 1993.

Periodicals

Bulletin of the Atomic Scientists (*BAS*)
Life
Los Angeles Times
The Nation
New Republic
New York Times (*NYT*)
Washington Monthly
Washington Post

Index

CAMBRIDGE STUDIES IN INTERNATIONAL RELATIONS

48 *William I. Robinson*
Promoting polyarchy
Globalization, US intervention, and hegemony

47 *Roger Spegele*
Political realism in international theory

46 *Thomas J. Biersteker and Cynthia Weber (eds.)*
State sovereignty as social construct

45 *Mervyn Frost*
Ethics in international relations
A constitutive theory

44 *Mark W. Zacher with Brent A. Sutton*
Governing global networks
International regimes for transportation and communications

43 *Mark Neufeld*
The restructuring of international relations theory

42 *Thomas Risse-Kappen (ed.)*
Bringing transnational relations back in
Non-state actors, domestic structures, and international institutions

41 *Hayward R. Alker*
Rediscoveries and reformulations
Humanistic methodologies for international studies

40 *Robert W. Cox with Timothy J. Sinclair*
Approaches to world order

39 *Jens Bartelson*
A genealogy of sovereignty

38 *Mark Rupert*
Producing hegemony
The politics of mass production and American global power

37 *Cynthia Weber*
Simulating sovereignty
Intervention, the state, and symbolic exchange

36 *Gary Goertz*
Contexts of international politics

35 *James L. Richardson*
Crisis diplomacy
The Great Powers since the mid-nineteenth century

34 *Bradley S. Klein*
Strategic studies and world order
The global politics of deterrence

33 *T. V. Paul*
Asymmetric conflicts: war initiation by weaker powers

32 *Christine Sylvester*
Feminist theory and international relations in a postmodern era

31 *Peter J. Schraeder*
US foreign policy toward Africa
Incrementalism, crisis, and change

30 *Graham Spinardi*
From Polaris to Trident: the development of US Fleet Ballistic Missile technology

29 *David A. Welch*
Justice and the genesis of war

28 *Russell J. Leng*
Interstate crisis behavior, 1816–1980: realism versus reciprocity

27 *John A. Vasquez*
The war puzzle

26 *Stephen Gill (ed.)*
Gramsci, historical materialism, and international relations

25 *Mike Bowker and Robin Brown (eds.)*
From Cold War to collapse: theory and world politics in the 1980s

24 *R. B. J. Walker*
Inside/outside: international relations as political theory

23 *Edward Reiss*
The Strategic Defense Initiative

22 *Keith Krause*
Arms and the state: patterns of military production and trade

21 *Roger Buckley*
US–Japan alliance diplomacy, 1945–1990

20 *James N. Rosenau and Ernst-Otto Czempiel (eds.)*
Governance without government: order and change in world politics

19 *Michael Nicholson*
Rationality and the analysis of international conflict

18 *John Stopford and Susan Strange*
Rival states, rival firms
Competition for world market shares

17 *Terry Nardin and David R. Mapel (eds.)*
Traditions of international ethics

16 *Charles F. Doran*
Systems in crisis
New imperatives of high politics at century's end

15 *Deon Geldenhuys*
Isolated states: a comparative analysis

14 *Kalevi J. Holsti*
Peace and war: armed conflicts and international order, 1648–1989

13 *Saki Dockrill*
Britain's policy for West German rearmament, 1950–1955

12 *Robert H. Jackson*
Quasi-states: sovereignty, international relations, and the Third World

11 *James Barber and John Barratt*
South Africa's foreign policy
The search for status and security, 1945–1988

10 *James Mayall*
Nationalism and international society

9 *William Bloom*
Personal identity, national identity, and international relations

8 *Zeev Maoz*
National choices and international processes

7 *Ian Clark*
The hierarchy of states
Reform and resistance in the international order

6 *Hidemi Suganami*
The domestic analogy and world order proposals

5 *Stephen Gill*
American hegemony and the Trilateral Commission

4 *Michael C. Pugh*
The ANZUS crisis, nuclear visiting, and deterrence

3 *Michael Nicholson*
Formal theories in international relations

2 *Friedrich V. Kratochwil*
Rules, norms, and decisions
On the conditions of practical and legal reasoning in international relations and domestic affairs

1 *Myles L. C. Robertson*
Soviet policy towards Japan
An analysis of trends in the 1970s and 1980s